Rev   *s*

HÖR GUT ZU!

A BEGINNING GERMAN AUDIO-LINGUAL READER

GERARD F. SCHMIDT
HARPUR COLLEGE
STATE UNIVERSITY OF NEW YORK AT BINGHAMTON

THE MACMILLAN COMPANY

To Linnie

printing number
12 13 14 15 16 17 18 19 20

Library of Congress catalog card number: 64–14961

The Macmillan Company
Collier-Macmillan Canada, Ltd., Toronto, Ontario

Printed in the United States of America

ACKNOWLEDGMENTS

The author wishes to express appreciation for permission to adapt the plots of copyrighted short stories as follows:

3B adapted from "THE OLD MAN" *by Holloway Horn,* with permission of Christy Moore, Ltd., London.

4B adapted from "DEATH IN THE KITCHEN" *by Milward R. K. Burge,* with permission of the author.

5B adapted from "THE ACE OF TROUBLE" *by Hedley Barker,* with permission of John Farquharson Ltd., London.

9A adapted from "NO. 17" *by E. Nesbit,* with permission of John Farquharson Ltd., London.

Preface

Whether we, as teachers, believe that we should stress grammar and the development of reading ability, or whether we are convinced that our objectives can best be reached by emphasizing the oral use of the language, we are, I am sure, all agreed that listening comprehension is so fundamental a skill that we cannot afford to neglect developing it. Our students can best acquire it by listening to us in the classroom. Our own time permitting, we have done our best to give our classes this needed practice by telling them anecdotes, short stories, perhaps even longer tales. If we did it well and had a good story to tell, we had the rewarding experience of seeing our students sit up, listen, and understand. However, the price we had to pay for this experience was high. We know that it is not easy to collect a year's supply of material sufficiently interesting to make the students *want* to listen, and we are all aware of how time-consuming it is to adapt our aural comprehension stories to the class's progress in vocabulary, grammar, and syntax.

This book is designed to furnish sufficient material to meet this need and may be used as a companion to any basic first-year textbook. The stories have been adapted for this purpose; they are graded, and the introduction of major grammatical features, especially the tenses, the passive, and the subjunctive, follows the sequence adopted in most textbooks currently in use.

The *Reader* should be introduced at a fairly early stage, that is, as soon as the students have become acquainted with the genders and cases, the conjugational forms of the present tense, the personal pronouns, and the basic prepositions.

In selecting and adapting the stories, I have held as a cardinal principle that they must hold the students' attention.

The *Reader* provides enough comprehension material for two semesters. It contains ten Sets of two stories each. Each story is divided into Parts which, within a given story, are of approximately the same length; the Parts become longer as the *Reader* progresses and can easily be subdivided in later Sets if the teacher so desires. This division into Sets, Stories, and Parts makes the *Reader* flexible enough to meet the demands of practically any classroom situation. The book has been so designed as to take up only a minor portion of a class hour and of the student's home-study time. A single reading, that is, telling by the teacher of any one Part of the stories in Sets 3 or 4, for example, averages between six and seven minutes.

Since the process of listening to, and understanding, a story must not be interrupted by questions from the class or answers or explanations by the teacher, all difficulties in the text (words, idioms, constructions) are resolved for the student in the form of a running Visible Vocabulary. The nature and arrangement of the Visible Vocabulary are explained below.

The vocabulary has been rigidly controlled. To insure the acquisition and retention of a basic vocabulary, I have (with the exception of the names of most months) employed all of the starred words in C. M. Purin's *Standard German Vocabulary* (D. C. Heath). Excepting *das Salz* and the names of some days of the week, all of Purin's 500 double-starred words have been used a minimum of five times; all of his single-starred words of the second order of frequency have been used at least three times. From among words not starred in Purin's *Vocabulary,* I have chosen only those which were either essential or very desirable for a certain story or whose usefulness is so evident that their noninclusion would have seemed inexcusable (*aufhören, einladen, besonders, einfach, der Gedanke, das Geschenk,* etc.). These nonstarred words, which I have also used repeatedly, number approximately 300. Not counted among them are easy cognates, easy derivatives, and obvious compounds whose component parts are words starred in Purin (*Armstuhl, Haustür, ruhelos,* e.g.).

Words in the Visible Vocabulary are keyed as follows:

A new word is keyed at its first occurrence. The word is keyed again at its second occurrence, either within the same Set or in a subsequent one. It is keyed for a third time if it appears in a subsequent Set *and* has been used less than four times. The word is keyed for a fourth time when it appears again after an interval of at least two Sets. From Set 3 on, the principal parts of strong and irregular verbs are similarly listed. Numbers following a vocabulary item indicate the second, third, or fourth listing. Words which have multiple meanings, such as *Gesellschaft, Wesen, Zug, gelten,* etc., have been keyed more often. Also listed repeatedly are some idiomatic expressions and certain constructions which are likely to impede the student's comprehension until he has become thoroughly familiar with them through continued exposure.

Most stories are preceded by "Notes." They are not essential to the comprehension of the stories, nor are they grammatically exhaustive. Their purpose is to save valuable class time by obviating much explanation by the teacher if a particular major grammatical feature should be introduced in the *Reader* before its formal presentation in the student's basic textbook. The review sections in the "Notes" present convenient summaries of idioms and strong and irregular verbs used in the preceding story.

Abundant question-and-answer material for every Part of every story has been provided at the back of the book for the teacher who wishes to stress active oral participation.

The end vocabulary contains all words which occur in the stories and in the Visible Vocabulary.

Coupled with the aural comprehension practice is a method of measuring the student's progress by means of periodic tests. For each Set in the *Reader* there is an accompanying Test Story and Questions in the *Teacher's Manual.* The Test Stories are entirely different from those of the *Reader,* but contain only words, idioms, and grammatical features which have appeared in preceding stories. No word is used in the Test Stories which the student has not encountered at least twice before. The student is tested not on memorized words or phrases, but on his ability to understand an entire German narrative. The administration of these Tests and a suggested method of grading them are discussed in detail in the *Teacher's Manual.*

A large part of the book has been tested in the classroom. The results of experimentation have indicated that the following technique of presenting the material will be most successful:

1. A new Part of a story is read, or rather told, at the beginning

of the class hour either by the teacher or by tape recorder. During this reading, the student is allowed to use the Visible Vocabulary, as explained in the "Suggestions to the Student" below. No assignment is given in preparation for this first hearing of new material, and the student has been advised against reading a new Part of a story ahead of time. It is only *after* the first hearing that he should read at home what he has heard in class, study the Visible Vocabulary, and, if feasible, listen again to the text in the language laboratory. A study of the "Notes" relevant to a story or Set can be made before the story is begun; it is, however, not necessary.

2. Before the next Part of a story is told to the students on the following class day, the previous day's Part should be read to them again either in the classroom or the language laboratory. During this second reading the students' books should be *closed*. A student who has adequately prepared his assignment will have no difficulty understanding the text during a second reading without the help of the Visible Vocabulary.

While the book was written as a first-year aural-comprehension *Reader,* it may also fit the special needs of a teacher who, for one reason or another, wishes to use it as a conventional companion *Reader.* In such a case, the teacher should caution the students against relying too heavily upon the Visible Vocabulary.

SUGGESTIONS TO THE STUDENT

This book has been designed to develop your ability to understand spoken German. Beyond acquiring this important skill, you will find that continued practice in listening will facilitate your general progress in learning German: it will help you to learn and retain a basic vocabulary and will develop and confirm sound habits of German sentence structure.

You will find the following suggestions helpful:

1. If the *Reader* is to accomplish its purpose, your first contact with a new Part of a story must be by ear. You should not follow the text on the right-hand page while the story is being told to you, nor should you read a new Part ahead of time, for this will only impair the development of your aural-comprehension ability.

2. While listening to a new Part of a story, you will probably find it less distracting if you keep the right-hand page covered. Your attention must be focused on the left-hand page where you will follow the running Visible Vocabulary.

The Visible Vocabulary is arranged in the following manner:

a. The words farthest to the left in the column are the first keyed words of new sentences. If you should "get lost," you will find your place by waiting for the next word at the extreme left.
b. The slightly indented words are the remaining keyed words within a given sentence.
c. A blank line indicates the beginning of a new paragraph. At this point, a perceptible pause will ordinarily occur.
Note: Remember that, as the *Reader* progresses, a whole sentence or more may intervene between two successive words in the Visible Vocabulary. Try to develop the habit of glancing at the next word and of holding it mentally in reserve until you have heard the word.
d. The words in parentheses, farthest to the right in the column, might be called "for home-study" because they are not immediately necessary for understanding the story and should, therefore, be disregarded while you listen. These words should be studied, along with the others, in preparation for the next Part of the story. A thorough study of both text and vocabulary *after* the initial hearing is of great importance because the words and constructions of every Part form the basis for the understanding of succeeding Parts and stories.

I am indebted to many friends and colleagues for their advice and criticism. Special thanks are due to Mr. Drayton Miller of the University of Illinois, Urbana, for his cooperation in testing the materials of the book in the classroom, and to Mr. Marshall Glasier of New York City, for his original drawings.

Binghamton, New York — Gerard F. Schmidt

Contents

DIE WETTE

[1A]

NOTES

I. 1. Your textbook may not have discussed the way in which a German speaks to someone with whom he is on particularly informal or intimate terms.

a. The grammatical form used for this purpose is the second person singular with the pronoun **du;** the verb ending of the second person singular is **–st.** Thus: **geh-en, du gehst; mach-en, du machst; tu-n, du tust.**

b. The ending is **–est** when the stem of the verb ends in a **d, t** or a consonant plus **n** or **m.** Thus: **arbeit-en, du arbeitest; wett-en, du wettest; wart-en, du wartest; find-en, du findest; öffn-en** (to open), **du öffnest.**

c. The **s** in the **–st** ending is dropped when the stem of the verb ends in an **s**-like sound (s, ss, ß, tz, x, z). Thus: **reis-en** (to travel), **du reist; fass-en** (to seize), **du faßt; grüß-en, du grüßt; sitz-en, du sitzt.**

d. With verbs whose stem vowels change in the third person singular of the present tense (**ich sehe, er sieht; ich verspreche, er verspricht; ich nehme, er nimmt; ich lasse, er läßt; ich laufe, er läuft,** etc.), the vowel change appears also in the second person singular. Thus: **du siehst, du versprichst, du nimmst, du läßt, du läufst.**

e. The conjugation of the following verbs is irregular in the singular:

sein	haben	werden	wissen
ich bin	ich habe	ich werde	ich weiß
du bist	du hast	du wirst	du weißt
er ist	er hat	er wird	er weiß

2. The second person singular is used in speaking to (a) a member of one's family (b) a very close friend (after the two friends have agreed to drop the formal **Sie**) (c) a child of up to about 12–14 years of age (d) God or a Saint (e) an animal.

In narratives of past or imaginary times, such as fairy tales, legends, animal stories, the **du**-form is used almost exclusively for addressing any one character in such stories.

3. The dative form of the personal pronoun of the second person singular is **dir,** the accusative form is **dich.** The basic form of the possessive adjective and pronoun is **dein** (your, yours).

II. Certain verbs, in English and in German, do not express an action, but merely the fact that an action is intended or willed, possible, necessary, advisable, desirable, permissible: I *can* go, you *must* eat, he *should* come, *may* I smoke? These verbs, called "modal auxiliaries," are used so frequently in both languages that their early introduction in this Reader seemed advisable.

Of the six German modal auxiliaries, four appear in Story 1A: **wollen, können, müssen, sollen.**

wollen expresses the idea of volition or will power.
können expresses what is possible.
müssen expresses the idea of strong or inevitable necessity.
sollen most often presupposes the existence of an authority and expresses the idea of obligation.

The conjugation of the modal auxiliaries is irregular in the singular of the present tense:

wollen	**können**	**müssen**	**sollen**
ich will	**ich kann**	**ich muß**	**ich soll**
du willst	**du kannst**	**du mußt**	**du sollst**
er will	**er kann**	**er muß**	**er soll**

While the German modal auxiliaries have infinitives and an almost complete conjugational system, the English modals are incomplete; none of them have an infinitive, for example, and missing forms must, therefore, be expressed by substitute phrases, especially in the infinitive and the past tenses. The following examples in the present tense show how a German modal auxiliary can be expressed in English.

er will gehen he wants to go, he is determined to go, he intends to go, he is willing to go
ich kann laufen I can run, I am able to run, I am capable of running, I am in a position to run
sie muß arbeiten she must work, she has to work, she is forced, obliged, compelled, to work
du sollst es tun you are to do it, you shall do it, you should do it, you are supposed to do it, you are expected to do it; you are said to do it

III. A German infinitive is placed at the end of the clause to which it belongs.

Zuerst muß sie die Kinder *waschen*.
Warum nicht einen kleinen Spaziergang *machen* und *sehen*, wie meine Kartoffeln wachsen?

IV. Dependent clauses are clauses introduced by subordinating conjunctions or relative pronouns, or clauses containing an indirect question. In such clauses, the finite verb, i.e., the inflected, conjugated verb form, stands at the very end of the clause.

Ich weiß, *daß* es besser *ist, wenn* ich nichts gegen den Willen meiner Frau *tue.*

Ich habe Zeit, *bis* das Frühstück fertig *ist.*

Er sieht den Hasen, *der* auch einen Spaziergang *macht.*

Ich weiß nicht, *was* du gegen mich *hast.*

Sie will immer wissen, *wo* ich *bin* oder *was* ich *tue.*

V. An infinitive in a dependent clause immediately *precedes* the finite verb.

Vielleicht sollten wir wetten, wer wirklich schneller *laufen kann.*

Ich muß ihr sagen, was wir beide *tun wollen.*

Note: Because the second part of a comparison is actually an incomplete sentence, it may *follow* an infinitive in a main clause or the finite verb in a dependent clause.

Ich kann mit meinen krummen Beinen schneller *laufen* als du (laufen kannst).

VI. Certain prepositions can be contracted with some dative and accusative forms of the definite article (**dem, der, den, das**).

Die Sonne scheint am Himmel.

Er geht zum Hasen.

Er kommt nur bis zur Mitte des Feldes.

The following contractions are possible:

am, ans, aufs, beim, durchs, fürs, hinterm, hintern, hinters, im, ins, überm, übern, übers, ums, unterm, untern, unters, vom, vorm, vors, zum, zur

VII. To emphasize a word in print, German does not use italics, but spaces the word.

S i e hat die Hände voll. *She* has her hands full.

IDIOMS FOR REVIEW

heute morgen this morning
immer noch still
einen Spaziergang machen to go for a walk, to take a walk
so etwas Dummes something stupid like that

Angst haben to be afraid
nach Haus(e) gehen to go home
noch einmal once more
ich warte schon über eine halbe Stunde I have been waiting for over half an hour
hin und zurück back and forth
stehen-bleiben to stop

---

die Wette the bet

schön beautiful, nice
der Sonntagmorgen Sunday morning
[**die Sonne** the sun]
[**der Tag, die Tage** the day]
[**der Morgen, die Morgen** the morning]
stehen to stand
der Igel the hedgehog
vor before, in front of
die Tür the door
[**die Tür, die Türen**]
das Haus the house
[**das Haus, die Häuser**]
der Sommer the summer
die Sonne the sun (2)
scheinen to shine
hell brightly
[**hell** light, bright; clear]
blau blue
der Himmel the sky; heaven
frisch fresh
der Wind the wind
bläst is blowing
[**blasen, er bläst**]
die Felder the fields
[**das Feld, die Felder**]
der Igel the hedgehog (2)
rauchen to smoke
zufrieden contentedly
[**zufrieden** satisfied, contented]
die Pfeife the pipe
[**die Pfeife, die Pfeifen**]
denken to think
wie how

[1 A]

(FOUR PARTS)

Die Wette

1.

An einem schönen Sonntagmorgen steht ein Igel vor der Tür seines Hauses. Es ist Sommer, die Sonne scheint hell am blauen Himmel, und ein frischer Wind bläst über die Felder. Der Igel raucht zufrieden seine Pfeife und denkt: „Wie schön das Wetter ist! Ein wunderbarer Morgen! Wenigstens für mich. Leider nicht für meine Frau. S i e hat die Hände voll. Zuerst muß sie die Kinder waschen, und dann macht sie das Früh-

---

schön beautiful, nice (2)
das Wetter the weather
wunderbar wonderful
der Morgen the morning (2)
wenigstens at least
leider unfortunately
meine Frau my wife
[**die Frau, die Frauen** the woman; wife; Mrs.]
die Hände the hands
[**die Hand, die Hände**]
voll full
zuerst first
muß sie she must
[**müssen** must, to have to]
die Kinder the children
[**das Kind, die Kinder**]
waschen to wash
[**waschen, er wäscht**]
dann then
machen to make; to do
das Frühstück the breakfast

nun well
[**nun** well; now]
arbeiten to work
ganz whole, entire
die Woche the week
[**die Woche, die Wochen**]
wenn when
[**wenn** when, whenever; if]
sechs six
Tage days
[**der Tag, die Tage** (2)]
schwer hard
[**schwer** heavy, difficult]
arbeiten to work (2)
dann then (2)
brauchen to need
meine Frau my wife (2)
am Sonntag on Sunday
[**am = an dem**]
[**der Sonntag, die Sonntage**]
helfen to help
[**helfen, er hilft**]
der Mann the man
[**der Mann, die Männer** the man; husband]
brauchen to need (2)
die Ruhe the rest
also therefore
die Zeit the time
bis until
das Frühstück the breakfast (2)
fertig finished, ready
warum why
einen kleinen Spaziergang machen to take a little walk
[**klein** little, small]
[**der Spaziergang, die Spaziergänge**]
sehen to see
[**sehen, er sieht**]
wie how (2)
die Kartoffeln the potatoes
[**die Kartoffel, die Kartoffeln**]
wachsen to grow
[**wachsen, er wächst**]

wie as, when
auf das Feld to the field
[**das Feld, die Felder** (2)]
kommen to come
sieht er he sees
[**sehen, er sieht** (2)]

stück. Nun, ich arbeite die ganze Woche, und wenn ich sechs Tage schwer arbeite, dann brauche ich meiner Frau am Sonntag nicht zu helfen. Ein Mann braucht seine Ruhe. Ich habe also Zeit, bis das Frühstück fertig ist. Warum nicht einen kleinen Spaziergang machen und sehen, wie meine Kartoffeln wachsen?"

Wie er auf das Feld kommt, sieht er seinen Nachbarn, den Hasen, der auch einen Spaziergang macht. Der Hase ist sein Nachbar, aber nicht sein Freund. Er, der große Hase mit den langen Beinen, denkt, er ist etwas Besseres als der kleine Igel mit seinen kurzen Beinen. Trotzdem grüßt der Igel ihn freundlich und sagt: „Guten Morgen, Nachbar Langbein! Wunderbares Wetter, was?"

---

der Nachbar the neighbor
[**der Nachbar, die Nachbarn**]
der Hase the hare
der auch einen Spaziergang macht who is also taking a walk
[**einen Spaziergang machen** to take a walk (2)]
der Hase the hare (2)
der Nachbar the neighbor (2)
der Freund the friend
[**der Freund, die Freunde**]
groß big, large, tall
lang long
die Beine the legs
[**das Bein, die Beine**]
denken to think (2)
etwas Besseres als something better than
[**etwas** something; some, a little; somewhat]
[**besser** better]
klein little, small (2)
kurz short
die Beine the legs (2)
trotzdem nevertheless
grüßen to greet, to salute
freundlich in a friendly way
[**freundlich** friendly]
sagen to say; to tell
gut good
Langbein "Long Legs"
wunderbar wonderful (2)
das Wetter the weather (2)
was what

unhöflich impolite
[**höflich** polite]
sagen to say (2)
gut good (2)
sondern but
antworten to answer
ganz quite; very
unfreundlich in an unfriendly way
[**freundlich** friendly (2)]
was what (2)
tust du are you doing
[**tun** to do]
hier here
früh early
schon already
die Hausarbeit the housework
[**das Haus, die Häuser** (2)]
[**die Arbeit** the work]
fertig finished (2)
heute morgen this morning
[**heute** today]
immer noch still
höflich polite (2)
heute today (2)
ich will nur sehen I only want to see
[**wollen** to want]
[**nur** only]
die Kartoffeln the potatoes (2)
wachsen to grow (2)
lachen to laugh
dünn thin
krumm crooked
jetzt now
genug enough
unhöflich impolite (2)
die Antwort the answer
[**die Antwort, die Antworten**]
machen to make (2)
böse angry
jetzt now (2)
unfreundlich unfriendly (2)
wird becomes
[**werden, er wird** to become)
ich weiß nicht I don't know
[**wissen, er weiß** to know]
gegen against
glauben to believe, to think
ich kann I can
[**können** can, to be able]

2.

Der unhöfliche Hase sagt nicht „Guten Morgen", sondern antwortet ganz unfreundlich: „Was tust du hier so früh auf dem Felde? Bist du schon mit der Hausarbeit fertig? Braucht deine Frau dich heute morgen nicht?" Der Igel ist immer noch höflich und sagt: „Oh, heute ist Sonntag; heute arbeite ich nicht. Ich will nur sehen, wie meine Kartoffeln wachsen, und mache einen kleinen Spaziergang."—„Einen Spaziergang?" lacht der Hase; „du, mit deinen dünnen und krummen Beinen?" Jetzt hat der Igel genug. Die unhöfliche Antwort des Hasen macht ihn so böse, daß er jetzt auch unfreundlich wird und sagt: „Ich weiß nicht, was du gegen mich hast, aber ich glaube, ich kann mit meinen krummen Beinen schneller laufen als du!"—„Ich kann nur lachen, wenn du so etwas Dummes sagst", antwortet der Hase; „aber vielleicht sollten wir wetten, wer

---

krumm crooked (2)
schneller faster
[**schnell** fast, quick]
laufen to run
[**laufen, er läuft**]
als than (2)
ich kann I can
[**können** can, to be able (2)]
nur only (2)
lachen to laugh (2)
wenn when (2)
so etwas Dummes something stupid like that
[**etwas** something (2)]
[**dumm** stupid]
antworten to answer (2)
vielleicht perhaps
sollten wir we should
[**sollen** shall, should, ought to]
wetten to bet
wer who

wirklich really
[**wirklich** real, really]
schneller faster
[**schnell** fast, quick (2)]
laufen to run (2)
zehn ten
Mark marks
[**die Mark** the mark]
die Flasche the bottle
[**die Flasche, die Flaschen**]
der Wein the wine
[**der Wein, die Weine**]
oder or
hast du Angst are you afraid
[**Angst haben** to be afraid]
[**die Angst** the fear]
wetten to bet (2)
„Ich Angst?“ “I, afraid?”
natürlich of course, naturally
[**natürlich** natural]
die Flasche the bottle (2)
der Wein the wine (2)
nein no
trinken to drink
der Mensch the man
[**der Mensch, die Menschen** the man; human being]
wetten um to bet for
nie never
der Alkohol the alcohol
warum why (2)
zwanzig twenty
Mark marks (2)
anstatt instead
zehn ten (2)
oder or (2)
das that
zu viel too much
[**viel** much, a lot]
natürlich of course, naturally (2)
zwanzig twenty (2)
wann when
beginnen to begin, to start

sofort right away, at once, immediately
bevor before
anfangen to begin, to start
[**an-fangen, er fängt an**]
muß ich I must
[**müssen** must, to have to]

wirklich schneller laufen kann. Zehn Mark und eine gute Flasche Wein? Oder hast du Angst zu wetten?"—„Ich Angst?" antwortet der Igel; „natürlich nicht. Aber eine Flasche Wein? Nein. Ich trinke keinen Wein. Ich bin ein guter Mensch und wette nie um Alkohol. Warum nicht zwanzig Mark anstatt zehn? Oder ist dir das zu viel?"—„Natürlich nicht", antwortet der Hase. „Gut. Zwanzig Mark. Wann beginnen wir?"

3.

„Nicht sofort", sagt der Igel. „Bevor wir anfangen, muß ich zuerst nach Hause gehen. Meine Frau wartet auf mich, und sie wird böse, wenn ich nicht komme. Sie will immer wissen, wo ich bin und was ich tue. Ich muß ihr also sagen, was wir beide tun wollen. Ohne ihre Erlaubnis kann ich nicht mit dir

---

zuerst first (2)
nach Haus(e) home
gehen to go
warten auf to wait for
[**warten** to wait]
sie wird she becomes
[**werden, er wird** (2)]
böse angry (2)
kommen to come (2)
sie will she wants
[**wollen** to want (2)]
immer always
wissen to know (2)
wo where
tun to do (2)
also therefore (2)
sagen to tell
wir beide the two of us
[**beide** both]
wollen to want
ohne without
die Erlaubnis the permission

ich weiß I know
[**wissen** to know (3)]
besser better (2)
nichts nothing, not anything
gegen against (2)
der Wille the will
hab keine Angst don't be afraid
[**Angst haben** to be afraid (2)]
[**die Angst** the fear (2)]
versprechen to promise
[**versprechen, er verspricht**]
halb half
die Stunde the hour
[**die Stunde, die Stunden**]
zurück back
warten auf to wait for (2)
hier here (2)
nach Haus(e) home (2)
holen to get, to fetch
das Scheckbuch the checkbook
[**der Scheck, die Schecks** the check]
[**das Buch, die Bücher** the book]
bleiben to stay, to remain
zu lange too long
[**lange** long, a long time]

wie as, when (2)
lassen to let
[**lassen, er läßt** to let, to leave]
die Kinder the children
[**das Kind, die Kinder** (2)]
allein alone
essen to eat
[**essen, er ißt**]
schicken to send
der Garten the garden
[**der Garten, die Gärten**]
unterwegs on the way
erzählen to tell, to relate
die Wette the bet (2)
sagen to tell (2)
was sie tun soll what she is to do
[**sollen** shall, should, ought to (2)]
führen to lead, to take
das Loch the hole
[**das Loch, die Löcher**]
am Ende at the end
[**am = an dem**]
[**das Ende** the end]

wetten. Ich weiß, daß es besser ist, wenn ich nichts gegen den Willen meiner Frau tue. Aber hab keine Angst! Ich verspreche dir, daß ich in einer halben Stunde zurück bin. Warte hier auf mich!"–„Gut", sagt der Hase; „dann laufe ich jetzt auch nach Haus und hole mein Scheckbuch. Bleib nicht zu lange!"

Wie der Igel nach Hause kommt, sagt er zu seiner Frau: „Komm schnell, Olga, ich brauche dich! Laß die Kinder allein ihr Frühstück essen oder schick sie in den Garten! Komm!" Unterwegs erzählt der Igel seiner Frau von der Wette mit dem Hasen und sagt ihr, was sie tun soll. Er führt sie zu einem Loch am Ende des Feldes, wo ein Busch steht. Dann geht er selbst zum Hasen, der am anderen Ende des langen Feldes wartet. Der Hase ist böse. Er ruft: „Schnell, Krummbein! Ich warte schon über eine halbe Stunde. Komm, laß uns anfangen!"– „Wir können sofort beginnen", sagt der Igel; „aber wohin

---

wo where (2)
der Busch the bush
[**der Busch, die Büsche**]
stehen to stand (2)
gehen to go (2)
er selbst he himself
zum Hasen, der to the hare who
[**zum = zu dem**]
ander other
das Ende the end (2)
lang long (2)
rufen to call
Krummbein "Crooked Legs"
ich warte schon über eine halbe Stunde I've been waiting for over half an hour already
[**schon** already (2)]
[**halb** half (2)]
[**die Stunde, die Stunden** the hour (2)]
lassen to let (2)
anfangen to begin, to start
[**an-fangen, er fängt an** (2)]
sofort at once, right away, immediately (2)
beginnen to begin (2)
wohin whereto, where

sollen wir shall we
vielleicht perhaps (2)
dieser, diese, dieses this
der Busch the bush (2)
bis zu up to
dort there, over there
du läufst you run
rechts to the right
links to the left

zählen to count
laut aloud
[**laut** loud, aloud, loudly]
eins–zwei–drei one–two–three
rennen to run
so schnell wie as fast as
[**so . . . wie** as . . . as]
die Rakete the rocket
[**die Rakete, die Raketen**]
läuft runs
drei three (2)
Schritte steps
[**der Schritt, die Schritte** the step, pace]
vorwärts forward
langsam slowly
[**langsam** slow, slowly]
zurück back (2)
wie as, when
am anderen Ende at the other end
[**am = an dem**]
[**ander** other (2)]
steigen to climb
das Loch the hole (2)
rufen to call (2)
da here
[**da** here; there; then]
reibt sich die Augen rubs his eyes
[**reiben** to rub]
[**das Auge, die Augen** the eye]
glauben to think, to believe (2)
recht right
wie how
das that (2)
möglich possible
das Gesicht the face
[**das Gesicht, die Gesichter**]
einmal once, one time
genug enough (2)
wir müssen we must

sollen wir laufen? Vielleicht von diesem Busch hier bis zu dem Busch dort am Ende des Feldes, was? Du läufst rechts, und ich laufe links.“

4.

„Gut“, sagt der Hase und zählt laut: „Eins–zwei–drei.“ Dann rennt er so schnell wie eine Rakete. Aber der Igel läuft nur drei Schritte vorwärts. Dann geht er langsam zurück und wartet. Wie der Hase zu dem Busch am anderen Ende des Feldes kommt, steigt die Frau des Igels aus dem Loch und ruft: „Haha! Ich bin schon da!“ Der Hase reibt sich die Augen und glaubt, er sieht nicht recht. „Wie ist das möglich?“ denkt er und macht ein langes Gesicht. Dann sagt er: „Einmal ist nicht genug. Wir müssen noch einmal laufen!“ Und er läuft zurück. Die Frau des Igels bleibt in ihrem Loch. Wie der Hase wieder zum ersten Busch kommt, sieht er den Igel schon dort sitzen und rufen: „Hahaha! Ich bin schon da!“ Jetzt ist der Hase wirklich böse und schreit ganz laut: „Noch einmal!“ Und nun

---

noch einmal once more
bleiben to stay, to remain (2)
wie when
wieder again
zum ersten Busch to the first bush
[**zum** = **zu dem**]
[**erst** first]
dort there (2)
sitzen to sit
da here
[**da** here; there; then (2)]
wirklich really (2)
schreien to shout, to scream
ganz quite, very (2)
laut loudly (2)
noch einmal once more (2)
nun now
[**nun** now; well (2)]

rennen to run (2)
hin und zurück back and forth
jedesmal every time
[**jeder, jede, jedes** every, each]
[**das Mal** the time]
hören to hear
viermal four times
fünf five
sechs six (2)
sieben seven
acht eight
neun nine
zehn ten (3)
elf eleven
beim zwölften Mal at the twelfth time
[**zwölf** twelve]
bis zur Mitte to the middle
[**bis zu** up to (2)]
[**zur = zu der**]
[**die Mitte** the middle]
bleibt er stehen he stops
[**stehen-bleiben** to stop]
das Blut the blood
fließen to flow
müde tired
die Füße the feet
[**der Fuß, die Füße**]
langsam slowly (2)
ich kann nicht mehr I can't (go on) any more
[**nicht mehr** no more, no longer]
der Scheck the check (2)
zweihundertvierzig 240
[**zwei** two (2)]
[**hundert** hundred]
[**vierzig** forty]
die Tasse the cup
[**die Tasse, die Tassen**]
stark strong
der Kaffee the coffee
das Fußbad the footbath
[**der Fuß, die Füße** the foot (2)]
[**das Bad, die Bäder** the bath]

nimmt takes
[**nehmen, er nimmt**]
holen to get, to fetch (2)
wie as, when
beide both (2)
zeigen to show

rennt er hin und zurück, hin und zurück, und jedesmal, wenn er zu einem Busch kommt, hört er den Igel oder seine Frau rufen: „Hahahaha! Ich bin schon da!" So geht es viermal, fünfmal, sechsmal, siebenmal, achtmal, neunmal, zehnmal, elfmal. Beim zwölften Mal kommt er nur bis zur Mitte des Feldes. Dort bleibt er stehen. Das Blut fließt von seinen müden Füßen. Ganz langsam geht er zum Igel. „Ich kann nicht mehr", sagt er. „Hier ist dein Scheck. Zweihundertvierzig Mark. Ich muß jetzt nach Hause gehen. Ich brauche eine Tasse starken Kaffee und ein Fußbad."

Der Igel nimmt den Scheck und holt seine Frau aus dem Loch am anderen Ende des Feldes. Wie beide langsam nach Hause gehen, zeigt der Igel seiner Frau den Scheck und sagt zufrieden: „Nicht schlecht, was? Zweihundertvierzig Mark ohne viel Arbeit. Siehst du, Olga, wir haben zwar kurze und krumme Beine, aber wir sind nicht so dumm, wie manche Leute glauben."

---

zufrieden contentedly (2)
schlecht bad
zweihundertvierzig 240 (2)
ohne without (2)
viel much (2)
die Arbeit the work (2)
siehst du you see
zwar to be sure
kurz short (2)
so dumm wie as stupid as
[**so . . . wie** as . . . as (2)]
[**dumm** stupid (2)]
manche some
die Leute (the) people

DIE VIER MUSIKER

[1B]

NOTES

I. 1. In English and in German, prepositions can be used as verbal modifiers: *to underline, to withdraw, to bypass, to overlook, to look someone over, to get up,* etc. Many German prepositions and other verbal modifiers, such as **weiter, stehen** in **stehenbleiben,** etc., used for the purpose of forming verbal compounds, may be detached from the verb. If they are detachable, they are called "separable prefixes."

2. The place of a separable prefix in an *independent* clause is *at the end.*

Sie macht den Mund wieder *zu.*
Schnell fliegt er vom Baum *herunter.*
Alle vier gehen voller Hoffnung *weiter.*
Er bleibt bei dem Esel *stehen.*

3. When the verb to which the separable prefix belongs is at the end of a clause (finite verbs in dependent clauses; infinitives, present or past participles), the separable prefix *precedes and joins* its verb.

Bevor der Hahn die Augen *zu*macht, dankt er Gott im Himmel.
„Nun?" fragen die anderen, als er *zurück*kommt.
Ich muß Tag und Nacht auf sein Haus *auf*passen.
Ich möchte so schnell wie möglich von hier *weg*gehen.
Was wird der Schmied sagen, wenn er hört, daß ich *weg*gehen will?

4. If the infinitive of a verbal compound is used with *zu,* the position of *zu* is *between* the separable prefix and the infinitive.

Ich schlafe, anstatt auf*zu*passen.

Note: To make it possible for you to recognize and learn the verbs with separable prefixes, such verbs are listed in the Visible Vocabulary with a hyphen between the prefix and the infinitive.

II. The remaining two modal auxiliaries are **dürfen** and **mögen.**

dürfen expresses the idea of permission.

Darf ich gegen seinen Willen das Haus verlassen? May I leave the house . . . ? Am I allowed, am I permitted to leave the house . . . ?

mögen expresses the idea of liking.

Ich möchte hinter dem Ofen liegen. I would (should) like to lie behind the stove.

Of all the forms of **mögen,** the (subjunctive) forms **ich möchte, du möchtest, er möchte,** etc. are used most frequently.

The conjugation of **dürfen** and **mögen** in the singular of the present tense is as irregular as that of the other four modal auxiliaries **wollen, können, müssen, sollen:**

dürfen	**mögen**
ich darf	**ich mag**
du darfst	**du magst**
er darf	**er mag**

III. 1. German often uses the present tense to express time in the future when the future meaning is clear from the context.

Morgen *bin* ich tot. Tomorrow *I shall be* dead.

Ich verspreche dir, daß ich in einer halben Stunde zurück *bin*. I promise you that *I'll be* back in half an hour.

2. German has, however, a separate future tense. It is formed by combining **werden,** in the present tense, with the infinitive of the main verb.

Ich glaube, ich *werde* bald vor Hunger *sterben*. I think *I'll* soon *die* from hunger.

Was *wird* der Schmied *sagen?* What *will* the blacksmith *say?*

Deshalb *werden* wir Ihnen das Ende ein anderes Mal *erzählen*. We *shall,* therefore, *tell* you the end another time.

IV. Note the following constructions in German and in English:

anstatt* sie *zu fangen *instead of* catch*ing* them
anstatt aufzupassen *instead of* watch*ing*
ohne* nach rechts oder links *zu sehen *without* look*ing* to the right or left

IDIOMS FOR REVIEW

zu Haus(e) at home
eines Tages one day

in der Zeitung steht
es steht in der Zeitung } it says in the newspaper

Freude machen to give pleasure

das Leben macht mir keine Freude mehr I don't enjoy life any more

ich lache gern I like to laugh

von Natur by nature

das gefällt mir nicht (that is not pleasing to me =) I don't like it

die Idee gefällt dem Hund the dog likes the idea

noch nicht not yet

auf deutsch in German

am Morgen, am Abend in the morning, in the evening

ich bin zu alt zum Arbeiten I am too old to work

du bist zu jung zum Sterben you are too young to die

etwas zum Essen und zum Trinken something to eat and drink

zu Ende at an end, over, finished, all gone

morgen ist mein Leben zu Ende tomorrow my life shall come to an end

nach Herzenslust to one's heart's content

vier four (2)
  Musiker musicians
    [**der Musiker, die Musiker**]

die Straße the road
    [**die Straße, die Straßen** the street, road]
  nach to
  Bremen city in northwestern Germany
  alt old
  der Esel the donkey
    [**der Esel, die Esel**]
schwach weak
  müde tired (2)
  denn er ist schon . . . unterwegs for he has already been on his way
    [**denn** for, because]
  ganz whole, entire (2)
    [**unterwegs** on the way (2)]
der Weg the way, road
    [**der Weg, die Wege**]
hoffen to hope
  als Musiker as a musician (2)
  finden to find
  das Symphonieorchester the symphony orchestra
    [**die Symphonie, die Symphonien**]
    [**das Orchester, die Orchester**]
  die Trompete the trumpet
  blasen to blow (2)
zu Haus(e) at home
  nicht mehr no longer (2)
  denn for, because (2)
  der Herr the master
    [**der Herr, die Herren** the gentleman; master; lord; Mr.; God]
  der Müller the miller
  länger longer
    [**lang** long]
fünfzehn fifteen
  Jahre years
    [**das Jahr, die Jahre**]
  alt old (2)
  die Säcke, die the sacks which
    [**der Sack, die Säcke** the sack, bag]
  zur Mühle to the mill
    [**die Mühle, die Mühlen**]
  tragen to carry
    [**tragen, er trägt** to carry; to wear]
  zu schwer too heavy
    [**schwer** heavy; difficult (2)]
weil because
  schwer hard (2)

[1 B]

(FOUR PARTS)

Die vier Musiker

I.

Auf der Straße nach Bremen steht ein alter Esel. Er ist schwach und müde, denn er ist schon den ganzen Tag unterwegs. Warum ist er auf dem Wege nach Bremen? Er hofft, dort als Musiker Arbeit zu finden; vielleicht kann er im Symphonieorchester die Trompete blasen. Zu Hause kann er nicht mehr arbeiten, denn sein Herr, ein Müller, will ihn nicht länger behalten. Er ist schon fünfzehn Jahre alt, und die Säcke, die er zur Mühle tragen muß, sind jetzt zu schwer. Und weil er nicht mehr schwer arbeiten kann, bekommt er auch von seinem Herrn nichts zu essen. So muß er also von zu Haus weggehen, weil niemand ihn dort braucht. Nun steht er auf der Straße, schwach, hungrig und müde. Da kommt ein Hund. Der Esel

---

bekommen to get, to receive
der Herr the master (2)
nichts nothing (2)
essen to eat (2)
von zu Haus from home
[**zu Haus** at home (2)]
weg-gehen to go away, to leave
weil because (2)
niemand no one, nobody
die Straße the street (2)
schwach weak (2)
hungrig hungry
der Hund the dog
[**der Hund, die Hunde**]
der Esel the donkey (2)

der Hund the dog (2)
er selbst he himself (2)
vor Hunger from hunger
[**der Hunger** the hunger]
er bleibt . . . stehen he stops
[**stehen-bleiben** to stop (2)]

arm poor
hungrig hungry (2)
wohin where
ach! alas!
was ich machen soll what I should do
noch still
gesund healthy
zum Arbeiten to work
der Schmied the blacksmith, smith
böse wicked, bad
der Mann the man (2)
sage ich dir I tell you
die Nacht the night
[**die Nacht, die Nächte**]
auf sein Haus aufpassen watch his house
[**auf-passen** to watch]
bellen to bark
jemand someone, somebody
das Geld the money
hat immer Angst is always afraid
[**immer** always (2)]
Diebe thieves
[**der Dieb, die Diebe**]
Räuber robbers
[**der Räuber, die Räuber**]
das Geld the money (2)
stehlen to steal
[**stehlen, er stiehlt** to steal]
auf-passen to watch (2)
arm poor (2)
Augen eyes
[**das Auge, die Augen** (2)]
die Nase the nose
[**die Nase, die Nasen**]
sehr very
die Stimme the voice
[**die Stimme, die Stimmen**]
am Abend in the evening
[**der Abend, die Abende**]
schlafen to sleep
[**schlafen, er schläft**]
anstatt aufzupassen instead of watching

sieht sofort, daß der Hund so müde ist wie er selbst. Der Hund geht ganz langsam; er ist vor Hunger so schwach, daß er nicht mehr laufen kann. Er bleibt bei dem Esel stehen.

„Du armer Hund", sagt der Esel; „ich glaube, du bist so müde und hungrig wie ich. Wohin gehst du?"—„ Ach!" antwortet der Hund, „ich weiß wirklich nicht, was ich machen soll. Ich bin noch gesund, aber ich bin zu alt zum Arbeiten. Mein Herr ist ein Schmied. Ein böser Mann, sage ich dir! Ich muß Tag und Nacht auf sein Haus aufpassen und laut bellen, wenn jemand kommt. Mein Herr hat viel Geld im Haus und hat immer Angst, daß Diebe oder Räuber kommen und sein Geld stehlen. Ich weiß, ich soll aufpassen, aber ich bin jetzt schon so alt, daß meine armen Augen nicht mehr viel sehen; meine Nase ist nicht mehr sehr gut, und meine Stimme ist schwach. Schon am Abend bin ich immer so müde, daß ich schlafe, anstatt aufzupassen, und wenn mein Herr das sieht, dann nimmt er seinen Hammer und schlägt mich. Er gibt mir auch nie genug zu essen. Ich glaube, ich werde bald vor Hunger sterben; ich bin jetzt schon ganz dünn. Und—wer weiß?—wenn eines Tages wirklich Diebe und Räuber kommen und das Geld

---

[**anstatt** instead of (2)]
nimmt er he takes
[**nehmen, er nimmt** (2)]
der Hammer the hammer
schlägt beats
[**schlagen, er schlägt** to beat, to strike]
er gibt he gives
[**geben, er gibt** to give]
nie never (2)
ich werde bald . . . sterben I shall soon die
[**bald** soon]
[**sterben, er stirbt** to die]
dünn thin (2)
wer who (2)
eines Tages one day, some day
Diebe thieves
[**der Dieb, die Diebe** (2)]
Räuber robbers
[**der Räuber, die Räuber** (2)]

stehlen to steal (2)
der Schmied the blacksmith (2)
schwer heavy (2)
der Hammer the hammer (2)
schlägt mich tot beats me to death
[**schlagen, er schlägt** to beat, to strike (2)]
[**tot** dead]
sage ich dir I tell you (2)
der Wunsch the wish
[**der Wunsch, die Wünsche**]
ich möchte I would like (to)
möglich possible (2)
weg-gehen to go away, to leave (2)
der Wunsch the wish (2)
den ich leicht erfüllen kann which I can easily fulfill
[**leicht** easy; light]
[**erfüllen** to fulfill]
weißt du was? you know what?
weil because (2)
zusammen together
in der Zeitung steht it says in the newspaper
[**die Zeitung, die Zeitungen** the newspaper]
hoffen to hope (2)
als Trompeter as a trumpet player
[**der Trompeter** the trumpet player]
das Orchester the orchestra (2)
finden to find (2)
musikalisch musical
wenn if
Hände hands
[**die Hand, die Hände**]
noch nicht not yet
die Trommel the drum
[**die Trommel, die Trommeln**]
die Leute the people (2)
wie like
braucht man one needs
[**man** one; they; people]
was wird . . . sagen what will . . . say
hören to hear (2)
darf ich may I
[**dürfen** may; to be allowed, permitted]
gegen seinen Willen against his will
[**der Wille** the will (2)]
verlassen to leave
[**verlassen, er verläßt**]
der Teufel the devil
[**der Teufel, die Teufel**]
schlecht bad, wicked (2)

stehlen, dann nimmt der Schmied vielleicht seinen schweren Hammer und schlägt mich tot. Ich habe Angst, sage ich dir! Ich habe nur einen Wunsch: Ich möchte so schnell wie möglich von hier weggehen. Aber wohin?"–„Das ist ein Wunsch, den ich leicht erfüllen kann", sagt der Esel. „Weißt du was? Mein Herr braucht mich auch nicht mehr, weil ich so alt bin. Warum gehen wir nicht beide zusammen nach Bremen? In der Zeitung steht, daß man dort Musiker braucht. Ich hoffe, als Trompeter im Orchester Arbeit zu finden. Bist du musikalisch? Wenn deine Hände noch nicht zu schwach sind, kannst du vielleicht die Trommel schlagen. Gute Leute wie dich braucht man in einem Orchester immer. Komm!"–„Aber was wird der Schmied sagen, wenn er hört, daß ich weggehen will?" antwortet der Hund; „darf ich gegen seinen Willen das Haus verlassen?"– „Dein Herr ist ein Teufel", sagt der Esel; „er ist so schlecht, daß du von ihm keine Erlaubnis brauchst. Nimm deine Sachen und folge mir!"

2.

Die Idee gefällt dem Hund, und er folgt dem Esel. Nach einer Weile sehen sie eine schwarze Katze am Wege sitzen. Sie

---

die Erlaubnis the permission (2)
deine Sachen your things
[**die Sache, die Sachen** the thing; matter; affair]
folgen to follow

die Idee gefällt dem Hund the dog likes the idea
[**die Idee, die Ideen**]
[**gefallen, er gefällt** to please]
folgen to follow (2)
nach after
die Weile the while
schwarz black
die Katze the cat
[**die Katze, die Katzen**]
am Wege by the road(side)
[**der Weg, die Wege** the way, road (2)]
sitzen to sit (2)

jung young
das Gesicht the face (2)
traurig sad
fragen to ask
ach! alas! (2)
die Katze the cat (2)
das Leben macht mir keine Freude mehr I don't enjoy life any more
[**das Leben** the life]
[**Freude machen** to bring, give joy, pleasure]
[**die Freude, die Freuden** the joy, pleasure]
keine Zähne mehr no teeth any more
[**der Zahn, die Zähne** the tooth]
deshalb therefore, because of that
Mäuse mice
[**die Maus, die Mäuse**]
fangen to catch
[**fangen, er fängt**]
ich möchte I would like (2)
hinter behind
der Ofen the stove
[**der Ofen, die Öfen** the stove, oven]
liegen to lie
warm warm
die Milch the milk
trinken to drink (2)
schlafen to sleep
[**schlafen, er schläft** (2)]
von Mäusen of mice
[**die Maus, die Mäuse** (2)]
träumen to dream
anstatt sie zu fangen instead of catching them
[**fangen, er fängt** (2)]
nichts mehr nothing any more
[**nichts** nothing (2)]
die Herrin the mistress
länger longer (2)
behalten to keep
[**behalten, er behält**]
leider unfortunately (2)
reich rich
um mir falsche Zähne zu kaufen to buy false teeth for me
[**um . . . zu** (in order) to]
[**falsch** false, wrong]
[**der Zahn, die Zähne** the tooth (2)]
[**kaufen** to buy]
ich selbst I myself
wenn ich an . . . zurückdenke when I think back on . . .
[**denken an** to think of]
die Jugend the youth

ist auch nicht mehr jung; sie ist schwach und müde und macht ein langes Gesicht. „Warum so traurig?" fragt der Esel.—„Ach!" antwortet die Katze, „das Leben macht mir keine Freude mehr. Ich bin alt und habe keine Zähne mehr, und deshalb kann ich keine Mäuse mehr fangen. Ich bin immer müde. Ich möchte hinter dem Ofen liegen und warme Milch trinken; ich will schlafen und von Mäusen t r ä u m e n , anstatt sie zu fangen. Weil ich jetzt nichts mehr fangen kann, will meine Herrin mich nicht länger im Haus behalten. Sie ist leider auch nicht reich genug, um mir falsche Zähne zu kaufen. Ich selbst habe natürlich auch nicht genug Geld. Ach, wenn ich an meine Jugend und an meine schönen weißen Zähne zurückdenke, dann werde ich ganz melancholisch! Ich bin von Natur optimistisch und lache gern; aber wenn ich jetzt den Mund aufmache, um zu lachen, dann sieht man, daß ich keine Zähne mehr habe, und jeder weiß sofort, wie alt ich bin. Ach, das Leben ist für eine alte Katze nicht leicht. Es ist bitter, alt zu sein. Aber was kann man machen?"—„Warum kommst du nicht mit uns nach Bremen?"

---

weiß white
werde ich I become
melancholisch melancholy
von Natur by nature
[**die Natur** the nature]
optimistisch optimistic
und (ich) lache gern and (I) like to laugh
[**lachen** to laugh (2)]
[**gern(e)** gladly, with pleasure]
der Mund the mouth
auf-machen to open
um zu lachen in order to laugh
sieht man one sees
[**man** one; they; people; (2)]
jeder everyone, everybody
[**jeder, jede, jedes** every, each (2)]
das Leben life (2)
leicht easy (2)
bitter bitter
alt zu sein to be old
machen do

jeder everybody (2)
ziemlich fairly, rather
gut well
singen to sing
besonders especially
die Nacht the night (2)
versprechen to promise
[**versprechen, er verspricht** (2)]
das Symphonieorchester the symphony orchestra (2)
jemand someone, somebody
wie like (2)
besonders especially (2)
Serenaden serenades
[**die Serenade, die Serenaden**]
spielen to play
herrlich wonderful, splendid
die Idee the idea (2)
schreien to screech
[**schreien** to scream, shout, screech (2)]
voller Freude full of joy
[**voll** full (2)]
[**die Freude** the joy, pleasure (2)
froh glad, happy
jemand someone, somebody (2)
noch still (2)
verdienen to earn
eines Tages some day, one day (2)
neu new
kaufen to buy (2)
wenn ich an . . . denke when I think of . . .
[**denken an** to think of (2)]
[**neu** new (2)]
fast almost
vor Freude with joy
ich schäme mich I am ashamed
[**sich schämen** to be ashamed]
wegen because of, on account of
sie macht . . . zu she closes, shuts
[**zu-machen** to close, to shut]
der Mund the mouth (2)
wieder again (2)
zeigen to show (2)
die Freunde the friends
[**der Freund, die Freunde** (2)]
die Zeit the time (2)
weiter-gehen to go on, to keep going
[**weiter** farther, further]
spät late

sagt der Esel; „jeder weiß, daß Katzen ziemlich gut singen, besonders in der Nacht. Ich kann dir nichts versprechen, aber ich glaube, das Symphonieorchester von Bremen braucht jemand wie dich—besonders wenn es Serenaden spielt."—„Das ist eine herrliche Idee!" schreit die Katze voller Freude; „ich bin so froh, daß jemand mich in meinen alten Tagen noch braucht. Vielleicht verdiene ich dort auch so viel Geld, daß ich mir eines Tages neue Zähne kaufen kann. Wenn ich an neue Zähne denke, möchte ich fast vor Freude lachen; aber ich schäme mich wegen meiner Zähne. Zähne? Hahaha!" Und sie macht den Mund sofort wieder zu, denn sie will nicht zeigen, daß sie keine Zähne mehr hat. „Komm!" sagen die zwei Freunde; „wir haben nicht viel Zeit. Wir müssen weitergehen. Es ist schon spät."

3.

Die drei gehen weiter. Nach einer Weile hören und sehen sie einen Hahn in einem Garten neben der Straße. Er sitzt auf einem Apfelbaum und schreit; aber er schreit nicht vor Freude. „Warum schreist du so laut?" fragt der Esel; „macht dir das

---

drei three (2)
  gehen weiter go on
    [**weiter-gehen** to go on, to keep going (2)]
nach after (2)
  die Weile the while (2)
  der Hahn the rooster
    [**der Hahn, die Hähne**]
  der Garten the garden
    [**der Garten, die Gärten** (2)]
  neben next to, beside
der Apfelbaum the apple tree
    [**der Apfel, die Äpfel** the apple]
    [**der Baum, die Bäume** the tree]
  vor Freude with joy (2)
fragen to ask (2)

macht dir das Leben keine Freude mehr? don't you enjoy life any more?
[**Freude machen** to give, bring joy, pleasure (2)]
singen to sing (2)
der Hahn the rooster (2)
traurig sad (2)
das Lied the song
[**das Lied, die Lieder**]
erzählen to tell, to relate (2)
die Geschichte the story, the tale
[**die Geschichte, die Geschichten**]
jung young (2)
gesund healthy, in good health (2)
erst only
fünf five (2)
Jahre years
[**das Jahr, die Jahre** (2)]
liegen to lie (2)
noch still (2)
vor mir before me
morgen tomorrow
ist es zu Ende it is (all) over
[**zu Ende** at an end, finished, over]
morgen tomorrow (2)
letzt last
die Herrin the mistress (2)
der Geburtstag the birthday
[**die Geburt** the birth]
der Festtag the day of celebration, holiday
[**das Fest, die Feste** the holiday; the festival]
schrecklich terrible
das Weib the woman
[**das Weib, die Weiber** the woman; wife; "old hag"]
am Abend in the evening (2)
die Suppe the soup
das gefällt mir natürlich nicht I don't like that, of course
[**gefallen, er gefällt** to please (2)]
ich habe Angst I am afraid
vor dem Tod of death
[**der Tod** the death; Death]
noch nicht not yet (2)
sterben to die
[**sterben, er stirbt** (2)]
nein no (2)
leben to live
bevor before (2)
niemand no one, nobody (2)
die Welt the world
machen do
wenn if (2)

Leben keine Freude mehr?"—„Ich schreie nicht, ich s i n g e", antwortet der Hahn; „ich singe ein trauriges Lied." Und nun erzählt er seine traurige Geschichte. „Ich bin jung, gesund und schön. Ich bin erst fünf Jahre alt, und das Leben liegt noch vor mir. Aber morgen ist es zu Ende, morgen ist mein letzter Tag. Morgen hat meine Herrin Geburtstag, und weil das ein Festtag ist, will das schreckliche Weib mich am Abend in der Suppe essen. Das gefällt mir natürlich nicht. Ich habe Angst vor dem Tod. Ich will noch nicht sterben. Nein, nein! Ich will leben! Ich möchte von hier weggehen, bevor ich sterben muß; aber ich habe niemand in der ganzen Welt.—Aber was kann man machen! Wenn Gott niemand schickt, um mir zu helfen, dann ist mein kurzes Leben zu Ende. Nun, morgen bin ich tot, und deshalb singe ich jetzt, auf deutsch, das herrliche Lied aus dem letzten Akt der Oper ‚Aida': ‚Leb wohl, o Erde, o du Tal der Tränen!' Arme Aida! Zu jung und schön zum Sterben! Wie ich."—„Schrecklich!" rufen die drei Freunde. Aber sie wissen

---

Gott God
schicken to send (2)
um mir zu helfen to help me
[**um . . . zu** (in order) to (2)]
zu Ende over, finished, at an end (2)
nun well
tot dead (2)
deshalb therefore (2)
auf deutsch in German
herrlich wonderful (2)
das Lied the song (2)
letzt last (2)
der Akt the act
[**der Akt, die Akte**]
die Oper the opera
[**die Oper, die Opern**]
Leb' wohl, o Erde Farewell, o Earth
o du Tal der Tränen! o, thou vale of tears!
[**die Erde** the earth; ground]
[**das Tal, die Täler** the valley]
[**die Träne, die Tränen** the tear]
zum Sterben to die
wie ich like me
schrecklich! terrible! (2)

die Situation the situation
[**die Situation, die Situationen**]
machen do
komm herunter come down
der Baum the tree (2)
alle all
die Stadt the town
[**die Stadt, die Städte** the town, city]
zum Sterben to die (2)
alle all (2)
um zu . . . spielen in order to play
[**spielen** to play (2)]
die Stimme the voice (2)
rein pure
modern modern
die Musik the music
immer noch still (2)
deine Sachen your things
[**die Sache, die Sachen** the thing, matter; affair (2)]
voller Freude full of joy (2)
größt greatest
[**groß** great, large, big, tall (2)]
erfüllt fulfilled
[**erfüllen** to fulfill (2)]
vor einem großen Publikum before a large audience
[**das Publikum** the public, audience]
das Weib the woman (2)
die Suppe the soup (2)

froh glad, happy (2)
die Hoffnung the hope
spät late (2)
es wird dunkel it is getting dark
[**dunkel** dark]
die Stadt the town (2)
ziemlich rather (2)
weit far
der Wald the forest, woods
[**der Wald, die Wälder**]
bis until
steigen to climb (2)
der Zweig the branch
[**der Zweig, die Zweige**]
fliegen to fly
die Spitze the top
[**die Spitze, die Spitzen** the point, tip, top]
zumacht closes
[**zu-machen** to close, to shut (2)]
danken to thank

natürlich sofort, was der traurige Hahn in dieser Situation machen muß. „Komm herunter von deinem Baum", rufen alle drei, „und geh mit uns in die Stadt Bremen! Du bist zu jung und viel zu schön zum Sterben. Wir sind alle Musiker und gehen nach Bremen, um im Symphonieorchester zu spielen und zu singen. Du hast eine schöne und laute Stimme. Sie ist vielleicht nicht mehr ganz rein, aber für moderne Musik ist sie immer noch gut genug. Geh, hole deine Sachen und komm mit uns!"–„Herrlich!" schreit der Hahn voller Freude; „dann ist mein größter Wunsch erfüllt: ich kann vor einem großen Publikum singen!–Und meine Herrin, dieses schreckliche Weib, kann ihre Suppe ohne mich essen."

4.

Alle vier gehen nun froh und voller Hoffnung weiter. Es ist schon spät, der Abend kommt, es wird dunkel, aber die Stadt ist noch ziemlich weit. Sie kommen in einen großen Wald. Hier müssen sie bleiben, bis der Morgen kommt. Der Esel und der Hund schlafen unter einem Baum, die Katze steigt auf einen Zweig, der Hahn fliegt in die Spitze des Baumes. Bevor der Hahn die Augen zumacht, dankt er Gott im Himmel, daß sein kurzes Leben morgen nicht in der Suppe endet. Wie er fertig ist, sieht er weit weg zwischen den Bäumen etwas Helles, etwas Weißes. „Was ist das?" sagt er und reibt sich die Augen. „Ah, ein Stern!"

Gott God (2)
der Himmel heaven
[**der Himmel** the sky, heaven (2)]
enden to end
weit weg far away (2)
zwischen between
etwas Helles something bright
[**hell** light, bright, clear (2)]
weiß white (2)
reibt sich die Augen rubs his eyes
[**reiben** to rub (2)]
der Stern the star
[**der Stern, die Sterne**]

die Oper the opera (2)
hold lovely
der Abendstern the evening star
mitten im Lied in the middle of the song
[**mitten in** in the middle of]
das Licht the light
[**das Licht, die Lichter**]
warm warm (2)
das Zimmer the room
[**das Zimmer, die Zimmer**]
kalt cold
der Wald the forest, woods (2)
zum Essen und zum Trinken to eat and drink
fliegen to fly (2)
vom Baum herunter down from the tree
wecken to wake up, to awaken
die anderen the others
leise softly
[**leise** soft, gentle]
bis until (2)
das Licht the light (2)
Menschen men, people
[**der Mensch, die Menschen** the man, human being (2)]
wohnen to live, to reside
böse wicked, bad (2)
leben to live (2)
allein alone (2)
sag uns tell us
leise softly (2)
die Tür the door
[**die Tür, die Türen** (2)]
sieht looks
das Schlüsselloch the keyhole
[**der Schlüssel, die Schlüssel** the key]
nun well (2)
die anderen the others (2)
als when (2)
zurück-kommen to come back, to return
das Schlüsselloch the keyhole (2)
alles everything, all
gefällt mir nicht I do not like
das Zimmer the room (2)
der Tisch the table
[**der Tisch, die Tische**]
viele many
Weinflaschen wine bottles
[**die Weinflasche, die Weinflaschen**]
die Mitte the middle, center, midst (2)
das Schwein the pig

denkt er und singt sofort das schöne Lied aus Richard Wagners Oper ,Tannhäuser': „O du, mein holder Abendstern . . ." Aber mitten im Lied sieht er, daß es kein Stern ist. Das Licht kommt von einem Haus. „Nun, wenn dort ein Haus steht, dann ist es natürlich viel besser für uns, wenn wir in einem warmen Zimmer schlafen als hier im kalten Wald. Und–wer weiß?– vielleicht finden wir dort auch etwas zum Essen und zum Trinken." Schnell fliegt er vom Baum herunter und weckt die anderen, und nun gehen alle vier so leise wie möglich durch den Wald, bis das Haus vor ihnen liegt. „Wo Licht ist, müssen Menschen wohnen", sagt der Esel; „aber ich glaube nicht, daß die Leute in diesem Haus gute Menschen sind. Nur böse Menschen leben ganz allein in einem großen Wald."–„Geh zum Haus und sag uns, was du siehst", sagt der Hund zum Esel. Der Esel geht leise zur Tür und sieht durch das Schlüsselloch. „Nun?" fragen die anderen, als er zurückkommt; „was siehst du?"–„Ich kann durch das kleine Schlüsselloch nicht alles sehen", sagt der Esel; „aber was ich sehe, gefällt mir nicht. Im Zimmer steht ein Tisch mit vielen Weinflaschen, und in der Mitte liegt ein kleines Schwein mit einem Apfel im Maul."– „Hm!" sagt der dünne, hungrige Hund; „das ist etwas für uns." –„Nein", sagt der Esel, „das ist leider noch nicht alles. Um den Tisch sitzen Männer. Sie essen, trinken und rauchen ihre Pfeifen, und vor ihnen auf dem Tisch liegt ein großer Sack mit Geld. Ich glaube, diese Männer sind Diebe und Räuber."–

[**das Schwein, die Schweine** the pig, swine]
der Apfel the apple (2)
das Maul the mouth
[**das Maul, die Mäuler** the mouth (of an animal)]
Hm! yum-yum!
alles all, everything (2)
um around
der Tisch the table (2)
rauchen to smoke (2)
die Pfeife the pipe (2)
vor ihnen before them
der Sack the sack, the bag (2)

solch such

sollten should (2)

treiben to drive

intelligent intelligent

legen to lay, to put, to place

das Fenster the window

[**das Fenster, die Fenster**]

springen to jump, to spring

der Rücken the back

[**der Rücken, die Rücken**]

der Kopf the head

[**der Kopf, die Köpfe**]

wie musikalisch how musical (2)

bellen to bark (2)

miauen to miaow

krähen to crow

fallen to fall

[**fallen, er fällt** to fall]

zusammen together (2)

das Fenster the window (2)

wie when

die Musik the music (2)

der Tod Death (2)

der Teufel the devil (2)

um sie zu holen to get them

ohne . . . zu sehen without looking

nach rechts oder links to the right or left (2)

so schnell as fast as

tragen to carry (2)

setzen sich sit down

[**sich setzen** to sit down]

nach Herzenslust to their hearts' desire

[**das Herz, die Herzen** the heart]

[**die Lust** the desire, pleasure, delight]

die Geschichte the story, tale (2)

werden wir . . . erzählen we shall tell you

das Mal the time (2)

„Solch schlechte Menschen sollten es nicht so gut haben“ sagen die anderen drei; “wir sollten sie aus dem Haus treiben! Aber wie?“ Die intelligente Katze hat eine gute Idee. Der Esel legt seine Füße leise an das Fenster, der Hund springt auf den Rücken des Esels, die Katze steigt auf den Hund, und der Hahn fliegt auf den Kopf der Katze. Und nun zeigen sie, wie musikalisch sie sind. Der Esel schreit, der Hund bellt, die Katze miaut, und der Hahn kräht. Dann fallen sie alle vier zusammen durch das Fenster in das Zimmer. Wie die Räuber diese schreckliche Musik hören, glauben sie, der Tod und der Teufel sind im Haus, um sie zu holen. Ohne nach rechts oder links zu sehen, rennen sie aus dem Haus so schnell ihre Beine sie tragen können. Nun setzen sich unsere vier Freunde an den Tisch und essen und trinken nach Herzenslust.

Die Geschichte von den vier Musikern ist hier noch nicht zu Ende. Die ganze Geschichte ist ziemlich lang, und deshalb werden wir Ihnen das Ende ein anderes Mal erzählen.

DIE DREI FREUNDE

[2A]

NOTES

I. 1. With five exceptions, the forms of the definite articles are also those of the relative pronoun. The five exceptions are the four genitives and the dative plural in which the forms of the definite articles are lengthened: **des** (genitive singular masculine and neuter) is lengthened to **dessen; der** (genitive singular feminine and genitive plural) to **deren;** and **den** (dative plural) to **denen.**

Das wilde Leben, *das* sie führen . . . The wild life *that (which)* they lead

Du bist der Diener des Todes, *der* dich hinausschickt . . . . . . *who* sends you out

Er klopft an alle Häuser, in *denen* der Tod zu Gast ist. . . . in *which* . . .

2. The relative pronoun agrees in *gender and number* with the noun(s) or pronoun(s) to which it refers; its *case,* however, depends on its function within its own clause. See above.

3. If the antecedent is neither a noun nor a pronoun, but a word such as **alles, nichts, etwas, viel(es), das** (that), or a substantived neuter adjective denoting the *quality* of something, the relative pronoun used to refer to such words is **was.**

***alles, was* ich habe** everything that I have

das ist *etwas, was* ich noch nicht weiß that is something that I do not yet know

ich habe *nichts, was* ich Ihnen geben kann I have nothing that I can give you

es ist nicht *das, was* ich suche it isn't (that) what I am looking for

es ist *das Beste, was* ich habe it is the best that I have

II. 1. The comparative of all German adjectives and adverbs is formed by adding **–er** to the stem (**–r** if the stem ends in **–e; leise,** for example).

The English *than* after a comparison is expressed by **als.**

Jeder von uns bekommt *weniger als* die Hälfte. . . . *less than* half

Der Gedanke an das Geld wiegt *schwerer als* . . . weighs *more heavily than*

Ich kann *schneller* laufen *als* du. . . . *faster than*

2. In a relatively small number of very common adjectives, the **–er** ending of the comparative causes umlaut of the stem vowel.

Er macht die Armen ärmer. He makes the poor poorer.
Sind wir zwei nicht stärker als er? Are the two of us not stronger than he?

The most frequently used adjectives of this group are: **alt, arm, dumm, groß, hart** (hard), **jung, kalt, klug** (intelligent), **krank** (sick, ill), **kurz, lang, nah, oft** (often, frequent), **scharf, schwach, stark, warm.** The comparative of **hoch** (high, tall) is **höher.**

3. The adjectives and adverbs **viel, gut,** and **gern** are irregular in their comparison:

viel—mehr; gut—besser; gern—lieber

III. 1. The superlative is formed by adding **–st** to the stem of the adjective (or to a present participle used as an adjective); **–est** if the stem of the adjective ends in a **d, t,** or an **s**-sound.

Der Tod ist unser schlimm*st*er Feind.
Wer die niedrig*st*e Karte zieht . . .

2. Adjectives which have umlaut in the comparative also have it in the superlative.

Der jung*st*e zieht die niedrig*st*e Karte.

3. The following adjectives and adverbs are irregular in the superlative:

groß—größt-; gut—best-; hoch—höchst-; nah—nächst-; viel—meist-; gern—am liebsten

IV. 1. In speaking to two or more persons with whom one is on particularly informal or intimate terms, German uses the second person plural with the pronoun **ihr**; the verb ending of the second person plural is **–t** (or, under certain conditions, **–et**; see Notes to Story 1A, **I.** 1.b.).

Geh*t* diesen Weg entlang, bis *ihr* einen großen Nußbaum erblick*t*.

Note: The second person plural of the verb **sein** is irregular: **ihr seid.**

2. The dative and accusative form of the personal pronoun of the second person plural is **euch.**

Gott sei mit *euch!*

The basic form of the possessive adjective (and pronoun) is **euer** your (yours).

Wenn *euer* Herz verlangt, den Tod zu finden . . .

V. 1. The present participle is formed by adding **–d** to the infinitive.

lachen*d* laughing; **schreien*d*** shouting

2. A present (and past) participle can be used as an adjective. It must then be inflected like other adjectives.

ein schnell wirkendes Gift
(dies muß gestohlenes Gut sein)

Note: Depending on the context, **meinen** can mean (a) to say (b) to think (c) to mean.

„Du hast recht", meint der zweite. . . . says the second
Was meinst du? (Story 2A, Part 4) What do you think?
Ich meine nur dich und mich. I mean only you and myself.

IDIOMS FOR REVIEW

er ist seit langem tot he has been dead for a long time
wieder einmal once again
auf einmal suddenly
recht haben to be right
  du hast recht you are right
dann muß es uns gelingen then we must succeed
  es gelingt mir I succeed
noch ein Glas! one more glass!
er ist außer sich he is beside himself
  ich bin außer mir I am beside myself
sich Sorgen machen to worry
  macht euch keine Sorgen don't worry
  ich mache mir große Sorgen I am greatly worried
sich auf den Weg machen to set out on one's way; to leave
  sie machen sich auf den Weg they set out on their way
aufs Land to the country
um den Hals fallen to embrace
  er fällt ihm um den Hals he embraces him

drei three (3)
Freunde friends
[**der Freund, die Freunde** (3]

folgend following
[**folgen** to follow; to obey (3)]
die Geschichte the story, tale (3)
die Erzählung the tale
[**die Erzählung, die Erzählungen**]
vierzehnt fourteenth
das Jahrhundert the century
[**das Jahrhundert, die Jahrhunderte**]
früh early (2)
das Gasthaus the inn
[**das Gasthaus, die Gasthäuser**]
[**der Gast, die Gäste** the guest]
spielen to play (3)
Karten cards
[**die Karte, die Karten** the card; post card; map]
ein Glas one glass
[**das Glas, die Gläser**]
der Teufel the devil (3)
wild wild
führen to lead (2)
die Stadt the town, city (3)
bekannt known, well-known
die Mütter the mothers
[**die Mutter, die Mütter**]
fürchten to fear, to be afraid
die Töchter the daughters
[**die Tochter, die Töchter**]
jeder every, each (3)
der Vater the father
[**der Vater, die Väter**]
wünschen to wish
trinken weiter keep drinking
finden to find (3)
die Morgensonne the morning sun
[**die Sonne** the sun (3)]
das Gasthaus the inn (2)
bis in die Nacht into the night
[**bis** until (3)]
[**die Nacht, die Nächte** (3)]
bei Karten at cards
[**die Karte, die Karten** (2)]
auf ihre eigene Weise genießen enjoy in their own way
[**eigen** own]
[**die Weise** the way, manner]
[**genießen** to enjoy]

(FOUR PARTS)

Die drei Freunde

I.

Die folgende Geschichte ist eine Erzählung aus dem vierzehnten Jahrhundert.

Drei junge Männer sitzen schon am frühen Morgen in einem Gasthaus. Sie spielen Karten, trinken ein Glas nach dem anderen und lachen über Gott und Teufel. Das wilde Leben, das sie führen, ist in der ganzen Stadt bekannt. Die Mütter fürchten für ihre Töchter, und jeder Vater wünscht den dreien ein frühes Ende. Sie aber lachen nur und trinken weiter. Jeden Tag findet die Morgensonne sie in einem anderen Gasthaus, wo sie bis in die Nacht bei Karten und Wein sitzen und das Leben auf ihre eigene Weise genießen.

Wie sie an jenem Morgen wieder einmal den Tag mit einer Flasche Wein beginnen, hören sie auf einmal draußen auf der

---

wie as
jener, jene, jenes that
wieder einmal once again
die Flasche the bottle (3)
beginnen to begin
auf einmal suddenly
draußen outside

die Straße the street (3)
hell clear
[**hell** bright, light, clear (3)]
der Ton the sound
[**der Ton, die Töne** the sound, tone]
das Glöcklein the little bell
[**die Glocke, die Glocken** the bell]
das Fenster the window (3)
erblicken to see, to catch sight of
der Zug the procession
[**der Zug, die Züge** the procession; train; feature]
der Leichenwagen the hearse
[**die Leiche, die Leichen** the corpse]
[**der Wagen, die Wagen** the carriage; car, auto; wagon]
an der Spitze at the head
[**die Spitze, die Spitzen** the top, tip, point, head (2)]
der Zug the procession (2)
Mädchen girls
[**das Mädchen, die Mädchen** the girl]
die Mutter the mother (2)
die Töchter the daughters
[**die Tochter, die Töchter** (2)]
hinaus out
befehlen command
[**befehlen, er befiehlt** to order, to command]
die drei jungen Leute the three young men
der Wirt the innkeeper
fragen to ask (3)
wen man da zu Grabe trägt whom they are carrying to his grave
[**das Grab, die Gräber** the grave]
[**tragen, er trägt** to carry; to wear (3)]
der Wirt the innkeeper (2)
bald soon (2)
berichten to report, to tell
kennen to know
gut well (2)
es sind Bauern they are peasants
[**der Bauer, die Bauern** the farmer, peasant]
nah near
das Dorf the village
[**das Dorf, die Dörfer**]
der Tote the dead man
[**tot** dead (3)]
einzig only, sole; unique
der Sohn the son
[**der Sohn, die Söhne**]
die Familie the family
[**die Familie, die Familien**]
den . . . zur letzten Ruhe bringen whom . . . are laying to rest

Straße den hellen Ton eines Glöckleins. Sie sehen durch das Fenster und erblicken einen kleinen Zug von Menschen, die langsam einem Leichenwagen folgen. An der Spitze des Zuges geht eine Frau mit zwei jungen Mädchen. Es ist eine Mutter mit ihren Töchtern. „Geh hinaus", befehlen die drei jungen Leute dem Wirt, „und frage, wen man da zu Grabe trägt!" Der Wirt kommt bald zurück und berichtet: „Hört, ihr Herren! Ich kenne die Leute gut. Es sind Bauern aus einem nahen Dorfe. Der Tote ist der einzige Sohn einer armen Familie, den seine Mutter und seine Schwestern zur letzten Ruhe bringen. Der Vater ist seit langem tot. Ach, die armen Frauen! Was für ein trauriges Leben liegt jetzt vor ihnen! Auf sie wartet nichts als schwere Arbeit und bittere Armut."—„Schade!" sagt der erste; „die hübschen Mädchen verdienen etwas Besseres."—„Das ist wahr", entgegnet der Wirt; „der Tod ist wirklich unser bösester

---

[**letzt** last (2)]
[**die Ruhe** the rest, peace, quiet]
[**bringen** to bring, to take]
Schwestern sisters
[**die Schwester, die Schwestern**]
der Vater the father (2)
ist seit langem tot has been dead for a long time
ach! alas! (3)
was für ein . . .! what a . . .!
auf sie wartet nichts als . . . nothing but . . . await them
[**warten auf** to wait for (3)]
schwer hard (3)
bitter bitter (2)
die Armut the poverty
schade! it's a pity!
der erste the first (3)
hübsch pretty
Mädchen girls
[**das Mädchen, die Mädchen** (2)]
verdienen to deserve
[**verdienen** to earn; to deserve (2)]
etwas Besseres something better (2)
wahr true
entgegnen to reply, to answer
der Tod Death (3)
bösest worst
[**böse** bad, wicked; angry (2)]

der Feind the enemy
[der Feind, die Feinde]
nimmt takes
[nehmen, er nimmt (3)]
der Sohn the son (2)
der Bruder the brother
[der Bruder, die Brüder]
die Armen the poor (people)
ärmer poorer
wer wird . . . heiraten wollen who will want to marry
[heiraten to marry]
die beiden the two
Schwestern sisters
[die Schwester, die Schwestern (2)]
du hast recht you are right
[recht haben to be right]
meint says
[meinen to mean; to say; to think]
der zweite the second
ohne zu fürchten without being afraid
[fürchten to fear, to be afraid (2)]
und . . . ein plötzliches Ende macht and puts a sudden end to . . .
[plötzlich sudden]
die Lust the pleasure, delight; desire (2)
froh happy, glad (3)
noch lebt is still alive
[leben to live, to be alive (3)]
Gott God (3)
der dritte the third
wahr true (2)
schlimmst worst
[schlimm bad]
der Feind the enemy (2)
töten to kill
und . . . werden and become
[werden, er wird (3)]
Helden heroes
[der Held, die Helden the hero]
Brüder brothers
[der Bruder, die Brüder the brother (2)]
geben to give (2)
eure Hand your hand
[die Hand, die Hände (3)]
lassen to let
[lassen, er läßt (3)]
beschließen to resolve
trotz aller Gefahren in spite of all dangers
[trotz in spite of]
[die Gefahr, die Gefahren the danger]

Feind. Er nimmt den Vater und den Sohn und Bruder und macht die Armen ärmer. Wer wird die beiden Schwestern jetzt heiraten wollen?"–„Du hast recht", meint der zweite; „der Tod wartet auf uns alle. Ich möchte trinken, trinken, Tag und Nacht trinken, ohne zu fürchten, daß der Tod kommt und meiner Lust ein plötzliches Ende macht. Wie kann ich wirklich froh sein, wenn ich weiß, daß der Tod noch lebt?"–„Bei Gott!" ruft der dritte; „es ist wahr, der Tod ist unser schlimmster Feind. Ha! Warum den Tod nicht töten und große Helden werden? Kommt, Brüder, gebt mir eure Hand und laßt uns beschließen, trotz aller Gefahren den Tod zu suchen und zu fangen! Wenn wir einander helfen und versprechen, einander in Not und Gefahr nicht zu verlassen, dann muß es uns gelingen. Kommt, Brüder, noch ein Glas, aber diesmal auf den Tod des Todes, und dann hinaus nach jenem Dorf, um ihn zu fangen und zu töten!"

---

suchen to look for, to seek, to search
fangen to catch
[**fangen, er fängt** (3)]
wenn if
einander one another, each other
helfen to help
[**helfen, er hilft** (3)]
versprechen to promise
[**versprechen, er verspricht** (3)]
einander one another (2)
die Not the need
[**die Not** the need, distress, misery]
die Gefahr the danger (2)
verlassen to abandon
[**verlassen, er verläßt** to leave, to abandon]
dann muß es uns gelingen then we must succeed
[**es gelingt mir** I succeed]
noch ein Glas one more glass
auf den Tod des Todes to the death of Death
hinaus out (2)
nach jenem Dorf to that village
[**das Dorf, die Dörfer** the village (2)]
um . . . zu fangen to catch
töten to kill (2)

die Tür the door (3)
wie how
lachend laughing
wild schreiend shouting wildly
[**wild** wild (2)]
[**schreien** to shout, scream (3)]
aufs Land to the country
[**das Land, die Länder** the country]
hinaus-eilen to hurry out
[**eilen** to hurry, to hasten]
solch such (2)
schütteln to shake
weise wisely
[**weise** wise]
grau gray
der Kopf the head (2)

etwa about, approximately
die Stunde the hour (3)
treffen to meet
[**treffen, er trifft** to meet, to encounter]
an einem Stock on a cane
[**der Stock, die Stöcke** the stick; cane; floor (of a building)]
die Landstraße the country road, highway
[**das Land, die Länder** the country (2)]
entlanggeht goes along
[**entlang** along]
die Farbe the color
[**die Farbe, die Farben**]
das Haar the hair
[**das Haar, die Haare**]
weiß white (3)
das Gesicht the face (3)
bleich pale
der Rücken the back
wie when
erblicken to see, to catch sight of (2)
grüßen to greet, to salute (2)
freundlich in a friendly way (3)
sei mit euch! be with you!
ganz allein all alone (3)
bei deinem Alter at your age
[**das Alter** the (old) age]
noch nicht not yet (3)
der Menschen sucht who is looking for men
[**suchen** to look for, to seek, to search (2)]
ach nein! oh no!
erwidern to reply, to answer
der Alte the old man

2.

Der Wirt steht an der Tür seines Gasthauses und sieht, wie die drei laut lachend und wild schreiend aufs Land hinauseilen, um den Tod zu fangen. „Solch wilde Freude nimmt ein wildes Ende", sagt er und schüttelt weise den grauen Kopf.

Nach etwa einer Stunde treffen die drei einen alten Mann, der langsam an einem Stock die Landstraße entlanggeht. Die Farbe seines Haares ist weiß, sein Gesicht ist bleich, sein Rücken krumm. Wie er die drei erblickt, bleibt er stehen und grüßt sie freundlich: „Gott sei mit euch, ihr jungen Herren!" —„Haha! Gott mit uns?" lacht der eine. „Sag, was tust du hier ganz allein bei deinem Alter? Warum bist du noch nicht tot? Ich glaube, du bist der Tod, der Menschen sucht."—„Ach nein", erwidert der Alte; „ich bin so alt, weil es Gottes Wille ist, daß ich so lange lebe, und deshalb muß ich mein Alter tragen, bis der Tod mich holen kommt. Aber er kommt nicht, und so wandere ich ruhelos von Dorf zu Dorf und klopfe früh und spät mit meinem Stock an alle Häuser, in denen der Tod zu Gast ist. Doch jedesmal, wenn ich ihn finde und ihn bitte, mich

---

der Wille the will (3)
deshalb therefore, for that reason (3)
das Alter the (old) age (2)
mich holen kommt comes to fetch me
wandern to wander
[**wandern** to wander, to hike, to go, to walk]
ruhelos without rest
[**–los** less, without]
klopfen to knock
spät late (3)
der Stock the cane (2)
in denen der Tod zu Gast ist in which Death is a guest
[**der Gast, die Gäste** the guest (2)]
doch yet, still, nevertheless
bitten to ask

in sein Reich to his kingdom
[**das Reich, die Reiche** the kingdom, empire, realm]
Alter old man
[**der Alte** the old man (2)]
die Zeit the time (3)
weiter-wandern keep on going
[**wandern** to wander, hike, walk, go (2)]
der zweite the second (2)
so . . . wie as . . . as (3)
sondern but (2)
der Diener the servant
[**der Diener, die Diener**]
um ihm zu berichten to tell him
[**berichten** to report, to tell (2)]
wen er . . . holen soll whom he should fetch
dunkel dark (2)
das Reich the kingdom (2)
der dritte the third (2)
der Narr the fool
[**der Narr, die Narren**]
wenn if
sogleich at once
tot-schlagen to beat to death (2)
sprich! speak!
[**sprechen, er spricht** to speak, to say]
stirb! die!
[**sterben, er stirbt** to die (3)]
entgegnen to reply, to answer (2)
schütteln to shake (2)
wenn if
euer Herz your heart
[**das Herz, die Herzen (2)**]
verlangen to demand, to ask
geht . . . entlang walk along
[**entlang** along (2)]
recht right (3)
die Seite the side
[**die Seite, die Seiten** the side; page]
der Nußbaum the walnut tree
[**die Nuß, die Nüsse** the nut]
wohnen to live, to dwell, to reside (2)
sei mit euch! be with you! (2)

eilen . . . entlang hurry along
[**eilen** to hurry, to hasten (2)]
der Weg the road
[**der Weg, die Wege** the way, road (3)]

so schnell as fast as

in sein Reich zu nehmen, höre ich ihn sagen: ‚Nein, Alter, deine Zeit ist noch nicht zu Ende.‘–Nun aber laßt mich weiterwandern, ihr Herren!“–„Nein, Alter“, sagt der zweite, „nicht so schnell! Kein Mensch kann so alt sein wie du. Du bist kein Mensch, sondern der Diener des Todes, der dich hinausschickt, um ihm zu berichten, wen er in sein dunkles Reich holen soll.“ –„Ha!“ ruft der dritte; „du bist ein Narr, wenn du denkst, daß wir dir glauben. Der Tod läßt dich so lange leben, weil er dich braucht, du böser Feind der Menschen! Wenn du uns nicht sogleich sagst, wo dein Herr ist, schlagen wir dich tot! Sprich oder stirb!“–„Nun, ihr Herren“, entgegnet der Alte und schüttelt traurig den Kopf, „wenn euer Herz verlangt, den Tod zu finden, dann geht diesen Weg entlang, bis ihr auf der rechten Seite einen großen Nußbaum erblickt. Unter diesem Baum wohnt und wartet der Tod. Dort werdet ihr ihn finden. Gott sei mit euch, ihr Herren!“

Wild lachend eilen die drei den Weg entlang.

3.

Sie laufen so schnell ihre Beine sie tragen können. Schon von fern erblicken sie den Nußbaum, der allein auf einem weiten Felde steht. Sie gehen langsam und leise, um den Tod nicht zu wecken, der vielleicht unter dem Baum schläft. Sie suchen, aber statt des Todes finden sie unter den Büschen am

---

von fern from afar
  [**fern** far, distant]
 der Nußbaum the walnut tree (2)
  [**die Nuß, die Nüsse** the nut (2)]
 weit wide
  [**weit** wide; far, distant (3)]
leise softly (3)
 um . . . nicht zu wecken in order not to wake up
  [**wecken** to awaken, to wake up (2)]
statt instead of

der Fuß the foot

[**der Fuß, die Füße** (3)]

herrlich wonderful (3)

der Schatz the treasure

[**der Schatz, die Schätze**]

Gold- und Silberstücke gold and silver coins

[**das Gold** the gold]

[**das Silber** the silver]

[**das Stück, die Stücke** the piece]

sieben seven (2)

Säcke sacks

[**der Sack, die Säcke** the sack, bag (3)]

springen to jump (2)

fast almost

die Brust the breast

[**die Brust** the breast, chest]

als when

der Schatz the treasure (2)

glänzen to glitter, to shine

außer sich beside themselves

[**außer** beside; except]

sogleich at once (2)

vergessen to forget

[**vergessen, er vergißt**]

an-fangen begin

[**an-fangen, er fängt an** (3)]

zählen to count (2)

was für ein . . .! what (a) . . .! (2)

das Glück the luck

[**das Glück** the luck, good fortune; happiness]

vor den Bergen before the mountains, mounds

[**der Berg, die Berge** the mountain]

das Gold the gold (2)

das Silber the silver (2)

träumen to dream (2)

offen open

angenehm pleasant

das . . . liegt which lies

ohne Sorgen without worries

[**die Sorge, die Sorgen** the worry, care]

voller full of

plötzlich suddenly (2)

gestohlen stolen

wie how

sicher safely

[**sicher** sure, safe; certain, certainly]

bringen to bring, to take (2)

das Problem the problem

[**das Problem, die Probleme**]

Fuß des Baumes einen herrlichen Schatz von Gold- und Silberstücken. Sieben volle Säcke! Das Herz springt ihnen fast vor Freude in der Brust, als sie den Schatz in der Sonne glänzen sehen. Sie sind so außer sich vor Freude, daß sie sogleich den Tod vergessen und anfangen, das Geld zu zählen. Was für ein Glück! Sie stehen vor den Bergen von Gold und Silber und träumen mit weit offenen Augen von dem angenehmen Leben, das ohne Sorgen und voller Lust vor ihnen liegt. Da sagt plötzlich der eine: „Dies muß gestohlenes Geld sein. Wie können wir es sicher nach Haus in die Stadt bringen? Es ist kein kleines Problem. Wenn die Leute uns sehen, werden sie glauben, daß wir Diebe sind, und ihr kennt die Strafe für Diebe: man wird uns hängen. Und damit ist dann unser frohes Leben sofort zu Ende."—„Richtig", sagt der zweite; „das Geld ist sicher gestohlenes Gut, aber das ist wirklich kein Grund, warum der Schatz nicht uns gehören sollte."—„Macht euch keine Sorgen!" spricht der älteste. „Das Problem ist leicht

---

werden sie glauben they will think
  Diebe thieves
    [**der Dieb, die Diebe** (3)]
  kennen to know
  die Strafe the punishment
    [**die Strafe, die Strafen**]
  man wird uns hängen they will hang us
    [**hängen** to hang]
damit with that
richtig right
    [**richtig** right, correct; real]
  sicher certainly, surely (2)
  gestohlenes Gut stolen goods
    [**das Gut, die Güter** the goods, property; estate]
  der Grund the reason
    [**der Grund, die Gründe** the reason, ground, bottom]
  gehören to belong
    [**gehören** to belong, to be part of]
macht euch keine Sorgen! don't worry!
    [**die Sorge, die Sorgen** the worry, care (2)]
  spricht says
    [**sprechen, er spricht** to speak, to say (2)]
  der älteste the oldest
das Problem the problem (2)
  leicht easy (3)

lösen to solve
im geheimen in secret, secretly
[**geheim** secret]
der Rat the advice
bleiben to stay (3)
auf-passen to watch (3)
um . . . zu kaufen to buy
etwas some
das Brot the bread
das Fleisch the meat
das Mittagessen lunch
[**der Mittag** noon, midday]
[**das Essen** the meal, food]
das Abendbrot supper
[**das Brot, die Brote** the (loaf of) bread (2)]
entscheiden to decide
wer whoever; he who
niedrigst lowest
[**niedrig** low]
ziehen to draw
[**ziehen** to draw, to pull; to go, march, move]
soll . . . gehen is to go
mischt shuffles
[**mischen** to mix]
der jüngste the youngest
ziehen to draw (2)
niedrigst lowest (2)
macht sich auf den Weg sets out on his way
[**ich mache mich auf den Weg** I set out on my way, I leave]

sobald as soon as
der jüngste the youngest (2)
fort away
der älteste the oldest (2)
hör gut zu! listen well!
[**zu-hören** to listen]
gleich equal
[**gleich** equal, same]
Teile parts
[**der Teil, die Teile** the part, share]
teilen to divide
[**teilen** to divide, to share]
bekommen to get, to receive (2)
weniger als less than
[**wenig** little]
die Hälfte the half
[**die Hälfte, die Hälften**]
behalten to keep
[**behalten, er behält** (3)]

zu lösen. Wir brauchen nur zu warten, bis die Nacht kommt. Dann tragen wir die Säcke im geheimen in die Stadt. Mein Rat ist, daß zwei von uns hier bei dem Schatz bleiben und auf das Geld aufpassen, und daß der dritte in die Stadt geht, um etwas Brot, Fleisch und Wein für unser Mittagessen und Abendbrot zu kaufen. Hier, laßt die Karten entscheiden! Wer die niedrigste Karte zieht, soll in die Stadt gehen." Er mischt die Karten. Der jüngste zieht die niedrigste Karte und macht sich auf den Weg zur Stadt.

4.

Sobald der jüngste fort ist, spricht der älteste: „Hör gut zu, Bruder! Wenn wir das Geld in drei gleiche Teile teilen, dann bekommt jeder von uns weniger als die Hälfte. Glaubst du nicht, daß es vielleicht besser ist, wenn jeder eine Hälfte behalten kann?"—„Natürlich", entgegnet der andere, der nicht sofort versteht, was sein Freund im Sinn hat; „nur verstehe ich nicht, wie es möglich ist, daß jeder eine Hälfte bekommt."—„Du Dummkopf!" antwortet der erste; „ich meine nicht jeden von uns d r e i e n . Ich meine nur dich und mich. Hör gut zu!" Und nun erklärt er, was er meint: „Wenn unser Freund zurückkehrt, ist er in unserer Gewalt. Sind wir zwei nicht stärker als

---

verstehen to understand
  im Sinn hat has in mind
    [**der Sinn, die Sinne** the sense, mind]
  verstehen to understand (2)
  die Hälfte the half (2)
der Dummkopf the blockhead
    [**dumm** stupid (3)]
  meinen to mean
    [**meinen** to mean; to think; to say (3)]
hör gut zu! listen well! (2)
    [**zu-hören** to listen (2)]
erklären to explain
zurück-kehren to come back, to return
  die Gewalt the power
stärker als stronger than
    [**stark** strong (2)]

scharf sharp
das Messer the knife
[**das Messer, die Messer**]
stehe auf! get up!
[**auf-stehen** to get up, to rise]
falle ihm um den Hals embrace him
[**fallen, er fällt** to fall (2)]
[**der Hals** the neck, throat]
als ob as if
küssen to kiss
hältst du ihn fest you hold him fast
[**halten, er hält** to hold]
[**fest** fast]
der Augenblick the moment
[**der Augenblick, die Augenblicke**]
stoße ich I thrust
[**stoßen, er stößt** to push, to thrust]
das Messer the knife (2)
was meinst du? what do you think?
denken an to think of (2)
der Gedanke the thought
[**der Gedanke, die Gedanken**]
wiegen to weigh
schwerer als more heavily than
die Liebe the love
beschließen to decide, to resolve (2)

indes meanwhile
[**indes, indessen** meanwhile; however]
teilen to share
[**teilen** to divide, to share (2)]
das Fleisch the meat (2)
nächst nearest
[**nah** near (2)]
die Apotheke the pharmacy, apothecary
verlangen to ask for, to demand (2)
schnell wirkend fast working
[**wirken** to work, to have an effect]
das Gift the poison
der Apotheker the pharmacist, apothecary, druggist
die Füchse the foxes
[**der Fuchs, die Füchse**]
brechen to break
[**brechen, er bricht**]
der Gänsestall the goose pen
[**die Gans, die Gänse** the goose]
[**der Stall, die Ställe** the stable, pen]
fressen to eat
[**fressen, er frißt**]

er? Siehst du dieses scharfe Messer hier? Wenn unser Freund kommt, dann stehe auf und falle ihm um den Hals, als ob du ihn vor Freude küssen willst. Dann hältst du ihn fest, und in diesem Augenblick stoße ich ihm das Messer in den Rücken. Was meinst du? Denke an das herrliche Leben, das wir beide dann führen können!" Der Gedanke an das Geld wiegt schwerer als die Liebe zum Freund, und so beschließen beide, den dritten zu töten.

Indes eilt der jüngste zur Stadt und denkt: „Warum soll ich das Geld mit den anderen teilen? Ist es nicht besser, wenn ich a l l e s für mich behalte?" In der Stadt kauft er Brot, Fleisch und drei Flaschen Wein. Dann geht er in die nächste Apotheke und verlangt ein starkes und schnell wirkendes Gift, „denn", so sagt er zu dem Apotheker, „die Füchse brechen oft in meinen Gänsestall und fressen meine Gänse." Wie er wieder aufs Land kommt, gießt er das Gift in die zwei Flaschen für seine Freunde. Die dritte Flasche behält er für sich selbst und steckt sie in die Tasche, denn er wird sie heute nacht brauchen, wenn er ganz allein die schweren Geldsäcke nach Haus tragen muß.

Brauchen wir mehr zu sagen? Wie er am frühen Nachmittag ankommt, fällt ihm der eine Freund um den Hals, während der andere ihm das kalte Eisen in den Leib stößt. Bevor die beiden

---

Gänse geese (2)
aufs Land to the country (2)
gießen to pour
das Gift the poison (2)
stecken to put, to place
die Tasche the pocket
[**die Tasche, die Taschen** the pocket; bag, purse]
heute nacht tonight

der Nachmittag the afternoon
an-kommen to arrive
fällt ihm . . . um den Hals embraces him (2)
[**der Hals** the neck, throat (2)]
während while
kalt cold (2)
das Eisen the iron
der Leib the body
stößt thrusts
[**stoßen, er stößt** to push, to thrust (2)]

legen to lay (2)
  an die Arbeit to work
  auf eine frohe Zukunft to a happy future
    [**die Zukunft** the future]
in denen in which
  auf die Gesundheit to the health
    [**die Gesundheit** the health]
    [**gesund** healthy (3)]

scheinen to shine (2)
  das Licht the light (3)
  der Tau the dew
  das Gras the grass
  die Blumen the flowers
    [**die Blume, die Blumen**]
  still quiet, silent, still
  bleich pale (2)

ihren toten Freund zur letzten Ruhe legen und an die Arbeit gehen, beschließen sie, auf eine frohe Zukunft zu trinken. Jeder nimmt eine der zwei Flaschen, in denen der Tod wartet, und trinkt auf die Gesundheit des anderen.

Am nächsten Morgen scheint das Licht der Sonne auf den Tau im Gras, die Blumen auf dem Felde und auch auf die stillen, bleichen Gesichter der drei Freunde.

Der Tod, wenn man ihn sucht, ist leicht zu finden.

DER SCHLAUE KAUFMANN

[2B]

NOTES

I. 1. Reflexive verbs are verbs which have a reflexive pronoun as their object. They indicate that the action of the verb is directed back upon the subject or that the meaning of the verb applies to the subject: **sich ändern** to change; **sich wundern** to be surprised, amazed; **sich ärgern** to be annoyed; **sich freuen** to be glad, happy; **sich auf den Weg machen** to set out on one's way, to leave; etc.

2. With the exception of the third person singular and plural, the reflexive pronouns are the same as the personal pronouns: **mir–mich; dir–dich; uns–uns; euch–euch.** There is just one form for both the dative and the accusative of the third person singular and plural (which includes the formal **Sie**-form): **sich.**

3. When the reflexive object is not the *direct* object of the sentence, the dative form of the reflexive pronoun must be used: **mir, dir.**

   Ich reibe *mir* die Hände. I rub my hands.

4. a. The reflexive meaning is sometimes expressed in English.

   Er schließt *sich* in sein Zimmer. He locks *himself* into his room.

   Die gleiche Szene wiederholt *sich*. The same scene repeats *itself*.

   b. More often, the reflexive meaning is understood in English.

   Die Preise ändern *sich*. The prices change.

   Sie wundern *sich* über ihre Dummheit. They are surprised at their stupidity.

   Ärgert er *sich* oder freut er *sich*? Is he annoyed or is he happy?

   c. Sometimes English expresses the reflexive meaning in other ways.

   er setzt *sich* he sits down

   ***sich* erkälten** to catch cold

   ***sich* unterhalten** to have a chat

5. In independent clauses, the reflexive pronoun comes immediately after the finite verb.

   Er schließt *sich* in sein Zimmer.

In dependent clauses it follows a pronoun subject, but precedes *or* follows a noun subject.

Man sieht nicht, ob *er sich* ärgert.
Man sieht nicht, ob *der Kaufmann sich* ärgert.
Man sieht nicht, ob *sich der Kaufmann* ärgert.

II. Kennen means to be acquainted with someone or something, to be able to recognize a person or a thing.

Die Zollbeamten *kennen* die Preise aller Waren.

Wissen means to know *about* something, to have information about something.

Die Zollbeamten *wissen* genau, wieviel dies oder das wert ist.

III. Da can mean

a. here, there

Ich bin schon *da!* I am already here.
Frage, wen man *da* zu Grabe trägt. Ask whom they are carrying to his grave there.

b. then

***Da* sagt plötzlich der eine:** Then, suddenly, one says:

c. since (as a subordinating conjunction)

***Da* aber der Preis immer noch sehr niedrig ist . . .** But since the price is still very low . . .

d. when

Jemand öffnet gerade den Mund, *da* sagt der Freund des Kaufmanns auf einmal . . .

This meaning of **da** is not very frequent.

IV. Während is a preposition and requires the genitive case: **während des Krieges** during the war. It is, however, also a subordinating conjunction meaning *while:*

Während er sich die Hände reibt . . . While he is rubbing his hands . . .

IDIOMS FOR REVIEW

ins Ausland reisen to go abroad
aus dem Ausland from abroad
im Ausland wohnen to live abroad
zu Mittag essen to have lunch

sich freuen to be happy, glad
sich freuen auf to look forward to
es hat wenig Zweck, es hat keinen Zweck there is little point, there is no point
es hat wenig Zweck, süß zu lächeln there is little point in smiling sweetly

schlau clever
[**schlau** sly, cunning, clever, crafty]
der Kaufmann the merchant
[**der Kaufmann, die Kaufleute**]

die Ferien the vacation
ins Ausland abroad
[**das Ausland** the foreign country]
reisen to travel
überall everywhere
viele many
Dinge things
[**das Ding, die Dinge**]
die uns gefallen which we like
[**gefallen, er gefällt** to please (3)]
weniger less
[**wenig** little (2)]
kosten to cost
manche kaufen wir some (of them) we buy
[**mancher, manche, manches** many a; **manche** (plural) some]
entweder . . . oder either . . . or
als Geschenke as gifts
[**das Geschenk, die Geschenke**]
die Familie the family (2)
die Eltern the parents
das Geschenk the gift (2)
aus dem Ausland from abroad (2)
interessanter als more interesting than
[**interessant** interesting]
etwas, was something that
das Geschäft the store
[**das Geschäft, die Geschäfte** the business; shop, store]
die Dinge the things
[**das Ding, die Dinge** (2)]
Koffer suitcases
[**der Koffer, die Koffer** the suitcase, trunk]
Taschen pockets
[**die Tasche, die Taschen** the pocket; bag; purse (2)]
kehren wir . . . zurück we return
die Ferien the vacation (2)
amerikanisch American
die Grenze the border
[**die Grenze, die Grenzen** the border, boundary, limit]
die Überraschung the surprise

wir kommen . . . zurück we come back
zum Beispiel (z.B.) for example
[**das Beispiel, die Beispiele**]

[2 B]

(FOUR PARTS)

Der schlaue Kaufmann

1.

Wenn wir Ferien haben und ins Ausland reisen, sehen wir überall viele Dinge, die uns gefallen und die weniger kosten als zu Haus. Manche kaufen wir, entweder für uns selbst oder als Geschenke für unsere Familie, Eltern, Brüder und Schwestern, oder für unsere Freunde. Ein Geschenk aus dem Ausland ist immer interessanter als etwas, was man in jedem Geschäft zu Haus finden kann. Mit all diesen Dingen in unseren Koffern und wenig Geld in unseren Taschen kehren wir am Ende der Ferien aus dem Ausland zurück und kommen zur amerikanischen Grenze. Was wartet dort auf uns? Eine kleine Überraschung.

Wir kommen z.B. (zum Beispiel) mit dem Auto von einer Ferienreise nach Mexiko zurück. Am amerikanischen Zollamt müssen wir halten. Hier steht die Polizei, höflich und freund-

---

das Auto the car
[**das Auto, die Autos**]
die Ferienreise the vacation trip
[**die Reise, die Reisen** the trip, journey, voyage]
amerikanisch American (2)
das Zollamt the customhouse
[**der Zoll** the customs; (customs) duty]
[**das Amt, die Ämter** the office]
halten to stop
[**halten, er hält** to hold; to stop (2)]
die Polizei the police
höflich polite (2)

prüfen to examine
[**prüfen** to examine, test, check]
zunächst first
unsere Pässe our passports
[**der Paß, die Pässe**]
wichtig important
Papiere papers
[**das Papier, die Papiere**]
sobald as soon as (2)
damit with that
die Zollbeamten the customs officials
[**der Zoll** the customs; (customs) duty (2)]
[**der Beamte, die Beamten** the official]
die Polizei the police (2)
ob whether
verzollen to declare
[**verzollen** to declare (at customs); to pay duty]
Silberwaren silver goods, silverware
[**die Ware, die Waren** the ware, goods, merchandise]
Edelsteine precious stones
[**edel** noble; precious]
[**der Stein, die Steine** the stone]
Wertgegenstände articles of value
[**der Wert** the value, worth]
[**der Gegenstand, die Gegenstände** the object; subject; topic]
der Kaffee the coffee
Zigaretten cigarettes
[**die Zigarette, die Zigaretten**]
und so weiter (usw.) and so on
man sieht they look
das Auto the car (2)
man sucht they search
oft often
müssen wir . . . aufmachen we must open
[**auf-machen** to open (2)]
sogar even
der Kofferraum the trunk (of a car)
[**der Koffer, die Koffer** the suitcase, trunk (2)]
die Sachen the things
[**die Sache, die Sachen** the thing, matter, affair (3)]
weniger less (2)
kosten to cost (2)
Amerika America, the U.S.
der Wert the value (2)
höher higher
[**hoch** high, tall]
gewiß certain
zollfrei duty-free
[**frei** free]

lich, und prüft zunächst unsere Pässe und andere wichtige Papiere. Sobald wir damit fertig sind, kommen die Zollbeamten. Sie sind auch höflich, aber nicht ganz so freundlich wie die Polizei. Man fragt uns, ob wir etwas zu verzollen haben: Silberwaren, Edelsteine, andere Wertgegenstände, Kaffee, Zigaretten usw. (und so weiter). Man sieht in das Auto, man sucht vielleicht, und oft müssen wir sogar den Kofferraum des Autos und unsere Koffer aufmachen. Wenn die Sachen, die wir haben, weniger kosten als in Amerika, und wenn ihr Wert höher ist als eine gewisse zollfreie Summe, so müssen wir sie verzollen, d.h. (das heißt), wir müssen Zoll bezahlen. Das Zollamt hat lange Preislisten und weiß also genau, wieviel dies oder das im Ausland wert ist. Es hat darum wenig Zweck, süß zu lächeln und falsche

---

die Summe the amount
  [**die Summe, die Summen** the sum; amount]
so müssen wir (then) we must
verzollen to pay duty (2)
das heißt (d.h.) that is to say
  [**heißen** to be called, to be named]
bezahlen to pay
das Zollamt the customhouse (2)
Preislisten price lists
  [**der Preis, die Preise** the price; prize]
  [**die Liste, die Listen** the list]
genau exactly
  [**genau** exact, precise, accurate]
wieviel how much
im Ausland abroad
wert worth
es hat darum wenig Zweck there is, therefore, little point
  [**darum** therefore]
  [**der Zweck, die Zwecke** the purpose, aim, object]
süß zu lächeln to smile sweetly
  [**süß** sweet]
  [**lächeln** to smile]
falsche Preise false prices
  [**falsch** false, incorrect, wrong (2)]
  [**der Preis, die Preise** (2)]

nennen to name
wenn if
entsteht eine Situation a situation arises
[**entstehen** to originate, to come about]
[**die Situation** the situation (2)]
sehr very (2)
angenehm pleasant (2)
der Zollbeamte the customs official (2)
lächelt nicht zurück doesn't smile back
[**lächeln** to smile (2)]
geschehen to happen
[**geschehen, es geschieht** to happen]
entweder . . . oder either . . . or (2)
die Strafe the fine
[**die Strafe, die Strafen** the punishment; fine (2)]
zahlen to pay
einfach simply
[**einfach** simple]
wenn wir . . . nennen if we name (2)
gleich immediately, at once (= **sogleich**)
richtig right, correct (2)
und . . . bezahlen and pay (2)
sauer sour
der Staat the government
[**der Staat, die Staaten** the state, the government]
dürfen wir . . . schließen we may . . . shut
[**dürfen, er darf** may; to be allowed, permitted]
[**schließen** to close, to shut]
der Kofferraum the trunk (of a car) (2)]
und . . . zumachen and close
[**zu-machen** to close, to shut (3)]
leer empty
die Brieftasche the wallet, billfold
[**der Brief, die Briefe** the letter]
[**die Tasche, die Taschen** the pocket; bag; purse (3)]
wir steigen we get (into)
[**steigen** to climb, to rise (3)]
das Zeichen the signal
[**das Zeichen, die Zeichen** the sign, signal]
uns durchzulassen to let us through
weiter-fahren go on
[**fahren, er fährt** to drive, to ride, to go]

alles everything
gut organisiert well organized
[**organisieren** to organize]
das System the system
kompliziert complicated
paßt gut auf pays close attention

Preise zu nennen. Wenn wir das tun, dann entsteht eine Situation, die für uns nicht sehr angenehm ist. Der Zollbeamte lächelt nicht zurück, sondern wird unfreundlich, und es kann geschehen, daß wir entweder Strafe zahlen oder daß man die Sachen einfach behält. Es ist also besser, wenn wir gleich den richtigen Preis nennen und mit saurem Gesicht dem Staat bezahlen, was er verlangt. Dann dürfen wir die Koffer und den Kofferraum wieder schließen und die leere Brieftasche zumachen; wir steigen ins Auto, der Beamte gibt ein Zeichen, uns durchzulassen, und wir können weiterfahren.

Heute ist alles sehr gut organisiert. Das System ist nicht kompliziert, die Polizei paßt gut auf, und die Zollbeamten kennen die genauen Preise aller Waren.

2.

Um das Jahr 1815 (achtzehnhundertfünfzehn) ist das anders, wenigstens in Europa und besonders in Deutschland. Die Preise für dieselben Waren sind damals überall in Europa sehr

---

genau exact (2)
aller Waren of all goods
[**die Ware, die Waren** the goods, merchandise (2)]

um das Jahr around the year
achtzehnhundertfünfzehn 1815
ist das anders this is different
[**anders** different]
wenigstens at least (2)
Europa Europe
besonders especially (3)
Deutschland Germany
dieselben Waren the same goods
[**derselbe, dieselbe, dasselbe** the same]
überall everywhere (2)

verschieden different
ändern sich change
[**ändern** to change]
wegen des Krieges because of the war
[**der Krieg, die Kriege** the war]
von Monat zu Monat from month to month
[**der Monat, die Monate**]
die Zollämter the customhouses
Listen lists
[**die Liste, die Listen** (2)]
gebrauchen to use
zwecklos useless, pointless
[**der Zweck, die Zwecke** the purpose, aim, object (2)]
woher from where
gewiß certain (2)
wieviel how much (2)
gebrauchen to use (2)
das System the system (2)
das zwar . . . ist which is, to be sure . . .
[**zwar** to be sure (2)]
kompliziert complicated (2)
wenn if
zum Beispiel (z.B.) for example
[**das Beispiel, die Beispiele** (2)]
deutsch German (2)
der Geschäftsmann the businessman
[**das Geschäft, die Geschäfte** the business; shop, store (2)]
[**der Geschäftsmann, die Geschäftsleute** the businessman]
irgendwo somewhere
[**irgend** some, any]
Frankreich France
Deutschland Germany (2)
um . . . zu verkaufen to sell
[**verkaufen** to sell]
so muß er (then) he must
die Grenze the border (2)
erklären to declare
[**erklären** to explain; to declare (2)]
Papiere papers
[**das Papier, die Papiere** the paper (2)]
Rechnungen bills, invoices
[**die Rechnung, die Rechnungen** the bill, invoice; check; account]
notwendig necessary
gelten nicht are not valid, do not count
[**gelten, er gilt** to be worth, valid; to be considered]
die Rechnung the invoice (2)
französisch French
der meisten Waren of most goods
[**die meisten** most]

verschieden und ändern sich wegen des Krieges von Monat zu Monat, so daß die Zollämter keine Listen gebrauchen können. Eine Liste ist zwecklos, wenn man nicht genau weiß, woher eine gewisse Ware kommt und wieviel sie dort kostet. Die Zollbeamten gebrauchen deshalb ein System, das zwar nicht sehr genau, aber auch nicht zu kompliziert ist. Wenn z.B. (zum Beispiel) ein deutscher Geschäftsmann irgendwo in Frankreich eine gewisse Ware kauft und nach Deutschland bringt, um sie dort zu verkaufen, so muß er an der Grenze erklären, wieviel die Ware wert ist. Papiere oder Rechnungen sind nicht notwendig, ja sie gelten nicht, denn eine Rechnung kann falsch sein. Jeder deutsche Zollbeamte an der französischen Grenze kennt die Preise der meisten Waren, die aus Frankreich kommen. Wenn der Kaufmann die Wahrheit sagt und den richtigen Preis nennt, ist alles gut; er bezahlt den Zoll, den der Beamte verlangt, man läßt ihn und die Waren durch, und er darf weiterfahren. Wenn er aber einen falschen Preis nennt, d.h. (das heißt) einen Preis, der viel zu niedrig ist, dann hat der Beamte das Recht, die Ware für diesen niedrigen Preis selbst zu kaufen. Ob der Geschäftsmann will oder nicht, er muß die Ware dem Beamten verkaufen. Aber er darf zehn Prozent mehr

---

Frankreich France (2)
wenn if
der Kaufmann the merchant (2)
die Wahrheit the truth
bezahlen to pay (2)
man läßt ihn . . . durch one lets him through (2)
er darf he is allowed (to)
[**dürfen, er darf** may; to be allowed, permitted (2)]
weiter-fahren go on
[**fahren, er fährt** to drive, to ride, to go (2)]
das heißt (d.h.) that is to say (2)
das Recht the right
selbst zu kaufen to buy himself
ob whether (2)
er muß . . . verkaufen he has to sell (2)
zehn Prozent ten percent

der Profit the profit
  in einem solchen Fall in such a case
    [**der Fall, die Fälle** the case; the fall]
  wirklich real (3)

geschieht happens
    [**geschehen, es geschieht** to happen (2)]
  welche which
  auf diese Weise in this manner
    [**die Weise** the way, manner (2)]
bestimmt certain, fixed
  einmal . . . im Monat once a month
    [**der Monat, die Monate** the month (2)]
der Verkauf the sale
  öffentlich public
  steht . . . in der Zeitung is (announced) in the newspaper
    [**die Zeitung, die Zeitungen** the newspaper (2)]
  einige Tage vorher a few days before
    [**einige** some, a few]
    [**vorher** before]
zufrieden satisfied, contented (3)
hübsch pretty, nice (2)
  der Profit the profit (2)
  weil sie . . . verlangen because they demand
  ziemlich rather (3)
  hohen Preis high price
    [**hoch,** high, tall (2)]
da aber since, however . . .
  immer noch still (2)
  wert worth (2)

schlecht bad (3)
  gewinnen to win
  keiner no one
  verlieren to lose
  außer except
    [**außer** beside; except (2)]
  Geschäftsleute businessmen
    [**der Geschäftsmann, die Geschäftsleute** (2)]
  versuchen to try
    [**versuchen** to try, to attempt; to tempt]
  zu billig too cheaply
    [**billig** cheap, inexpensive]
hindert . . . nicht, . . . zu stecken does not prevent . . . from putting
    [**hindern** to prevent, to hinder]
    [**stecken** to put, to place (2)]
  einfach simple (2)
  der Trick the trick
  enorm enormous

verlangen. Diese zehn Prozent sind sein Profit—ein Profit, der in einem solchen Fall natürlich kein wirklicher Profit mehr ist.

Was geschieht nun mit den Waren, welche die Zollbeamten auf diese Weise kaufen? An einem bestimmten Tage, einmal oder zweimal im Monat, verkaufen die Zollbeamten diese Waren im Zollamt. Der Verkauf ist öffentlich und steht einige Tage vorher in der Zeitung. Es ist ein Tag, an dem jeder zufrieden nach Hause geht. Warum? Die Beamten machen einen hübschen Profit, weil sie natürlich einen ziemlich hohen Preis verlangen. Da aber dieser Preis immer noch sehr niedrig ist, kosten die Waren viel weniger als sie wirklich wert sind.

Es ist kein schlechtes System. Jeder gewinnt, keiner verliert—außer jenen Geschäftsleuten, die versuchen, eine Ware zu billig über die Grenze zu bringen. Aber dieses wunderbare System hindert einen deutschen Kaufmann nicht, durch einen einfachen Trick einen enormen Profit in seine eigene Tasche zu stecken. Während er sich in Deutschland vor Vergnügen die Hände reibt, stehen zwei deutsche Zollbeamte mit sauren Gesichtern an der Grenze und wundern sich über ihre Dummheit.

Und hier fängt nun endlich die Geschichte von dem schlauen Kaufmann an.

---

eigen own (2)
während while
er sich . . . reibt he rubs
[**reiben** to rub (3)]
vor Vergnügen with pleasure
[**das Vergnügen** the pleasure, enjoyment; amusement]
sauer sour (2)
und wundern sich and are surprised
[**ich wundere mich** I am surprised]
über ihre Dummheit at their stupidity
[**die Dummheit** the stupidity]

fängt . . . an begins
endlich finally
schlau clever (2)

die Geschäftsreise the business trip
[**die Reise, die Reisen** the trip, journey, voyage (2)]
der Gegenwert the equivalent
achthundert eight hundred
Kästen boxes
[**der Kasten, die Kästen** the box, chest, case]
feinster Herren– und Damenhandschuhe of the finest men's and women's gloves
[**fein** fine]
[**die Dame, die Damen** the lady, woman]
[**der Handschuh, die Handschuhe** the glove]
[**der Schuh, die Schuhe** the shoe]
fährt er he goes
die Kästen the boxes (2)
schließt er sich he locks himself
[**schließen** to shut, to close, to lock (2)]
das Abendessen the supper
[**das Essen** the meal, food (2)]
nimmt . . . heraus takes out
[**heraus** out]
dauern to last, to take
einige a few, some (2)
geht . . . aus goes out
erst kurz vor Mitternacht only shortly before midnight
[**kurz** short, brief (3)]
[**die Mitternacht** the midnight]
zu Bett to bed
[**das Bett, die Betten**]

läßt er . . . zurück he leaves behind
[**zurück-lassen** to leave behind]
das Frühstück the breakfast (3)
hält stops
läßt . . . ihn öffnen has him open, makes him open
[**öffnen** to open (2)]
teuer expensive
[**teuer** expensive; dear]
erwidern to reply, to answer (2)
süß sweetly (2)
hundertfünfzig one hundred fifty
gleich immediately, at once (= **sogleich**) (2)
best best
die Qualität the quality
teuer expensive (2)
meint er he says
[**meinen** to mean, to say, to think (3)]
wenn if
billig cheap (2)
kaufe ich sie selbst I'll buy them myself

3.

Unser Kaufmann macht eine Geschäftsreise nach Frankreich und kauft dort für den Gegenwert von achthundert Mark zwei Kästen feinster Herren- und Damenhandschuhe. Dann fährt er mit den Kästen in eine kleine Stadt, die nahe an der Grenze liegt, und geht in ein Gasthaus. Dort schließt er sich nach dem Abendessen in sein Zimmer, nimmt die Handschuhe heraus und fängt an zu arbeiten. Was er tut, dauert einige Stunden, denn das Licht unter seiner Tür geht erst kurz vor Mitternacht aus. Zufrieden mit seiner Arbeit geht er zu Bett und träumt. Er träumt natürlich von Handschuhen.

Am nächsten Morgen läßt er einen Kasten im Zimmer zurück, fährt mit dem anderen nach dem Frühstück zur Grenze und hält am Zollamt. Dort läßt der Beamte ihn den Kasten öffnen. „Wieviel sind die Handschuhe wert?“ fragt er. „Nicht sehr teuer“, erwidert der Kaufmann und lächelt süß; „hundertfünfzig Mark.“ Der Beamte sieht natürlich gleich, daß der Preis viel zu niedrig ist, denn die Handschuhe sind von bester Qualität und kosten wenigstens dreihundert bis vierhundert Mark. „Das ist wirklich nicht teuer“, meint er; „wenn sie s o billig sind, kaufe ich sie selbst.“ Er nimmt Feder, Tinte und Papier, schreibt eine Quittung für die Handschuhe und bezahlt dem Kaufmann hundertfünfundsechzig Mark. „Vielen Dank!“ sagt der Beamte freundlich lächelnd, indem er dem

---

die Feder the pen
  [**die Feder, die Federn** the pen; the feather]
 die Tinte the ink
 schreiben to write
 die Quittung the receipt
 hundertfünfundsechzig one hundred and sixty-five
  [**sechzig** sixty]
vielen Dank many thanks, thank you very much
  [**der Dank** the thanks, gratitude]
 indem er . . . bezahlt while . . . paying
  [**indem** while; by]

wieder einmal once again (2)
bitte please
der Ausdruck the expression
zeigen to show (3)
ob er sich ärgert whether he is annoyed
[**sich ärgern** to be annoyed]
ob er sich freut whether he is happy
[**sich freuen** to be happy, glad; to rejoice]
die Brieftasche the wallet, billfold (2)
ißt er zu Mittag he has lunch
[**zu Mittag essen** to have lunch]
[**der Mittag** noon, midday (2)]
genießen to enjoy (2)
nachher afterwards
die Tasse the cup (2)
der Kaffee the coffee (2)
köstlich delicious
die Zigarre the cigar
[**die Zigarre, die Zigarren**]
das Mittagessen the lunch (2)
der Nachmittag the afternoon (2)
wählen to choose
als er dort ankommt when he arrives there
[**an-kommen** to arrive (2)]
wiederholt sich die gleiche Szene the same scene repeats itself
[**wiederholen** to repeat]
[**gleich** same (2)]
[**die Szene, die Szenen** the scene]
für denselben Preis for the same price
[**derselbe, dieselbe, dasselbe** the same (2)]

voneinander of each other
erzählen to tell (3)
der . . . bringen will who wants to take
und dabei . . . verliert and loses in the process
[**dabei** in doing so, in the process]
[**verlieren** to lose (2)]
eine Menge Geld a lot of money
[**die Menge** the crowd, quantity, lot]
beide freuen sich auf both are looking forward to
[**sich freuen auf** to look forward to]
der Verkauf the sale
zählen to count (3)
im voraus ahead of time
[**voraus** ahead]
den sie machen werden (which) they will make
der Verkaufstag the day of the sale

Kaufmann sein Geld bezahlt; „wenn Sie wieder einmal billige Handschuhe haben, dann kommen Sie bitte zu mir zurück!"– „Das werde ich tun", entgegnet unser Freund. Der Ausdruck seines Gesichtes zeigt nicht, ob er sich ärgert oder ob er sich freut. Er steckt das Geld in seine Brieftasche und fährt zu seinem Gasthaus in Frankreich zurück. Dort ißt er zu Mittag, genießt nachher eine gute Tasse Kaffee und eine köstliche Zigarre, bezahlt die Rechnung für sein Zimmer und das Mittagessen und fährt am frühen Nachmittag mit dem zweiten Kasten zur Grenze. Nur wählt er diesmal einen anderen Weg und ein anderes Zollamt. Als er dort ankommt, wiederholt sich die gleiche Szene: ein anderer Zollbeamter kauft den zweiten Kasten für denselben Preis wie der Beamte im ersten Zollamt.

Beide Beamten wissen nichts voneinander, aber beide erzählen am Abend ihren Familien die gleiche Geschichte: die Geschichte von einem dummen Kaufmann, der teure Handschuhe billig über die Grenze bringen will und dabei eine Menge Geld verliert. Und beide freuen sich auf den Tag des Verkaufes und zählen schon im voraus den hohen Profit, den sie machen werden.

Aber auch unser Freund, der Kaufmann, wartet auf den Verkaufstag.

4.

An dem Tage, an dem der öffentliche Verkauf im ersten Zollamt stattfindet, geht unser Kaufmann nicht selbst hin, weil

---

[**der Verkauf** the sale (2)]

an dem Tage, an dem . . . stattfindet . . ., on which . . . takes place
[**statt-finden** to take place]
öffentlich public (2)
geht . . . nicht selbst hin doesn't go there himself
[**hin** there]

erkennen to recognize
senden to send
unterrichtet ihn über das, was instructs him as to what
[**unterrichten** to instruct; to inform]
[**über das, was** about that which]
hinter behind
Berge mountains, heaps
[**der Berg, die Berge** the mountain (2)]
offen open (2)
damit so that
die Qualität the quality (2)
fühlen to feel
meine Herren! gentlemen!
französisch French (2)
feinst finest
[**fein** fine (2)]
er nimmt . . . heraus he takes out
[**heraus** out (2)]
das Paar the pair
[**das Paar, die Paare**]
damit so that (2)
bieten to offer
jemand, der . . . sieht someone who sees
das Doppelte twice as much
[**doppelt** double]
öffnet gerade is just opening
[**öffnen** to open (2)]
[**gerade** just, just then; straight]
der Mund the mouth (3)
um . . . zu nennen in order to name, call
höher higher
[**hoch** high, tall (2)]
da sagt . . . when . . . says
auf einmal suddenly (2)
hier stimmt etwas nicht there is something wrong here
[**stimmen** to be correct]
unmöglich impossible
hat . . . recht is right
[**recht haben** to be right (2)]
in Paaren in pairs
[**das Paar, die Paare**]
jeder einzelne every single one
[**einzeln** single, individual]
bieten to offer (2)
hundertfünfzig one hundred fifty (2)
fünfzig fifty
dessen Gesicht whose face
vor Ärger with anger
[**der Ärger** the annoyance, vexation, anger]

er fürchtet, daß man ihn dort erkennt. Er sendet einen Freund und unterrichtet ihn über das, was er zu tun hat. Das Zollamt ist voller Menschen, die alle billig kaufen wollen. Hinter langen Tischen stehen die Beamten, vor ihnen liegen Berge von Waren in offenen Koffern und Kästen, damit jeder die Qualität sehen und fühlen kann. „Hier, meine Herren!" ruft ein Beamter; „ein ganzer Kasten mit französischen Handschuhen feinster Qualität!" Er nimmt ein Paar heraus und hält es hoch, damit alle die Handschuhe sehen können. „Wer bietet mehr als zweihundert Mark?" Jemand, der sofort sieht, daß die Handschuhe wenigstens das Doppelte wert sind, öffnet gerade den Mund, um laut einen höheren Preis zu nennen, da sagt der Freund des Kaufmanns auf einmal: „Ich glaube, hier stimmt etwas nicht. Die Handschuhe, die Sie da hoch halten, sind beide für die rechte Hand."—„Unmöglich", sagt der Beamte; aber der Freund hat natürlich recht. Alle Handschuhe im Kasten sind zwar in Paaren, aber jeder einzelne Handschuh ist für die rechte Hand. Jetzt will natürlich niemand mehr die Handschuhe kaufen. „Wer bietet hundertfünfzig Mark?—Hundert?—Fünfzig?" schreit der Beamte, dessen Gesicht vor Ärger rot wird, als keiner antwortet. „Nun", sagt endlich unser Freund, „wenn niemand die Handschuhe will, dann biete ich dreißig Mark. Vielleicht kann ich einige an Soldaten verkaufen, die aus dem Krieg mit nur einem Arm zurückkommen. Aber mehr als dreißig Mark bezahle ich nicht." Was kann der Zollbeamte

---

rot red
als keiner when no one
endlich finally (2)
wenn if
dreißig thirty
einige an Soldaten verkaufen sell a few to soldiers
[**einige** some, a few (2)]
[**der Soldat, die Soldaten**]
die . . . zurückkommen who (will) return
aus dem Krieg from the war
[**der Krieg, die Kriege** (2)]
mit nur einem Arm with only one arm
[**der Arm, die Arme**]
dreißig thirty (2)

wenn er . . . bekommen will if he wants to get
überhaupt etwas anything at all
[**überhaupt** at all; on the whole; altogether; in general]

die Szene the scene (2)
wiederholt sich repeats itself
[**wiederholen** to repeat (2)]
einzeln single (2)
link left (3)

trifft er he meets
[**treffen, er trifft** to meet, to encounter (2)]
Dienste services
[**der Dienst, die Dienste**]
legt . . . zusammen puts together
[**legen** to put, to place, to lay (3)]
[**zusammen** together (3)]
ein paar a few (2)
Wochen weeks
[**die Woche, die Wochen** (2)]
das Doppelte twice the amount (2)
[**doppelt** double (2)]
den sie . . . wert sind (which) they are worth

wenn Sie gut rechnen können if you are good at figures
[**rechnen** to calculate, to figure, to count]
bitte please (2)
der Bleistift the pencil
[**der Bleistift, die Bleistifte**]

machen? Wenn er überhaupt etwas für die Handschuhe bekommen will, muß er sie für dreißig Mark verkaufen.

Die gleiche Szene wiederholt sich einige Tage später im zweiten Zollamt. Auch hier bezahlt der Freund dreißig Mark für den ganzen Kasten von einzelnen Handschuhen für die linke Hand.

Am folgenden Tage trifft er den Kaufmann in Deutschland. Er gibt ihm die zwei Kästen und bekommt für seine Dienste hundert Mark. Der Kaufmann legt die Handschuhe in richtige Paare zusammen und verkauft sie in ein paar Wochen für das Doppelte des Preises, den sie in Frankreich wert sind.

Wenn Sie gut rechnen können, dann sagen Sie bitte schnell (aber ohne Papier und Bleistift!), wieviel Profit der Kaufmann macht!

DER SCHWEINEHIRT

[3A]

NOTES

I. 1. The simple past and the past participle of most English verbs are formed by adding **–(e)d** to the infinitive. The stem vowel remains unchanged.

to wipe	I wipe*d*	I had wipe*d*
to end	it end*ed*	it had end*ed*

Most German verbs follow this pattern. They do not change the stem vowel and form

a. the simple past (or imperfect) tense by adding **–te, –test, –te; –ten, –tet, –ten** to the stem;

b. the past participle by prefixing **ge–** and adding **–t** to the stem. (In certain cases, **ge–** is not prefixed; see Notes to Story 4A, in which the compound tenses and the use of the past participles are discussed.)

Note: Verbs whose stem vowel ends in **d** or **t** (or a consonant plus **n**) insert an **e** after the stem.

leb-en	**er leb*te***	**er hatte *ge*leb*t***
arbeit-en	**er arbeit*ete***	**er hatte *ge*arbeit*et***
öffn-en	**er öffn*ete***	**er hatte die Tür *ge*öffn*et***

Verbs following this pattern are called "weak" verbs.

2. Past time is also expressed by a change of the stem vowel.

to sing	she sang	she had sung

German verbs using this pattern are called "strong" verbs.

a. In the simple past, no endings are added to the first and third person singular; the other persons have the same endings as in the present tense: **—, –(e)st, —; –en, –(e)t, –en.**

ich sang, du sang*st*, er sang; wir sang*en*, ihr sang*t*, sie sang*en*

ich fand, du fand*est*, er fand; wir fand*en*, ihr fand*et*, sie fand*en*

b. The past participle is formed by prefixing **ge–** and adding **–en** to the stem. (In certain cases, **ge–** is not prefixed; see Notes to Story 4A.)

c. In addition to changing the stem vowel, some strong verbs also change the consonant(s) of the stem. Some examples:

bitten **er bat**

gehen **er ging**
sitzen **er saß**
ziehen **er zog**

3. Some weak verbs form the simple past and the past participle in an irregular manner. Their endings are weak, but they change the stem vowel and, in the case of **bringen** and **denken**, even the final consonants of the stem. Examples:

kennen	**er k*a*nnt*e***	**er hatte ihn gek*a*nn*t***
bringen	**er br*achte***	**er hatte es gebr*acht***
denken	**er d*achte***	**er hatte ged*acht***

4. The simple past of the modal auxiliaries and of **wissen** is formed on the model of the weak verbs. Note that only **wollen** and **sollen** do not change the stem vowel.

können **ich k*o*nnte**
müssen **ich m*u*ßte**
dürfen **ich d*u*rfte**
mögen **ich m*och*te**
wollen **ich wollte**
sollen **ich sollte**
wissen **ich w*u*ßte**

(The past participle of **wissen** is **gewußt.**)

5. The simple past tense of **haben, sein** and **werden** is
ich hatte, du hattest, er hatte; wir hatten, ihr hattet, sie hatten
ich war, du warst, er war; wir waren, ihr wart, sie waren
ich wurde, du wurdest, er wurde; wir wurden, ihr wurdet, sie wurden

6. The simple past tense is sometimes called the narrative past. It is most frequently used in telling a connected narrative or in describing a *state* in the past.

II. German uses the prefixes **hin–** and **her–** to indicate whether the direction of motion is *toward* or *away* from the *speaker* or *observer.*

ich muß *hinunter*gehen
er trieb seine Schweineherde *hinaus* auf die Felder
geh *hin!* go (there)!
geh *hinein!* go in!
Hinaus! out!
wenn man in die Pfeife *hinein*blies
da kam die Nachtigall *heraus*
allerlei Walzer und Polkas kamen *heraus*

III. A personal pronoun (or the demonstrative pronoun **der, die, das**) which is governed by a preposition and does *not* refer to *persons* is often replaced by the word **da–** (**dar–** before vowels). This **da–** (**dar–**) precedes and joins the preposition.

man wußte nicht, was die Leute *darin* aßen (**darin** = in them = in the houses)
sagt niemand etwas *davon* (of it, about it)
sie bekam *dafür* den Topf (**dafür** = for them = the kisses)
und *damit* wandte er sich von ihr (**damit** = with that = with these words)
was hast du jetzt *dafür*? (for it = for what you have done)

IDIOMS FOR REVIEW

vor vielen Jahren many years ago
es gibt Hunderte von Königstöchtern there are hundreds of princesses
gab es nicht Hunderte von Königstöchtern? weren't there hundreds of princesses?
es gab keine Wohnung there was no apartment
es gibt keine schönere Musik there is no more beautiful music
sie war dem Weinen nahe she was close to tears
einige Augenblicke lang for a few moments
sie war seit vielen Jahren tot she had been dead for many years
auf keine Weise in no way
auf diese Weise in this way, in this manner
er bat um ihre Hand he asked for her hand (in marriage)
etwas anderes something else, something different
spazieren-gehen to go for a walk, to take a walk
sie ging mit den Hofdamen spazieren she went for a walk with . . .
von fern from afar
vor allem above all
nicht in Frage kommen to be out of the question
Küsse kommen nicht in Frage kisses are out of the question
das tun wir gar nicht gern we do not like to do that at all
sich Zeit nehmen to take one's time
er nahm sich Zeit he took his time
auf kurze Zeit for a short time

heute abend tonight
am Nachmittag in the afternoon
was für ein Rosenbusch das war! what a rosebush that was!
was für ein Zufall! what a coincidence!
was für ein Unsinn! what nonsense!
was für eine Menschenmenge! what a crowd of people!

---

der Schweinehirt the swineherd
[**das Schwein, die Schweine** the pig (2)]
[**der Hirt, die Hirten** the shepherd]

vor vielen Jahren many years ago
lebte einmal there once lived
der Prinz the prince
hatte had
er besaß he owned
[**besitzen, besaß, hat besessen** to own, to possess]
zwar to be sure (3)
das Königreich the kingdom
[**der König, die Könige** the king]
[**das Reich, die Reiche** the empire, kingdom, realm (3)]
war was
daß man es . . . nennen konnte that one could . . . call it
[**können, er kann, konnte, hat gekonnt**]
kaum mehr hardly any more
[**kaum** hardly, barely, scarcely]
das Königreich the kingdom (2)
indessen however
[**indes, indessen** meanwhile; however (2)]
immer noch still (3)
um . . . zu erlauben to allow
[**erlauben** to allow, to permit]
der Prinz the prince (2)
sich zu verheiraten to get married
[**sich verheiraten** to get married, to marry]
der Wunsch the wish (3)

wen whom
dachte thought
[**denken, er dachte, hat gedacht** to think]
irgendeine some
[**irgendein, irgendeine** some, any]
die Prinzessin the princess

[3 A]

(FOUR PARTS)

Der Schweinehirt

I.

Vor vielen Jahren lebte einmal ein Prinz, der nicht viel Geld hatte. Er besaß zwar ein Königreich, aber das war so klein, daß man es kaum mehr ein Königreich nennen konnte. Es war indessen immer noch groß genug, um dem Prinzen zu erlauben, sich zu verheiraten. Und sich zu verheiraten war sein größter Wunsch.

„Aber wen soll ich fragen?" dachte der Prinz. „Irgendeine kleine Prinzessin? Nein! Ich möchte die Tochter des Kaisers!"

Doch wie konnte er, der arme Prinz, zur Tochter des Kaisers sagen: „Willst du mich haben?" Nun, wer nicht wagt, gewinnt nicht. War sein Name nicht weit und breit bekannt,

---

die Tochter the daughter
  [die Tochter, die Töchter (3)]
 der Kaiser the emperor

doch yet (2)
 wie konnte er . . . sagen how could he say
  [**können, er kann, konnte, hat gekonnt** (2)]
 der Kaiser the emperor (2)
wer nicht wagt he who does not take a chance
  [**wer** he who, whoever (2)]
  [**wagen** to dare, to risk]
 gewinnen to win (2)
der Name the name
  [**der Name, die Namen**]
 weit und breit far and wide
  [**breit** broad, wide]
 bekannt known, well-known (2)

gab es nicht weren't there
[**es gibt** there is, there exists; there are]
[**geben, er gibt, gab, hat gegeben** to give]
Hunderte hundreds
Königstöchter princesses, kings' daughters
[**der König, die Könige** the king (2)]
die ihn . . . haben wollten who wanted to have him
[**wollen, er will, wollte, hat gewollt**]
zum Mann as their husband
beschloß decided
[**beschließen, beschloß, hat beschlossen**]
das Glück the luck
[**das Glück** the luck, good fortune; happiness (2)]
versuchen to try
[**versuchen** to try, to attempt; to tempt (2)]

das Grab the grave
[**das Grab, die Gräber** (2)]
der Vater the father
[**der Vater, die Väter** (3)]
wuchs grew
[**wachsen, er wächst, wuchs, ist gewachsen** to grow]
der Rosenbusch the rosebush
[**die Rose, die Rosen** the rose]
was für ein . . .! what a . . .! (2)
blühen to bloom, to blossom
jedes fünfte Jahr every fifth year
trug bore
[**tragen, er trägt, trug, hat getragen** to carry, to bear; to wear]
einzig single (2)
die Blume the flower
[**die Blume, die Blumen** (2)]
die Rose the rose (2)
selten rare
[**selten** rare; rarely, seldom]
die Schönheit the beauty
roch smelled
[**riechen, roch, hat gerochen** to smell]
daß man . . . vergaß that one forgot
[**vergessen, er vergißt, vergaß, hat vergessen** to forget]
Sorgen worries
[**die Sorge, die Sorgen** the worry, care (3)]
Schmerzen pains
[**der Schmerz, die Schmerzen** the pain, grief]
sobald man . . . kam as soon as one came
[**sobald** as soon as (3)]
[**kommen, kam, ist gekommen** to come]
in ihre Nähe near it
[**die Nähe** the vicinity, proximity]

und gab es nicht Hunderte von Königstöchtern, die ihn zum Mann haben wollten? Warum sollte dann die Tochter des Kaisers nicht ja sagen? Der Prinz beschloß also, sein Glück zu versuchen.

Auf dem Grabe seines Vaters wuchs ein Rosenbusch, und was für ein Rosenbusch das war! Er blühte nur jedes fünfte Jahr und trug dann nur eine einzige Blume, aber das war eine Rose von ganz seltener Schönheit, die so wunderbar roch, daß man alle seine Sorgen und Schmerzen vergaß, sobald man in ihre Nähe kam. Der Prinz hatte auch eine Nachtigall, die so schön sang, daß jeder andere Vogel sofort schwieg, wenn er ihre süße Stimme hörte. Diese Rose und diese Nachtigall bestimmte der Prinz für die Tochter des Kaisers. Er tat sie in zwei große Kästen aus Gold und Silber und schickte sie an den Hof.

Die Prinzessin spielte gerade mit den Hofdamen Ball, als

---

die Nachtigall the nightingale
  sang sang
    [**singen, sang, hat gesungen** to sing]
  der Vogel the bird
    [**der Vogel, die Vögel**]
  schwieg was silent
    [**schweigen, schwieg, hat geschwiegen** to be silent]
  süß sweet (3)
  die Stimme the voice (3)
bestimmte der Prinz the prince intended, chose
    [**bestimmen** to intend for; to fix, determine, appoint]
er tat sie he put them
    [**tun, tat, hat getan** to do]
  das Gold the gold (3)
  an den Hof to (the emperor's) court
    [**der Hof, die Höfe** the court; the yard, the courtyard; the farm]

die Prinzessin the princess (2)
  spielte gerade . . . Ball was just playing ball
    [**gerade** just, just then; straight (2)]
    [**der Ball, die Bälle** the ball]
  Hofdamen ladies-in-waiting
    [**die Hofdame, die Hofdamen** the lady-in-waiting]
    [**die Dame, die Damen** the lady]
  als der Wagen . . . fuhr when the carriage drove
    [**der Wagen, die Wagen** the carriage, wagon, car (2)]
    [**fahren, er fährt, fuhr, ist gefahren** to drive, go, ride]

Geschenke gifts
[**das Geschenk, die Geschenke** (3)]
in den Schloßhof into the courtyard of the castle
[**das Schloß, die Schlösser** the castle; the lock]
[**der Hof, die Höfe** the yard, courtyard; farm (2)]
sie hörte . . . auf she stopped
[**auf-hören** to stop, to cease]
welche vier Diener . . . hoben which four servants lifted
[**der Diener, die Diener** the servant (2)]
[**heben, hob, hat gehoben** to lift, to raise]
und . . . trugen and carried
[**tragen, er trägt, trug, hat getragen** (2)]
ins Schloß into the castle
[**das Schloß, die Schlösser** the castle; the lock (2)]
um sie . . . zu stellen in order to put them
[**stellen** to place, to put]
auf den Boden on the floor
[**der Boden** the floor; ground, soil]

rief sie she exclaimed
[**rufen, rief, hat gerufen** to call, to exclaim]
außer sich beside herself
[**außer** beside; except (3)]
hoffen to hope (3)
das Kätzchen the kitten
hervorkam came out
[**hervor** out]
[**kommen, kam, ist gekommen** (2)]
als man . . . öffnete when they opened
[**öffnen** to open (3)]

hübsch pretty (3)
riefen exclaimed
[**rufen, rief, hat gerufen** (2)]
Hofdamen ladies-in-waiting
[**die Hofdame, die Hofdamen** the lady-in-waiting (2)]
[**die Dame, die Damen** the lady (2)]

als . . . näher ging when . . . went closer
[**gehen, ging, ist gegangen**]
merken to notice
richtig real
da war sie dem Weinen nahe then she was close to tears
[**weinen** to cry, to weep]
künstlich artificial
[**die Kunst, die Künste** the art; skill]

wiederholen to repeat (3)
sogleich at once (3)

der Wagen mit den Geschenken in den Schloßhof fuhr. Sie hörte sofort auf zu spielen und folgte den Kästen, welche vier Diener des Prinzen von dem Wagen hoben und ins Schloß trugen, um sie vor dem Kaiser auf den Boden zu stellen.

„Oh, Geschenke!" rief sie und war vor Freude außer sich; „ich hoffe, es ist ein Kätzchen!" Aber was hervorkam, als man den ersten Kasten öffnete, war kein Kätzchen, sondern der Rosenbusch mit der herrlichen Rose.

„Eine Blume! Wie hübsch!" riefen alle Hofdamen.

„Sie ist mehr als hübsch", sagte der Kaiser, „sie ist schön!"

Als die Prinzessin aber näher ging und merkte, daß es eine richtige Blume war, da war sie dem Weinen nahe und sagte: „Pfui, Papa, es ist keine künstliche, sondern eine natürliche Blume!"

„Pfui!" wiederholten sogleich alle Hofdamen, „sie ist nicht künstlich!"

„Nun", meinte der Kaiser, „laßt uns erst sehen, was in dem anderen Kasten ist, bevor wir böse werden!" Und da kam die Nachtigall heraus und sang so schön, daß einige Augenblicke lang niemand ein böses Wort gegen sie zu sagen wagte.

„*Superbe! Charmant!*" riefen die Hofdamen, denn sie

Hofdamen ladies-in-waiting (2)
künstlich artificial (2)

meinte said
böse angry
kam . . . heraus came out
[**heraus** out]
sang sang
[**singen, sang, hat gesungen** (2)]
daß . . . niemand . . . zu sagen wagte that . . . no one dared to say
einige Augenblicke lang for a few moments
[**der Augenblick, die Augenblicke** (2)]
[**wagen** to dare; to risk (2)]
ein böses Wort an angry word
[**das Wort, die Worte (die Wörter)** the word]

superbe superb
charmant charming

sprachen spoke
[**sprechen, er spricht, sprach, hat gesprochen**]
fließend fluently
[**fließen** to flow (2)]
französisch French (3)
eine schlechter als die andere one worse than the other

dachte thought
[**denken, dachte, hat gedacht** (2)]
heiß hot
Tränen tears
[**die Träne, die Tränen** (2)]
liefen ran
[**laufen, er läuft, lief, ist gelaufen**]
ihm über die Backen down his cheeks
[**die Backe, die Backen** the cheek]
der Bart the beard
erinnerte ihn an reminded him of
[**erinnern** to remind]
[**sich erinnern** to remember]
lieb dear
die . . . tot war who had been dead

hoffentlich I hope
[**hoffentlich** I hope, let's hope]
der Vogel the bird (2)

doch! oh yes!
richtig real (2)

fliegen to fly (3)
sie wollte . . . gestatten she wanted . . . permit
[**wollen, er will, wollte, hat gewollt** (2)]
[**gestatten** to permit, to allow]
auf keine Weise in no way
[**die Weise** the way, manner (3)]
um ihre Hand zu bitten to ask for her hand
[**bitten** to ask, to request]

verlor lost
[**verlieren, verlor, hat verloren** to lose]
der Mut the courage
nahm took
[**nehmen, er nimmt, nahm, hat genommen**]
braun brown
schwarz black (2)
die Farbe the paint
[**die Farbe, die Farben** the color, paint (2)]
strich smeared
[**streichen, strich, hat gestrichen** to spread, smear, stroke]

sprachen alle fließend französisch, eine schlechter als die andere.

„Wie schön!“ dachte der Kaiser, und heiße Tränen liefen ihm über die Backen in den Bart, denn die süße Stimme der kleinen Nachtigall erinnerte ihn an seine liebe Frau, die schon seit vielen Jahren tot war.

„Hoffentlich ist es kein natürlicher Vogel!“ rief die Prinzessin.

„Doch!“ antworten die Diener, „es ist ein richtiger Vogel!“

„Dann laßt ihn fliegen!“ sagte die Prinzessin ganz böse, und sie wollte dem Prinzen auf keine Weise gestatten, sie zu sehen und um ihre Hand zu bitten.

2.

Aber der Prinz verlor nicht den Mut. Er nahm braune und schwarze Farbe und strich sie auf sein Gesicht. Dann zog er einen alten Rock und ein Paar schmutzige Hosen an, drückte den Hut tief ins Gesicht, ging an den Hof und klopfte an die Tür. „Guten Morgen, Kaiser!“ sagte er. „Ich suche Arbeit und möchte fragen, ob ich hier auf dem Schloß dienen kann.“

---

dann zog er . . . an then he put on
[**an-ziehen** to put on]
[**ziehen, zog, hat gezogen** to pull, to draw]
der Rock the coat
[**der Rock, die Röcke** the coat, jacket; skirt]
das Paar the pair (3)]
schmutzig dirty
Hosen pants
[**die Hose, die Hosen** the pants, trousers]
drückte den Hut tief ins Gesicht pulled his hat low over his face
[**drücken** to press, to push]
[**der Hut, die Hüte** the hat]
[**tief** deep]
ging an den Hof went to court
[**gehen, ging, ist gegangen** (2)]
klopfen to knock (2)
dienen be of service
[**dienen** to serve, to be of service]

was für ein Zufall! what a coincidence!
  [**der Zufall** the chance, coincidence, accident]
eben just now, just
  der . . . aufpassen kann who can watch
  die Schweineherde the herd of pigs
    [**die Herde, die Herden** the herd]
wenn if
  die Stelle the position
    [**die Stelle, die Stellen** the place, spot; position, job]
  ist sie dein it is yours

wurde became
    [**werden, er wird, wurde, ist geworden**]
  kaiserlich imperial
  der Schweinehirt swineherd (2)
    [**der Hirt, die Hirten** the shepherd (2)]
bekam received
    [**bekommen, bekam, hat bekommen** to get, receive]
  der Schweinestall the pigsty
    [**der Stall, die Ställe** the stable, pen (2)]
  unten down
  am Ufer des Sees on the shore of the lake
    [**das Ufer, die Ufer** the shore, bank]
    [**der See, die Seen** the lake]
  der Strohhaufen the pile of straw
    [**das Stroh** the straw]
    [**der Haufen, die Haufen** the heap, pile]
  dienen to serve (2)
  als Bett as bed
    [**das Bett, die Betten**]
  wohnen to live (3)
  tat did
    [**tun, tat, hat getan** (2)]
trieb drove
    [**treiben, trieb, hat getrieben** to drive]
  die Schweineherde the herd of pigs (2)
    [**die Herde, die Herden** the herd (2)]
  hinaus out
  führen to lead (3)
  heim home
    [**das Heim** the home]
  saß sat
    [**sitzen, saß, hat gesessen**]
  das Feuer the fire
  das Eisen the iron (2)
  der Topf the pot
an den Seiten on the sides
    [**die Seite, die Seiten** the side; page (2)]

„Was für ein Zufall!“ rief der Kaiser. „Wir brauchen eben jemand, der auf unsere Schweineherde aufpassen kann. Wenn du die Stelle willst, ist sie dein.“

So wurde der Prinz kaiserlicher Schweinehirt. Er bekam ein ganz kleines Zimmer neben dem Schweinestall unten am Ufer des Sees; ein Strohhaufen diente ihm als Bett; und dort wohnte er nun und tat seine Arbeit. Am Morgen trieb er seine Schweineherde hinaus auf die Felder, am Abend führte er sie wieder heim; in der Nacht aber saß er in seinem Zimmer und arbeitete mit Feuer und Eisen an einem kleinen Topf. Was für ein hübscher Topf das war! An den Seiten hingen runde Glöckchen, die klingelten, wenn der Topf kochte, und was sie spielten, war ein altes Liedchen:

„Ach, du lieber Augustin, Augustin, Augustin,
Ach, du lieber Augustin,
Alles ist hin!“

Aber das war noch nicht alles. Wenn man den Finger in den Topf hielt, wußte man sogleich, was auf jedem Ofen der Stadt

---

hingen hung
[**hängen, hing, hat gehangen** to hang]
rund round
Glöckchen little bells
[**das Glöckchen, die Glöckchen**]
klingeln to ring, to tinkle
der Topf the pot (2)
kochen to boil
[**kochen** to cook; to boil]
das Liedchen the little song
lieb dear (2)
Augustin Augustine
alles ist hin everything is gone

wenn man . . . hielt if one held
[**halten, er hält, hielt, hat gehalten** to hold]
der Finger the finger
[**der Finger, die Finger**]
wußte man one knew
[**wissen, er weiß, wußte, hat gewußt**]
was . . . stand what stood
[**stehen, stand, hat gestanden**]
der Ofen the stove (2)

und . . . hing and hung
[**hängen, hing, hat gehangen** (2)]
das Feuer the fire (2)
riechen to smell
[**riechen, roch, hat gerochen** (2)]
backen to bake
kochen to cook (2)
brieten roasted
[**braten, er brät, briet, hat gebraten** to roast, fry, broil]
war doch etwas ganz anderes als was indeed something quite different from

spazierenging went for a walk
[**spazieren-gehen** to go for a walk]
von fern from afar
[**fern** far, distant]
blieb sie . . . stehen she stopped
[**bleiben, blieb, ist geblieben** to stay, to remain]
überrascht surprised, in surprise
[**überraschen** to surprise]
freute sich was pleased
[**sich freuen** to be glad, happy, pleased; to rejoice (2)]
das Klavier the piano
mit einem Finger with one finger
[**der Finger, die Finger** (2)]
wenn er . . . kann if he can . . .
gebildet educated, cultured
[**bilden** to form, to shape; to educate]
geh hin go there, go down
das Instrument the instrument
[**das Instrument, die Instrumente**]

mußte had to
[**müssen, er muß, mußte, hat gemußt**]
eines der Fräulein one of the ladies
[**das Fräulein, die Fräulein** the young lady, miss; Miss]
hinein-gehen go in
[**hinein** in, into]
zog . . . an put on
[**an-ziehen** to put on (2)]
[**ziehen, zog, hat gezogen** (2)]
vorher before
Holzschuhe wooden shoes
[**das Holz** the wood]
[**der Schuh, die Schuhe** the shoe (2)]
hob . . . hoch lifted up
[**heben, hob, hat gehoben** to raise, to lift (2)]
der Rock the skirt
[**der Rock, die Röcke** the coat, jacket, skirt (2)]

stand und über jedem Feuer hing, denn man konnte riechen, was die Leute backten, kochten oder brieten. Ja, solch ein Topf war doch etwas ganz anderes als eine natürliche Rose!

Als die Prinzessin am folgenden Tage mit allen ihren Hofdamen spazierenging und von fern das Liedchen hörte, das der Topf spielte, blieb sie überrascht stehen. „Wie hübsch!“ sagte sie und freute sich, denn es war das einzige Lied, das sie auf dem Klavier spielen konnte, und das spielte sie mit einem Finger. „Es muß der Schweinehirt sein“, sagte sie. „Wenn er etwas spielen kann, was ich auch kann, dann ist er wirklich gebildet. Geh hin und frage ihn, wieviel das Instrument kostet!“

Und da mußte eines der Fräulein hineingehen; aber sie zog vorher ein Paar Holzschuhe an und hob ihren Rock hoch, weil der Hof vor dem Schweinestall so schmutzig war.

„Was verlangst du für das Ding?“ fragte sie.

„Ich will zehn Küsse von der Prinzessin haben“, erwiderte der Schweinehirt.

„Pfui!“ sagte das Fräulein, „du solltest dich schämen!“

„Zehn Küsse, oder der Topf bleibt hier!“ antwortete der Schweinehirt.

„Nun, wieviel will er?“ fragte die Prinzessin, als das Fräulein wiederkam.

---

der Schweinestall the pigsty (2)
schmutzig dirty (2)

das Ding the thing (3)

Küsse kisses
[**der Kuß, die Küsse**]
erwidern to reply (3)

das Fräulein the young lady (2)
du solltest dich schämen you should be ashamed of yourself
[**sich schämen** to be ashamed (2)]

Küsse kisses
[**der Kuß, die Küsse** (2)]

als . . . wiederkam when . . . came back
[**wieder-kommen** to come back, to return]

schrecklich terrible (3)

das Ohr the ear
[**das Ohr, die Ohren**]
befahl commanded
[**befehlen, er befiehlt, befahl, hat befohlen** to order, to command]

als aber . . . begann but when . . . began
[**beginnen, begann, hat begonnen**]
die Weile the while (3)
zum zweiten Male for the second time
sandte . . . hinunter sent . . . down
[**senden, sandte, hat gesandt**]
[**hinunter** down (3)]
dieselbe the same
noch einmal once more (3)

danke thank you; thanks

ärgerlich annoying
um mich herumstehen stand around me
[**um . . . herum** around]
damit so that
stellten sich placed themselves
[**stellen** to place, to put (2)]
ihre Mäntel their coats
[**der Mantel, die Mäntel** the coat, overcoat]
gab gave
[**geben, er gibt, gab, hat gegeben** (2)]
bekam received
[**bekommen, bekam, hat bekommen** (2)]
dafür for it; in exchange

die Lust the delight
[**die Lust** the desire, pleasure, delight (3)]
die Ruhe the rest (3)
mußte er it had to
[**müssen, er muß, mußte, hat gemußt** (2)]
es gab there was
die Wohnung the home
[**die Wohnung, die Wohnungen** the apartment; residence]
von der man nicht wußte of which one didn't know
[**wissen, er weiß, wußte, hat gewußt**]
darin in it, in them
aßen were eating
[**essen, er ißt, aß, hat gegessen** to eat]
tanzen to dance
schrien screamed
[**schreien, schrie, hat geschrien**]

„Ich kann es nicht wiederholen", antwortete das Fräulein, „es ist zu schrecklich."

„Dann sage es mir leise ins Ohr!" befahl die Prinzessin.

„Pfui!" sagte dann auch sie und ging weg. Als aber nach einer Weile der Topf zum zweiten Male zu spielen begann, blieb sie wieder stehen und sandte dieselbe Hofdame noch einmal hinunter. „Frage ihn, ob er zufrieden ist, wenn er zehn Küsse von einer Hofdame bekommt!" sagte sie.

„Nein, danke!" sagte der Schweinehirt. „Zehn Küsse von der Prinzessin, oder ich behalte meinen Topf."

„Wie ärgerlich!" rief die Prinzessin, als sie das hörte. „Nun, dann müßt ihr alle um mich herumstehen, damit niemand es sieht!" Und so stellten sich die Hofdamen um sie und hoben ihre Mäntel hoch, und dann gab die Prinzessin dem Schweinehirten zehn Küsse und bekam dafür den Topf.

3.

Nun, war das eine Lust und Freude, als die Prinzessin ihren Topf hatte! Sie gab ihm keine Ruhe; den ganzen Abend und den ganzen Tag mußte er kochen. Es gab in der ganzen Stadt keine Wohnung, von der man nicht wußte, was die Menschen darin aßen. Die Hofdamen lachten, tanzten und schrien vor Vergnügen. „Wir wissen, wer heute abend Schweinefleisch mit Erbsen bekommt! Fräulein Müller hat Eier mit Schinken! Frau Schulz gibt morgen sicher eine Gesellschaft,

---

heute abend tonight
  das Schweinefleisch pork
    [**das Fleisch** the meat, flesh(3)]
  Erbsen peas
    [**die Erbse, die Erbsen**]
Eier eggs
    [**das Ei, die Eier**]
  der Schinken the ham
sicher certainly (3)
  die Gesellschaft the party
    [**die Gesellschaft** the company; society; party (2)]

bäckt is baking
[**backen, er bäckt, backte (buk), hat gebacken**]
der Kuchen the cake
[**der Kuchen, die Kuchen**]
dick fat, thick
brät is frying
[**braten, er brät, briet, hat gebraten** to roast, fry, broil (2)]
Fische fish
[**der Fisch, die Fische**]
interessant interesting (2)
tanzen to dance (2)
plötzlich suddenly (3)
vor allem above all
etwas davon anything about it

ließ . . . vorbeigehen let . . . go by
[**lassen, er läßt, ließ, hat gelassen**]
[**vorbei** past]
ohne etwas zu tun without doing something
das Instrument the instrument (2)
die Pfeife the whistle
[**die Pfeife, die Pfeifen** the pipe; the whistle (2)]
aus Holz of wood
[**das Holz** the wood (2)]
der Mund the mouth (3)
stecken to put (3)
und hineinblies and blew into it
[**hinein** in, into]
[**blasen, er bläst, blies, hat geblasen** to blow]
kamen . . . heraus came out
[**heraus** out (2)]
allerlei all sorts of
Walzer und Polkas waltzes and polkas
[**der Walzer, die Walzer**]
[**die Polka**]
lustig merry, jolly
daß jeder . . . zu tanzen anfing that everyone . . . began to dance
[**an-fangen, er fängt an, fing an, hat angefangen**]
ach oh
superbe superb
als sie . . . spazierenging when she . . . went for a walk
[**spazieren-gehen** to go for a walk (2)]
wieder einmal once again (3)
am Ufer des Sees at the shore of the lake
[**das Ufer, die Ufer** the shore, bank (2)]
[**der See, die Seen** the lake (2)]
um . . . zu genießen in order to enjoy (3)
frisch fresh (2)
die Luft the air

denn sie bäckt Kuchen! Und die dicke Frau Meier brät Fische! Wie interessant!" Die Prinzessin lachte und tanzte mit den anderen, aber dann sagte sie plötzlich: „Schreit nicht so laut und sagt vor allem niemand etwas davon, denn ich bin des Kaisers Tochter!"–„Natürlich nicht!" antworteten die Hofdamen.

Der Schweinehirt ließ keinen Tag vorbeigehen, ohne etwas zu tun. Das nächste Instrument, das er machte, war eine Pfeife aus Holz. Wenn man sie in den Mund steckte und hineinblies, dann kamen allerlei Walzer und Polkas heraus, die so lustig waren, daß jeder, der sie hörte, sofort zu tanzen anfing. „Ach, das ist wirklich *superbe!*" sagte die Prinzessin, als sie wieder einmal mit ihren Hofdamen am Ufer des Sees spazierenging, um die frische Luft zu genießen. „Schönere Musik als diese gibt es in der ganzen Welt nicht. Geh hinein und frage, was das Instrument kostet. Aber Küsse kommen nicht in Frage!"

„Diesmal will er hundert Küsse von der Prinzessin haben", berichtete die Hofdame, als sie zurückkam. „Unter hundert tut er es nicht, sagt er."

„Der Narr!" rief die Prinzessin und begann weiterzugehen. Allein nach einer Weile blieb sie stehen und sagte: „Nein, ich

---

schönere Musik als diese gibt es . . . nicht there is no more beautiful music than this
[**die Musik** the music (3)]
die Welt the world (2)
geh hinein go in
[**hinein** in, into (2)]
kommen nicht in Frage are out of the question
[**die Frage, die Fragen** the question]

berichten to report (3)
unter hundert under a hundred

der Narr the fool
[**der Narr, die Narren** (2)]
begann began
[**beginnen, begann, hat begonnen** (2)]
allein but
blieb sie stehen she stopped
[**bleiben, blieb, ist geblieben** (2)]

ich darf nicht I must not
an mich selbst denken think of myself
als solche as such
die Aufgabe the obligation
[**die Aufgabe, die Aufgaben** the lesson, assignment, task]
ja indeed
die Pflicht the duty
[**die Pflicht, die Pflichten**]
die Kunst zu fördern to promote art
[**die Kunst, die Künste** the art, skill (2)]
[**fördern** to further, to advance, to promote]
die übrigen the remaining
[**übrig** remaining, left (over)]

das tun wir gar nicht gern we don't like to do that at all
[**gar** at all]

was für ein Unsinn what nonsense
[**der Unsinn** the nonsense]
[**der Sinn, die Sinne** the sense; mind (2)]
damit so that

entweder . . . oder either . . . or (3)
die Pfeife the whistle (2)

um mich herum around me
[**um . . . herum** around (2)]
ihren Rock her skirt
während sie . . . ging while going
bis zu (up) to
dann fing das Küssen an then the kissing started
[**an-fangen, fängt an, fing an, hat angefangen** (2)]
[**küssen** to kiss]
und so weiter (usw.) and so on
nahm sich Zeit took his time
[**nehmen, er nimmt, nahm, hat genommen** (2)]
wurde rot blushed
[**werden, er wird, wurde, ist geworden** to become, to get (2)]
[**rot** red (2)]
bis auf die Haarwurzeln to the roots of her hair
[**das Haar, die Haare** the hair (2)]
[**die Wurzel, die Wurzeln** the root]
ließen . . . niederfallen let . . . (fall) down
[**lassen, er läßt, ließ, hat gelassen** (2)]
[**nieder** down]
[**fallen** to fall (3)]
das Küssen the kissing (2)
dauern to last (2)

darf nicht immer nur an mich selbst denken. Ich bin des Kaisers Tochter, und als solche habe ich die Aufgabe, ja die Pflicht, die Kunst zu fördern. Lauf schnell zurück und sage ihm, er soll zehn Küsse von mir haben. Die übrigen Küsse bekommt er von meinen Hofdamen!"

„Aber das tun wir gar nicht gern", antworteten die Damen; „der Mann ist so schmutzig!"

„Was für ein Unsinn!" erwiderte die Prinzessin; „wenn i c h ihn küssen kann, dann könnt ihr es auch. Vergeßt bitte nicht, daß mein Vater euch bezahlt, damit ihr tut, was ich befehle!"

„Oh nein!" sagte der Schweinehirt; „entweder ich bekomme meine hundert Küsse von der Prinzessin, oder ich behalte meine Pfeife für mich."

„Dann stellt euch wieder um mich herum!" rief die Prinzessin und hob ihren Rock mit beiden Händen, während sie durch den schmutzigen Hof bis zu dem Schweinestall ging, und die Hofdamen hoben wieder ihre Mäntel hoch, damit niemand etwas sehen konnte, und dann fing das Küssen an. Eins, zwei, drei, vier, fünf usw. (und so weiter). Der Schweinehirt nahm sich Zeit, die Prinzessin wurde rot bis auf die Haarwurzeln, und die Hofdamen lachten. Aber sie lachten so leise, daß die Prinzessin sie nicht hören konnte. Zehn, zwanzig, dreißig, vierzig. Und nun wurden die Hofdamen müde und ließen eine nach der anderen ihre Mäntel niederfallen, weil das Küssen so lange dauerte.

4.

Während all dies geschah, lag der Kaiser auf seinem Bett oben im Schloß und schlief und träumte von Rosen und Nachti-

---

während while
geschah was happening
[**geschehen, es geschieht, geschah, ist geschehen** to happen]
lag was lying
[**liegen, er lag, hat gelegen** to lie]
oben upstairs
[**oben** upstairs; above]
schlief was sleeping
[**schlafen, er schläft, schlief, hat geschlafen** to sleep]

er kannte he knew
[**kennen, kannte, hat gekannt** to know]
als . . . zu schlafen than to sleep
der Nachmittag the afternoon (3)
und . . . zu vergessen and to forget
auf kurze Zeit for a short time
die Mühen the troubles
[**die Mühe, die Mühen** the effort, pain, trouble]
auf einmal suddenly (3)
wachte er auf he woke up
[**auf-wachen** to wake up]
es klang wie it sounded like
[**klingen, klang, hat geklungen** to sound]
das Lachen the laughter
er sprang he jumped
[**springen, sprang, ist gesprungen** to spring, to jump]
zog . . . an put on
gelb yellow
der Schlafrock the dressing gown
Hausschuhe slippers
lief ran
[**laufen, er läuft, lief, ist gelaufen** (2)]
offen open (3)
was für eine Menschenmenge what a crowd (of people)
[**die Menge, die Mengen** the crowd, quantity, lot (2)]
unten down (2)
rieb rubbed
[**reiben, rieb, hat gerieben** to rub]
was tun sie nur dort? what on earth are they doing there?
setzte er . . . auf he put on
[**setzen** to put, to place (2)]
die Krone the crown
vergaß forgot
[**vergessen, er vergißt, vergaß, hat vergessen** (2)]
daß er noch . . . anhatte that he still had on
der Schlafrock the dressing gown (2)
Hausschuhe slippers (2)
sobald er in die Nähe . . . kam as soon as he came close to
[**die Nähe** the vicinity, proximity (2)]
der Eifer the eagerness
[**der Eifer** the zeal, eagerness]
damit so that
weder zu viele noch zu wenige neither too many nor too few
[**weder . . . noch** neither . . . nor]
merken to notice (2)
gar nicht not at all
[**gar** at all (2)]
stand stood
[**stehen, stand, hat gestanden** (2)]

gallen und seiner lieben Frau. Er kannte kein größeres Vergnügen, als am Nachmittag ein wenig zu schlafen und auf kurze Zeit die Mühen und Sorgen des Tages zu vergessen. Auf einmal wachte er auf. Was war das? Hörte er richtig? Es klang wie lautes Lachen. Er sprang aus dem Bett, zog seinen gelben Schlafrock und seine Hausschuhe an und lief zum offenen Fenster. „Was für eine Menschenmenge dort unten beim Schweinestall!" sagte er und rieb sich die Augen, denn er konnte nicht sehen, w e r es war. „Ich glaube, es ist meine Tochter mit ihren Hofdamen", sagte er dann. „Was tun sie nur dort? Ich muß hinuntergehen." Schnell setzte er seine Krone auf, vergaß aber, daß er noch Schlafrock und Hausschuhe anhatte, und lief hinunter. Sobald er in die Nähe des Schweinestalles kam, ging er ganz leise, und weil die Hofdamen die Küsse mit solchem Eifer zählten, damit der Schweinehirt weder zu viele noch zu wenige bekam, merkten sie gar nicht, daß der Kaiser plötzlich hinter ihnen stand. „Was ist das?" rief der Kaiser und streckte seinen Hals, denn er war dick und klein und mußte über die Schultern der Hofdamen sehen. Und nun wurde er ganz rot vor Zorn, als er sah, daß die beiden sich küßten. So böse war er, daß sogar die Krone auf seinem Haupt zitterte. „Hinaus mit euch!" schrie er und schlug beide mit

---

strecken to stretch
  der Hals the neck
  dick fat, thick (2)
  die Schultern the shoulders
    [die Schulter, die Schultern]
vor Zorn with rage
    [**der Zorn** the anger, rage]
  als er sah when he saw
    [sehen, er sieht, sah, hat gesehen]
sogar even (2)
  die Krone the crown (2)
  das Haupt the head
  zittern to tremble
schrie er he shouted
    [schreien, schrie, hat geschrien (2)**]**
  schlug beat
    [schlagen, er schlägt, schlug, hat geschlagen (2)**]**

der Kopf the head (3)
sechsundachtzigst eighty-sixth
befahl commanded
[**befehlen, er befiehlt, befahl, hat befohlen** to order, to command (2)]

saß sat
[**sitzen, saß, hat gesessen** (2)]
hart hard
die Erde the ground, earth (2)
draußen outside (2)
vor den Mauern before the walls
[**die Mauer, die Mauern**]
klagen to complain
die Ungerechtigkeit the injustice
[**die Gerechtigkeit** the justice]
weinen to weep
[**weinen** to cry, to weep (2)]
heiß hot (2)
schwieg was silent
[**schweigen, schwieg, hat geschwiegen** to be silent (2)]
der Regen the rain
fiel. . . nieder fell down
[**fallen, er fällt, fiel, ist gefallen**]
[**nieder** down (2)]
in Strömen in torrents
[**der Strom, die Ströme** the large river; stream, current]

das Mädchen the girl (3)
selbst wenn er . . . sandte even if he sent
[**selbst wenn** even if]
[**senden, sandte, hat gesandt** (2)]
unglücklich unhappy
[**glücklich** happy]

wischen to wipe (2)
braun brown (2)
warf . . . zu Boden threw to the ground
[**werfen, er wirft, warf, hat geworfen** to throw]
[**der Boden** the ground, earth (2)]
die Kleider the clothes
[**das Kleid, die Kleider** the dress]
trat stepped
[**treten, er tritt, trat, ist getreten** to step, to walk]
trauen to trust

du verstandest nicht you did not understand
[**verstehen, verstand, hat verstanden**]

einem seiner Hausschuhe an den Kopf, gerade in dem Augenblick, in dem die Prinzessin dem Schweinehirten seinen sechsundachtzigsten Kuß gab. „Hinaus mit euch!" Und er rief seine Soldaten und befahl, beide an die Grenze zu bringen und aus seinem Reich zu treiben.

Da saß nun die Prinzessin auf der harten Erde draußen vor den Mauern des Königreiches und klagte über die Ungerechtigkeit der Welt und weinte heiße Tränen, und der Schweinehirt stand neben ihr und schwieg, und der Regen fiel in Strömen auf sie nieder.

„Ach, ich armes Mädchen!" sagte die Prinzessin. „Warum nahm ich nicht den Prinzen, selbst wenn er mir diese dummen Geschenke sandte? Ach, wie unglücklich ich bin!"

Da ging der Schweinehirt hinter einen Baum, wischte die braune und schwarze Farbe aus dem Gesicht, warf die alten schmutzigen Kleider zu Boden und trat nun als ein herrlicher Prinz vor sie, so schön, daß die Prinzessin ihren Augen nicht traute, als sie ihn erblickte.

„Ja", sagte er, „ich bin der Prinz, den du nun haben möchtest. Jetzt aber will ich dich nicht. Du wolltest keinen richtigen Prinzen, du verstandest nicht die Rose und die Nachtigall, aber einen Schweinehirten konntest du küssen wegen einer dummen Pfeife aus Holz und eines Topfes aus Eisen! Und was hast du jetzt dafür? Nichts!" Und damit wandte er sich von ihr und ging in sein Königreich und machte ihr die Tür vor der Nase zu.

---

aus Eisen of iron
[**das Eisen** the iron (2)]
dafür for it, in exchange for it (2)
damit with that
wandte er sich he turned
[**wenden, wandte, hat gewandt** to turn]
machte . . . zu shut
vor der Nase in her face
[**die Nase** the nose (2)]

der Regen the rain (2)

das ihr nun wirklich tief aus dem Herzen kam which now really came from the depth of her heart

[**tief** deep]

[**das Herz, die Herzen** the heart (3)]

Sie aber stand jetzt draußen im Regen und konnte, wenn sie wollte, ein Liedchen singen, das ihr nun wirklich tief aus dem Herzen kam:

„Ach, du lieber Augustin, Augustin, Augustin,
Ach, du lieber Augustin,
Alles ist hin!“

DER ALTE

[3B]

NOTES

The subordinating conjunction **indem** may mean

a. *while* if its meaning is *temporal.* It expresses *simultaneity.*

> ***Indem* er das sagte, starb er.** While saying this, he died.

b. *by* (plus present participle) if it indicates the *way in which something is done.*

> **Sie taten der menschlichen Gesellschaft einen Gefallen, *indem* sie ihn ins Gefängnis schickten.** . . . *by* send*ing* him to jail
>
> **Er bildete seinen Geist, *indem* er die Zeitung las.** . . . *by* read*ing* the paper

REVIEW OF STRONG AND IRREGULAR VERBS USED IN STORY 3A

The principal parts are listed in the following order: infinitive; third person singular of the present tense if the second and third persons singular are irregular; third person of the simple past; past participle. The form "ist" before a past participle indicates that the compound tenses are formed with the auxiliary *sein.*

backen	bäckt	backte *or* buk	gebacken	*to bake*
befehlen	befiehlt	befahl	befohlen	*to command, order*
beginnen		begann	begonnen	*to begin*
bekommen		bekam	bekommen	*to get, receive*
beschließen		beschloß	beschlossen	*to decide*
besitzen		besaß	besessen	*to possess, own*
bitten		bat	gebeten	*to ask, beg*
blasen	bläst	blies	geblasen	*to blow*
(bleiben		blieb	ist geblieben	*to remain, stay*)
stehen-bleiben		blieb stehen	ist stehengeblieben	*to stop*
braten	brät	briet	gebraten	*to roast*
denken		dachte	gedacht	*to think*
essen	ißt	aß	gegessen	*to eat*
fahren	fährt	fuhr	ist gefahren	*to go, drive, ride*
fallen	fällt	fiel	ist gefallen	*to fall*
(fangen	fängt	fing	gefangen	*to catch*)
an-fangen	fängt an	fing an	angefangen	*to begin, start*

geben	gibt	gab	gegeben	*to give*
gehen		ging	ist gegangen	*to go*
geschehen	es geschieht	es geschah	es ist geschehen	*to happen*
haben	hat	hatte	gehabt	*to have*
halten	hält	hielt	gehalten	*to hold, stop*
hängen		hing	gehangen	*to hang*
heben		hob	gehoben	*to lift, raise*
kennen		kannte	gekannt	*to know*
klingen		klang	geklungen	*to sound*
kommen		kam	ist gekommen	*to come*
können	kann	konnte	(gekonnt)	*can, to be able*
lassen	läßt	ließ	gelassen	*to let, leave*
laufen	läuft	lief	ist gelaufen	*to run*
liegen		lag	gelegen	*to lie*
mögen	mag	mochte	(gemocht)	*to like*
müssen	muß	mußte	(gemußt)	*must, to have to*
nehmen	nimmt	nahm	genommen	*to take*
reiben		rieb	gerieben	*to rub*
riechen		roch	gerochen	*to smell*
rufen		rief	gerufen	*to call*
schlafen	schläft	schlief	geschlafen	*to sleep*
schlagen	schlägt	schlug	geschlagen	*to beat, strike*
schreien		schrie	geschrien	*to shout, scream*
schweigen		schwieg	geschwiegen	*to be silent*
sehen	sieht	sah	gesehen	*to see, look*
sein	ist	war	ist gewesen	*to be*
senden		sandte	gesandt	*to send*
singen		sang	gesungen	*to sing*
sitzen		saß	gesessen	*to sit*
sollen	soll	sollte	(gesollt)	*shall, should, ought*
sprechen	spricht	sprach	gesprochen	*to speak, say*
springen		sprang	ist gesprungen	*to jump, spring*
stehen		stand	gestanden	*to stand*
streichen		strich	gestrichen	*to stroke, strike, spread*
tragen	trägt	trug	getragen	*to carry, wear*
treiben		trieb	getrieben	*to drive; float*
treten	tritt	trat	ist getreten	*to step, go, walk*
tun		tat	getan	*to do*
vergessen	vergißt	vergaß	vergessen	*to forget*
verlieren		verlor	verloren	*to lose*
verstehen		verstand	verstanden	*to understand*
wachsen	wächst	wuchs	ist gewachsen	*to grow*
wenden		wandte *or* wendete	gewandt	*to turn*
werden	wird	wurde	ist geworden	*to become*
werfen	wirft	warf	geworfen	*to throw*
wissen	weiß	wußte	gewußt	*to know*
wollen	will	wollte	(gewollt)	*to want*
(ziehen		zog	gezogen	*to pull, draw*)
an-ziehen		zog an	angezogen	*to put on, dress*

IDIOMS FOR REVIEW

halten für to believe to be, to consider (as), to take for
man hielt ihn für einen Geschäftsmann people thought he was a businessman
es ging ihm gut he was doing all right
es geht mir gut I am fine, I'm doing all right
auf Kosten des Staates at the expense of the government
auf meine Kosten at my expense
vor allen Dingen above all
warten auf to wait for
er wartet auf mich he is waiting for me
ihm wurde heiß he was getting hot
mir ist kalt I am cold
je mehr, desto besser the more the better
desto besser! all the better!
auf keinen Fall under no circumstances, in no case
der Zeitung nach according to the newspaper
immer wieder again and again
sich fertig machen to get ready
er hatte ein kleines Heft bei sich he had a small notebook with him
gegen elf Uhr toward eleven o'clock
das war ihm gleich that was all the same to him
im voraus ahead, ahead of time
Lust haben to feel like
ich habe keine Lust . . . I don't feel like . . . , I have no desire to . . .
heute nachmittag this afternoon
er brachte kein Wort über die Lippen he could not utter a word

kein Mann von Charakter not a man of character
[**der Charakter** the character]
wer whoever (2)
kannte knew
[**kennen, kannte, gekannt** (2)]
hielt ihn für believed him to be
[**halten für** to believe, to consider to be]
[**halten, er hält, hielt, hat gehalten** to hold (2)]
der Geschäftsmann the businessman (3)
der Buchhalter the accountant
[**das Buch, die Bücher** the book (2)]
die Kleidung the clothing
einfach simple (3)
weder . . . noch neither . . . nor (2)
elegant elegant
seine Art zu reden his manner of speaking
[**die Art, die Arten** the kind, manner, way]
[**reden** to talk, to speak]
ungebildet uneducated
[**gebildet** educated (2)]
[**bilden** to form; to educate (2)]
er besaß he possessed
[**besitzen, besaß, hat besessen** to own, to possess (2)]
angenehm pleasant (3)
die Manieren the manners
die Zwecke the purposes
[**der Zweck, die Zwecke** the purpose, aim, object (3)]
gewinnend winning
[**gewinnen** to win (2)]
das Wesen the personality
[**das Wesen, die Wesen** the being, creature; nature, character, manner, personality; essence, substance; system]
der Eindruck the impression
[**der Eindruck, die Eindrücke**]
der Grund the reason
[**der Grund, die Gründe** the reason, cause; ground, bottom (2)]
fand found
[**finden, fand, hat gefunden** to find]
täglich daily
das Brot the bread (3)
die Mühe the effort
[**die Mühe, die Mühen** the effort, trouble (2)]
verdienen to earn
[**verdienen** to earn; to deserve (3)]
die er kennenlernte whom he got to know
[**kennen-lernen** to get to know, to make the acquaintance of]
trauen to trust (2)
er machte . . . Geschäfte he did business

[3 B]

(FOUR PARTS)

Der Alte

1.

Tobias Puff war kein Mann von Charakter. Wer ihn nicht kannte, hielt ihn für einen kleinen Geschäftsmann, vielleicht einen Buchhalter. Seine Kleidung war einfach, aber gut, weder elegant noch billig; seine Art zu reden war nicht ungebildet; er besaß angenehme Manieren und, wenn es seinen Zwecken diente, ein freundliches, gewinnendes Wesen. Tobias Puff wußte, daß er keinen schlechten Eindruck machte, und daß dieser Eindruck der Grund war, warum er es nicht schwer fand, sein tägliches Brot ohne große Mühe zu verdienen. Die Menschen, die er kennenlernte, trauten ihm, und Tobias Puff brauchte solche Leute. Er machte zwar Geschäfte, aber er war kein Geschäftsmann im gewöhnlichen Sinne, denn seine Geschäfte waren etwas dunkler Art, und einem Buchhalter war er nur insofern

---

im gewöhnlichen Sinne in the ordinary sense
[**gewöhnlich** ordinary]
[**der Sinn, die Sinne** the sense, mind (3)]
etwas dunkler Art of a somewhat shady kind
[**die Art, die Arten** the kind, manner, way (2)]
einem Buchhalter war er nur insofern ähnlich he resembled an accountant only insofar
[**der Buchhalter** the accountant (2)]
[**insofern** insofar]

[**ähnlich** similar, like]
[**ähnlich sein** to resemble]
als auch er as he too
nur waren es only they were
gewöhnlich ordinary (2)
um es . . . kurz zu sagen to say it briefly
mit einem Wort in one word
[**das Wort, die Worte (Wörter)** (2)]
der Buchmacher the bookmaker
der Schwindler the swindler, crook
als solchem ging es ihm ganz gut as such he was doing quite well
[**es geht mir gut** I am doing well, I am fine]
solange er . . . atmete as long as he breathed
[**atmen** to breathe]
die Luft the air (2)
der Freiheit of freedom
[**die Freiheit** the liberty, freedom]
und . . . sah and saw
[**sehen, er sieht, sah, hat gesehen** (2)]
fest solid
[**fest** fast, firm, solid (2)]
Mauern walls
[**die Mauer, die Mauern** (2)]
des Stadtgefängnisses of the city jail
[**das Gefängnis, die Gefängnisse** the prison, jail]
von außen from the outside
[**außen** outside]
es ging ihm weniger gut he did less well
die Polizei the police (3)
die Richter the judges
[**der Richter, die Richter**]
es für richtig hielten considered it right
[**halten für** to consider, to believe (to be) (2)]
der menschlichen Gesellschaft einen Gefallen zu tun to do human society a favor
[**menschlich** human]
[**die Gesellschaft** the company, society, party (2)]
[**der Gefallen** the favor; pleasure]
indem sie ihn . . . schickten by sending him
von Zeit zu Zeit from time to time
das Gefängnis the jail (2)
wo Tobias Puff . . . studieren durfte where Tobias Puff was allowed to study
[**studieren** to study]
[**dürfen, er darf, durfte, hat gedurft** to be allowed, permitted]
einige Zeit lang for some time
die Außenwelt the outside world
[**außen, draußen** outside (2)]

ähnlich, als auch er etwas mit Büchern zu tun hatte. Nur waren es wieder keine gewöhnlichen Bücher. Um es kurz mit einem Wort zu sagen: Tobias Puff war ein Buchmacher und ein Schwindler. Als solchem ging es ihm ganz gut, solange er die frische Luft der Freiheit atmete und die dicken, festen Mauern des Stadtgefängnisses von außen sah. Es ging ihm weniger gut, wenn die Polizei und die Richter es für richtig hielten, der menschlichen Gesellschaft einen Gefallen zu tun, indem sie ihn von Zeit zu Zeit ins Gefängnis schickten, wo Tobias Puff dann einige Zeit lang die Außenwelt von innen studieren durfte.

Gefängnisse waren für Tobias Puff nichts Neues. Er klagte seit langem nicht mehr über die Ungerechtigkeit von Richtern, die ihm nicht erlaubten, in Ruhe und Frieden für sich zu leben und seine kleinen Geschäfte zu machen, denn er wußte, daß die Welt ihn nicht verstand. Und er trauerte auch nicht zu sehr um die Wochen, Monate, manchmal sogar Jahre, während deren er auf Kosten des Staates im Gefängnis saß. Erstens

---

von innen from the inside
[**innen, drinnen** inside]

klagen to complain (2)
seit langem since a long time
die Ungerechtigkeit the injustice (2)
von Richtern of judges
[**der Richter, die Richter** (2)]
erlauben to allow (2)
der Friede(n) the peace
für sich for himself
verstand understood
[**verstehen, verstand, hat verstanden** (2)]
er trauerte auch nicht zu sehr um he also did not grieve too much for
[**trauern um** to mourn, lament, grieve]
die Wochen the weeks
[**die Woche, die Wochen** (3)]
die Monate the months
[**der Monat, die Monate** (3)]
manchmal sometimes
während deren er . . . saß during which he sat
auf Kosten des Staates at the expense of the government
[**die Kosten** the cost(s), the expense]
[**der Staat, die Staaten** the state; government (2)]
erstens first(ly)

neu new (3)
Pläne plans
[**der Plan, die Pläne**]
die Zukunft the future (2)
zweitens second(ly)
der Geist the mind
[**der Geist, die Geister** the ghost, spirit; mind, intellect]
indem er . . . las by reading
[**lesen, er liest, las, hat gelesen** to read]
mit besonderem Eifer with special eagerness
[**besonder** special]
[**der Eifer** the zeal, eagerness (2)]
die Seiten studierte studied the pages
[**die Seite, die Seiten** the side; page (3)]
[**studieren** to study (2)]
die Pferderennen the horse races
[**das Pferd, die Pferde** the horse]
[**das Rennen, die Rennen** the race]
er kannte . . . auswendig he knew by heart
[**auswendig** by heart]
die Namen the names
[**der Name, die Namen** (3)]
fast aller Pferde of almost every horse
[**fast** almost (3)]
[**das Pferd, die Pferde** (2)]
ihre Chancen their chances
[**die Chance, die Chancen**]
bei jedem with each
verdienen to earn (3)
besonderes Fach special field
[**besonder** special (2)]
[**das Fach, die Fächer** the subject, field; drawer; compartment]
sie gehörten . . . zu they were . . . part of
[**gehören** to belong, to be part of (2)]
schließlich after all
[**schließlich** after all; finally]
drittens third(ly)
selbst im Gefängnis even in jail
Wetten bets
[**die Wette, die Wetten** (3)]
organisieren to organize (2)

auf diese Weise in this manner
durchaus nicht not at all, by no means
unangenehm unpleasant
er fürchtete sich nicht vor he was not afraid of
[**sich fürchten vor** to be afraid of]
klar clear
reich rich (2)

machte er dort neue und bessere Pläne für die Zukunft. Zweitens bildete er seinen Geist, indem er jeden Tag die Zeitung las und mit besonderem Eifer die Seiten studierte, auf denen die Pferderennen standen. Er kannte die Namen fast aller Pferde auswendig, er wußte, wie gut ihre Chancen waren und wieviel man bei jedem verdienen konnte. Pferde waren Tobias Puffs besonderes Fach; sie gehörten schließlich zu seinem Geschäft. Und drittens war Tobias Puff nie ohne Geld, weil er selbst im Gefängnis kleine Wetten organisierte.

Das Leben, das er auf diese Weise führte, war also durchaus nicht unangenehm. Er hatte, was er brauchte, und er fürchtete sich nicht vor der Zukunft. Es war ihm klar, daß man nicht hoffen konnte, im Gefängnis ein reicher Mann zu werden, aber er tröstete sich mit dem Gedanken, der eigentlich das Motto seines Lebens darstellte: „Für jeden Dummkopf, der stirbt, kommen zehn neue Dummköpfe zur Welt." Warum sich also Sorgen machen?

2.

In dem Augenblick, in dem diese Geschichte anfängt, war Tobias Puff seit einigen Tagen wieder einmal ein freier Mann. Was er vor allen Dingen brauchte, dachte er, war Geld, und

---

er tröstete sich he consoled himself
[**trösten** to console]
der Gedanke the thought
[**der Gedanke, die Gedanken**]
der eigentlich . . . darstellte which actually represented
[**eigentlich** actually, really]
[**dar-stellen** to represent, to present, to perform]
das Motto the motto
der Dummkopf the fool
[**der Dummkopf** the fool, idiot, dumbbell, blockhead (2)]
der stirbt who dies
kommen . . . zur Welt are born
warum sich also Sorgen machen? why worry, therefore?
[**sich Sorgen machen** to worry]

vor allen Dingen above all things

sprach spoke
[**sprechen, er spricht, sprach, hat gesprochen** (2)]
Pfennige pennies
[**der Pfennig, die Pfennige**]
ein paar a few (2)
große Summen large amounts
[**die Summe, die Summen** the sum, the amount (2)]
es genügte nicht it was not enough
[**genügen** to be sufficient, to be enough]
um . . . wieder anzufangen to start . . . again
dazu for that
das Kapital the capital
je mehr, desto besser the more, the better
[**je . . . desto** the . . . the]
der Freitag Friday
der Sonnabend Saturday
fand . . . statt took place
[**statt-finden** to take place (2)]
[**finden, fand, hat gefunden** to find (2)]
das Pferderennen the horse race (2)
das Problem the problem (3)
gelöst solved
[**lösen** to solve (2)]
sicher with certainty
rechnen to count
[**rechnen** to figure, to calculate, to count (2)]

als er . . . nach Haus ging when he went home
das Abendessen the supper (2)
und eben . . . bog and was just turning
[**eben** just, just then (2)]
[**biegen, bog, gebogen** to turn]
die Ecke the corner
[**die Ecke, die Ecken** the corner]
sah er jemand . . . stehen he saw someone standing
an einer Hauswand against the wall of a house
[**die Wand, die Wände** the wall]
die Gestalt the figure
[**die Gestalt, die Gestalten** the figure, shape, form]
klar clearly (2)
es schien jemand zu sein it seemed to be someone
[**scheinen, schien, hat geschienen** to shine; to seem, to appear]
die Gestalt the figure (2)
fing . . . an began
[**an-fangen, er fängt an, fing an, hat angefangen** (2)]
nannten ihn called him
[**nennen, nannte, genannt** to call, to name]
wandte sich um turned around
[**wenden, wandte, hat gewandt** to turn (2)]

wenn Tobias Puff von Geld sprach, dann meinte er nicht Pfennige oder ein paar Mark, sondern große Summen. Für sich selbst hatte er noch mehr als genug, um während der nächsten Monate ohne Sorgen zu leben, aber es genügte nicht, um seine kleinen dunklen Geschäfte wieder anzufangen. Dazu brauchte er Kapital. Je mehr, desto besser. Nun, heute war Freitag, und morgen, am Sonnabend, fand das größte Pferderennen des Jahres statt. Morgen war sein Problem gelöst. Er wußte, auf welche Pferde er sicher rechnen konnte.

Als er nach einem späten Abendessen durch die engen, dunklen Straßen nach Haus ging und eben um die letzte Ecke bog, sah er jemand zu seiner Linken an einer Hauswand stehen. Er konnte die Gestalt nicht klar sehen, aber es schien jemand zu sein, der ihn kannte und auf ihn wartete, denn die Gestalt fing plötzlich an zu sprechen und rief ihn sogar bei seinem Namen. „Hallo, Puffer!" sagte die Stimme. Nur seine wirklichen Freunde nannten ihn Puffer. Tobias Puff wandte sich um. Es war zu dunkel, um die Gesichtszüge zu erkennen; alles, was er sah, waren weiße Haare und ein langer, weißer Bart. „Ja?" erwiderte Tobias Puff und wartete. Er war sicher, daß er den Mann nicht kannte; unter seinen Freunden war niemand mit einem weißen Bart.

„Was wollen Sie? Wer sind Sie?" fragte er kurz, als der Alte nicht antwortete.

„Ich bin alt und schwach, Puffer", sagte der Fremde, „und es ist kalt."

---

um . . . zu erkennen to recognize
[**erkennen** to recognize (2)]
die Gesichtszüge the features (of the face)
[**der Zug, die Züge** the train; procession; feature (3)]
der Bart the beard (2)
unter seinen Freunden among his friends

kurz curtly
der Fremde the stranger
[**fremd** foreign; strange]
kalt cold (3)

suchte . . . nach searched for
die Westentasche the vest pocket
[**die Weste** the vest, waistcoat]
das Fünfzigpfennigstück the fifty-pfennig piece
[**der Pfennig, die Pfennige** the pfennig, penny (2)]
[**das Stück, die Stücke** the piece; play (2)]
reichen to hand
[**reichen** to hand (to), to pass; to reach]
der Fremde the stranger
[**fremd** foreign; strange (2)]

überrascht surprised
[**überraschen** to surprise (2)]

was wollen Sie damit sagen? what do you mean by that?
[**damit** with that]

die Abendzeitung the evening paper

trotzdem nevertheless
etwas nervös a little nervous
[**nervös** nervous]
eng narrow
die Seitenstraße the side street
in der er sich befand where he was
[**sich befinden** to find oneself, to be]
weit und breit far and wide (2)
[**breit** broad, wide (2)]
keine Seele not a soul
[**die Seele, die Seelen** the soul]

am Ärmel by the sleeve
[**der Ärmel, die Ärmel**]
flüstern to whisper
wichtig important (2)
Sie werden . . . sein you will be
was . . . passieren wird what will happen
[**passieren** to happen]

Unsinn! nonsense! (2)
jetzt wurde ihm now he was getting
zugleich at the same time

doch! oh, yes!
drücken to press (2)

das Geldstück the coin
fiel fell
[**fallen, er fällt, fiel, ist gefallen** (2)]

„Er will Geld", dachte Puffer und suchte in seiner Westentasche nach einem Fünfzigpfennigstück. „Hier!" sagte er und reichte es dem Alten. Aber der Fremde nahm es nicht.

„Ich wollte Ihnen etwas verkaufen, Puffer", sagte er.

„Verkaufen?" fragte Tobias Puff überrascht. Er traute dem Mann nicht. „Ich kenne Sie nicht."

„Aber ich kenne S i e , Puffer", entgegnete der Alte. „Ich wollte Ihnen eine Zeitung verkaufen. Es ist keine gewöhnliche Zeitung."

„Was wollen Sie damit sagen . . . keine gewöhnliche Zeitung?" fragte Tobias Puff.

„Es ist die Abendzeitung von morgen", entgegnete der Alte.

„Der arme Narr", dachte Tobias Puff. Aber er wurde trotzdem etwas nervös. Die enge Seitenstraße, in der er sich befand, war dunkel, und weit und breit war keine Seele zu sehen.

„Ich brauche keine Zeitung", sagte er kurz, aber nicht unfreundlich, und wollte gehen, als der Alte ihn am Ärmel festhielt und flüsterte: „Nehmen Sie die Zeitung! Sie wissen nicht, wie wichtig sie für Sie ist. Sie werden der einzige Mensch in der Welt sein, der weiß, was in den nächsten vierundzwanzig Stunden passieren wird. Wissen Sie, was in der Zeitung steht? Die Pferde, die morgen gewinnen werden!"

„Unsinn!" rief Puffer. Aber jetzt wurde ihm heiß und kalt zugleich.

„Doch!" sagte der Alte und drückte ihm die Zeitung in die Hand. „Lesen Sie selbst!"

Das Geldstück, das Tobias Puff in der Hand hielt, fiel zur Erde und rollte auf die Straße. Tobias Puff hörte jemand leise lachen. Es mußte der alte Mann sein, aber Tobias Puff sah ihn nicht mehr.

Er war allein. Sein Herz schlug so schnell, daß er nicht zu

---

rollen to roll

schlug beat
[**schlagen, er schlägt, schlug, hat geschlagen** to strike, to beat]

brannten were burning
[**brennen, brannte, hat gebrannt** to burn]
der Sonnabend Saturday (2)
stand darauf it said (on it)
das Datum the date
[**das Datum, die Daten**]
der neunundzwanzigste the twenty-ninth
der Juli July
der achtundzwanzigste the twenty-eighth
ohne Zweifel without doubt
[**der Zweifel, die Zweifel** the doubt]

so etwas something like that
letzt last (3)
das Datum the date (2)
stimmen to be correct (2)
stand mehr there was more
über einen Mord about a murder
[**der Mord, die Morde** the murder]
von gestern from yesterday
die Blätter the pages
[**das Blatt, die Blätter** the leaf, page, sheet]
der Arm the arm
[**der Arm, die Arme** (2)]
trat in entered
[**treten, er tritt, trat, ist getreten** the step; to walk (2)]
die . . . Bar the bar
setzte er sich he sat down
[**sich setzen** to sit down (2)]
leer empty (2)
bis der Kellner . . . brachte until the waiter brought
[**der Kellner, die Kellner** the waiter]
[**bringen, brachte, hat gebracht** to bring]
das Glas the glass (3)
erst dann only then
auf die er . . . setzen wollte on which he wanted to bet
gewann won
[**gewinnen, gewann, hat gewonnen** to win]
ein einziges a single one
„Blitz“ "Lightning"
wahrscheinlich probably
zwei zu eins two to one
desto besser all the better

wischte sich wiped
[**wischen** to wipe (2)]
der Schweiß the perspiration, sweat
die Stirn the forehead
bestellen to order

laufen wagte. Er ging langsam, bis er zu einem Geschäft kam, in dem noch einige Lichter brannten. Dort sah er auf die erste Seite. „Sonnabend" stand darauf, und das Datum war der 29. (neunundzwanzigste) Juli. Heute war der 28. (achtundzwanzigste). Es war ohne Zweifel die Zeitung von morgen.

3.

Wie war so etwas möglich? Vielleicht war die Zeitung vom letzten Jahr. Aber nein, das Datum stimmte, und auf der ersten Seite stand mehr über einen Mord, den Puffer von gestern kannte. Er wandte die Blätter, bis er zu der Seite kam, wo die Rennen standen. Ja, hier! Das mußte er studieren. Aber nicht hier auf der Straße. Er steckte die Zeitung unter den Arm und trat in die nächste Bar. Dort setzte er sich an einen leeren Tisch und wartete, bis der Kellner ihm ein Glas Wein brachte; erst dann legte er die Zeitung auf den Tisch und öffnete sie. Von den fünf Pferden, auf die er morgen setzen wollte, gewann nur ein einziges, im zweiten Rennen, und das war „Blitz", ein Pferd, von dem jedes Kind wußte, daß es gewinnen m u ß t e. Wahrscheinlich zwei zu eins. In der Zeitung stand drei zu eins. Nun, desto besser! Aber die anderen! Mein Gott!

Tobias Puff wischte sich den Schweiß von der Stirn und bestellte ein zweites Glas Wein, obwohl er die ernste Stimme des Arztes in seinen Ohren klingen hörte: „Ihr Herz ist nicht sehr stark, Herr Puff. Milch, Herr Puff, Milch! Vielleicht etwas

---

obwohl er . . . klingen hörte although he heard . . . ring
[**obwohl, obgleich** although]
[**klingen** to ring, to sound (2)]
ernst earnest
[**ernst** earnest, serious, grave]
der Arzt the doctor
[**der Arzt, die Ärzte** the physician, doctor]
die Ohren the ears
[**das Ohr, die Ohren** (2)]
stark strong (3)
die Milch the milk (2)

der Tee the tea
auf keinen Fall in no case
[**der Fall, die Fälle** the case; fall (2)]
der Alkohol the alcohol (3)
der Doktor the doctor
[**der Doktor, die Doktoren**]
hatte . . . recht was . . . right
[**recht haben** to be right (3)]
hatte Durst was thirsty
[**der Durst** the thirst]
fühlen to feel (2)

der Kellner the waiter (2)
verstecken to hide
las er weiter continued to read
[**lesen, er liest, las, hat gelesen** (2)]
verloren lost
[**verlieren, verlor, hat verloren** to lose (2)]
auf die er setzen wollte on which he wanted to bet (2)
die Pferde, die . . . zuerst durch das Ziel liefen the horses which finished first
[**zuerst** first (2)]
[**das Ziel, die Ziele** the aim, goal, target]
übrig remaining (2)
unbekannt unknown
[**bekannt** known, well-known (2)]
bedeuten to mean
zittern to tremble (2)
was für eine Chance what a chance
[**die Chance, die Chancen** (2)]
das Vermögen the fortune
sechs six (3)
fünfzehn fifteen (2)
neun nine (2)
sieben seven (3)

trocknete sich die Stirn dried his forehead
[**trocknen** to dry]
[**die Stirn** the forehead (2)]
bestellen to order (2)
schien seemed
[**scheinen, schien, hat geschienen** to seem, to appear; to shine (2)]
und doch! and yet!
am besten best
wenn er . . . setzte if he bet
der Zeitung nach according to the newspaper
konnte er . . . ändern he could change
[**ändern** to change (2)]

schwachen Tee, aber auf keinen Fall Kaffee oder Alkohol!"
Der Doktor hatte natürlich recht, aber Tobias Puff hatte Durst, und er fühlte sich nicht wohl. Er brauchte etwas Starkes.

Als der Kellner zurückkam, versteckte Tobias Puff das Datum der Zeitung mit der Hand. Dann las er weiter. Nicht nur, daß alle anderen Pferde verloren, auf die er setzen wollte; die Pferde, die in den vier übrigen Rennen zuerst durch das Ziel liefen, waren mehr oder weniger unbekannt, und was das bedeutete, wußte jedes Kind. Tobias Puffs Hand zitterte leicht. Was für eine Chance, ein richtiges Vermögen zu verdienen! Sechs zu eins, fünfzehn zu zwei, neun zu zwei, und das letzte Rennen sogar hundert zu sieben!

Tobias Puff trocknete sich die Stirn und bestellte ein drittes Glas. Er wußte nicht, ob er seinen Augen trauen konnte. Was er sah, schien unmöglich zu sein. Und doch! Vielleicht war es am besten, wenn er morgen im ersten Rennen hundert Mark auf s e i n Pferd setzte und fünfzig Mark auf das Pferd, das der Zeitung nach gewinnen sollte. Während des zweiten Rennen konnte er dann immer noch seine Meinung über die anderen Pferde ändern. Was wirklich zählte, waren die letzten drei Rennen.

Nun, die ganze Sache konnte bis morgen warten. Er brauchte sich nicht zu eilen. Er beschloß, auf jeden Fall sein ganzes Geld auf den Rennplatz mitzunehmen. Wenn er noch größere Summen setzen wollte, konnte er immer noch vom

---

seine Meinung über his opinion about
[**die Meinung, die Meinungen** the opinion]

sich eilen to hurry (3)
er beschloß . . . mitzunehmen he decided to take along
[**beschließen, beschloß, hat beschlossen** (2)]
[**mit-nehmen** to take along]
auf jeden Fall in any case
wenn if
noch größere Summen still larger amounts
konnte er . . . anrufen he could call
[**an-rufen** to call, to telephone]

vom Rennplatz from the racecourse
[**der Rennplatz** the racecourse]
[**der Platz, die Plätze** the place, seat; the square]
einige Buchmacher a few bookmakers
[**der Buchmacher** the bookmaker (2)]

einige Mühe . . . aufzustehen a little trouble getting up
[**auf-stehen** to get up, to stand up]
der Stuhl the chair
[**der Stuhl, die Stühle**]
die Rechnung the check (3)
bat er he asked
[**bitten, bat, hat gebeten** to ask, to request]
das Taxi the taxi
fuhr went
[**fahren, er fährt, fuhr, ist gefahren** (2)]
das Bad the bath (2)
tief deep (2)
der Schlaf the sleep
immer wieder again and again

dünn thin (3)
deutete er auf he pointed at
[**deuten** to point]

die Morgensonne the morning sun (2)
fand found
[**finden, fand, hat gefunden** (2)]
gesund healthy (3)
der Fisch the fish
[**der Fisch, die Fische** (2)]
das Wasser the water
sein Glück his fortune
er machte sich fertig he got himself ready
schrieb wrote
[**schreiben, schrieb, hat geschrieben** to write]
die Telephonnummern the telephone numbers
[**das Telephon** the telephone]
[**die Nummer, die Nummern** the number]
mehrerer of several
[**mehrere** several]
das Heft the notebook
[**das Heft, die Hefte**]
bei sich with him
verließ left
[**verlassen, er verläßt, verließ, hat verlassen** to leave]
gegen elf Uhr around eleven o'clock
[**die Uhr, die Uhren** the watch, clock]

Rennplatz einige Buchmacher in der Stadt anrufen, die ihn kannten und ihm noch trauten.

Tobias Puff hatte einige Mühe, von seinem Stuhl aufzustehen. Er fühlte sich gar nicht wohl. Als er mit zitternder Hand seine Rechnung bezahlte, bat er einen Kellner, ihm ein Taxi zu bestellen. Er fuhr nach Haus, nahm ein heißes Bad und fiel bald in einen tiefen Schlaf. Er träumte nicht von Pferden oder Geld, sondern von einem alten Mann mit weißen Haaren und einem langen Bart. Tobias Puff konnte das Gesicht nicht genau sehen, weil es zu dunkel war, aber er hörte ganz klar seine Stimme, die immer wieder dieselben Worte wiederholte: „Hundert zu sieben, hundert zu sieben, hundert zu sieben . . ."

Und mit seinem dünnen Finger deutete er immer auf eine Zeitung.

4.

Die Morgensonne fand Tobias Puff gesund und frisch. Er fühlte sich wie ein Fisch im Wasser. Heute war der große Tag, an dem er vielleicht sein Glück machen konnte. Er machte sich fertig, schrieb die Telephonnummern mehrerer Buchmacher in ein kleines Heft, das er immer bei sich trug, nahm die Zeitung und verließ das Haus gegen elf Uhr. Es war eine ziemlich lange Fahrt mit der Eisenbahn, aber er kam früh genug an, um einen Platz zu finden, der ihm erlaubte, während des zweiten Rennens schnell zu verschwinden—wenn es notwendig sein sollte.

---

die Fahrt the ride
  [**die Fahrt, die Fahrten** the trip, journey, ride]
mit der Eisenbahn by train
  [**die Eisenbahn** the railroad]
er kam . . . an he arrived
  [**an-kommen, kam an, ist angekommen** (3)]
der Platz the seat
  [**der Platz, die Plätze** the place, seat; square (2)]
zu verschwinden to disappear
  [**verschwinden** to disappear]
wenn if
notwendig necessary (2)

gewann won
    [**gewinnen, gewann, hat gewonnen** (2)]
verschwand disappeared
    [**verschwinden, verschwand, ist verschwunden** to disappear]
  mehrere several (2)
  tausend thousand
  der Zeitung nach according to the newspaper (2)
das Telephon the telephone (2)
  und rief . . . an and called
    [**an-rufen, rief an, hat angerufen** to call, to telephone]
sie mochten they might
    [**mögen, er mag, mochte, hat gemocht** may, might; to like]
  unbekannt unknown (2)
das war ihm gleich that was all the same to him
    [**es ist mir gleich** I don't care, it is all the same to me]
was er tat what he was doing

der Sitz the seat
    [**der Sitz, die Sitze**]
  zurück-kehren to return (3)
  lief „Blitz" gerade durchs Ziel "Lightning" was just winning
    [**das Ziel, die Ziele** the aim, goal, target (2)]
Zweifel doubts
    [**der Zweifel, die Zweifel** the doubt (2)]
interessieren to interest
im voraus in advance (2)
erst only
  vorüber over, finished
beobachten to observe
  gewiß certain (3)
  der Ärger the annoyance
    [**der Ärger** the annoyance, anger, vexation, irritation (2)]
  seiner Nachbarn of his neighbors
    [**der Nachbar, die Nachbarn** (3)]
das gleiche Glück the same luck
    [**gleich** same (3)]

vorüber over, finished (2)
drang pushed his way
    [**dringen, drang, ist gedrungen** to press, push, penetrate; urge]
  schreiend shouting
  das Taxi the taxi (2)
  der Bahnhof the station
außer sich beside himself
enorm enormous (2)

im Zug in the train
  setzte er sich he sat down
  die Ecke the corner
    [**die Ecke, die Ecken** (2)]

Das erste Rennen begann. Tobias Puff verlor hundert Mark und gewann dreihundert. Die Zeitung hatte recht. Tobias Puff verschwand und setzte sein ganzes Geld, mehrere tausend Mark, auf die übrigen Pferde, die der Zeitung nach gewinnen sollten. Dann lief er zum nächsten Telephon und rief die Buchmacher in der Stadt an. Sie mochten große Augen machen und ihn für einen Narren halten, wenn er so viel Geld auf unbekannte Pferde setzte. Aber das war ihm gleich. Er wußte, was er tat.

Als er zu seinem Sitz zurückkehrte, lief „Blitz" gerade durchs Ziel. Drei zu eins. Tobias Puff hatte keine Zweifel mehr. Was jetzt folgte, interessierte ihn wenig. Er wußte im voraus, was kommen mußte. Aber er blieb bis zum Ende, weil er sein Geld erst bekommen konnte, wenn alles vorüber war. Indessen beobachtete er mit einem gewissen Vergnügen den Ärger auf den Gesichtern seiner Nachbarn, die ein Rennen nach dem anderen verloren. Nun, so war das Leben. Nicht jeder konnte das gleiche Glück haben.

Als das letzte Rennen vorüber war, wußte Tobias Puff, daß er ein reicher Mann war. Er drang durch die schreienden Menschenmengen, holte sein Geld und fuhr im Taxi zum Bahnhof. Er war außer sich vor Freude. Was er jetzt in seinen vollen Taschen trug, war nichts, wenn er an die enormen Summen dachte, die in der Stadt auf ihn warteten.

Im Zug setzte er sich in eine Ecke. Er liebte die Gesellschaft von Menschen, aber diesmal hatte er keine Lust, mit Personen zu sprechen, die er nicht kannte; besonders nicht, wenn sein Kopf so voller Gedanken war.

„Wie heiß es ist!" dachte er plözlich. „Und diese schreckliche Luft! Kein Wunder, wenn die Leute alle rauchten!" Er

---

lieben to love
die Gesellschaft the company (3)
keine Lust no desire
Personen persons
[**die Person, die Personen**]

kein Wunder no wonder
[**das Wunder, die Wunder** the wonder, miracle]
rauchen to smoke (3)

er versuchte . . . aufzumachen he tried to open
    [**auf-machen** to open (3)]
  es gelang ihm nicht he did not succeed
    [**gelingen, gelang, ist gelungen** to succeed]
    [**es gelingt mir** I succeed]
dessen Bild . . . erschien whose picture appeared
    [**das Bild, die Bilder** the picture]
    [**erscheinen, erschien, ist erschienen** to appear]
  immer wieder again and again (2)
die Rocktasche the coat pocket
die Abendzeitung the evening paper (2)
  dieselben the same

der Blick the glance
    [**der Blick, die Blicke** the glance, look; view]
  die Stelle the place
    [**die Stelle, die Stellen** the place, spot; position (2)]
starren to stare
  der Satz the sentence
    [**der Satz, die Sätze** the sentence; leap, jump]
Ludwig-Straße siebzehn Ludwig Street seventeen
  starb died
    [**sterben, er stirbt, starb, ist gestorben** to die]
  heute nachmittag this afternoon
die Buchstaben the letters
    [**der Buchstabe, die Buchstaben** the letter (of the alphabet)]
  schwammen swam
    [**schwimmen, schwamm, ist geschwommen** to swim]
atmen to breathe (2)
weiß wie Kreide white as chalk
    [**die Kreide** the chalk]
  er brachte kein Wort über die Lippen he could not utter a word
    [**bringen, brachte, hat gebracht** to bring (2)]
    [**die Lippe, die Lippen** the lip]
warf threw
    [**werfen, er wirft, warf, hat geworfen** to throw (2)]
  sank sank
    [**sinken, sank, ist gesunken** to sink]
  die Brust the breast (2)
  zu Boden to the ground

einer one
  riß . . . auf tore . . . open
    [**reißen, riß, hat gerissen** to tear, to pull]
  mit Gewalt with great effort
    [**die Gewalt** the force, power, might, violence (2)]
  um . . . hereinzulassen in order to let in
    [**herein** in]

versuchte, ein Fenster aufzumachen, aber es gelang ihm nicht. Er setzte sich wieder. Ob er wollte oder nicht, seine Gedanken kehrten zu dem alten Mann zurück, dessen Bild immer wieder vor seinen Augen erschien. Wer war der Alte? Wie war es möglich, daß er gestern eine Zeitung von heute hatte? Tobias Puff zog die Zeitung aus der Rocktasche. Gut, daß er sie noch hatte! Er beschloß, in der Stadt eine Abendzeitung zu kaufen, um zu sehen, ob die beiden Zeitungen wirklich dieselben waren. Die Sache war jetzt nicht mehr wichtig, aber . . . Plötzlich fiel sein Blick auf eine Stelle auf der ersten Seite. Sah er richtig? War das nicht sein Name? Er las. „Tod im Zug." Dann starrte er auf den ersten Satz: „Herr Tobias Puff, Ludwig-Straße 17 (siebzehn), starb plötzlich heute nachmittag, als er im Zug von den Pferderennen zurückkehrte . . ." Tobias Puff konnte nicht weiterlesen. Die Buchstaben schwammen ihm vor den Augen. Er atmete schwer. Die Zeitung fiel ihm aus den Händen, sein Gesicht wurde weiß wie Kreide, er versuchte zu sprechen, aber er brachte kein Wort über die Lippen. Dann warf er die Arme in die Luft, sein Kopf sank auf die Brust, und er fiel zu Boden.

Seine Nachbarn versuchten, ihm zu helfen. Einer riß mit Gewalt das Fenster auf, um frische Luft hereinzulassen. Jemand öffnete sein Hemd. Aber es war zu spät. Tobias Puffs Herz schlug nicht mehr.

Niemand schien die Zeitung zu sehen, die unter dem Sitz lag. Aber ob sie jemand sah oder nicht, war nicht wichtig. In zwei Stunden konnte jeder die gleiche Zeitung überall in der ganzen Stadt kaufen. Dann war es eine Zeitung wie jede andere.

---

das Hemd the shirt
    [**das Hemd, die Hemden**]

der Sitz the seat
    [**der Sitz, die Sitze** (2)]
  lag lay
    [**liegen, lag, hat gelegen** to lie (2)]
überall everywhere (3)
wie jede andere like any other

JANS UND JENS

[4A]

NOTES

I. 1. As in English, the German present perfect and the past perfect are formed by combining the past participle with an auxiliary verb. The important difference is that German uses both **haben** and **sein** as auxiliaries.

2. The auxiliary **sein** must be used with verbs which do not have a direct object *and* denote a change of condition or place (motion toward or from an object or place): **sterben, wachsen, werden,** for example; **fallen, gehen, kommen, laufen, springen,** etc.

3. With a few exceptions, all other verbs use the auxiliary verb **haben.**

   The most important exceptions are:

   begegnen: Ich *bin* ihm auf der Straße begegnet. I met him in the street.

   bleiben: Er *war* zu Hause geblieben. He had stayed at home.

   folgen: *Ist* er Ihnen gefolgt? Did he follow you?

   gelingen: Es *war* mir nicht gelungen, ihn zu finden. I had not succeeded in finding him.

   geschehen: Was *ist* geschehen? What happened?

   passieren: Ihm *war* nichts passiert. Nothing had happened to him.

4. Verbs with separable prefixes insert the **ge–** of the past participle between the prefix and the stem. The entire combination is written as one word.

   voraus-gehen: Jans, der im Dunkeln voraus*ge*gangen war, fiel in das Loch.

5. Verbs with inseparable prefixes (**be–, emp–, ent–, er–, ge–, miß–, ver–, zer–**) omit the **ge–** in the present participle. So do verbs ending in **–ieren.**

   verschwinden: Der Mond war hinter den Wolken verschwunden.

   geschehen: Er wollte wissen, was geschehen war.

   studieren: Er hat Literatur studiert.

6. The past participle stands at the end of its clause. It stands at the very end in independent clauses, and just *before* the

auxiliary in dependent clauses since the finite verb must be at the very end of a dependent clause.

Mein Nachbar hat mir meine Uhr *gestohlen.*

Wenn er ihn *gefunden hatte,* konnten sie Partner werden.

II. 1. The present perfect is used

a. where English uses it.

Haben Sie ihn gesehen? Have you seen him?

b. When a single event in the past is reported as a fact or happening isolated from what preceded or followed it.

Mitten durch den Kopf geschossen, wie ich gesagt habe! . . . as I said

Note: The present perfect is *the* past tense ordinarily used in everyday conversational language. It is sometimes called the conversational past.

2. The past perfect is used where English uses it.

Keiner konnte ihm sagen, wie es geschehen war. . . . how it had happened

Jens hatte einen Mann aus Stroh gemacht. Jens had made a man out of straw.

III. As in English, the past infinitive is formed by combining the past participle with the infinitive of an auxiliary verb (he must *have done* it). Unlike English, German places the infinitive of the auxiliary verb (**haben** or **sein**) *after* the past participle. **Haben** and **sein** must be used in accordance with the rule stated above under **I.** 2. and **I.** 3.

Jeder behauptete, niemanden *gesehen zu haben.*

Keiner konnte ihm sagen, wer es *getan haben* mochte.

Nur Jans oder Jens können es *getan haben.*

Wenn jemand morgen Fleisch kauft, dann wirst du deinen Dieb *gefangen haben.*

Sie verließen das Haus, ohne den Dieb *gefunden zu haben.*

REVIEW OF STRONG AND IRREGULAR VERBS USED IN STORY 3B

an-kommen		kam an	ist angekommen	*to arrive*
(sich) befinden		befand	befunden	*to be*
biegen		bog	gebogen	*to bend, turn*
bleiben		blieb	ist geblieben	*to remain, stay*
brennen		brannte	gebrannt	*to burn*
bringen		brachte	gebracht	*to bring*
dringen		drang	ist gedrungen	*to penetrate*
dürfen	darf	durfte	(gedurft)	*to be allowed*
erscheinen		erschien	ist erschienen	*to appear*
finden		fand	gefunden	*to find*
statt-finden		fand statt	stattgefunden	*to take place*
gelingen		es gelang	es ist gelungen	*to succeed*
gewinnen		gewann	gewonnen	*to win, gain*
lesen	liest	las	gelesen	*to read*
nennen		nannte	genannt	*to name*
reißen		riß	gerissen	*to tear*
scheinen		schien	geschienen	*to seem; shine*
schreiben		schrieb	geschrieben	*to write*
schwimmen		schwamm	ist geschwommen	*to swim*
sinken		sank	ist gesunken	*to sink*
sterben	stirbt	starb	ist gestorben	*to die*
verlassen	verläßt	verließ	verlassen	*to leave*
verschwinden		verschwand	ist verschwunden	*to disappear*
ziehen		zog	gezogen	*to pull, draw*

IDIOMS FOR REVIEW

vor etwa 200 Jahren about 200 years *ago*
vor einigen Minuten a few minutes *ago*
durch Zufall by chance
es gelang ihnen they succeeded
es hilft nichts it's no use
heute abend tonight
zu Abend essen to have dinner
im Dunkeln in the dark
am Abend in the evening

Jans und Jens names of the two main characters

fern distant (3)
das Land the country (3)
überm Meer across the sea
[**das Meer, die Meere** the sea, ocean]
der Norden the north
Europa Europe (3)
gab es einst there was once
[**einst** once, once upon a time]
vor etwa . . . Jahren about . . . years ago
[**etwa** about, approximately]
berühmt famous
nannte called
[**nennen, nannte, hat genannt** to call, to name (2)]
ein solcher Meister such a master
[**der Meister, die Meister**]
die Kunst the art
[**die Kunst, die Künste** the art; skill (2)]
niemand . . . gefangen hatte that no one had caught
[**fangen, er fängt, fing, hat gefangen** to catch]
bisher as yet
[**bisher** until now, hitherto]
irgendwo somewhere
berühmt famous (2)
der . . . hieß whose name was
[**heißen, hieß, hat geheißen** to be called]
er beschloß he decided
[**beschließen, beschloß, hat beschlossen** to decide (3)]
reisen to travel (2)
kennen-lernen to make the acquaintance of (2)
gefunden hatte had found
[**finden, fand, hat gefunden** to find (3)]
Partner partners
[**der Partner, die Partner**]
vor ihnen sicher safe from them

geschah es it happened
[**geschehen, es geschieht, geschah, ist geschehen** to happen (2)]
sich . . . trafen met
[**treffen, er trifft, traf, hat getroffen** to meet, to encounter]
und daß beide . . . saßen and that both sat
[**sitzen, saß, hat gesessen** to sit (3)]
durch Zufall by chance
[**der Zufall, die Zufälle** the chance, coincidence, accident (2)]
während sie . . . aßen while they were eating
[**essen, er ißt, aß, hat gegessen** to eat (2)]
tranken were drinking
[**trinken, trank, hat getrunken** to drink]

[4 A]

(FOUR PARTS)

Jans und Jens

I.

In einem fernen Land weit überm Meer im Norden Europas gab es einst vor etwa zweihundert Jahren einen berühmten Dieb, den man Jans nannte. Er war ein solcher Meister in seiner Kunst, daß niemand ihn bisher gefangen hatte. Jans hatte gehört, daß irgendwo in Deutschland ein anderer berühmter Dieb lebte, der Jens hieß. Er beschloß, nach Deutschland zu reisen, um ihn kennenzulernen. Wenn er ihn gefunden hatte, dachte er, konnten sie vielleicht Partner werden, und dann war kein Schatz der Welt vor ihnen sicher.

Nun geschah es eines Tages, daß Jans und Jens sich in demselben Gasthaus trafen, ohne es zu wissen, und daß beide durch Zufall auch an demselben Tisch saßen. Während sie zusammen aßen und tranken und über dies und das sprachen, stahl Jens dem Jans die Uhr. Als dieser nach einer Weile in die

---

sprachen were speaking
[**sprechen, er spricht, sprach, hat gesprochen** (3)]
stahl stole
[**stehlen, er stiehlt, stahl, hat gestohlen** to steal]
die Uhr the watch
[**die Uhr, die Uhren** the watch, clock (2)]
als dieser . . . griff when the latter reached
[**greifen, griff, hat gegriffen** to seize, to grasp]

die Westentasche the vest pocket (2)
[**die Weste** the vest, waistcoat (2)]
entdecken to discover
fehlte was missing
[**fehlen** to be missing, not to be there]
hat . . . gestohlen has stolen
[**stehlen, er stiehlt, stahl, hat gestohlen** to steal (2)]
ohne daß ich etwas gemerkt habe without my having noticed anything
[**merken** to notice (3)]
und damit and with that
die Brieftasche the wallet (3)
wie der andere sie . . . ziehen wollte as the other wanted to take it
etwas später a little later
fort gone
[**fort** away, gone (2)]
da wandte er sich he then turned
[**wenden, wandte, hat gewandt** to turn (3)]
nicken to nod
lächelnd smiling; with a smile

nachdem beide . . . geschüttelt hatten after both had shaken
[**nachdem** after]
[**schütteln** to shake (3)]
glücklich happy, fortunate (2)
uns zusammengebracht hat has brought us together
[**bringen, brachte, hat gebracht** (3)]
ich habe . . . gehört I have heard
oft often (2)
daß ich . . . gewünscht habe that I have wished
[**wünschen** to wish, to desire (2)]
was meinst du? what do you think?
die Idee the idea (3)
Partner partners
[**der Partner, die Partner** (2)]
von jetzt an from now on
fein! fine! (3)
übers Meer across the sea
[**das Meer, die Meere** the sea, ocean (2)]
als einer allein than one alone
da sie since they
verließen left
[**verlassen, er verläßt, verließ, hat verlassen** to leave (3)]
nahm . . . mit took along
[**mitnehmen, er nimmt mit, nahm mit, hat mitgenommen** to take along (2)]
ein Salzfaß a saltcellar
[**das Salz** the salt]
[**das Faß, die Fässer** the barrel, keg, cask]
silbern of silver

Westentasche griff, um zu sehen, wie spät es war, entdeckte er, daß seine Uhr fehlte. Da sagte er sich: „Aha! Mein Nachbar hat mir meine Uhr gestohlen, ohne daß ich etwas gemerkt habe. Das kann nur der berühmte Jens sein. Nun, ich werde ihm zeigen, wer neben ihm sitzt!" Und damit stahl er ihm die Brieftasche. Wie der andere sie etwas später aus der Tasche ziehen wollte, um seine Rechnung zu bezahlen, fand er, daß sie fort war. Da wandte er sich zu seinem Nachbarn und sagte: „Du mußt Jans sein!" Jans nickte und sagte lächelnd: „Und du bist Jens!"

Nachdem beide sich die Hände geschüttelt hatten, sagte Jans: „Ich glaube, daß ein glücklicher Zufall uns zusammengebracht hat. Ich habe schon so oft von dir und deiner Kunst gehört, daß ich mehr als einmal gewünscht habe, dich kennenzulernen und eines Tages vielleicht mit dir zusammen zu arbeiten. Was meinst du?"—„Das ist keine schlechte Idee", antwortete Jens. „Ja, laß uns Partner werden und von jetzt an zusammen stehlen!"—„Fein!" rief Jans; „dann komm mit mir übers Meer in mein Land, wo mehr Arbeit auf uns wartet, als einer allein tun kann!" Da sie nie ein Haus verließen, ohne etwas zu stehlen, nahm Jans noch schnell ein Salzfaß mit, und Jens eine silberne Gabel.

Als sie in die Hauptstadt kamen, wo Jans mit seiner Frau wohnte, entwickelten sie einen Plan, den Schatz des Königs zu stehlen. Der König hatte sein Schloß und vor allem das Schatzhaus mit Soldaten umgeben, aber für Jans und Jens war keine

---

die Gabel the fork
 [**die Gabel, die Gabeln**]

die Hauptstadt the capital
 [**Haupt-** chief, main; head]
entwickeln to develop
der Plan the plan
 [**der Plan, die Pläne** (2)]
hatte . . . umgeben had surrounded
 [**umgeben, er umgibt, umgab, hat umgeben** to surround]
vor allem above all
das Schatzhaus the treasure house
mit Soldaten with soldiers
 [**der Soldat, die Soldaten**(3)]

keine Aufgabe no task
[**die Aufgabe, die Aufgaben** the task, assignment, lesson (2)]
schwierig difficult
die Mauer the wall
[**die Mauer, die Mauern** (3)]
die . . . umgab which surrounded
[**umgeben, er umgibt, umgab, hat umgeben** to surround (2)]
gruben dug
[**graben, er gräbt, grub, hat gegraben** to dig]
gelang es ihnen they succeeded
[**gelingen, es gelingt, gelang, ist gelungen** to succeed (2)]
in . . . zu dringen in entering
[**dringen** to penetrate, to enter; to urge, to press (2)]
lag lay
[**liegen, lag, hat gelegen** to lie (3)]

erfuhr learned
[**erfahren, er erfährt, erfuhr, hat erfahren** to learn, to find out]
daß er . . . verloren hatte that he had lost
[**verlieren, verlor, hat verloren** to lose (3)]
rot red (3)
vor Zorn und Ärger with anger and vexation
[**der Zorn** the anger, wrath (2)]
[**der Ärger** the annoyance, vexation (2)]
sich . . . erklären explain to himself
[**erklären** to explain; to declare (3)]
in . . . gedrungen waren had entered
er ließ . . . kommen he had . . . come, he sent for
[**lassen, er läßt, ließ, hat gelassen** to let; to leave; to have someone do something, to have something done (3)]
vor sich before him
fragte interrogated, questioned
jeden einzelnen every single one
[**einzeln** single, individual (3)]
es half nichts it was of no avail
[**helfen, er hilft, half, hat geholfen** to help]
behaupten to maintain, to assert
niemanden gesehen zu haben that he had not seen anyone
[**sehen, er sieht, sah, hat gesehen** to see (3)]
geschehen war had happened
[**geschehen, es geschieht, geschah, ist geschehen** to happen (3)]
wer es getan haben mochte who might have done it
[**tun, tat, hat getan** to do (3)]
[**mögen, er mag, mochte, hat gemocht** may, might; to like (2)]
weise wise (2)
der schon seit Jahren . . . saß who had already been sitting for years
entdecken to discover (2)
wer . . . genommen hat who has taken
[**nehmen, er nimmt, nahm, hat genommen** to take (3)]

Aufgabe zu schwierig. Am Fuß der Mauer, die das Schloß umgab, gruben sie ein Loch, und auf diese Weise gelang es ihnen, während der Nacht, als alle schliefen, in das Schloß und das Gebäude zu dringen, wo der Schatz lag, und ihn zu stehlen, ohne daß jemand etwas merkte.

2.

Als der König erfuhr, daß er seinen ganzen Schatz verloren hatte, wurde er rot vor Zorn und Ärger, weil er sich nicht erklären konnte, wie die Diebe in das Schloß gedrungen waren. Er ließ die Soldaten vor sich kommen und fragte jeden einzelnen; aber es half nichts. Jeder behauptete, niemanden gesehen zu haben, und keiner konnte ihm sagen, wie es geschehen war oder wer es getan haben mochte. Da ließ der König einen alten, weisen Dieb kommen, der schon seit Jahren im Gefängnis saß, und sprach zu ihm: „ Wenn du entdecken kannst, wer meinen Schatz genommen hat, lasse ich dich frei."—„Nur Jans oder Jens oder beide können es getan haben", antwortete der Dieb, „und ich werde dir sagen, wie du sie fangen kannst. Befiehl, daß von nun an ein Pfund Fleisch hundert Mark kostet! Kein Bürger der Stadt ist so reich, daß er Fleisch zu einem solch hohen Preis kaufen kann—außer Jans oder Jens, die deinen Schatz haben. Wenn morgen jemand Fleisch kauft, dann wirst du deinen Dieb gefangen haben."

---

frei free (3)
können es getan haben can have done it
befiehl command
[**befehlen, er befiehlt, befahl, hat befohlen** (3)]
das Pfund the pound
kein Bürger no citizen
[**der Bürger, die Bürger**]
reich rich (3)
zu einem solch hohen Preis at such a high price
außer except (3)
dann wirst du . . . gefangen haben then you will have caught
[**fangen, er fängt, fing, hat gefangen** to catch (2)]

geraten hatte had advised
[**raten, er rät, riet, hat geraten** to advise; to guess]
die Bürger the citizens
[**der Bürger, die Bürger** (2)]
die Butter the butter
Eier eggs
[**das Ei, die Eier** the egg (2)]
Kartoffeln potatoes (3)
das Obst the fruit
die Marktpolizei the market police
[**der Markt, die Märkte** the market]
hatte . . . beobachtet had observed
[**beobachten** to observe (2)]
mehrere Pfund several pounds
[**mehrere** several (3)]
[**das Pfund** the pound (2)]
jedoch however
verschwand disappeared
[**verschwinden, verschwand, ist verschwunden** to disappear (2)]
die Menschenmenge the crowd (of people)
[**die Menge, die Mengen** the crowd, quantity, lot (3)]
der Marktplatz the market place
[**der Markt, die Märkte** the market (2)]
[**der Platz, die Plätze** the place, square; room; seat (3)]
füllen to fill

der Zweifel the doubt (3)
heute abend tonight
klopfen to knock (3)
riechen to smell (3)
zum Abendessen for supper
[**das Abendessen** the supper (3)]
brät oder ißt roasts or eats
[**braten, er brät, briet, hat gebraten** to roast, to fry, to grill (3)]
werde ich . . . zeichnen I shall draw
[**zeichnen** to draw]
außen outside (3)
gelb yellow (2)
die Kreide the chalk (2)
das Zeichen the sign
[**das Zeichen, die Zeichen** the sign, signal (2)]

und dessen Frau and the latter's wife
zu Abend gegessen hatte had eaten supper
[**essen, er ißt, aß, hat gegessen** to eat (3)]
[**zu Abend essen** to have supper]
bedeuten to mean (2)
ähnlich similar (2)

Der König tat, was der weise Dieb ihm geraten hatte. Am nächsten Tag kauften die Bürger Brot, Butter, Eier, Fisch, Kartoffeln und Obst, aber kein Fleisch. Die Marktpolizei, die überall aufpaßte, hatte nur einen Mann beobachtet, der mehrere Pfund Fleisch kaufte. Man hatte versucht, ihm zu folgen. Als der Mann jedoch merkte, daß man ihn gesehen hatte, begann er zu laufen und verschwand bald in der Menschenmenge, die den Marktplatz füllte.

„Nun", sagte der alte Dieb, als er das hörte, „der Mann war ohne Zweifel entweder Jans oder Jens. Ich werde heute abend von Haus zu Haus gehen und an jede Tür klopfen. Wo ich rieche oder sehe, daß man zum Abendessen Fleisch brät oder ißt, werde ich außen mit gelber Kreide ein gewisses Zeichen an die Tür zeichnen, so daß die Soldaten das Haus am Morgen sofort finden können."

Als Jens später das Haus verließ, wo er mit Jans und dessen Frau zu Abend gegessen hatte, sah er das Zeichen an der Haustür und wußte sogleich, was es bedeutete. Er nahm gelbe Kreide und machte in der Nacht ähnliche Zeichen an Dutzende von Häusern in jeder Straße der Stadt, so daß die Soldaten am Morgen nicht wußten, wo sie zuerst anfangen sollten, die zwei Diebe zu suchen.

„Habe ich dir nicht gesagt, daß Jans und Jens schlaue Füchse sind?" sagte der alte Dieb zum König. „Aber wir werden sie dennoch fangen. Laß am Fuß der Treppe, die ins Schatz-

---

Dutzende dozens
[**das Dutzend, die Dutzende** the dozen]

schlaue Füchse sly foxes
[**schlau** sly, clever (3)]
[**der Fuchs, die Füchse** the fox (2)]
dennoch nevertheless
laß . . . ein tiefes Loch graben have a deep hole dug
[**tief** deep (3)]
[**das Loch, die Löcher** the hole (4)]
[**graben, er gräbt, grub, hat gegraben** to dig (2)]
die Treppe the stairs
[**die Treppe, die Treppen** the stairs, staircase, steps]
das Schatzhaus the treasure house (2)

  das Wasser the water (2)
  füllen to fill (2)

neues zu stehlen to steal some more
der . . . vorausgegangen war who had gone ahead
    [**voraus** ahead (3)]
    [**gehen, ging, ist gegangen** to go (3)]
  starb died
    [**sterben, er stirbt, starb, ist gestorben** to die (2)]
wunderte sich was surprised, wondered
    [**sich wundern** to wonder, to be surprised (2)]
der Mond the moon
  aus den Wolken trat came out of the clouds
    [**die Wolke, die Wolken** the cloud]
    [**treten, er tritt, trat, ist getreten** to step, to walk, to go (3)]
  die Leiche the corpse
    [**die Leiche, die Leichen** (2)]
  schwimmen to float, to swim (2)
da since
  schwer heavy
  der Körper the body
    [**der Körper, die Körper**]
  schnitt er . . . ab he cut off
    [**schneiden, schnitt, hat geschnitten** to cut]
  damit so that
  erkennen to recognize (3)
  gefallen war had fallen
    [**fallen, er fällt, fiel, ist gefallen** to fall (3)]

an das Loch trat went to the hole
  ob . . . etwas geschehen war whether anything had happened
    [**geschehen, es geschieht, geschah, ist geschehen** to happen (3)]
  eine Gestalt a figure
    [**die Gestalt, die Gestalten** the figure, shape, form (3)]
  oben auf dem Wasser on top of the water
    [**oben** above, on top, upstairs (2)]
  schwamm was floating
    [**schwimmen, schwamm, ist geschwommen** to float, to swim (3)]
jedoch however (2)
  ein Körper a body
    [**der Körper, die Körper** (2)]
bleibt nur noch ein Mittel there remains only one more way
    [**das Mittel, die Mittel** the means, way, measure]
binde tie
    [**binden** to tie, to bind]
  des Toten of the dead man
  laß ihn . . . ziehen have him dragged
ein Weib a woman
    [**das Weib, die Weiber** the woman; wife (3)]

haus führt, ein tiefes Loch graben und es mit Wasser füllen. Wenn Jans und Jens kein Geld mehr haben und ins Schloß zurückkommen, werden sie in das Loch fallen."

3.

Als Jans und Jens nach einigen Monaten mit ihrem Geld zu Ende waren, gingen sie, neues zu stehlen. Jans, der im Dunkeln vorausgegangen war, fiel in das Loch und starb. Jens wartete und wartete und wunderte sich, daß Jans nicht zurückkam. Als nach einer Weile der Mond aus den Wolken trat, folgte er Jans, kam zu dem Loch und sah seine Leiche im Wasser schwimmen. Da es zu weit war, um den schweren Körper nach Haus zu tragen, schnitt er Jans den Kopf ab und nahm ihn mit, damit niemand erkennen konnte, wer in das Loch gefallen war.

Als der König am nächsten Morgen an das Loch trat, um zu sehen, ob während der Nacht etwas geschehen war, erblickte er eine Gestalt, die oben auf dem Wasser schwamm, und schrie: „Ha! Wir haben ihn!" Was man jedoch aus dem Loch zog, war ein Körper ohne Kopf. Da sprach der alte Dieb zum König: „Der schlaue Fuchs! Jetzt bleibt nur noch e i n Mittel, ihn zu entdecken. Binde den Körper des Toten an ein Paar Pferde und laß ihn durch alle Straßen der Stadt ziehen. Wo man ein Weib weinen und klagen hören wird, daß sie ihren Mann verloren hat, dort wohnt die Frau des Toten, und wenn wir s i e haben, wird sie uns sagen müssen, wer der andere Dieb ist."

Als die Frau die Volksmenge hörte, die der Leiche folgte, trat sie ans Fenster und sah, daß es ihr toter Mann war, den die Pferde durch die Straße zogen. „Oh, ich arme Frau!" rief sie

---

weinen to cry, to weep (3)
klagen to lament (3)
wird sie uns sagen müssen she will have to tell us

die Volksmenge the crowd of people
[**das Volk, die Völker** the people, nation]

unten below
[**unten** below, at the bottom, downstairs (3)]
gekommen war had come
[**kommen, kam, ist gekommen** to come (3)]
trösten to console (2)
mit Schrecken with horror
[**der Schreck(en)** the fright, shock, alarm, horror]
die Haut the skin
retten to save
Tassen und Teller cups and plates
[**die Tasse, die Tassen** the cup (3)]
[**der Teller, die Teller** the plate]
warf threw
[**werfen, er wirft, warf, hat geworfen** to throw (3)]
der Fußboden the floor
Stücke pieces
[**das Stück, die Stücke** (3)]
brachen broke
[**brechen, er bricht, brach, hat gebrochen** to break]
der Stock the stick
[**der Stock, die Stöcke** the stick, cane; floor, story (3)]
vorher before (3)
die Diener the servants
[**der Diener, die Diener** (3)]
die Treppe the stairs
[**die Treppe, die Treppen** the stairs, steps, stairway (2)]
hinaufeilten hurried up
Teller plates
[**der Teller, die Teller** (2)]
der Fußboden the floor (2)
ein streitendes Ehepaar a fighting couple
[**streiten** to fight, to quarrel]
[**das Ehepaar** the married couple]
[**die Ehe** the marriage]
baten um Entschuldigung begged their pardon
[**bitten, bat, hat gebeten** to ask, to beg, to request (2)]
[**die Entschuldigung** the excuse, pardon, apology]
Ehepaare married couples
[**die Ehe** the marriage (2)]
die sich stritten which quarreled
[**(sich) streiten, stritt, hat gestritten** to fight, to quarrel (2)]

Bürger citizens
[**der Bürger, die Bürger** (2)]
seines Staates of his state
[**der Staat, die Staaten** the state; government (3)]
dienen to serve (3)
als wenn than if
der Feind the enemy (3)

und weinte so laut, daß das Volk sie unten auf der Straße hören konnte. Jens, der am Morgen ins Haus gekommen war, um der Frau von dem traurigen Ende ihres Mannes zu erzählen und sie zu trösten, hörte mit Schrecken, wie sie laut um ihren Mann klagte, und wußte sofort, daß er etwas tun mußte, wenn er seine Haut retten wollte. Schnell nahm er alle Tassen und Teller, die er finden konnte, und warf sie auf den Fußboden, wo sie in tausend Stücke brachen. Dann schlug er die Frau mit einem Stock, bis sie noch lauter schrie als vorher. Als die Diener des Königs die Treppe hinaufeilten, fanden sie nur Stücke von Tassen und Tellern auf dem Fußboden liegen und einen Mann, der seine Frau schlug. „Ein streitendes Ehepaar", dachten sie, baten um Entschuldigung und machten die Tür gleich wieder zu. Ehepaare, die sich stritten, waren nichts Neues. Sie verließen das Haus und kehrten zu dem König zurück, ohne den zweiten Dieb gefunden zu haben.

Als der König sah, daß der Dieb schlauer war als er und alle Bürger seines Staates, sagte er sich: „Ist es nicht besser, wenn der Mann mir und dem Staat dient, als wenn er mein Feind ist und mir schadet?" Er beschloß also, ihm zu verzeihen und ihm sogar seine Tochter zur Frau zu geben, wenn es dem Dieb gelingen sollte, ihm das Bettuch unter dem Leibe wegzustehlen.

---

und mir schadet and does me harm
[**schaden** to damage, to harm, to injure, to hurt]
verzeihen to pardon
zur Frau as a wife
wenn es dem Dieb gelingen sollte if the thief should succeed
ihm . . . unter dem Leibe wegzustehlen in stealing . . . from under his body
das Bettuch the bed sheet
[**das Tuch, die Tücher** the cloth, fabric]
[**der Leib** the body (2)]

lösen to solve (2)
  gefangen caught
    [**fangen, er fängt, fing, hat gefangen** to catch (2)]
  hatte . . . gewonnen had won
    [**gewinnen, gewann, hat gewonnen** to win, to gain (3)]
  auf den man stolz sein konnte of whom one could be proud
    [**stolz sein auf** to be proud of]

stellte placed
    [**stellen** to put, to place (3)]
  das Gewehr the gun
    [**das Gewehr, die Gewehre** the gun, rifle]
blies er . . . aus he blew out
    [**blasen, er bläst, blies, hat geblasen** to blow (2)]
  die Kerze the candle
    [**die Kerze, die Kerzen**]
lange for a long time (2)
  still quiet, calm, still (3)

aus Stroh out of straw
    [**das Stroh** the straw (2)]
und der Mond . . . verschwunden war and the moon had disappeared
    [**der Mond** the moon (2)]
    [**verschwinden, verschwand, ist verschwunden** to disappear (3)]
schlich sneaked
    [**schleichen, schlich, ist geschlichen** to sneak, to creep]
  stieg climbed
    [**steigen, stieg, ist gestiegen** to climb, to rise]
das Dach, unter dem the roof, under which
    [**das Dach, die Dächer** the roof]
  das Schlafzimmer the bedroom
    [**der Schlaf** the sleep (2)]
um Mitternacht at midnight
    [**die Mitternacht** midnight (2)]
  ließ er . . . hinuntergleiten he let . . . slide down
    [**gleiten** to slide, to glide]
  der Strohmann the straw man

als draußen . . . erschienen when . . . appeared outside
    [**draußen** outside (3)]
    [**erscheinen, erschien, ist erschienen** to appear (2)]
die Schultern the shoulders
    [**die Schulter, die Schultern** (2)]
der sich . . . herunterließ who let himself down
    [**herunter** down (3)]
  vom Dach from the roof
    [**das Dach, die Dächer** the roof (2)]
  stieg climbed
    [**steigen, stieg, ist gestiegen** to climb, to rise (2)]

4.

Am Abend ging der König zufrieden zu Bett. Was heute nacht geschah, dachte er, mußte das Problem lösen: entweder war der Dieb am Morgen gefangen oder tot, oder der Staat hatte einen Diener gewonnen, auf den man stolz sein konnte.

Bevor er sich ins Bett legte, stellte er ein Gewehr neben sich, das er mitgenommen hatte. Dann blies er die Kerze aus und wartete. Lange blieb alles still.

Jens hatte am Nachmittag einen Mann aus Stroh gemacht. Er wartete, bis es dunkel wurde und der Mond hinter den Wolken verschwunden war. Dann schlich er ins Schloß und stieg auf das Dach, unter dem des Königs Schlafzimmer lag. Um Mitternacht ließ er den Strohmann langsam an der Mauer zum Fenster hinuntergleiten.

„Aha!" dachte der König, als draußen am Fenster die Füße eines Mannes erschienen. Jetzt kamen die Beine, die Schultern, der Kopf. Das mußte der Dieb sein, der sich vom Dach herunterließ und jetzt ins Zimmer stieg. „Erschrick nicht!" flüsterte der König seiner Frau ins Ohr, nahm das Gewehr und schoß. Bums! Mitten durch den Kopf! Der Mann war ohne Zweifel tot, denn er schrie nicht einmal, sondern fiel sofort in den Garten. „Der steht nicht wieder auf", sagte der König und

---

erschrick nicht don't be frightened
  [**erschrecken, er erschrickt, erschrak, ist erschrocken** to be scared, frightened]
  flüstern to whisper (2)
  das Ohr the ear (3)
  das Gewehr the gun
  [**das Gewehr, die Gewehre** the gun, rifle (2)]
  schoß fired
  [**schießen, schoß, hat geschossen** to shoot, to fire]
mitten durch right through
nicht einmal not even
  der Garten the garden (3)
der steht nicht wieder auf *he* won't get up again
  [**auf-stehen** to get up, to stand up (3)]

zündete . . . an lit
[**an-zünden** to light]
die Kerze the candle
[**die Kerze, die Kerzen** (2)]
dennoch nevertheless (2)
wie . . . aussieht what . . . looks like
[**aus-sehen, er sieht aus** to look, to appear]

das Schlafzimmer the bedroom (2)
geschossen shot
[**schießen, schoß, hat geschossen** to shoot, to fire (2)]
sieht . . . aus looks
[**aus-sehen, er sieht aus** to look, to appear (2)]
kaum hardly (2)
das Bettuch the bed sheet (2)
[**das Tuch, die Tücher** the cloth, fabric (2)]
damit so that

der Strohmann the straw man (2)
heraufkam came up
[**herauf** up]
fehlte was missing
[**fehlen** to be missing, not to be there (2)]
erst als only when
vor einigen Minuten a few minutes ago
[**die Minute, die Minuten** the minute]
verstand understood
[**verstehen, verstand, hat verstanden** to understand (2)]

verzieh pardoned
[**verzeihen, verzieh, hat verziehen** to excuse, to pardon]
wie er versprochen hatte as he had promised
[**versprechen, er verspricht, versprach, hat versprochen** to promise]

gemein common
[**gemein** common; mean]
heiraten to marry (2)
verzieh pardoned
[**verzeihen, verzieh, hat verziehen** to pardon, to excuse (2)]
die Antwort the answer
[**die Antwort, die Antworten** (2)]
noch einmal once more (3)
wenn . . . aber if, however
wenigstens at least (3)
die Familie the family
[**die Familie, die Familien** (3)]

zündete die Kerze an; „aber ich werde dennoch hinuntergehen, um zu sehen, wie Jans oder Jens aussieht."

Dies war der Augenblick, auf den Jens gewartet hatte. Er stieg vom Dach, ging ins dunkle Schlafzimmer und sagte: „Mitten durch den Kopf geschossen, wie ich gesagt habe! Der Mann sieht so schrecklich aus, daß man ihn kaum erkennen kann. Komm, gib mir mein Bettuch, damit ich es auf den armen Teufel legen kann!"

Der König hatte im Garten natürlich nur einen Strohmann gefunden. Als er mit der Kerze wieder heraufkam, sah er, daß sein Bettuch fehlte. Erst als seine Frau ihm sagte, daß er selbst es vor einigen Minuten verlangt hatte, verstand er, was geschehen war.

Als Jens am nächsten Morgen mit dem Bettuch erschien, verzieh ihm der König und gab ihm seine Tochter zur Frau, wie er versprochen hatte.

Am Ende dieser Geschichte kann man nun fragen, warum der König wollte, daß ein gemeiner Dieb seine Tochter heiratete. War es nicht genug, wenn er ihm verzieh? Die einfache Antwort ist natürlich, daß er nicht wissen konnte, ob Jens seinen Schatz nicht noch einmal stehlen wollte. Wenn er es aber jetzt tat, dann blieb das Geld wenigstens in der Familie.

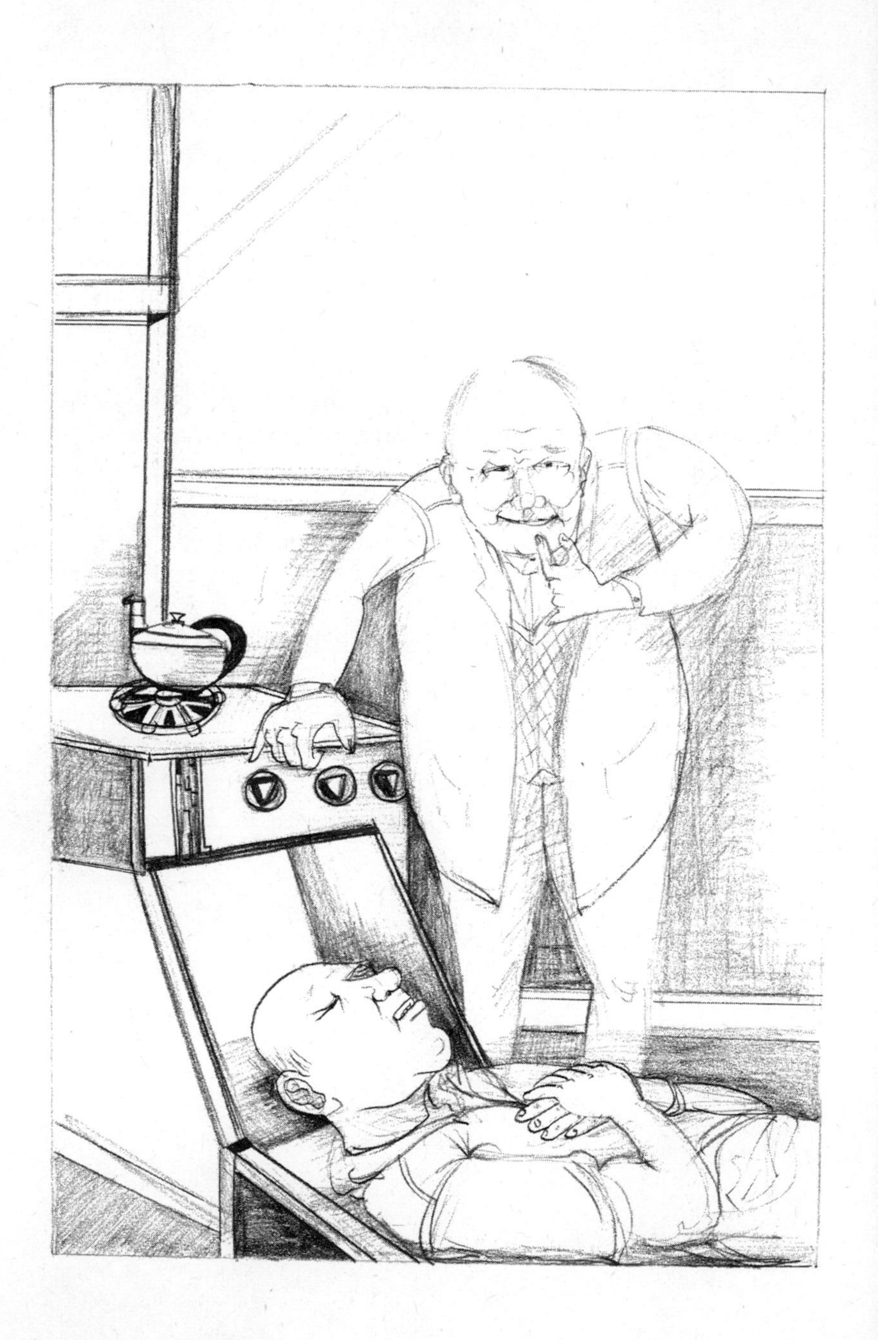

HERRN MEIERBACHS FEHLER

[4B]

NOTES

The most frequent meanings of **lassen** are:

1. to let

   Laß die Kinder ihr Frühstück allein essen! Let the children . . . (1A)

   Laßt uns beschließen, den Tod zu fangen! Let us resolve . . . (2A)

2. to leave

   Einen Kasten läßt der Kaufmann im Zimmer zurück . . . leaves behind . . . (2B)

3. to cause, order, have someone do something; to cause, order that something be done

   Laß ein tiefes Loch graben! Have a deep hole dug! (4A)

   Laß ihn durch die Straßen ziehen! Have him dragged through the streets! (4A)

4. **fallen lassen** to drop

   kommen lassen to send for

   Meierbach ließ fast die Gabel fallen. . . . almost dropped the fork (4B)

   Der König ließ einen alten Dieb kommen. . . . sent for . . . (4A)

REVIEW OF STRONG AND IRREGULAR VERBS USED IN STORY 4A

brechen	bricht	**brach**	**gebrochen**	*to break*
erfahren	erfährt	**erfuhr**	**erfahren**	*to learn, find out*
fangen	fängt	**fing**	**gefangen**	*to catch*
graben	gräbt	**grub**	**gegraben**	*to dig*
greifen		**griff**	**gegriffen**	*to grasp, seize, reach*
heißen		**hieß**	**geheißen**	*to be called*
helfen	hilft	**half**	**geholfen**	*to help*
raten	rät	**riet**	**geraten**	*to advise; guess*
schießen		**schoß**	**geschossen**	*to shoot*
schleichen		**schlich**	**ist geschlichen**	*to sneak, creep*
schneiden		**schnitt**	**geschnitten**	*to cut*
stehlen	stiehlt	**stahl**	**gestohlen**	*to steal*
steigen		**stieg**	**ist gestiegen**	*to climb*
streiten		**stritt**	**gestritten**	*to fight, quarrel*
treffen	trifft	**traf**	**getroffen**	*to meet, hit*
trinken		**trank**	**getrunken**	*to drink*
umgeben	umgibt	**umgab**	**umgeben**	*to surround*
versprechen	verspricht	**versprach**	**versprochen**	*to promise*
verzeihen		**verzieh**	**verziehen**	*to forgive*

IDIOMS FOR REVIEW

es blitzt there is lightning
es donnert there is thunder
zu dieser Stunde at this (that) hour
zum Mörder werden to become a murderer
vor ein paar Tagen a few days ago
fünf Jahre lang for five years
zur gleichen Zeit at the same time
nicht einmal not even
nichts als Schulden nothing but debts
Boltes Regenschirm sah neuer aus Bolte's umbrella looked newer
Boltes Tod sah wie Selbstmord aus Bolte's death looked like suicide
er kam auf den Gedanken he got the idea
heute früh this morning

---

der Fehler the mistake
[**der Fehler, die Fehler** the mistake, error, fault, defect]

streckte sich stretched
[**(sich) strecken** to stretch, to extend (2)]
atmen to breathe (3)
trocknen to dry (2)
der Ärmel the sleeve
[**der Ärmel, die Ärmel** (2)]
der Schweiß the perspiration, sweat (2)
die Stirn the forehead (2)
blickte sich . . . um looked around
[**sich um-blicken** to look around]
die Küche the kitchen
[**die Küche** the kitchen; cuisine]
soweit as far as
der Ort place
[**der Ort, die Orte** the place; locality; village]
die Hauptsache the main thing
[**Haupt-** main, chief; head (2)]

[4 B]

(FOUR PARTS)

Herrn Meierbachs Fehler

1.

Ernst Meierbach stand vom Fußboden auf, streckte sich und atmete tief. Dann trocknete er sich mit dem Ärmel den Schweiß von der Stirn und blickte sich in der kleinen Küche um. Soweit er sehen konnte, war alles am richtigen Ort. Nichts, was nicht natürlich aussah, und das war die Hauptsache. Sein Blick kehrte zu der Gestalt zurück, die zu seinen Füßen lag. Es hatte ihn einige Mühe gekostet, den schweren Körper aus dem Wohnzimmer in die Küche zu tragen und die einzelnen Glieder in eine solche Stellung zu bringen, daß niemand auf den Gedanken kommen konnte, daß der Mann sich nicht selbst auf den Fußboden gelegt hatte. Ja, die Stellung war gerade richtig;

---

der Blick the glance
  [**der Blick, die Blicke** the glance, look (2)]
einige Mühe some effort
  [**die Mühe** the effort, trouble, pain (3)]
 das Wohnzimmer the living room
 die Küche the kitchen
  [**die Küche** the kitchen; cuisine (2)]
 und . . . zu bringen and to put
 die einzelnen Glieder the individual limbs
 in eine solche Stellung in such a position
  [**die Stellung, die Stellungen** the position; job]
 auf den Gedanken kommen konnte could get the idea
die Stellung the position (2)
 gerade richtig just right

von der man nicht behaupten konnte of which one could not say
[**behaupten** to assert, to maintain (2)]
gewöhnlich normal
[**gewöhnlich** common, ordinary, usual, customary, habitual (2)]
bequem comfortable
Bruno Bolte name of the second principal character of the story
nämlich you see
[**nämlich** you see; namely]
der Gasofen the gas stove
[**das Gas** the gas]
[**der Ofen, die Öfen** the stove, oven (3)]

fortgegangen war had left
[**fort-gehen** to go away, to leave]
[**fort** away, gone (3)]
hatte es geblitzt und gedonnert there had been lightning and thunder
[**blitzen; es blitzt** there is lightning]
[**donnern; es donnert** there is thunder]
der Herbststurm the autumn storm
[**der Herbst** the fall, autumn]
[**der Sturm, die Stürme** the storm]
der Regen the rain (2)
die Mitternacht midnight (2)
bei einem solchen Wetter in such a weather
[**das Wetter** the weather (3)]
zu so später Stunde at such a late hour
besuchen to visit
da er . . . gezogen war since he had moved
erst vor ein paar Wochen only a few weeks ago
auf-wachen to wake up (2)
hatte . . . getrunken had drunk
[**trinken, trank, hat getrunken** to drink (2)]
gefüllt filled
und . . . reichte and handed
[**reichen** to hand, pass; to reach, extend (2)]
das Glas that glass
in dem sich . . . befand in which there was
[**sich befinden** to be, to find oneself, to be found (2)]
[**befinden, befand, hat befunden**]
das Eis the ice
[**das Eis** the ice, ice cream]
der Teelöffelvoll the teaspoonful
[**der Tee** the tea (2)]
[**der Löffel, die Löffel** the spoon]
das Schlafmittel the sleeping potion
[**das Mittel, die Mittel** the means, way, measure (2)]
das Fläschchen the little bottle
wirken to work
[**wirken** to work, to have an effect (2)]

so natürlich wie möglich für eine Stellung, von der man nicht behaupten konnte, daß sie entweder gewöhnlich oder bequem war. Bruno Boltes Kopf steckte nämlich im Gasofen.

Er brauchte sich nicht zu eilen. Als er von zu Haus fortgegangen war, hatte es geblitzt und gedonnert. Ein richtiger Herbststurm. Jetzt fiel draußen ein starker Regen, es war fast Mitternacht, und bei einem solchen Wetter und zu so später Stunde setzte niemand den Fuß auf die Straße, um Bolte zu besuchen, der allein wohnte und kaum viele Freunde haben konnte, da er erst vor ein paar Monaten in die Stadt gezogen war. Und daß Bolte nicht aufwachte, war sicher. Der Narr hatte während des Abends so viel getrunken, daß er nichts gemerkt hatte, als Meierbach mit zwei gefüllten Gläsern aus der Küche zurückkam und ihm d a s Glas reichte, in dem sich außer Whisky und Eis jetzt auch ein Teelöffelvoll von dem Schlafmittel befand, das Meierbach in einem Fläschchen von zu Haus mitgebracht hatte. Es hatte fast sofort gewirkt. Bolte war eingeschlafen, bevor er die Hälfte getrunken hatte. Meierbach war sofort ans Werk gegangen und hatte Bolte in die Küche getragen.

Vielleicht war es besser, wenn er sich etwas ausruhte und eine Zigarette rauchte, bevor er anfing, die Briefe zu suchen. Er

---

war eingeschlafen had fallen asleep
  [**ein-schlafen, er schläft ein, schlief ein, ist eingeschlafen** to fall asleep]
die Hälfte the half (2)
getrunken hatte had drunk
  [**trinken, trank, hat getrunken** to drink (3)]
ans Werk to work
  [**das Werk, die Werke** the work]
hatte getragen had carried
  [**tragen, er trägt, trug, hat getragen** to carry, to wear (3)]

wenn er sich . . . ausruhte if he rested
  [**sich aus-ruhen** to rest, to take a rest]
die Zigarette the cigarette
  [**die Zigarette, die Zigaretten** (2)]
anfing began
  [**an-fangen, er fängt an, fing an, hat angefangen** to begin, start (3)]
die Briefe the letters
  [**der Brief, die Briefe** (3)]

das Wohnzimmer the living room (2)
seine Schuld his fault
[**die Schuld** the fault, guilt, debt]
[**die Schulden** the debts]
daß er zum Mörder geworden war that he had become a murderer
[**der Mörder, die Mörder** the murderer]
[**werden, er wird, wurde, ist geworden** to become, to get (3)]
hatte ihn dazu getrieben had driven him to it
[**treiben, trieb, hat getrieben** to drive (2)]
seine Schuld his fault
[**die Schuld** the fault, guilt, debt (2)]
[**die Schulden** the debts (2)]
gesessen hatte had been
[**sitzen, saß, hat gesessen** to sit (3)]
weder er noch neither he nor (3)
früher former
hatten damals . . . gesagt had then told
[**damals** then, at that time (2)]
vor Gericht in court
[**das Gericht, die Gerichte** the court, tribunal]
die Wahrheit the truth (2)
irgendwie somehow
der Richter the judge
[**der Richter, die Richter** (3)]
als Bolte . . . schrieb when Bolte wrote
[**schreiben, schrieb, hat geschrieben** to write (2)]
vor ein paar Tagen a few days ago
hatte er . . . erfahren he had found out
[**erfahren, er erfährt, erfuhr, hat erfahren** to learn, to find out (2)]
wahr true (3)
der Grund the reason
[**der Grund, die Gründe** the reason, cause; ground, bottom (3)]
weggeworfen thrown away
[**werfen, er wirft, warf, hat geworfen** to throw (4)]
wie er zuerst gedacht . . . hatte as he had first thought
[**denken, dachte, hat gedacht** to think (3)]
hatte sie . . . behalten had kept them
[**behalten, er behält, behielt, hat behalten** to keep]
fünf Jahre lang for five years
statt . . . zu bringen instead of putting
hatte . . . es vorgezogen had preferred
[**vor-ziehen, zog vor, hat vorgezogen** to prefer]
teuer at a high price
[**teuer** expensive (3)]
wer weiß wie lange for who knows how long
[**lange** (for) a long time (3)]
auf seine Kosten at his expense
[**die Kosten** the cost, the expense (2)]

ging ins Wohnzimmer zurück und setzte sich. War es seine Schuld, daß er zum Mörder geworden war? Nein, der Mann hatte ihn dazu getrieben. War es seine Schuld, daß Bolte fünf Jahre im Gefängnis gesessen hatte? Weder er noch sein früherer Freund hatten damals vor Gericht die Wahrheit gesagt, aber irgendwie hatte man i h m geglaubt, nicht Bolte. Er hatte sich damals gewundert, daß Bolte dem Richter die Briefe nicht gezeigt hatte. Jetzt, nach fünf Jahren, als Bolte ihm vor ein paar Tagen plötzlich schrieb, hatte er endlich den wahren Grund erfahren. Bolte hatte die Briefe nicht weggeworfen, wie er zuerst gedacht und gehofft hatte. Nein, er hatte sie fünf Jahre lang behalten. Statt ihn damals auch ins Gefängnis zu bringen, hatte Bolte es vorgezogen, zu warten, bis er wieder ein freier Mann war, um ihm die Briefe teuer zu verkaufen und wer weiß wie lange auf seine Kosten zu leben.

2.

Der Mann hatte für jeden Brief die runde Summe von fünftausend Mark gefordert. Fünftausend Mark! Sollte er für den ersten Brief bezahlen? Nein, damit war nichts gewonnen. Wenn er zahlte und wenn das so weiterging, war er bald ein armer Mann. Das Beste, was er tun konnte, war, daß er der ganzen Sache ein Ende machte, bevor es zu spät war. Er hatte Bolte angerufen und versprochen zu zahlen. Aber er hatte ihn

---

hatte . . . gefordert had demanded
  [**fordern** to demand]
 rund round (2)
damit by that
 gewonnen gained
zahlen to pay (2)
 und wenn das so weiterging and if it continued that way
er hatte . . . angerufen he had called
  [**an-rufen, rief an, hat angerufen** to call (3)]
 versprochen promised
  [**versprechen, er verspricht, versprach, hat versprochen** to promise (2)]

er hatte . . . gebeten he had asked
[**bitten, bat, hat gebeten** to ask, request, beg (3)]
zur gleichen Zeit at the same time
war . . . gewesen had been
[**sein, er ist, war, ist gewesen** to be (2)]
als er . . . vorschlug when he suggested
[**vor-schlagen, er schlägt vor, schlug vor, hat vorgeschlagen** to suggest, to propose]
gestern yesterday (3)
gefordert hatte had demanded
[**fordern** to demand (2)]
es war dem Dummkopf nicht eingefallen it had not occurred to the blockhead
[**der Dummkopf** the blockhead, fool, dumbbell, idiot (3)]
[**ein-fallen, es fällt ein, fiel ein, ist eingefallen** to occur]
daß er . . . gegraben hatte that he had dug
[**graben, er gräbt, grub, hat gegraben** to dig (2)]
damit in so doing
das Grab the grave
[**das Grab, die Gräber** (3)]

ans Werk to work
[**das Werk, die Werke** the work (2)]
es blieb there remained
wie Selbstmord aussah was to look like suicide
[**der Selbstmord** the suicide]
[**der Mord, die Morde** the murder]
durfte er he must
[**dürfen, er darf, durfte, hat gedurft** may, to be allowed, permitted (2)]
[**dürfen** + negation must not]
der Fehler the mistake
[**der Fehler, die Fehler** the mistake, error, fault, defect (2)]
darauf deuten point to the fact
[**deuten** to point (2)]
je ever (2)
irgend etwas anything
zunächst first (2)
das Dutzend the dozen
[**das Dutzend, die Dutzende** (2)]

zog . . . an put on
[**an-ziehen, zog an, hat angezogen** to put on (3)]
der Schreibtisch the desk
leer empty (3)
unbezahlt unpaid
die Tinte the ink (2)

zur gleichen Zeit gebeten, ihm ein paar Tage Zeit zu geben, und Bolte war dumm genug gewesen, ja zu sagen, als er ihm gestern vorschlug, heute abend zu ihm zu kommen, um mit ihm über den Preis zu sprechen, den er für die Briefe gefordert hatte. Es war dem Dummkopf nicht eingefallen, daß er sich damit selbst sein Grab gegraben hatte.

Aber nun ans Werk! Es blieb noch genug zu tun. Wenn er wollte, daß Boltes Tod morgen wie Selbstmord aussah, dann durfte er jetzt keinen Fehler machen. Nichts im Haus durfte darauf deuten, daß er hier gewesen war oder je mit Bolte irgend etwas zu tun gehabt hatte. Zunächst die Briefe. Ein rundes Dutzend, hatte Bolte gesagt. Sie konnten nicht schwer zu finden sein.

Ernst Meierbach stand auf, zog die Handschuhe an, die er mitgebracht hatte, und begann zu suchen. Der Schreibtisch war fast leer; mehrere unbezahlte Rechnungen, Tinte und ein paar Bleistifte, das war alles. In dem alten Pult im Schlafzimmer lagen nur einige Hemden, schmutzige Unterwäsche, einzelne Strümpfe und ein paar Streichhölzer. Wo mochte Bolte die Briefe versteckt haben? Bolte hatte sie ihm nicht gezeigt, aber er war sicher, daß er sie behalten hatte und daß sie im Haus

---

ein paar Bleistifte a few pencils
[**ein paar** a few, some (3)]
[**der Bleistift, die Bleistifte** the pencil (2)]
das Pult the desk
Hemden shirts
[**das Hemd, die Hemden** (2)]
die Unterwäsche the underwear
Strümpfe socks
[**der Strumpf, die Strümpfe** the stocking, sock]
Streichhölzer matches
[**das Streichholz, die Streichhölzer** the match]
mochte . . . versteckt haben might . . . have hidden
[**verstecken** to hide (2)]
behalten hatte had kept
[**behalten, er behält, behielt, hat behalten** to keep (2)]

die Kleider the clothes
[**das Kleid, die Kleider** the dress; clothing, clothes (2)]
die Hosentaschen pants pockets
[**die Hose, die Hosen** the trousers, pants (2)]
die Jacke the jacket
[**die Jacke, die Jacken**]
der Kamm the comb
die Streichholzschachtel the matchbox
[**das Streichholz, die Streichhölzer** the match (2)]
[**die Schachtel, die Schachteln** the box]
er kroch he crawled
[**kriechen, kroch, ist gekrochen** to crawl, to creep]
die Bilder the pictures
[**das Bild, die Bilder** (2)]
die Wände the walls
[**die Wand, die Wände** (2)]
hingen hung
[**hängen, er hängt, hing, hat gehangen** to hang (3)]
hörte . . . auf stopped
[**auf-hören** to stop (2)]
es hatte keinen Zweck there was no point (2)
verstecken to hide (2)
wenn es mir nicht gelungen ist if *I* haven't succeeded
[**gelingen, es gelingt, gelang, ist gelungen** to succeed (3)]
nicht einmal not even (2)
mitten auf dem Schreibtisch in the middle of the desk
[**der Schreibtisch** the desk (2)]
das Blatt the sheet
[**das Blatt, die Blätter** the sheet, page; leaf (2)]
bewies proved
[**beweisen, bewies, hat bewiesen** to prove]
ein klarer Fall a clear case
[**klar** clear (3)]
[**der Fall, die Fälle** the case; fall (3)]
der Selbstmord the suicide (2)
[**der Mord, die Morde** the murder (2)]
was für ein Zufall what a coincidence
geschrieben hatte had written
[**schreiben, schrieb, hat geschrieben** to write (3)]
die Sätze the sentences
[**der Satz, die Sätze** the sentence; leap (2)]
gebrauchen to use (3)
ja indeed
hatte . . . überhaupt . . . gegeben had in fact given
[**geben, er gibt, gab, hat gegeben** to give (3)]
[**überhaupt** generally, on the whole, actually, in fact, altogether]
los-werden to get rid of
er durfte nicht he must not
nachher afterward, later (2)

waren. Vielleicht in den Kleidern? Nein, die Hosentaschen waren leer; in einer Jacke fand er einen Kamm, in einer anderen eine Streichholzschachtel. Er kroch unters Bett, sah hinter die wenigen Bilder, die an den Wänden hingen, suchte zwischen den Tassen und Tellern in der Küche. Nichts. Nach zwei Stunden hörte Meierbach auf. Es hatte keinen Zweck, weiterzusuchen. Die Briefe waren ohne jeden Zweifel im Haus, aber der schlaue Fuchs hatte sie so gut versteckt, daß niemand sie finden konnte. „Wenn es m i r nicht gelungen ist", sagte sich Meierbach, „dann findet auch die Polizei nichts. Sie wird nicht einmal suchen." Warum sollte die Polizei nach Briefen suchen, wenn mitten auf dem Schreibtisch ein Blatt Papier lag, mit dem Bolte selbst bewies, daß er sich das Leben genommen hatte? Für die Polizei war die Sache ein klarer Fall von Selbstmord. Was für ein Zufall, daß Bolte ihm diesen Brief geschrieben hatte! Als er ihn las, hatte er sofort gesehen, zu welchem Zweck er die letzten Sätze gebrauchen konnte. Ja, der Brief hatte ihm überhaupt die Idee gegeben, auf welche Weise er Bolte für immer loswerden konnte. Er durfte nicht vergessen, ihn nachher auf den Schreibtisch zu legen.

3.

Er ging ins Wohnzimmer zurück. Sein Blick fiel auf die zwei Gläser. Er nahm seins, trug es in die Küche und wusch es. Dann trocknete er es und stellte es zu den anderen zurück. Boltes Glas und die fast leere Flasche konnte er auf dem Tisch stehen lassen; die Polizei sollte sehen, wieviel Bolte getrunken hatte. Aber nein! Mein Gott, was für einen Fehler er fast gemacht hatte! Er hatte fast vergessen, daß das Schlafmittel

---

wusch washed
 [**waschen, er wäscht, wusch, hat gewaschen** to wash]
er hatte fast vergessen he had almost forgotten
 [**vergessen, er vergißt, vergaß, hat vergessen** to forget (3)]
 das Schlafmittel the sleeping potion (2)

zittern to tremble (3)
wusch washed
[**waschen, er wäscht, wusch, hat gewaschen** (2)]
halb half (3)
das Eis the ice
[**das Eis** the ice, ice cream (2)]
der Arm the arm (3)
drücken to press (3)
die Fingerspitzen the finger tips
[**die Spitze, die Spitzen** the point, tip (3)]
darauf on it

zwei Blätter two sheets
gebraucht hatte had used
dafür for them
schloß concluded
[**schließen, schloß, hat geschlossen** to shut, to lock; to conclude, to finish]
das Hundeleben the dog's life
fünf Jahre lang for five years (2)
nichts als Schulden nothing but debts
hatte nicht gewußt had not known
[**wissen, er weiß, wußte, hat gewußt** to know (3)]
daß es . . . gab that there was
schwierig difficult (2)
der Vorteil the advantage
[**der Vorteil, die Vorteile**]
daß es . . . rettete that it saved
[**retten** to save, to rescue]
vor einem Hundeleben from a dog's life (2)

dicht tightly
[**dicht** tight, dense, thick]
geschlossen shut
[**schließen, schloß, hat geschlossen** to shut, to lock; to conclude, to finish (2)]
prüfen to check
[**prüfen** to examine, to test, to check (2)]
das Gas the gas (2)
erfüllen to accomplish
[**erfüllen** to fulfill, to accomplish (3)]
hereingekommen war had come in
[**herein** in (2)]
der Regenschirm the umbrella
waren . . . gewesen had been
vollständig completely
[**vollständig** complete, whole, entire; completely, perfectly]
trocken dry

noch in Boltes Whisky war. Seine Hand zitterte, als er das Glas wusch und es wieder halb mit Whisky und Eis füllte. Dann hob er Boltes Arm, gab ihm das Glas in die Hand, drückte seine Fingerspitzen darauf und stellte es ins Wohnzimmer zurück.

Und nun der Brief. Wie gut es war, daß Bolte zwei Blätter gebraucht hatte! Das ganze erste Blatt hatte mit den Briefen zu tun und dem Geld, das Bolte dafür verlangte; das zweite Blatt begann und schloß mit den folgenden Worten: „Ich habe genug von dem Hundeleben, das ich fünf Jahre lang im Gefängnis geführt habe. Und jetzt? Seit drei Monaten keine Arbeit, kein Geld und nichts als Schulden. Warum soll ich es mir nicht leicht machen? Bruno Bolte." Meierbach lächelte. Bolte hatte nicht gewußt, daß es noch ein anderes Mittel gab, ein schwieriges Problem zu lösen. Nur hatte dieses andere Mittel den großen Vorteil, daß es nicht i h n , sondern Meierbach vor einem Hundeleben rettete. Er steckte das erste Blatt in seine Brieftasche zurück; das zweite legte er mitten auf den Schreibtisch, wo der erste, der heute ins Haus trat, es sofort sehen mußte.

Waren die Fenster dicht geschlossen? Er ging von einem zum anderen und prüfte sie. Eins stand halb offen. Er schloß es. Es war wichtig, daß das Gas lange genug im Haus blieb, um seinen Zweck zu erfüllen. Hatte er den Fußboden schmutzig gemacht, als er von draußen hereingekommen war? Nein, sein Regenschirm und seine Schuhe waren vollständig trocken gewesen. Der Regen hatte erst angefangen, nachdem er im Haus war, und als Bolte eingeschlafen war, hatte er sofort die Schuhe

---

hatte erst angefangen had only started
[**an-fangen, er fängt an, fing an, hat angefangen** (4)]
nachdem after (2)
eingeschlafen war had fallen asleep
[**ein-schlafen, er schläft ein, schlief ein, ist eingeschlafen** to fall asleep (2)]
hatte er . . . ausgezogen he had taken off
[**aus-ziehen, zog aus, hat ausgezogen** to take off (2)]

die Strümpfe the socks
[**der Strumpf, die Strümpfe** the stocking, sock (2)]

die Ordnung the order
noch eine Minute one more minute
[**die Minute, die Minuten** the minute (2)]
die Zündflamme the pilot light
[**die Flamme, die Flammen** the flame]
drehen to turn
der Knopf the knob
[**der Knopf, die Knöpfe** the button, knob]
die Flamme the flame (2)
drehte er . . . an he turned on
[**drehen** to turn (2)]
unten im Ofen in the oven below
der Regenschirm the umbrella (2)
sah neuer aus looked newer
seinen eigenen his own
[**eigen** own (3)]

einsamer als sonst more deserted than usual
[**einsam** lonely, solitary, deserted]
[**sonst** otherwise]
um diese Zeit at this time
der Nebel the fog
begegnen to meet, to encounter

der Nebel the fog (2)
hatte sich gehoben had lifted
[**heben, hob, hat gehoben** to lift, raise (3)]
die Ecke the corner
[**die Ecke, die Ecken** (3)]
bog turned
[**biegen, bog, hat gebogen** to bend, to turn (2)]
brannte was burning
[**brennen, brannte, hat gebrannt** to burn (2)]
er hatte . . . angelassen he had left on
[**an-lassen** to leave on]
[**lassen, er läßt, ließ, hat gelassen** (3)]
mit Absicht intentionally
[**die Absicht, die Absichten** the intention]
Lampen lamps
[**die Lampe, die Lampen**]
auf den Gedanken kommen get the idea (2)

kühl cool
der Schlüssel the key (3)
der Herbst the fall, autumn (2)
der Winter the winter

ausgezogen und war in Strümpfen durch die Zimmer gegangen.

Im Wohnzimmer war alles in Ordnung. Zurück zur Küche. Noch eine Minute, dann war er fertig. Ah, hier war das kleine Loch, unter dem die Zündflamme sein mußte. Er blies durch das Loch und drehte den Knopf. Keine Flamme. Gut. Dann drehte er auch das Gas unten im Ofen an, schloß die Küchentür hinter sich und zog die Schuhe an. Boltes Regenschirm sah neuer aus als seiner, und Bolte brauchte jetzt keinen Regenschirm mehr. Aber es war besser, wenn er seinen eigenen nahm.

Als er das Haus verließ, war es drei Uhr. Die Straßen waren noch einsamer als sonst um diese Zeit, ein leichter Nebel hatte sich auf die Stadt gelegt. Es war ein langer Weg, aber er begegnete niemand.

4.

Der Nebel hatte sich gehoben, als Meierbach um die letzte Ecke bog. Sein Haus war das einzige, in dem noch Licht brannte. Er hatte mit Absicht einige Lampen angelassen; seine Nachbarn sollten nicht auf den Gedanken kommen, daß er den ganzen Abend nicht zu Haus gewesen war.

Wie kühl es geworden war, dachte er, als er den Schlüssel aus der Tasche zog und leise ins Haus trat. Nun, es war Herbst, fast Winter. Hoffentlich hatte er sich nicht erkältet. Aber vielleicht war ihm nur so kalt, weil er müde war. Er machte sich eine Tasse Tee, nahm ein heißes Bad und ging ins Bett.

Er war todmüde, als er einige Stunden später aufwachte.

---

hoffentlich he hoped
 [**hoffentlich** I hope, we hope, he hoped, etc.; let's hope (2)]
hatte er sich nicht erkältet (that) he had not caught a cold
 [**sich erkälten** to catch a cold]
war ihm . . . kalt he was cold (2)
 [**mir ist kalt** I am cold]
das Bad the bath (3)

todmüde dead tired

wie gewöhnlich as usual
die Morgenzeitung the morning paper
  es lohnte nicht die Mühe it wasn't worth the effort
    [**lohnen** to be worth(while); to reward]
interessieren to interest (2)

schmecken to taste
  köstlich delicious (2)
  kam ihm . . . vor seemed to him
    [**vor-kommen, kam vor, ist vorgekommen** to occur, to happen; to seem, to appear]
  wie ein Festmahl like a feast
    [**das Fest, die Feste** the feast, holiday, celebration, festival (2)]
    [**das Mahl** the meal]
überhaupt actually
    [**überhaupt** generally, on the whole, actually, in fact, altogether (3)]
  der Festtag the day of celebration, feast day (2)

klingeln to ring (2)
ließ . . . fallen dropped
    [**fallen lassen** to drop]
  die Gabel the fork
    [**die Gabel, die Gabeln** (2)]
er hatte sich nicht geirrt he had not been mistaken
    [**sich irren** to be wrong, to be mistaken]
er zwang sich he forced himself
    [**zwingen, zwang, hat gezwungen** to force]
  ruhig calm
    [**ruhig** still, calm, quiet]
der Milchmann the milkman
  grüßen to greet (3)
erschrecken to frighten
die Butter the butter (2)
  griff eben was just reaching
    [**greifen, griff, hat gegriffen** to seize, grasp, reach (2)]
  sich entschuldigen to apologize
  später als sonst later than usual
    [**sonst** otherwise (2)]
aufgehalten held up
    [**auf-halten** to hold up, to delay]
    [**halten, er hält, hielt, gehalten** to hold; to stop (3)]
und will gerade . . . schieben and am about to push
    [**schieben** to push, to shove]
stürzen to rush
    [**stürzen** to fall, to rush]
  reiße . . . auf push open
    [**auf-reißen** to tear open]
    [**reißen, riß, hat gerissen** to tear (2)]
  will gerade . . . anrufen am about to call

Acht Uhr. Es war besser, wenn er aufstand und wie gewöhnlich zur Arbeit ging. Die Morgenzeitung lag sicher schon vor der Tür, aber es lohnte nicht die Mühe, sie zu holen. Was ihn heute interessierte, war Boltes Selbstmord in der Abendzeitung.

Das Frühstück schmeckte köstlich und kam ihm wie ein Festmahl vor. Von jetzt an, dachte er, war überhaupt jeder Tag ein Festtag. Bolte war tot; er konnte wieder frei atmen.

Was war das? Hatte jemand geklingelt? Ernst Meierbach ließ fast die Gabel fallen. Da, noch einmal! Er hatte sich nicht geirrt. Die Polizei? Unmöglich. Er zwang sich, ruhig zu erscheinen und öffnete die Tür. Es war nur der Milchmann, der draußen mit seinen Flaschen wartete und ihn nun freundlich grüßte. Wie der Mensch ihn erschreckt hatte! Er brachte die zwei Flaschen herein, Meierbach nahm ein halbes Pfund Butter und griff eben in die Tasche, um die Rechnung für die letzte Woche zu bezahlen, als der Milchmann sich entschuldigte, daß er heute etwas später als sonst gekommen war. „Und wissen Sie, was mich aufgehalten hat?" sagte er. „Sie werden es kaum glauben. Ich komme heute früh um fünf zu einem Haus, stelle zwei Flaschen draußen vor die Küche und will gerade die Rechnung unter die Tür schieben, als mein Blick durch Zufall in die Küche fällt. Das Licht war an. Und was, denken Sie, sehe ich auf dem Fußboden liegen? Herrn Bol . . . Aber es ist besser, wenn ich den Namen nicht nenne. Mit dem Kopf im Gasofen! ‚Tot. Selbstmord!' sage ich mir natürlich. Ich stürze ins Haus —die Tür war offen—, reiße ein paar Fenster auf und will gerade vom Wohnzimmer die Polizei anrufen, als ich sehe, daß der Mann sich bewegt. Er steht langsam auf, starrt in den Ofen, schüttelt den Kopf, kommt ins Wohnzimmer und geht zum Schreibtisch, auf dem ein Stück Papier liegt. ‚Soll ich einen Doktor rufen?' sage ich. ‚Doktor?' antwortet er und wundert sich gar nicht, daß ich im Zimmer stehe, sondern liest ruhig

---

sich bewegt is moving
  [**bewegen** to move]
starren to stare (2)
ruhig calmly
  [**ruhig** still, calm, quiet (2)]

ich bin vollständig in Ordnung I am perfectly all right
[**vollständig** complete, entire, whole; completely, perfectly (2)]
[**die Ordnung** the order (2)]
eigentlich actually
[**eigentlich** actual, real; actually, really (2)]
viel gesünder much better
[**gesund** healthy, in good health (4)]
als ich mich je gefühlt habe than I have ever felt
[**fühlen** to feel (3)]
die Schulden the debts (2)
die Gasgesellschaft the gas company
und danken and thank them
[**danken** to thank (3)]
daß man . . . abgedreht hat that they turned off
[**ab-drehen** to turn off]
fängt . . . an begins
auf einmal suddenly
wird . . . sich wundern will . . . be surprised
heute abend tonight (2)
na well
ich habe . . . dagestanden I . . . stood there
[**da-stehen** to stand there]
[**stehen, stand, hat gestanden** to stand (3)]
abgedreht ist has been turned off
[**ab-drehen** to turn off (2)]
darüber about it
so was such a thing
[**was = etwas**]

verstanden understood
[**verstehen, verstand, hat verstanden** to understand (3)]

weiter. ‚Doktor?' sagt er noch einmal. ‚Nein, ich brauche keinen Doktor. Ich bin vollständig in Ordnung. Eigentlich viel gesünder, als ich mich je gefühlt habe. Und wissen Sie warum? Weil ich meine Schulden nicht bezahlen konnte! Ich muß später die Gasgesellschaft anrufen und danken, daß man mir gestern das Gas abgedreht hat, weil ich seit zwei Monaten meine Gasrechnung nicht bezahlt habe.' Und dann fängt der Mann auf einmal laut zu lachen an und sagt: ‚Wird mein Freund Ernst sich wundern, wenn ich ihm heute abend die Geschichte von der Gasrechnung erzähle!' Na, ich sage Ihnen, ich habe nur mit offenem Mund dagestanden. Erst will der Mann sich das Leben nehmen und vergißt, daß das Gas abgedreht ist, und am nächsten Morgen lacht er darüber! Verstehen Sie so was?"

Herr Meierbach war plötzlich ganz weiß geworden. Er antwortete nicht. Er hatte nur zu gut verstanden, warum Bolte gelacht hatte.

DER HERR MIT DEM ZIEGENBART

[5A]

NOTES

There is, there are, there was, there were, there existed, there had been, etc., are expressed by

1. **es gibt, es gab, es hatte gegeben,** etc., if the statement is or was *generally true* at the time and under the mentioned circumstances. The **es** is the subject, the verb is always in the singular, and the noun or pronoun referred to is in the accusative.

   Es gab nicht mehr genug Häuser. There weren't enough houses left.

2. **es ist, es sind, es war, es waren, es ist gewesen, es sind gewesen, es war gewesen, es waren gewesen,** etc., if the reference is made to something *temporary*. If any element other than the **es** is placed at the beginning of the sentence, the **es** must be omitted.

   Es waren noch zwei Plätze frei. There were (still) two seats left.

   In dem Abteil waren noch zwei Plätze frei.

REVIEW OF STRONG AND IRREGULAR VERBS USED IN STORY 4B

aus-sehen	sieht aus	sah aus	ausgesehen	*to look (like)*
aus-ziehen		zog aus	ausgezogen	*to take off, undress*
behalten	behält	behielt	behalten	*to keep*
beweisen		bewies	bewiesen	*to prove*
ein-fallen	fällt ein	fiel ein	ist eingefallen	*to occur*
ein-schlafen	schläft ein	schlief ein	ist eingeschlafen	*to fall asleep*
kriechen		kroch	ist gekrochen	*to creep, crawl*
schließen		schloß	geschlossen	*to shut, lock; conclude*
vor-kommen		kam vor	ist vorgekommen	*to occur; seem*
vor-schlagen	schlägt vor	schlug vor	vorgeschlagen	*to suggest, propose*
vor-ziehen		zog vor	vorgezogen	*to prefer*
waschen	wäscht	wusch	gewaschen	*to wash*
zwingen		zwang	gezwungen	*to force*

IDIOMS FOR REVIEW

es schmeckt nach Wasser it tastes of water
es riecht nach Kaffee it smells of coffee
auf zwei Monate for two months

auf jeden Fall in any case, at any rate
bitten um to ask for
noch jemand someone else (i.e., in addition to the others)
heute nachmittag this afternoon
hoffen wir das Beste let's hope for the best
bestehen aus to consist of
danke schön thank you very much

---

der Ziegenbart the goatee
[**die Ziege, die Ziegen** the goat]

der Schmuggel smuggling
manchmal sometimes
notwendig necessary (3)
die Not the need
[**die Not** the need, misery, distress (2)]
zum Beispiel for example (3)
[**das Beispiel, die Beispiele** the example (3)]
der Weltkrieg the World War
[**der Krieg, die Kriege** the war (3)]
schlank slender
der Ziegenbart the goatee (2)
[**die Ziege, die Ziegen** the goat (2)]
kurz briefly
wie . . . damals aussah what . . . looked like at that time
[**damals** then, at that time (3)]
wenn Sie nämlich you see, if you
[**nämlich** you see; namely (3)]
die Zustände the conditions
[**der Zustand, die Zustände** the condition, state]
unter denen . . . litten from which . . . were suffering
[**leiden, litt, hat gelitten** to suffer]
die meisten most (2)
[**meist** most (2)]
wahrscheinlich probably (2)

nach jahrelangen Kämpfen after years of fighting
[**jahrelang** (lasting) for years]
[**der Kampf, die Kämpfe** the fight, battle]
der Friede(n) the peace (2)
deshalb therefore (4)

[5 A]

(THREE PARTS)

Der Herr mit dem Ziegenbart

1.

In guten Zeiten ist der Schmuggel ein dunkles Geschäft. In schlechten Zeiten ist er manchmal fast notwendig. Solch eine Zeit der Not waren zum Beispiel in Deutschland die ersten Jahre nach dem letzten Weltkrieg. Bevor wir Ihnen die Geschichte von dem schlanken Fräulein und dem Herrn mit dem Ziegenbart erzählen, möchten wir kurz berichten, wie Deutschland damals aussah. Wenn Sie nämlich die Zustände kennenlernen, unter denen nicht nur Deutschland, sondern auch die meisten Länder Europas nach dem Kriege litten, werden Sie die Geschichte wahrscheinlich besser verstehen.

Nach jahrelangen Kämpfen war endlich der Friede gekommen; aber die Zeiten waren deshalb nicht besser geworden. Bomben, Artillerie und Feuer hatten die meisten Städte in Ruinen verwandelt, so daß es nicht mehr genug Häuser gab

---

Bomben bombs
[**die Bombe, die Bomben**]
die Artillerie the artillery
das Feuer the fire (3)
hatten . . . verwandelt had transformed
[**verwandeln** to change, to transform]
Ruinen ruins
[**die Ruine, die Ruinen**]
so daß es . . . gab so that there were

die Wohnung the apartment
[**die Wohnung, die Wohnungen** the apartment, residence, dwelling (2)]
froren were cold
[**frieren, fror, ist/hat gefroren** to freeze, to be cold]
warme Kleider warm clothes
[**warm** warm (3)]
[**das Kleid, die Kleider** the dress; clothing, clothes (3)]
Kohlen coal
[**die Kohle, die Kohlen**]
diese Zustände these conditions
[**der Zustand, die Zustände** the condition, state (2)]
am besten best
die . . . passiert ist which happened
[**passieren** to happen (2)]
die Mutter the mother
[**die Mutter, die Mütter** (3)]
die Tränen the tears
[**die Träne, die Tränen** (3)]
das Krankenhaus the hospital
[**krank** sick, ill]
der Junge the boy
[**der Junge, die Jungen**]
du wirst . . . nicht mehr spielen können you will no longer be able to play
der Bruder the brother (4)
er ist . . . gestorben he died
[**sterben, er stirbt, starb, ist gestorben** to die (3)]
heute nachmittag this afternoon
der Kleine the little boy
der Mantel the overcoat
[**der Mantel, die Mäntel** (3)]

die Kälte the cold
schlimm bad (2)
nicht einmal not even (3)
das Holz the wood (3)
damit with it
die Suppe the soup
[**die Suppe, die Suppen** (3)]
kochen to cook (3)
wer whoever
beobachten to observe (3)
die Wälder the woods
[**der Wald, die Wälder** (3)]
wandern to wander (3)
Zweige branches
[**der Zweig, die Zweige** (2)]

und mehrere Familien oft in einer einzigen Wohnung leben mußten. Die Zimmer waren kalt, und die Menschen froren, weil sie weder warme Kleider noch Kohlen hatten. Wie schrecklich diese Zustände waren, sehen Sie am besten aus der folgenden kurzen Geschichte, die damals wirklich passiert ist: Eine Mutter kam mit Tränen in den Augen aus dem Krankenhaus zurück und sagte zu ihrem kleinen Jungen: „Hansel, du wirst mit deinem kleinen Bruder nun nicht mehr spielen können. Er ist heute nachmittag gestorben."—„Das ist fein, Mama!" sagte der Kleine; „dann kann ich jetzt seinen Mantel tragen."

Kälte ist schlimm genug; aber die Leute hatten nicht einmal genug Holz, um damit auf dem Ofen eine dünne Suppe zu kochen. Wer damals in Deutschland lebte, konnte beobachten, wie die Menschen jeden Tag in die Wälder wanderten, um dort Zweige zu suchen, die sie dann unter dem Arm oder auf dem Rücken nach Haus trugen. Um nicht vor Hunger zu sterben, sammelten sie während des Tages Nüsse und Beeren und waren glücklich über jedes Stück Obst, das auf den Landstraßen von den Bäumen gefallen war. Und in der Nacht gingen sie auf die Äcker und gruben mit ihren Fingern in der Erde, in der Hoff-

---

der Rücken the back
[**der Rücken, die Rücken** (3)]
vor Hunger from hunger
[**der Hunger** (3)]
sammeln to gather
Nüsse nuts
[**die Nuß, die Nüsse** (3)]
Beeren berries
[**die Beere, die Beeren** the berry]
glücklich happy (3)
das Obst the fruit (2)
die Landstraße the highway (2)
die Äcker the fields
[**der Acker, die Äcker** the (cultivated) field]
gruben dug
[**graben, er gräbt, grub, hat gegraben** to dig (3)]
die Erde the earth (3)
die Hoffnung the hope

die Bauern the farmers
[**der Bauer, die Bauern** the farmer, peasant (2)]

bedeuten to mean (3)
dafür for it
die Lebensmittelgeschäfte the food stores
[**die Lebensmittel** the food, provisions]
bekamen nicht did not get
[**bekommen, bekam, hat bekommen** to get, to receive (3)]
ja sogar indeed, even
berühmt famous (3)
das Bier the beer
nach Wasser . . . schmeckte tasted . . . of water
[**das Wasser** the water (3)]
[**schmecken** to taste (2)]
was für ein what a
nicht einmal not even
bei einem . . . Glas over a . . . glass
das Bier the beer (2)

gab es . . . überhaupt nicht zu kaufen could not be bought at all
Apfelsinen oranges
[**die Apfelsine, die Apfelsinen** the orange]
amerikanisch American (3)
Zigarren cigars
[**die Zigarre, die Zigarren** (2)]
Zigaretten cigarettes
[**die Zigarette, die Zigaretten** (3)]
Damenstrümpfe ladies' stockings
[**der Strumpf, die Strümpfe** the stocking; sock (3)]
der Tee the tea (3)
selbst even
richtig real
die Seife the soap
der Schwarzmarkt the black market
[**schwarz** black (3)]
[**der Markt, die Märkte** the market (3)]
enorm enormous (3)
das Wunder the wonder (2)
manche Leute some people
auf den Gedanken kamen got the idea
ins Ausland abroad
[**das Ausland** the foreign country (3)]
die Lebensmittel the foodstuffs (2)
Waren goods
[**die Ware, die Waren** the merchandise, goods (3)]
fehlen to be missing (3)
verboten prohibited
[**verbieten, verbot, hat verboten** to forbid, to prohibit]

nung, ein paar Kartoffeln zu finden, welche die Bauern vielleicht vergessen hatten.

Es gab zwar genug Geld, aber was bedeutete Geld, wenn man fast nichts dafür kaufen konnte? Die Lebensmittelgeschäfte standen leer, die Kinder bekamen nicht genug Milch, ja sogar das berühmte deutsche Bier war mit der Zeit so dünn geworden, daß es jetzt mehr nach Wasser als nach Bier schmeckte. Was für ein Leben, wenn ein Mann nicht einmal am Abend die Mühen des Tages bei einem guten Glas Bier vergessen konnte!

Viele Dinge gab es in den Geschäften überhaupt nicht zu kaufen. Apfelsinen, amerikanische Zigarren und Zigaretten, gute Damenstrümpfe, Kaffee und Tee oder selbst richtige Seife waren nur auf dem Schwarzmarkt zu finden. Doch zu welch enormen Preisen! Kein Wunder, daß in einer solchen Zeit manche Leute auf den Gedanken kamen, ins Ausland zu fahren und von dort Lebensmittel oder andere Waren nach Deutschland zu bringen, die zu Haus fehlten. Das war zwar verboten und deshalb gefährlich; aber was konnte schon passieren? Wenn der Zoll die Waren entdeckte, mußte man Strafe zahlen, oder der Zollbeamte nahm sie einfach weg. Das Schlimmste, was geschehen konnte, war, daß man vor Gericht zu erscheinen hatte und vielleicht auf zwei oder drei Monate ins Gefängnis mußte. Aber im Gefängnis bekam man auf jeden Fall zu essen, und das kostete nichts.

---

gefährlich dangerous
konnte schon passieren could actually happen
der Zoll the customs (people) (3)
entdecken to discover (3)
die Strafe the fine
[**die Strafe, die Strafen** the punishment; fine, penalty (3)]
zahlen to pay (3)
der Zollbeamte the customs official (3)
nahm sie . . . weg took them away
[**weg-nehmen** to take away]
vor Gericht in court
[**das Gericht, die Gerichte** the court, tribunal (2)]
erscheinen to appear (3)
und . . . mußte and had to go
auf zwei . . . Monate for two . . . months
auf jeden Fall in any case

die Schweiz Switzerland
gehören to belong (3)
gelitten hatten had suffered
[**leiden, litt, hat gelitten** to suffer (2)]
und denen es . . . gut ging and which were . . . doing well
[**es geht mir gut** I am fine, I am doing all right]
darum therefore (2)
die Schweiz Switzerland (2)
blühen flourish
[**blühen** to bloom, to blossom; to flourish (2)]
der Schmuggel smuggling (2)

wenige a few
Weihnachten Christmas
stieg . . . in boarded
[**steigen, stieg, ist gestiegen** to climb (3)]
das Abteil the compartment
[**das Abteil, die Abteile** the compartment]
trat ein entered
[**ein-treten** to enter]
das Gepäck the baggage
bestehen aus to consist of
[**bestehen, bestand, hat bestanden**]
die Handtasche the handbag
die Hutschachtel the hat box
[**der Hut, die Hüte** the hat (2)]
[**die Schachtel, die Schachteln** the box]
gestatten Sie allow me
[**gestatten** to allow, to permit]
das Abteil the compartment
[**das Abteil, die Abteile** (2)]
sprang auf jumped up
[**auf-springen** to jump up]
[**springen, sprang, ist gesprungen** (2)]
die Hutschachtel the hatbox (2)
[**die Schachtel, die Schachteln** the box (2)]
das Gepäcknetz the luggage rack
[**das Gepäck** the baggage, luggage (2)]
[**das Netz, die Netze** the net]
danke thank you
höflich politely (3)
ich behalte . . . lieber I'd rather keep

nervös nervous (2)
die . . . Reisenden the . . . travelers
[**der Reisende, die Reisenden** the traveler]
wird nicht auf den Gedanken kommen will not get the idea
hoffen wir das Beste let's hope for the best
kaum hardly (3)

Die Schweiz gehörte damals zu den wenigen Ländern Europas, die während des Krieges nicht so viel gelitten hatten und denen es darum jetzt ziemlich gut ging. Hier fand man alles, hier, zwischen der Schweiz und Deutschland, blühte deshalb der Schmuggel, und hier fängt unsere Geschichte nun endlich an.

2.

Wenige Tage vor Weihnachten stieg kurz vor der Grenze eine schlanke junge Dame in den Zug nach Frankfurt. In einem Abteil waren noch zwei Plätze frei. Sie trat ein. Ihr Gepäck bestand nur aus zwei Stücken: einer Handtasche und einer alten Hutschachtel. „Gestatten Sie", sagte einer der Herren im Abteil und sprang auf—denn die Dame war nicht nur jung, sondern auch hübsch—„gestatten Sie", und wollte ihr helfen, die Hutschachtel in das Gepäcknetz zu heben.—„Nein, danke", entgegnete die junge Dame höflich; „ich glaube, ich behalte meine Sachen lieber bei mir."

Das Fräulein schien etwas nervös zu sein. „Aha!" dachten die anderen Reisenden; „sie hat wahrscheinlich in der Schweiz einen Hut gekauft und ihn in die alte Hutschachtel gesteckt, und jetzt denkt sie, der Zollbeamte wird nicht auf den Gedanken kommen, daß in der alten Schachtel ein neuer Hut steckt. Nun, hoffen wir das Beste!"

Kaum hatte das Fräulein sich gesetzt und die Schachtel zwischen ihre Beine auf den Boden gestellt, als ein dicker Herr an der Tür des Abteils erschien. Da er noch einen freien Platz

---

der Boden the floor (3)
dick fat
[**dick** thick, fat (3)]
da er since he

trat . . . ein entered
[**ein-treten** to enter (2)]
der Schaffner the conductor
[**der Schaffner, die Schaffner** the conductor]
geholfen hatte had helped
[**helfen, er hilft, half, hat geholfen** to help (2)]
der Koffer the suitcase (3)
das Gepäcknetz the luggage rack (2)
[**das Netz, die Netze** the net (2)]
dem es nicht schlecht geht who is not badly off
blickten mit Neid auf looked with envy at
[**blicken** to look, to glance]
[**der Neid** the envy]
fest solid
[**fest** fast, firm, solid (3)]
die . . . Backen the . . . cheeks
[**die Backe, die Backen** the cheek (2)]
fett fat
das Doppelkinn the double chin
[**doppelt** double (3)]
[**das Kinn** the chin]
zu leiden gehabt hatte had had to suffer

ließ sich . . . nieder sat down
[**nieder-lassen** to let down]
[**nieder** down (3)]
atmend breathing
der Sitz the seat
[**der Sitz, die Sitze** the seat (3)]
er mußte gelaufen sein he must have run
[**laufen, er läuft, lief, ist gelaufen** to run (3)]
erreichen to reach
nachdem er . . . hervorgezogen after he had pulled out
[**hervor-ziehen** to pull out]
[**hervor** out (2)]
[**ziehen, zog, ist/hat gezogen** to pull, draw; to move (3)]
das Taschentuch the handkerchief
[**das Taschentuch, die Taschentücher**]
damit with it
der Schweiß the perspiration (3)
wischen to wipe (3)
strich er he stroked
[**streichen, strich, hat gestrichen** to stroke, pass, move, spread (2)]
die Brusttasche the breast pocket
[**die Brust** the breast (3)]
zündete . . . an lit
[**an-zünden** to light (2)]
blies blew
[**blasen, er bläst, blies, hat geblasen** to blow (2)]

sah, trat auch er ein, dankte dem Schaffner, der ihm geholfen hatte, grüßte freundlich und hob zwei schwere Koffer in das Gepäcknetz. „Ohne Zweifel ein Mann, dem es nicht schlecht geht", dachten die anderen Reisenden und blickten mit Neid auf die festen Schuhe, die teuren Kleider, die roten Backen und das fette Doppelkinn, an dem ein kleiner Ziegenbart hing. Es war klar, daß der Mann nie Hunger zu leiden gehabt hatte.

Der Herr ließ sich schwer atmend auf den leeren Sitz nieder. Er mußte gelaufen sein und den Zug im letzten Augenblick erreicht haben. Nachdem er ein Taschentuch hervorgezogen und sich damit den Schweiß von der Stirn gewischt hatte, strich er sich über den Ziegenbart, holte eine Zigarre aus der Brusttasche, bat seinen Nachbarn um Feuer, zündete die Zigarre an, blies mehrere Ringe in die Luft und lächelte zufrieden. „Feine Zigarre", dachten die Herren im Abteil, als ihnen der Rauch in die Nase stieg; „dem Mann geht's gut." Auf einmal blickte der Herr mit dem Ziegenbart auf, steckte die Nase in die Luft, und sein Gesicht verlor seinen freundlichen Ausdruck. „Hat hier jemand Kaffee?" sagte er; „ich rieche Kaffee."–„Stimmt", sagten die anderen. Sie brauchten die Nase nicht in die Luft zu stecken, denn jetzt roch das ganze Abteil nach Kaffee. Da es erst zu riechen begonnen hatte, nachdem die junge Dame ins Abteil getreten war, starrten jetzt alle auf die Hutschachtel, die das

---

Ringe rings
[**der Ring, die Ringe** the ring]
der Rauch the smoke
die Nase the nose (3)
dem Mann geht's gut the man is doing all right
auf einmal suddenly
blickte . . . auf looked up
[**auf-blicken** to look up]
[**blicken** to look, to glance (2)]
der Ausdruck the expression (2)
stimmt that's right
[**stimmen** to be right, to be correct]
roch . . . nach smelled of
[**riechen, roch, hat gerochen** to smell (3)]
da es erst . . . begonnen hatte since it had only begun
[**beginnen, begann, hat begonnen** to begin, to start (3)]
starren to stare (3)

die Knie the knees
[**das Knie, die Knie** the knee]
der Rock the skirt
blaß pale
ich habe . . . versteckt I hid
[**verstecken** to hide (3)]
das Pfund the pound
die Unterwäsche the underwear (2)
von . . . wegfuhr left
[**weg-fahren** to depart, to leave]
[**fahren, er fährt, fuhr, ist gefahren** to go, to drive, to ride (3)]
habe ich . . . versprochen I promised
[**versprechen, er verspricht, versprach, hat versprochen** to promise]
zu Weihnachten for Christmas (2)
mitgebracht brought along
[**mit-bringen** to bring along (2)]
ist doch is, after all
richtig real
selbst wenn even if
die Sahne the cream
der Zucker the sugar
die Hundenase the dog's nose
na well
ist der Zollinspektor . . . erkältet the customs inspector has a cold
[**der Inspektor** the inspector]
[**erkältet sein** to have a cold]
[**sich erkälten** to catch a cold (2)]

erreichen to reach (2)
hielt stopped
die Paßkontrolle the passport control
[**der Paß, die Pässe** the passport (2)]
[**die Kontrolle** the control]
die Zollkontrolle the customs inspection
der Schaffner the conductor (2)
der Bahnsteig the platform
damit so that
ihre Knie her knees
[**das Knie, die Knie** the knee (2)]
verzollen to declare (3)
alle schwiegen all were silent
[**schweigen, schwieg, hat geschwiegen** to be silent (3)]
streng stern
[**streng** severe, stern, strict]
wandte sich turned
[**wenden, wandte, hat gewandt** to turn (3)]
der Dame stieg das Blut ins Gesicht the blood rushed to the lady's face
[**das Blut** the blood (2)]
stimmt das? is that correct?

Fräulein zwischen den Beinen hielt. Jeder konnte sehen, wie ihr die Knie unter dem Rock zitterten. Sie war ganz blaß geworden. „Mein Gott, was tue ich jetzt?“ rief sie. „Ich habe zwei Pfund Kaffee unter meiner Unterwäsche in der Hutschachtel versteckt und dachte, daß niemand etwas merken wird. Als ich von Frankfurt wegfuhr, habe ich meinen Eltern etwas Kaffee zu Weihnachten versprochen und habe ihn jetzt mitgebracht. Weihnachten ohne eine gute Tasse Kaffee ist doch kein richtiges Weihnachten, selbst wenn man keine Sahne und keinen Zucker hat. Kaffee ist Kaffee und schmeckt auch gut ohne Zucker und Sahne. Und der Zoll ist so teuer! Ich kann nur hoffen, daß der Beamte nichts merken wird.“—„Hoffen kostet nichts, Fräulein“, sagte der dicke Herr mit dem Ziegenbart; „aber man braucht keine Hundenase zu haben, um zu riechen, daß jemand im Abteil Kaffee hat. Na, vielleicht ist der Zollinspektor heute erkältet. Man kann nie wissen.“

3.

Der Zug hatte jetzt die Grenze erreicht und hielt. „Paßkontrolle! Zollkontrolle!“ rief ein Schaffner laut auf dem Bahnsteig. Erst kam die Paßkontrolle, dann trat der Zollbeamte ins Abteil. Die Dame drückte die Beine fest an die Hutschachtel, damit der Beamte nicht sehen sollte, wie ihre Knie zitterten. „Hat jemand etwas zu verzollen?“ fragte der Zollbeamte. Seine klare und laute Stimme zeigte, daß er heute nicht erkältet war. Alle schwiegen. „Warum sagen Sie denn nichts, Fräulein?“ rief plötzlich der dicke Herr mit einem strengen Gesicht und wandte sich dann zu dem Zollbeamten. „Die Dame hier hat Kaffee. In der Hutschachtel, glaube ich.“ Der Dame stieg das Blut ins Gesicht. „Stimmt das, Fräulein?“ fragte der Beamte.— „Ja, Herr Inspe-spe-spektor“, stotterte sie; „aber sehen Sie, es ist doch jetzt bald Weihnachten, und meine armen alten Eltern

---

stottern to stutter
es ist doch after all, it is

bitte please
unterbrach interrupted
[**unterbrechen** to interrupt]
[**brechen, er bricht, brach, hat gebrochen** to break (2)]
das Pfund the pound (2)
was Sie . . . versprochen haben what you promised
[**versprechen, er verspricht, versprach, hat versprochen** to promise (2)]
interessiert mich . . . nicht does not interest me
[**interessieren** to interest (3)]
als Beamten as an official
das Recht the right
[**das Recht, die Rechte** the right (2)]
die Pflicht the duty
[**die Pflicht, die Pflichten** (2)]
wegzunehmen to take away
[**weg-nehmen** to take away (2)]
da jetzt . . . ist since it is now
streng strict
[**streng** severe, stern, strict (2)]
eigentlich actually
damit with that
der Bleistift the pencil (3)
die Brusttasche the breast pocket (2)
rechnen to figure
[**rechnen** to calculate, to figure (3)]
das Quittungsheft the receipt book
[**die Quittung, die Quittungen** the receipt (2)]
[**das Heft, die Hefte** the notebook (2)]
auf jeden Fall in any case
dreizehn thirteen
fünfzig fifty (3)
der Pfennig the pfennig
[**der Pfennig, die Pfennige** the pfennig, penny (3)]
bitte please (2)
sauer sour (3)
sonst noch jemand anyone else
[**sonst** otherwise, else, usual (3)]
danke schön thank you very much

fuhr ab left
[**ab-fahren** to leave]
sah . . . hinaus looked out
[**hinaus-sehen** to look out]
na well (2)
rollen to roll (2)
hinunter down
vor Ärger with vexation
[**der Ärger** the annoyance, vexation, anger, irritation (3)]

haben mich gebeten . . ."—„Machen Sie die Schachtel bitte auf!" unterbrach sie der Inspektor; „wieviel haben Sie?"—„Nur zwei Pfund, Herr Inspektor. Aber ich muß doch meinen armen alten Eltern etwas zu Weihnachten . . ."—„Was Sie Ihren Eltern versprochen haben, interessiert mich als Beamten nicht", erwiderte der Inspektor. „Zwei Pfund Kaffee, sagen Sie. Sie wissen wahrscheinlich, daß ich nicht nur das Recht, sondern sogar die Pflicht habe, Ihnen den Kaffee wegzunehmen und Sie Strafe zahlen zu lassen, weil Sie nichts gesagt haben. Aber"—und seine Stimme war jetzt etwas freundlicher—„da jetzt bald Weihnachten ist, brauchen wir vielleicht nicht ganz so streng zu sein, wie wir eigentlich sollten." Und damit zog er Bleistift und Papier aus der Brusttasche, rechnete eine Weile, nahm sein Quittungsheft und schrieb die Quittung. „Den Zoll müssen Sie auf jeden Fall zahlen. Dreizehn Mark und fünfzig Pfennig, bitte." Das Fräulein machte ein saures Gesicht und bezahlte. „Hat sonst noch jemand etwas zu verzollen?" fragte der Beamte und wandte sich an die anderen Reisenden. „Nein? Danke schön." Mit einem bösen Blick auf den Herrn mit dem Ziegenbart verließ er das Abteil

Der Zug fuhr ab. Man war in Deutschland. Der dicke Herr sah lächelnd aus dem Fenster hinaus. „Na, wissen Sie . . ." begann das Fräulein; aber jetzt rollten ihr die Tränen die Backen hinunter, und sie konnte vor Ärger und Zorn nicht weitersprechen.—„Na! Na! Es war ja nicht so schlimm", sagte ihr Nachbar, ein freundlicher älterer Herr, und klopfte ihr auf die Schulter; „schließlich haben Sie ja noch Ihren Kaffee, und das ist doch die Hauptsache."—„Das arme Ding!" rief plötzlich

---

der Zorn the rage (3)
weiter-sprechen go on speaking
ein . . . älterer Herr an elderly gentleman
klopfte patted
die Schulter the shoulder
[**die Schulter, die Schultern** (2)]
schließlich after all
[**schließlich** finally; after all (2)]
die Hauptsache the main thing (2)

wie kann man nur how *can* one
gemein mean
[**gemein** common; mean (2)]
es gibt überhaupt there is simply
die Entschuldigung the excuse
dafür for that
die geringste Absicht the slightest intention
[**gering** small, little, slight]
[**die Absicht, die Absichten** the intention (2)]
mich zu entschuldigen to apologize
[**(sich) entschuldigen** to beg pardon, to apologize (2)]
an-zünden to light (2)
gestatten Sie allow me
[**gestatten** to allow, to permit (2)]
unangenehm unpleasant
die Situation the situation (3)
da jeder wußte since everybody knew
danach roch smelled of it
der Zucker the sugar (2)
die Sahne the cream (2)
leider unfortunately (3)
ein paar Apfelsinen a few oranges
[**die Apfelsine, die Apfelsinen** (2)]
richtig real
die Seife the soap (2)
als Weihnachtsgeschenk as a Christmas present
wünschen to wish (3)
direkt directly
bitte sehr! help yourselves
er . . . herumreichte he passed around
[**herum** around (3)]
[**reichen** to pass, to hand; to be sufficient (3)]
sicher safely
erst nachher only afterward
[**nachher** afterward, later (3)]
ein bißchen a little
abergläubisch superstitious

ein anderer ganz laut und blickte böse auf den Herrn mit dem Ziegenbart; „wie kann man nur so gemein sein? Es gibt überhaupt keine Entschuldigung dafür."—„Ich habe auch nicht die geringste Absicht, mich zu entschuldigen", sagte der dicke Herr, der sich gerade eine zweite Zigarre angezündet hatte. Er stand auf, hob einen seiner Koffer aus dem Gepäcknetz und öffnete ihn. „Gestatten Sie!" sagte er zu der jungen Dame. „Hier!" Und er nahm zwei Pfund Kaffee aus dem Koffer. „Hier. Das ist für die unangenehme Situation, in die ich Sie gebracht habe. Da jeder wußte, daß Sie Kaffee hatten und das ganze Abteil danach roch, wollte ich den Inspektor nicht meine eigenen fünfzig Pfund finden lassen.—Und Zucker haben Sie auch nicht zu Hause? Hier. Ein Pfund Zucker, damit Sie zu Weihnachten den Kaffee mit Ihren Eltern süß trinken können. Sahne habe ich leider nicht, aber was sagen Sie zu ein paar Apfelsinen und einem richtigen Stück Seife als Weihnachtsgeschenk für Sie selbst?—Wünschen die Herren vielleicht eine gute Zigarre? Kommt direkt aus Amerika. Bitte sehr!—Sehen Sie", sagte er, während er die Zigarren im Abteil herumreichte, „jedesmal, wenn es mir gelungen ist, meine fünfzig Pfund Kaffee sicher über die Grenze zu bringen, bekommt jeder Herr im Abteil eine Zigarre. Aber erst nachher, nicht vorher. Ich bin nämlich ein bißchen abergläubisch."

PIK AS

[5B]

NOTES

REVIEW OF STRONG AND IRREGULAR VERBS USED IN STORY 5A

bestehen	bestand	bestanden	*to consist*
frieren	fror	gefroren	*to freeze, to be cold*
leiden	litt	gelitten	*to suffer*
verbieten	verbot	verboten	*to forbid*

IDIOMS FOR REVIEW

das taten sie nun seit Monaten they had been doing this for months
zu Mittag at noon
einige Stunden lang for several hours
ich interessiere mich für etwas I am interested in something
  ich bin an etwas interessiert I am interested in something
es ist mir recht it's all right with me
Glück haben to be lucky
es tut mir leid I am sorry
  er tut mir leid I am sorry for him
  sie tut mir leid I am sorry for her
  sie tun mir leid I am sorry for them
so etwas something like that
ein Gedanke fuhr ihm durch den Kopf a thought flashed through his head
am Anfang in the beginning
zur Arbeit gehen to go to work
Hunger (Durst) haben to be hungry (thirsty)
spätestens at the latest
am nächsten Morgen (Tag) the next morning (day)
alles in allem all in all
schade! that's a pity (2)

Pik As the ace of spades

mit schnellen Schritten with quick steps
[**der Schritt, die Schritte** the step, pace (2)]
das Bahnhofsrestaurant the station restaurant
[**der Bahnhof, die Bahnhöfe** the railroad station (2)]
[**das Restaurant, die Restaurants** the restaurant]
wurde er zum Mörder he became a murderer
[**der Mörder, die Mörder** the murderer (2)]
um halb sechs at half past five
den Bahnsteig entlangrannte ran along the platform
[**der Bahnsteig, die Bahnsteige** the platform (2)]
[**entlang-rennen** to run along]
[**rennen, rannte, ist gerannt** to run]

der Buchhalter the accountant (3)
bei einer . . . Münchener Firma at a . . . Munich firm
[**München** Munich]
[**die Firma, die Firmen** the firm]
jedoch however (2)
etwa about (2)
außerhalb outside
die Kleinstadt the small town
vor ein paar Monaten a few months ago
das Häuschen the little house
zwang ihn forced him
[**zwingen, zwang, hat gezwungen** to force (2)]
freilich to be sure
eine Stunde lang for an hour
außerhalb outside (2)
ruhig quiet (3)
die . . . Fahrt the . . . ride (2)
gefiel ihm sogar he liked even
[**gefallen, er gefällt, gefiel, hat gefallen** to please]
zuerst at first (3)
solange as long as
am Anfang in the beginning
[**der Anfang** the beginning]
hatte . . . gelesen had read
[**lesen, er liest, las, hat gelesen** to read (3)]
das Buch the book
[**das Buch, die Bücher** the book (3)]
hatte er . . . kennengelernt he had made the acquaintance of
[**kennen-lernen** to make the acquaintance of (3)]
der Polizeiinspektor the police inspector
abends in the evening
der Halbsechsuhrzug the 5:30 train

(THREE PARTS)

Pik As

I.

Als Herr Müller mit schnellen Schritten das Bahnhofsrestaurant verließ, war er noch ein Mensch wie die meisten anderen. Eine halbe Stunde später wurde er zum Mörder. Aber um halb sechs, als er den Bahnsteig entlangrannte und auf den Zug sprang, wußte er das noch nicht.

Herr Müller arbeitete als Buchhalter bei einer großen Münchener Firma. Er wohnte jedoch nicht in München selbst, sondern etwa eine Stunde außerhalb in einer Kleinstadt, wo er sich vor ein paar Monaten ein Häuschen gekauft hatte. Das zwang ihn freilich, jeden Tag zweimal etwa eine Stunde lang mit dem Zug zu fahren und so eine Menge Zeit zu verlieren. Aber das Leben außerhalb Münchens war angenehm, ruhig und billig, und die lange Fahrt am Morgen und Abend gefiel ihm sogar viel besser, als er zuerst gedacht hatte. Solange er am Anfang im Zug noch niemanden gekannt hatte, war er allein gefahren und hatte die Zeitung oder ein Buch gelesen. Später hatte er drei Herren kennengelernt, zwei Geschäftsleute und einen Polizeiinspektor, die auch jeden Morgen um dieselbe Zeit nach München zur Arbeit fuhren und abends den Halbsechsuhrzug nahmen. Die vier Männer waren bald Freunde geworden, und als einer von ihnen vorschlug, während der

---

vorschlug suggested
[**vor-schlagen** to suggest, to propose]
[**schlagen, er schlägt, schlug, hat geschlagen** to beat, to strike (2)]

sich . . . zu treffen to meet
[**treffen, er trifft** to meet, to encounter (3)]
morgens in the morning
abends in the evening (2)
der Eisenbahnwagen the coach
[**die Eisenbahn, die Eisenbahnen** the railroad (2)]
[**der Wagen, die Wagen** the carriage, wagon, coach, car (3)]
das taten sie nun seit they had been doing this for
bisher until now (2)

hatte . . . verlassen had left
das Büro the office
[**das Büro, die Büros** the office]
hungrig hungry (3)
zu Mittag at noon
[**der Mittag** noon (3)]
irgendwo somewhere
auf der Bank at the bank
[**die Bank, die Banken** the bank]
der Teil the part
[**der Teil, die Teile** the part (2)]
das Monatsgehalt the monthly salary
[**das Gehalt, die Gehälter** the salary]
dauern to last (3)
das Büro the office (2)
lassen . . . vergessen let . . . forget
einige Stunden lang for a few hours
der Magen the stomach
der Durst the thirst (2)
die Abfahrt the departure
absolut absolutely
er hatte . . . bestellt he had ordered
[**bestellen** to order (3)]
das Bahnhofsrestaurant the station restaurant
[**das Restaurant, die Restaurants** the restaurant (2)]
die Butter the butter (3)
der Schinken the ham (2)
der Kellner the waiter
[**der Kellner, die Kellner** (3)]
sich zu beeilen to hurry
[**sich beeilen** to hurry]
die Bahnhofsuhr the station clock
bewegte sich schon was already moving
[**bewegen** to move (2)]
er rannte he ran
[**rennen, rannte, ist gerannt** to run (2)]
auf den fahrenden Zug on the moving train
ärgerlich annoying (2)
bestimmt certainly

Fahrt Karten zu spielen, hatten sie beschlossen, sich morgens und abends in dem gleichen Abteil eines bestimmten Eisenbahnwagens zu treffen und zusammen zu spielen. Das taten sie nun seit Monaten, und bisher hatte keiner von ihnen einen einzigen Tag gefehlt. An dem Abend, an dem sie zum ersten Mal nicht zusammen spielten, wurde Herr Müller zum Mörder.

An diesem Abend hatte Herr Müller zur gleichen Zeit wie immer sein Büro verlassen und war schnell zum Bahnhof gegangen. Er war hungrig. Zu Mittag hatte ihm die Zeit gefehlt, schnell irgendwo etwas zu essen, weil er auf der Bank gewesen war. Heute war der Erste des Monats, und er hatte sich auf der Bank einen Teil seines Monatsgehaltes geholt; aber wegen der vielen Leute dort hatte es so lange gedauert, bis er sein Geld bekam, daß er wieder zur Arbeit ins Büro zurück mußte, ohne gegessen zu haben. Nun, dreihundert Mark sind eine hübsche Summe Geld und lassen einen Menschen einige Stunden lang seinen leeren Magen vergessen. Jetzt aber, um fünf Uhr, hatte er einen solchen Hunger und Durst, daß er vor der Abfahrt des Zuges absolut etwas essen und trinken mußte. Er hatte im Bahnhofsrestaurant Bier, Brot, Butter und gekochten Schinken bestellt und den Kellner gebeten, sich zu beeilen. Aber der Kellner war so langsam gewesen, daß die Bahnhofsuhr schon halb sechs zeigte, als Herr Müller die Rechnung bezahlte. Der Zug bewegte sich schon, als er auf den Bahnsteig trat. Er rannte so schnell er konnte, und es gelang ihm noch, den letzten Wagen zu erreichen und auf den fahrenden Zug zu springen. Nun, er war wenigstens nicht zu spät gekommen. Aber wie ärgerlich, daß er jetzt allein war und mit seinen Freunden nicht Karten spielen konnte! Die saßen in einem anderen Wagen, warteten auf ihn und fragten sich bestimmt, warum er nicht kam. Und ärgerten sich natürlich, daß sie ohne ihn nicht spielen konnten, weil er immer die Karten bei sich trug. Nun, es war nicht seine Schuld, daß man in diesem alten Zug nicht von einem Wagen in den

---

von einem Wagen in den anderen konnte could go from one coach to the next

zu schade too bad (2)
  nicht einmal not even

ihm gegenüber opposite him
  die Zeitschrift the magazine
    [**die Zeitschrift, die Zeitschriften** the magazine]
  aufgeblickt hatte had looked up
    [**auf-blicken** to look up (2)]
  stürzte plunged
    [**stürzen** to fall, to rush, to plunge (2)]
elegant elegant (2)
  die Jacke the jacket
    [**die Jacke, die Jacken**]
  die Hose the trousers (3)
  der Stoff the material
  braun brown (3)
  die Qualität the quality (3)
  die Armbanduhr the wrist watch
  der Goldring the gold ring
    [**der Ring, die Ringe** the ring (2)]
  das Vermögen the fortune (2)
ein bißchen a little
  der Geschmack the taste
er mochte auch . . . nicht nor did he like
  der Spitzbart the pointed beard
überhaupt in general
nach seinem Geschmack according to his taste
    [**der Geschmack** the taste (2)]

ein paar Minuten a few minutes
    [**die Minute, die Minuten** the minute (3)]
  sich langweilen to be bored
ihm gegenüber opposite him (2)
  das Kartenspiel the card game
    [**das Spiel, die Spiele** the play, game]
  war Herrn Müller jeder gut genug anyone was good enough for Mr. Müller
entschuldigen Sie excuse me
    [**entschuldigen** to excuse (3)]
  stören to disturb
legte . . . weg put aside
    [**weg-legen** to put away, to put aside]
  die Zeitschrift the magazine (2)
  mit Vergnügen with pleasure
    [**das Vergnügen, die Vergnügen** the pleasure (3)]
mischen to shuffle
    [**mischen** to mix; to shuffle (2)]
um wieviel for how much

anderen konnte.—Zu schade, daß er nicht einmal eine Zeitung oder ein Buch mitgebracht hatte!

Schwer atmend ließ er sich auf den Sitz fallen und sah, daß er nicht allein im Abteil war. Ihm gegenüber saß ein junger Herr, der eine Zeitschrift las und nur kurz aufgeblickt hatte, als er so plötzlich ins Abteil stürzte. Herr Müller beobachtete den Mann. Die elegante Jacke und die Hose waren aus feinstem Stoff, die braunen Schuhe von bester Qualität; die Armbanduhr war sicher sehr teuer gewesen, und der dicke Goldring hatte ohne Zweifel ein Vermögen gekostet. Alles in allem war der Mann ein bißchen z u elegant für Herrn Müllers Geschmack. Er mochte auch den kleinen Spitzbart nicht. Herr Müller war überhaupt gegen Bärte. Nun, jeder nach seinem Geschmack, dachte er.

2.

Nach ein paar Minuten begann Herr Müller sich zu langweilen. Der Herr ihm gegenüber gefiel ihm nicht, aber für ein kleines Kartenspiel war Herrn Müller jeder gut genug. Er zog die Karten aus der Tasche. „Entschuldigen Sie, wenn ich Sie störe", begann er; „aber darf ich Sie fragen, ob Sie vielleicht an einem kleinen Kartenspiel interessiert sind?"— „Karten?" erwiderte der andere und legte sofort seine Zeitschrift weg; „mit Vergnügen!" Herr Müller begann, die Karten zu mischen. „Um wieviel wollen wir spielen?" fragte er.—„Oh, vielleicht zwanzig Mark das Spiel, wenn es Ihnen recht ist", entgegnete der andere.—„Z-z-zwanzig Mark?—G-g-gut", stotterte Herr Müller, der in seinem ganzen Leben nur um Pfennige gespielt hatte. Aber er konnte jetzt nicht nein sagen. Und

---

das Spiel the game
  [**das Spiel, die Spiele** (2)]
 wenn es Ihnen recht ist if it's all right with you
  [**es ist mir recht** it is all right with me; I agree]
stottern to stutter (2)
 um Pfennige for pennies

keine Angst zu haben to have no fear
[**Angst haben** to be afraid]
[**die Angst** the fear, anxiety (3)]
ein geübter Spieler a practiced player
[**üben** to practice, to exercise]
[**der Spieler, die Spieler** the player]

die Pause the pause
[**die Pause, die Pausen** the pause; intermission]
der Meister the master (2)
hatte er nur Glück? was he only lucky?
[**Glück haben** to be lucky]
[**das Glück** the luck, fortune, happiness (3)]
er griff he reached
[**greifen, griff, hat gegriffen** to seize, to take hold of (2)]
das Taschentuch the handkerchief
[**das Taschentuch, die Taschentücher** the handkerchief (2)]
stieß auf encountered
[**stoßen, er stößt, stieß, hat gestoßen** to push, to thrust]
hart hard (2)
der Gegenstand the object
[**der Gegenstand, die Gegenstände** the object; subject; matter; topic (2)]
der Revolver the revolver
heute nachmittag this afternoon
die Bank the bank
[**die Bank, die Banken** the bank (2)]
zog . . . heraus drew . . . out
[**heraus-ziehen** to pull out]
die Bank the bench
[**die Bank, die Bänke** the bench]
trocknen to dry (3)
überrascht surprised
[**überraschen** to surprise (3)]
etwas gezwungen in a somewhat forced fashion
[**zwingen, zwang, hat gezwungen** to force (3)]
der Gangster the gangster
geladen loaded
[**laden, er lädt, lud, hat geladen** to load; to invite]
nicht einmal not even
wir wohnen nämlich you see, we live
ist es . . . vorgekommen it happened
[**vor-kommen** to happen, to occur]
fürchtet sich is afraid
als sonst than usual
damit so that
nicken to nod (2)

warum sollte er nein sagen, dachte er. Der Mann schien Geld zu haben, und wenn er es auf diese Weise verlieren wollte, dann war es seine eigene Schuld. Er selbst brauchte keine Angst zu haben; er war ein geübter Spieler und verlor nur selten.

Sie begannen zu spielen. Kein Spiel dauerte länger als ein oder zwei Minuten; eins folgte dem anderen ohne Pause. Nach etwa zehn Minuten hatte Herr Müller hundert Mark verloren. Er hatte seinen Meister gefunden. Es war kein Zweifel, daß der andere wirklich spielen konnte. Oder hatte er nur Glück? Herr Müller wurde nervös. Er griff in die Tasche und suchte nach seinem Taschentuch, um sich den Schweiß von der Stirn zu wischen. Seine zitternde Hand stieß auf einen harten Gegenstand, den er ganz vergessen hatte. Es war ein Revolver, den er heute nachmittag auf dem Weg von der Bank zum Büro gekauft und in die Tasche gesteckt hatte. Er zog ihn heraus, legte ihn neben sich auf die Bank und trocknete sich die Stirn. Der junge Mann blickte überrascht auf den Revolver. Herr Müller lachte etwas gezwungen. „Sie brauchen keine Angst zu haben“, sagte er; „ich bin kein Gangster. Das Ding ist zwar geladen, aber ich weiß nicht einmal, wie man damit schießt. Ich habe nur gedacht, daß es besser ist, einen Revolver im Haus zu haben. Wir wohnen nämlich am Ende der Stadt. In den letzten paar Wochen ist es mehrere Male vorgekommen, daß Diebe versucht haben, während des Tages in einige Häuser zu dringen. Meine Frau ist den ganzen Tag allein zu Haus und fürchtet sich jetzt natürlich noch mehr als sonst, und so habe ich heute einen Revolver gekauft, damit sie sich etwas sicherer fühlt. Sie wissen ja, wie die Frauen sind.“ Der andere nickte.

Sie spielten weiter. Der junge Mann gewann ein Spiel nach dem anderen. Hundertsechzig Mark, zweihundert, zweihundertvierzig Mark, und Herr Müller hatte immer noch kein einziges

---

hatte immer noch . . . gewonnen still had won
[**immer noch** still]
[**gewinnen, gewann, hat gewonnen** to win (3)]

auf-hören to stop (3)
  wenn das so weitergeht if things go on this way
zurück-gewinnen to win back
der Erfolg the result
    [**der Erfolg, die Erfolge** the success; the result]
es tut mir leid I am sorry
schade too bad (3)

verzweifelt in despair
    [**verzweifeln** to despair]
hören Sie listen
  so etwas something like that
  unter Spielern among players
    [**der Spieler, die Spieler** the player (2)]
das Monatsgehalt the monthly salary (2)
    [**das Gehalt, die Gehälter** the salary (2)]
  kann unmöglich cannot possibly
    [**unmöglich** impossible]
leihen to lend
spätestens at the latest
erstaunt in astonishment
    [**erstaunt** astonished]
so etwas something like that (2)
der Kindergarten the kindergarten
es tut mir leid I am sorry (2)
auf einmal suddenly
  direkt directly (2)
außer sich beside himself
leihen to lend (2)
  es passiert was something is going to happen
    [was = **etwas**]
Sekunden seconds
    [**die Sekunde, die Sekunden** the second]
eine geladene Feuerwaffe a loaded firearm
    [**laden, er lädt, lud, hat geladen** to load; to invite (2)]
    [**die Waffe, die Waffen** the weapon]
  gefährlich dangerous (2)
aufsprang jumped up
    [**auf-springen** to jump up (2)]
  schoß fired
    [**schießen, schoß, hat geschossen** to shoot, to fire (3)]

Spiel gewonnen. „Vielleicht sollte ich aufhören", sagte er sich; „wenn das so weitergeht, verliere ich meinen letzten Pfennig. Aber wenn ich jetzt nicht weiterspiele", dachte er sofort, „kann ich nichts zurückgewinnen." Er spielte weiter—mit dem Erfolg, daß er in den nächsten zehn Minuten sein letztes Geld verlor. „Ich muß jetzt leider aufhören", sagte er; „es tut mir leid, aber ich habe alles verloren, was ich bei mir hatte."—„Schade", entgegnete der andere und fing an, seine Zeitschrift weiterzulesen.

Herr Müller war verzweifelt. Er mußte etwas tun. „Hören Sie", sagte er; „ich weiß, daß man so etwas unter Spielern nicht tut, aber ich habe mein halbes Monatsgehalt verloren und kann unmöglich mit leeren Taschen nach Haus kommen. Darf ich Sie bitten, mir von den dreihundert Mark vielleicht hundert Mark zu leihen? Ich verspreche Ihnen, daß Sie sie spätestens nächsten Monat zurückbekommen." Der junge Mann sah ihn erstaunt an. „Mein lieber Herr", erwiderte er; „an so etwas denkt man, bevor man ein Kartenspiel anfängt, nicht nachher. Wir sind hier nicht in einem Kindergarten. Wenn Sie Geld brauchen, dann gehen Sie zu einer Bank. Es tut mir leid, aber von mir bekommen Sie nichts." Aber jetzt blickte er auf einmal nicht mehr auf Herrn Müller, sondern auf den Revolver, der ihm direkt ins Gesicht starrte. „Ich muß das Geld haben", schrie Herr Müller außer sich. „Entweder leihen Sie es mir sofort, oder es passiert was! Ich gebe Ihnen zehn Sekunden Zeit. Eins—zwei—drei . . ." Herr Müller hatte nicht die Absicht gehabt, zu schießen; aber eine geladene Feuerwaffe ist ein gefährliches Ding, mit dem man nicht spielen sollte. Als der junge Mann plötzlich aufsprang und sich auf ihn warf, machte Herr Müller die Augen zu und schoß. Alles war so schnell gegangen, daß er selbst kaum wußte, was geschehen war.

der Arzt the doctor
[**der Arzt, die Ärzte** the doctor, physician (2)]
die Mitte the middle (3)
rund round (3)
aus dem . . . floß from which . . . was flowing
[**fließen, floß, ist geflossen** to flow]
überlegen to think
wohl probably
am besten best
der Körper the body
[**der Körper, die Körper** the body (3)]
an den Armen by the arms
die Armbanduhr the wrist watch (2)
des Toten of the dead man
[**der Tote, die Toten** the dead man; the dead (3)]
fuhr flashed
er drehte . . . zurück he turned . . . back
[**drehen** to turn (3)]
und die Polizei . . . untersuchte and the police investigated
[**untersuchen** to examine, investigate]
der Mord the murder (2)

lehnte sich hinaus leaned out
[**lehnen** to lean]
aus Zufall by chance
[**der Zufall, die Zufälle** the chance, coincidence, accident (3)]
falsch wrong
[**falsch** wrong, false, incorrect (3)]
irgendein some
bei dem dichten Nebel in the thick fog
[**dicht** dense, thick (2)]
[**der Nebel** the fog, mist (3)]
inzwischen in the meantime
schob pushed
[**schieben, schob, hat geschoben** to shove, to push]
wischte er . . . ab he wiped off
die Ordnung the order (3)

ausgestiegen waren had gotten out
[**aus-steigen** to get out, to get off]
verschwand disappeared
[**verschwinden, verschwand, ist verschwunden** to disappear, to vanish (3)]

trafen sich met
[**treffen, er trifft, traf, hat getroffen** to meet, to encounter (2)]

3.

Herr Müller hatte während des Krieges genug Leichen gesehen, um zu wissen, daß hier kein Arzt mehr helfen konnte. In der Mitte der Stirn war ein rundes, schwarzes Loch, aus dem jetzt langsam etwas Blut auf den Fußboden floß. Was sollte er tun? Er überlegte einige Minuten. Es war wohl am besten, die Leiche aus dem Zug zu werfen. Als Herr Müller den Körper an den Armen zur Tür zog, fiel sein Blick auf die Armbanduhr des Toten. Ein Gedanke fuhr ihm durch den Kopf. Er drehte die Uhr eine Stunde zurück. Wenn der schwere Körper aus dem Zug fiel, mußte die Uhr stehenbleiben, und wenn man die Leiche später fand und die Polizei den Mord untersuchte, dann mußte sie glauben, daß der Mann nicht mit diesem, sondern einem früheren Zug gefahren war.

Herr Müller griff in die Brusttasche des Toten, nahm seine dreihundert Mark und steckte die dicke Brieftasche zurück. Dann öffnete er die Abteiltür und lehnte sich hinaus, um sicher zu sein, daß aus Zufall niemand im falschen Augenblick aus irgendeinem Fenster sah. Draußen war es dunkel, und bei dem dichten Nebel, der sich inzwischen auf das Land gelegt hatte, konnte niemand etwas sehen. Gut. Herr Müller schob den Toten aus dem Abteil. Dann wischte er das Blut mit dem Taschentuch vom Boden ab. Alles war in Ordnung.

Als der Zug die Stadt erreichte und hielt, wartete er eine Weile, bis er sicher war, daß die Reisenden ausgestiegen waren. Dann stieg er selbst aus und verschwand im Nebel.

Am nächsten Morgen trafen sich die vier Freunde wie gewöhnlich in ihrem Abteil. „Wo sind Sie denn gestern gewesen, Müller?“ rief Herr Schneider. „Wir wollten ohne Sie spielen und konnten es nicht, weil Sie die Karten hatten. Kann ich sie haben, damit wir anfangen können?“—„Hier“, erwiderte Müller und reichte ihm die Karten; „ich bin gestern leider zu spät zum Bahnhof gekommen und habe den nächsten Zug genommen.—Sagen Sie, haben Sie schon die Zeitung gelesen?

der Halbfünfuhrzug the 4:30 train
gestern abend last night
der Teufel the devil (4)
ermordet murdered
[**ermorden** to murder]
ein Fremder a stranger
[**der Fremde, die Fremden** the stranger (3)]
der Haufe(n) the heap
[**der Haufe(n), die Haufen** the heap, pile, quantity (2)]
erfährt man one learns
[**erfahren, er erfährt, erfuhr, hat erfahren** to learn, to find out (3)]
von dem, was of what
interessant interesting (3)
Sie wissen doch after all, you know
allerdings that is quite true
[**allerdings** to be sure]
muß man . . . geheimhalten one must keep . . . secret
[**geheim-halten** to keep secret]
[**geheim** secret (2)]
der Beruf the profession
[**der Beruf, die Berufe** the profession]
daß man mich . . . anrief that I had a call
[**an-rufen** to call (by telephone) (3)]
die Stelle the place (3)
unterbrach interrupted
[**unterbrechen, er unterbricht, unterbrach, hat unterbrochen** to interrupt (2)]
da stimmt etwas nicht there is something wrong
es fehlt . . . there is . . . missing
wohl probably (2)
ernst serious
[**ernst** earnest, serious, grave, stern (2)]
das Pik As the ace of spades (2)
wenn ich mich nicht irre if I am not mistaken
[**sich irren** to be wrong, to be mistaken (2)]
blaß pale (2)
damit by that
indem er . . . legte while putting
fest firmly
verhaftet under arrest
[**verhaften** to arrest]
gestern abend last night (2)
der Ärmel the sleeve (3)

Ich meine die Geschichte von dem Mord im Halbfünfuhrzug gestern abend." Herr Schneider nickte. „Ja", sagte er, während er die Karten mischte; „schreckliche Sache, was? Der arme Teufel. Erst ermordet und dann aus dem Zug geworfen. Es scheint ein Fremder gewesen zu sein, mit einem Haufen Geld in der Tasche. Weiß die Polizei schon, wer es war, Inspektor? Aus der Zeitung erfährt man ja immer nur die Hälfte von dem, was wirklich interessant ist. Sie wissen doch immer mehr über solche Sachen, Inspektor."—„Allerdings", entgegnete der Inspektor. „Nur muß man in meinem Beruf manchmal gewisse Dinge geheimhalten. Aber unter Freunden kann ich Ihnen sagen, daß man mich einige Stunden nach dem Mord anrief und daß ich sofort mit dem Auto zu der Stelle gefahren bin, wo man den Toten gefunden hat."—„Sagen Sie, Müller", unterbrach Herr Schneider den Polizeiinspektor, „da stimmt etwas nicht mit den Karten. Es fehlt eine Karte."—„Es fehlt eine Karte?" sagte Herr Müller. „Das verstehe ich nicht. Nun, wenn sie nicht da ist, muß sie wohl noch in meiner Tasche sein." Er griff in die Tasche. Aber er suchte nicht lange, denn plötzlich machte der Inspektor ein ernstes Gesicht. „Ich glaube, i c h habe sie", sagte er langsam und zog eine Karte aus seiner Tasche; „das Pik As, wenn ich mich nicht irre." Mit diesen Worten legte er das Pik As zu den anderen Karten. Dann wandte er sich zu Herrn Müller. „Wenn wir in München ankommen, muß ich Sie bitten, mit mir auf die Polizei zu kommen."—„Po-po-polizei?" stotterte Müller und wurde blaß. „Was meinen Sie damit? Was habe ich denn mit der Polizei zu tun?"—„Es tut mir schrecklich leid", sagte der Inspektor, indem er seine Hand fest auf Herrn Müllers Schulter legte, „aber ich muß meine Pflicht tun. Sie sind verhaftet. Sehen Sie, ich habe das Pik As gestern abend im Ärmel des Toten gefunden."

DIE VIER MUSIKER (ENDE)

[6A]

NOTES

1. As in English, the infinitive that normally accompanies a modal auxiliary is often omitted in German.

   Kannst du morgen kommen?—Nein, ich kann leider nicht.
   Warum hat er nicht das Auto seines Vaters genommen?—Warum? Er hat nicht gedurft! (He wasn't allowed to!)

2. The six modal auxiliaries have two sets of past participles. The regular participles (**gewollt, gemußt, gekonnt, gesollt, gemocht, gedurft**) are used in compound tenses when the infinitive which normally accompanies a modal auxiliary is omitted. See the last example above.

3. a. The other past participles are identical in form with the *infinitives* of the modal auxiliaries and must be used when the dependent complementary infinitive is *not* omitted. This creates the appearance of a "double infinitive," and the construction is therefore often called "double infinitive construction." Examples from Story 6B:

   Das letzte Dienstmädchen hatte sie gleich gehen lassen *müssen*. She had had to let the last maid go right away.

   Ihre Träume hatten Wünsche bleiben *müssen*. Her dreams had had to remain wishes.

   Vor vielen Jahren hatte einmal jemand das Haus kaufen *wollen*. Many years ago someone had wanted to buy the house.

   b. In dependent clauses containing a double infinitive construction, the finite verb, instead of being at the very end, *immediately precedes the infinitives.* This is the only exception to the rule that the finite verb stands last in a dependent clause. Examples from Stories 6A and 6B:

   Alles war so schnell gegangen, daß die Räuber nicht einmal ihre Jacken und Mäntel *hatten* mitnehmen können.

   Das Zimmer, das er vor einigen Stunden *hatte* verlassen müssen, war dunkel.

   Es war ihnen so gut gegangen, daß sie sogar ein Dienstmädchen *hatten* haben können.

   Die Ferien waren so kurz gewesen, daß sie und ihr Mann nie sehr weit *hatten* fortgehen können.

Sie kamen von Studentinnen, die schon lange einmal nach Amerika *hatten* fahren wollen.
Der Preis, den das junge Mädchen im voraus *hatte* bezahlen müssen . . .
Sie fuhr in eines der vielen Länder, von denen sie in ihrer Jugend nur *hatte* träumen können.

REVIEW OF STRONG AND IRREGULAR VERBS USED IN STORY 5B

fließen		floß	ist geflossen	*to flow*
gefallen	gefällt	gefiel	gefallen	*to please*
laden	lädt	lud	geladen	*to load*
rennen		rannte	ist gerannt	*to run*
schieben		schob	geschoben	*to shove, push*
stoßen	stößt	stieß	gestoßen	*to push, thrust*
unterbrechen	unterbricht	unterbrach	unterbrochen	*to interrupt*

IDIOMS FOR REVIEW

den Tisch decken to set the table
vor kurzem a short while ago
immer näher closer and closer
es ist eine Frage der Zeit it is a question of time
es regnet in Strömen it is pouring buckets
Hunger (Durst) bekommen to get hungry (thirsty)
was ist los? what is the matter?
das heißt that is; that is to say; that means; i.e.
wer immer es ist whoever it is
was konnte er anderes tun als . . . what else could he do but . . .
auf allen vieren on all fours
Gott sei Dank! thank God, thank Heavens
es fehlte nicht an Gras there was no lack of grass
auf die Jagd gehen to go hunting
in Ruhe und Frieden in peace and quiet

Musiker musicians
    [**der Musiker, die Musiker** the musician (4)]

seit langem for a long time
Sie erinnern sich hoffentlich let's hope that you remember
    [**sich erinnern** to remember (2)]
    [**erinnern** to remind]
    [**hoffentlich** we hope, I hope, let's hope (3)]
  der Esel the donkey (3)
  brav good
  schwach weak (4)
  optimistisch optimistic (2)
  die Katze the cat (4)
  melancholisch melancholy (2)
  der Hahn the rooster (3)
wenn Sie if you
  auf Seite on page
die Nummer the number (2)

an den schön gedeckten Tisch at the beautifully set table
    [**den Tisch decken** to set the table]
    [**decken** to cover]
  nach Herzenslust to their hearts' desire (2)
einander one another (3)
  bequem comfortable (2)
  der Ort the place
    [**der Ort, die Orte** the place; the village (2)]
das Essen the meal, the food (3)
  der Magen the stomach (2)
  träge lazy
eng narrow (3)
  und da er and since he
  darin in it
  aus-strecken to stretch out
    [**strecken** to stretch (3)]
  der Hof the yard
    [**der Hof, die Höfe** the yard; court; farm (3)]
  der Strohhaufen the pile of straw (2)
    [**der Haufe(n), die Haufen** the pile, heap, lot; crowd (3)]
nicht ganz wohl not quite well
dem Hund war der Alkohol in den Kopf gestiegen the alcohol had gone to the dog's head
    [**der Alkohol** the alcohol (3)]
  das Fieber the fever
  die Kopfschmerzen the headache
    [**der Schmerz, die Schmerzen** the pain, ache; grief (2)]
anstatt sich . . . zu legen instead of lying down
  kroch crawled

[6 A]

(THREE PARTS)

Die vier Musiker (Ende)

1.

Heute wollen wir Ihnen endlich das Ende der Geschichte von den vier Musikern erzählen, auf das Sie vielleicht schon seit langem gewartet haben. Sie erinnern sich hoffentlich noch an den armen, alten Esel, an den braven Hund mit den schwachen Augen, die optimistische Katze ohne Zähne und den melancholischen Hahn mit der schönen Stimme. Wenn Sie nicht mehr wissen sollten, wie die Geschichte aufhörte, dann müssen Sie Ihr Buch auf Seite 39 aufmachen. Es ist die zweite Geschichte, Nummer 1B.

Nachdem unsere vier Freunde sich an den schön gedeckten Tisch gesetzt und nach Herzenslust gegessen und mehrere Flaschen Wein getrunken hatten, waren sie so müde geworden, daß sie beschlossen, zu Bett zu gehen. Sie wünschten also einander eine gute Nacht und suchten sich einen bequemen Ort zum Schlafen. Der Esel versuchte zuerst, in ein Bett zu steigen, weil das gute Essen ihm schwer im Magen lag und der Wein ihn etwas träge gemacht hatte. Das Bett war zwar bequem; aber er fand es zu klein und eng, und da er seine langen Beine nicht darin ausstrecken konnte, ging er nach einer Weile hinaus auf den Hof und legte sich dort auf einen Strohhaufen. Die frische Luft tat ihm gut; er hatte sich nach dem Wein wirklich nicht ganz wohl gefühlt. Auch dem Hund war der Alkohol in den Kopf gestiegen; er klagte über hohes Fieber und starke Kopfschmerzen. Anstatt sich einfach auf die Erde zu legen, wie

[**kriechen, kroch, ist gekrochen** to crawl, to creep (2)]
eben just
die Wolldecke the woolen blanket
[**die Wolle** the wool]
[**die Decke, die Decken** the blanket, cover; ceiling]
er hatte keine Lust he had no desire
sich erkälten to catch a cold (3)
sah sich . . . um looked around
[**sich um-sehen** to look around]
miauen to miaow (2)
der Kamin the fireplace
das Kohlenfeuer the coal fire
[**die Kohle, die Kohlen** the coal (2)]
lustig merrily
[**lustig** merry, gay (2)]
gebrannt hatte had been burning
[**brennen, brannte, hat gebrannt** to burn (3)]
fortrannten ran away
[**fort-rennen** to run away]
[**rennen, rannte, ist gerannt** to run (3)]
war inzwischen ausgegangen had gone out in the meantime
[**inzwischen** meanwhile, in the meantime (3)]
[**aus-gehen** to go out]
die Asche the ashes
die sehr auf Ordnung achtete who paid great attention to orderliness
[**achten** to pay attention; to esteem, to respect]
blies . . . aus blew out
[**aus-blasen** to blow out]
[**blasen, er bläst, blies, hat geblasen** to blow (3)]
die Kerze the candle (3)
damit kein Feuer entstand so that no fire would start
[**entstehen, entstand, ist entstanden** to start, to originate, to come about]
wecken to wake up (3)
der Kamin the fireplace (2)
streckte . . . aus stretched out
[**aus-strecken** to stretch out (2)]
die Glieder the limbs
[**das Glied, die Glieder** the member; limb (2)]
die Asche the ashes (2)
war . . . hinausgegangen had . . . gone out
[**hinaus-gehen** to go out]
indessen meanwhile (3)
hatte . . . auf ihn gewirkt had had its effect on him
[**wirken** to have an effect, to work (3)]
tat ihm weh hurt him
[**weh tun** to hurt]
der Kamm the crest
[**der Kamm, die Kämme** the comb, crest, ridge (2)]

Hunde es gewöhnlich tun, kroch er in das warme Bett, das der Esel eben verlassen hatte, und zog eine Wolldecke über sich; er hatte keine Lust, sich zu erkälten. Die Katze sah sich nach einem guten Platz zum Schlafen um. „Aha!“ miaute sie, als sie den Kamin erblickte. Das Kohlenfeuer, das noch lustig gebrannt hatte, als die Räuber fortrannten, war inzwischen ausgegangen; aber die Asche war noch warm. Die Katze, die sehr auf Ordnung achtete, blies zuerst die Kerzen aus, damit kein Feuer entstand; dann ging sie leise, um den Hund nicht zu wecken, zum Kamin und streckte ihre müden Glieder neben der Asche aus. Der Hahn war indessen auf den Hof hinausgegangen. Der starke Wein hatte auch auf ihn gewirkt: der Kopf tat ihm weh, sein Kamm war ganz rot geworden, und er wußte nicht mehr recht, wo rechts und links war. Wie jeder weiß, können Vögel nicht auf der Erde schlafen, und so flog unser Hahn auf eine Linde, die mitten im Hofe stand. Bald waren unsere Freunde eingeschlafen. Weit, weit weg hörte man eine Dorfuhr zwölf schlagen. Mitternacht, die Stunde der bösen Geister und Hexen, war gekommen.

Draußen im Wald standen die Räuber und wußten nicht,

---

er wußte nicht mehr recht he didn't quite know any more
Vögel birds
[**der Vogel, die Vögel** the bird (3)]
flog flew
[**fliegen, flog, ist geflogen** to fly]
die Linde the linden tree
[**die Linde, die Linden**]
mitten im in the middle of (3)
waren . . . eingeschlafen had fallen asleep
[**ein-schlafen** to fall asleep (3)]
die Dorfuhr the village clock
[**das Dorf, die Dörfer** the village (3)]
Mitternacht midnight (3)
Geister ghosts
[**der Geist, die Geister** the ghost, spirit; mind, intellect (2)]
Hexen witches
[**die Hexe, die Hexen** the witch]

die Räuber the robbers (3)

der Mond, dessen the moon, whose (3)
vor kurzem a short time ago
mächtig mighty
Wolken clouds
[**die Wolke, die Wolken** the cloud (3)]
es hatte zu blitzen . . . begonnen it had begun to lightning
[**es blitzt** there is lightning]
donnern to thunder
gewaltig powerful
der Sturm the storm
[**der Sturm, die Stürme** the storm]
zog immer näher was coming closer and closer
nur noch only
die Frage the question
[**die Frage, die Fragen**]
Hemden shirts
[**das Hemd, die Hemden** the shirt (3)]
dastanden stood there
[**da-stehen** to stand there]
bei dem schneidenden Wind in the piercing wind
[**schneiden** to cut (2)]
[**der Wind, die Winde** the wind (2)]
vor Kälte with cold
[**die Kälte** the cold (2)]
die Tiere the animals
[**das Tier, die Tiere** the animal]
gesprungen jumped
[**springen, sprang, ist gesprungen** to jump (3)]
nicht einmal not even
die Jacken the jackets
[**die Jacke, die Jacken** the jacket (2)]
hatten mitnehmen können had been able to take along
froren sie they were cold
[**frieren, fror, hat gefroren** to freeze, to be cold (2)]
der Regen the rain (3)
in Strömen in buckets
[**der Strom, die Ströme** the (large) river; stream, current (2)]
nieder-fallen to fall down
der Räuberhauptmann the robber captain
[**der Hauptmann, die Hauptleute** the captain, chief]
der Durst the thirst (3)
irgend etwas something
was für Wesen what sort of creatures
[**das Wesen, die Wesen** the being, creature; system; essence; character; manner (2)]
gejagt haben have chased
[**jagen** to chase, to hunt; to race]
untersuchen to investigate (2)

was sie tun sollten. Der Mond, dessen freundliches Licht noch vor kurzem durch die Blätter der mächtigen Bäume geschienen hatte, war jetzt hinter dunklen Wolken verschwunden. Es hatte zu blitzen und zu donnern begonnen, ein gewaltiger Sturm zog immer näher, und es war nur noch eine Frage der Zeit, bis er die Räuber erreichte, die in ihren Hemden und Hosen dastanden und bei dem schneidenden Wind vor Kälte zu zittern angefangen hatten. Nachdem die vier Tiere so plötzlich durch das Fenster gefallen und in das Zimmer gesprungen waren, war alles so schnell gegangen, daß die Räuber nicht einmal ihre Jacken oder Mäntel hatten mitnehmen können. Nun froren sie, und als nach einer Weile der Regen in Strömen auf sie niederzufallen begann, sprach der Räuberhauptmann: „Wenn das so weitergeht, werden wir uns erkälten. Auch bekomme ich langsam Hunger und Durst. Wir müssen irgend etwas tun. Ich weiß nicht, was für Wesen uns aus dem Haus gejagt haben, aber jemand muß die Sache untersuchen. —Du! Komm her!" rief er und wandte sich an einen seiner Räuber; „du schleichst jetzt an das Haus und siehst, was los ist. Die Lichter sind aus, und das heißt, daß die Leute, oder wer immer es ist, entweder schlafen oder wieder fortgegangen sind."—„Ich?" erwiderte der Räuber, der vor Angst ganz blaß geworden war und am ganzen Körper zitterte; „zwischen Mitternacht und ein Uhr gehe ich nicht gern dunkle Häuser untersuchen. Warum gehst du nicht selbst?"—„Ich?" schrie der Hauptmann. „Warte, ich werde dich lehren, deinem Haupt-

---

du schleichst jetzt you are now going to sneak
[**schleichen, schlich, ist geschlichen** to creep, to prowl, to sneak (2)]
was los ist what's up
[**was ist los?** what is up? what is the matter? whats going on? etc.]
das heißt that means (3)
wer immer es ist whoever it is
fort-gehen to go away (2)
blaß pale (3)
gehe ich nicht gern I don't like to go
der Hauptmann the captain (2)
lehren to teach

wider-sprechen to contradict
[**wider** against]
je . . . desto the . . . the (3)
los! Sonst . . . get going! Or else . . .
anderes tun als do other than
folgen to obey
sich . . . auf den Weg zu machen to leave
wider seinen Willen
[**wider** against (2)]
[**der Wille** the will (4)]

kein Wunder no wonder (3)
die Gewalt the force
[**die Gewalt, die Gewalten** the power, force, violence (3)]
ihren Gipfel its peak
[**der Gipfel, die Gipfel** the peak, summit, top]
riß tore
[**reißen, riß, hat gerissen** to tear (2)]
vom Leib from his body
[**der Leib** the body (2)]
es goß in Strömen it was pouring buckets
[**gießen, goß, hat gegossen** to pour]
der Hals the neck (4)
die Zweige the branches
[**der Zweig, die Zweige** the branch (3)]
die Büsche the bushes
[**der Busch, die Büsche** the bush (4)]
vorn und hinten in front and in back
Hexen witches
[**die Hexe, die Hexen** the witch (2)]
fassen to seize
[**fassen** to seize, to grasp]
die Dunkelheit the darkness
stieß er he hit
[**stoßen, er stößt, stieß, hat gestoßen** to push, thrust (2)]
das Dutzend the dozen (3)
Baumstämme tree trunks
[**der Stamm, die Stämme** the stem, trunk, stalk; tribe]
Wurzeln roots
[**die Wurzel, die Wurzeln** the root (2)]
er stürzte he fell
[**stürzen** to fall, to plunge, to rush (3)]
immer wieder again and again
schließlich finally (3)

rührte sich moved
[**rühren** to touch, to stir, to move]
vor einigen Stunden a few hours ago
hatte verlassen müssen had had to leave

mann zu widersprechen! Weißt du nicht, daß ein guter Hauptmann seine Leute nicht verlassen darf? Fort mit dir! Und je schneller, desto besser! Los! Sonst . . ." Was konnte der arme Räuber anderes tun als dem Hauptmann zu folgen und sich wider seinen Willen auf den Weg zu machen?

2.

Kein Wunder, daß der Räuber sich fürchtete! Die Gewalt des Sturmes hatte jetzt ihren Gipfel erreicht. Der Wind riß dem Räuber fast das Hemd vom Leib, es goß in Strömen, das Wasser lief ihm den Hals und Rücken hinunter, die Zweige und Blätter der Bäume und Büsche schlugen ihm ins Gesicht; überall, vorn und hinten, rechts und links, glaubte er Geister und Hexen zu sehen, die ihre Arme nach ihm ausstreckten und ihn fassen wollten. In der Dunkelheit stieß er mit dem Kopf an ein gutes Dutzend Baumstämme und fiel über die dicken Wurzeln. Er stürzte mehrere Male zur Erde; aber er stand immer wieder auf und erreichte schließlich das Haus.

Alles war ruhig, nichts rührte sich. Auf allen vieren kroch der Räuber leise durch die Tür. Das Zimmer, das er vor einigen Stunden hatte verlassen müssen, war dunkel. Er griff nach den Streichhölzern, die er in der Hemdtasche trug; aber sie entzündeten sich nicht, da sie nicht mehr trocken genug waren. Da stieß er plötzlich mit der Hand an ein Stück Papier, das auf dem Fußboden lag. „Im Kamin brennt noch Feuer", dachte er, denn er sah etwas, was wie heiße Kohlen aussah, und wollte das Papier

---

er griff nach he reached for
 [**greifen, griff, hat gegriffen** to seize, take hold of (3)]
 die Streichhölzer the matches
 [**das Streichholz, die Streichhölzer** the match (3)]
 sich entzünden to catch fire
 [**entzünden** to light, to kindle]
 da sie since they
 trocken dry (2)
was wie . . . aussah what looked like

daran anzünden to light on it
[**an-zünden** to light, to kindle (3)]
nichts anderes als nothing but
sich nähern to approach
mit einem Satz with one leap
[**der Satz, die Sätze** the sentence; the leap, jump (3)]
erschrocken frightened
[**erschrecken, er erschrickt, erschrak, ist erschrocken** to be frightened]
sprang auf jumped up
[**auf-springen** to jump up (3)]
die Hintertür the back door
fliehen to flee
war . . . aufgewacht had awakened
[**auf-wachen** to awaken, to wake up (3)]
die Kehle the throat
bellen to bark (3)
krank sick (2)
lehnte er sich he leaned
[**lehnen** to lean (2)]
biß bit
[**beißen, biß, hat gebissen** to bite]
wild wild (3)
Gott sei Dank thank God
die Gefahr the danger
[**die Gefahr, die Gefahren** the danger, risk (3)]
vorüber gone (3)
jedoch however (3)
an dem Strohhaufen vorbeieilte was hurrying past the pile of straw
[**vorbei-eilen** to hurry past]
[**vorbei** past; over, finished (2)]
der Hinterfuß the hind foot
gewaltig powerful (2)
der Schlag the blow
[**der Schlag, die Schläge** the blow, stroke]
sank sank
[**sinken, sank, ist gesunken** to sink (2)]
beinahe almost
lehren to teach (2)
friedliebend peace-loving
[**der Friede(n)** the peace (3)]
der Schlaf the sleep (2)
schrecken to scare
auf einmal suddenly
die Linde the linden tree (2)
die Kraft the strength
[**die Kraft, die Kräfte** the strength, power, force]
floh fled
[**fliehen, floh, ist geflohen** to flee]

daran anzünden. Die Kohlen waren aber natürlich nichts anderes als die offenen Augen der Katze, die den Räuber gehört und die ganze Zeit beobachtet hatte. Als das Papier sich ihrer Nase näherte, sprang sie dem Räuber mit einem Satz ins Gesicht. Der war zu Tode erschrocken, schrie vor Schmerz, sprang auf und wollte durch die Hintertür fliehen. Indessen war der Hund aufgewacht. Er hatte eine zu trockene Kehle, um zu bellen, und fühlte sich auch zu krank, um aufzustehen. Deshalb lehnte er sich nur aus dem Bett und biß den Räuber ins Bein. Wie wild rannte dieser aus dem Haus. Gott sei Dank, jetzt war er endlich draußen! Die Gefahr war vorüber. Als er jedoch an dem Strohhaufen vorbeieilte, gab ihm der Esel mit seinem Hinterfuß einen solch gewaltigen Schlag, daß der Räuber zur Erde sank und beinahe die Sinne verlor. „So, das wird dich lehren, friedliebende Menschen aus dem Schlaf zu schrecken!" sagte sich der Esel. Als der Räuber aufstand und weiterlaufen wollte, rief auf einmal jemand über ihm in der Linde: „Kikeriki! Kikeriki!" Mit seiner letzten Kraft sprang der Räuber auf und floh in den Wald zurück, wo die anderen Räuber schon mit Ungeduld auf ihn warteten.

„Na, wie war's?" fragte der Räuberhauptmann; „ist alles in Ordnung?"—„Ach, leider gar nicht", entgegnete der Räuber. „Als ich in das Haus kam, saß dort eine furchtbare Hexe im Kamin. Sie war schwarz wie Tinte, hatte rote Augen und ist mir mit ihren langen Fingernägeln ins Gesicht gesprungen. An der Hintertür lag ein Mann, der wollte mich fassen und hat mich

---

die Ungeduld the impatience
[**die Geduld** the patience]

wie war's? how was it?
gar nicht not at all (3)
furchtbar frightful
die Tinte the ink (3)
die Fingernägel the fingernail
[**der Nagel, die Nägel** the nail]
die Hintertür the back door (2)
fassen to seize (2)

hat mich . . . gestochen stabbed me
[**stechen, er sticht, stach, hat gestochen** to sting, to stab, to prick]
scharf sharp (2)
das Messer the knife
[**das Messer, die Messer** the knife (3)]
von der habe ich . . . bekommen from it I got
der Schlag the blow
[**der Schlag, die Schläge** the blow, stroke (2)]
Knochen bones
[**der Knochen, die Knochen** the bone]
weh tun hurt
[**weh tun** to hurt (2)]
oben up
[**oben** above, upstairs (3)]
in der Krone in the top
[**die Krone, die Kronen** the crown (3)]
bringt ihn mir her! bring him here to me!

erschrocken frightened
[**erschrecken, er erschrickt, erschrak, ist erschrocken** to be frightened (2)]
kreideweiß white as chalk
[**die Kreide** the chalk (3)]
brachten . . . kein Wort über die Lippen could not utter a word
[**die Lippe, die Lippen** the lip (2)]
zunächst at first (3)
genügte ihnen was enough for them
[**genügen** to suffice, to be sufficient, to be enough (2)]
nachdem sie . . . Rat gehalten after they had held counsel
[**der Rat** the advice, counsel; council (2)]
miteinander with one another
zogen moved

stören to disturb (2)
das Dach the roof
[**das Dach, die Dächer** the roof (3)]
die Decke the ceiling
[**die Decke, die Decken** the blanket, cover; ceiling (2)]
die Reihe the row
[**die Reihe, die Reihen** the row]
fetter Schinken of fat hams
[**fett** fat (2)]
[**der Schinken, die Schinken** the ham (3)]
Würste sausages
[**die Wurst, die Würste** the sausage]
der Keller the cellar
[**der Keller, die Keller** the cellar, basement]
voller Weinfässer full of wine barrels
[**das Faß, die Fässer** the barrel, cask (2)]

mit einem scharfen Messer ins Bein gestochen. Mitten im Hofe wartete eine schwarze Gestalt; von der habe ich einen solchen Schlag in den Rücken bekommen, daß mir noch jetzt alle Knochen im Körper weh tun. Und oben in der Krone der großen Linde saß der Richter, der hat gerufen: ‚Bringt ihn mir her! Bringt ihn mir her!' "

Als die Räuber das hörten, waren sie zu Tode erschrocken; sie wurden kreideweiß und brachten zunächst kein Wort über die Lippen. Was sie gehört hatten, genügte ihnen. Nachdem sie kurz miteinander Rat gehalten hatten, verließen sie den Wald und zogen in ein anderes Land. In ihr Haus sind sie nie wieder zurückgekehrt.

Als in der nächsten Nacht niemand ihren Schlaf störte, wußten unsere vier Freunde, daß es ihnen gelungen war, die Räuber für immer aus dem Haus zu treiben. Sie hatten jetzt ein Dach überm Kopf, zu essen und zu trinken gab es genug, denn von der Decke hing eine lange Reihe fetter Schinken und dicker Würste, und der Keller stand voller Weinfässer. So wurde nun jeder Tag für sie ein Festtag, den sie mit einer herrlichen Mahlzeit feierten. Während der ersten Tage waren sie vor Freude so außer sich, daß sie sogar jedesmal nach dem Essen einen oder zwei Walzer tanzten. Das taten sie aber nur einige Tage, denn der Esel und der Hund empfanden, daß ihre Würde darunter litt. Der wahre Grund war natürlich, daß ihre Glieder zum Tanzen einfach zu alt waren.

---

der Festtag the holiday
den sie . . . feierten which they celebrated
[**feiern** to celebrate]
herrlich wonderful (4)
die Mahlzeit the meal
[**die Mahlzeit, die Mahlzeiten** the meal]
der Walzer the waltz (2)
tanzen to dance (3)
empfanden felt
[**empfinden, empfand, hat empfunden** to feel]
die Würde the dignity
darunter litt suffered from it
[**leiden, litt, hat gelitten** to suffer (3)]

die Wurst the sausage
[**die Wurst, die Würste** the sausage (2)]
darf man sich nicht one must not
die Lebensmittel the foodstuffs (3)
gefiel ihnen pleased them
[**gefallen, er gefällt, gefiel, hat gefallen** to please (2)]
gering slight
[**gering** small, little, slight (2)]
empfanden felt (2)
[**empfinden, empfand, hat empfunden** to feel (2)]
täglich daily (2)
fehlte es nicht an there was no lack of
das Gras the grass (2)
zart tender
Blumen flowers
[**die Blume, die Blumen** the flower (3)]
wuchsen grew
[**wachsen, er wächst, wuchs, ist gewachsen** to grow (2)]
ging . . . auf die Jagd went hunting
[**die Jagd** the hunt, chase]
trotz in spite of (2)
das Alter the age (3)
fing caught
[**fangen, er fängt, fing, hat gefangen** to catch (3)]
der Knochen the bone
[**der Knochen, die Knochen** the bone (2)]
in Ruhe in quiet
[**die Ruhe** the rest, peace, quiet (4)]
fraß ate
[**fressen, er frißt, fraß, hat gefressen** to eat (of beasts)]
die Jagd the hunt (2)
nach Mäusen for mice
[**die Maus, die Mäuse** the mouse (3)]
waren ihr were for her
sie zog es . . . vor she preferred
[**vor-ziehen** to prefer (2)]
aus Vogelnestern from bird's nests
[**das Vogelnest** the bird's nest]
[**das Nest, die Nester** the nest]
Eier eggs
[**das Ei, die Eier** the egg (3)]
der Bach the brook
[**der Bach, die Bäche** the brook]
der Honig the honey
die . . . Bienen the . . . bees
[**die Biene, die Bienen** the bee]
stachen stung
[**stechen, er sticht, stach, hat gestochen** to sting, stab, prick (2)]

3.

„Alles hat ein Ende, nur die Wurst hat zwei", sagt man in Deutschland, und so darf man sich nicht wundern, daß eines Tages in dem Haus unserer Freunde die Lebensmittel zu Ende gingen. Das angenehme Leben in ihrem neuen Haus gefiel ihnen jedoch so gut, daß sie nicht die geringste Lust empfanden, nach Bremen zu wandern und sich dort durch schwere Arbeit ihr tägliches Brot zu verdienen. Warum nicht bleiben, wo sie waren und wo es ihnen gut ging? Draußen vor dem Haus fehlte es nicht an Gras für den Esel, und zarte Blumen, mit denen er sich den Magen füllen konnte, wuchsen im Walde in großen Mengen. Der Hund ging trotz seines hohen Alters noch auf die Jagd und fing auch hier und da einen Hasen oder fand einen Knochen, den er dann nach Haus brachte und dort in Ruhe und Frieden fraß. Für die alte Katze bedeutete die Jagd nach Mäusen zu viel Arbeit; die Mäuse waren ihr jetzt etwas zu schnell. Sie zog es deshalb vor, aus Vogelnestern Eier zu stehlen, im nahen Bach Fische zu fangen und im Wald nach süßem wildem Honig zu suchen; nur mußte sie immer gut aufpassen, daß die bösen Bienen sie nicht in die Nase stachen. Und auch der Hahn brauchte sich keine Sorgen zu machen. Der köstliche Weizen in dem großen Strohhaufen auf dem Hof genügte für mehrere Winter, und die reifen Beeren auf den Büschen des Waldes, die er vorher nie gekostet, schmeckten ihm besser als

---

köstlich delicious (3)
  der Weizen the wheat
  Winter winters
    [**der Winter, die Winter** the winter (2)]
  reif ripe
    [**reif** ripe, mature]
  Beeren berries
    [**die Beere, die Beeren** the berry (2)]
  nie gekostet had never tasted
    [**kosten** to cost; to taste]
  schmecken to taste (3)

das Futter the feed
das Trinken drinking
stellte . . . dar presented
[**dar-stellen** to present, to represent, to perform (2)]
der Keller the cellar
[**der Keller, die Keller** the cellar, basement (2)]

sie konnten . . . nennen they could call
das Heim the home (2)
sich langweilen to be bored (2)
einen Musikverein zu bilden to form a music association
[**der Verein, die Vereine** the association, club, organization]
[**bilden** to form; to educate (3)]
die Kunst (the) art
[**die Kunst, die Künste** the art (3)]
sie hatten recht they were right
[**recht haben** to be right (4)]
schwierig difficult
ja unmöglich indeed impossible
richtig right
passieren to happen (3)
gab es noch there were as yet
die . . . geschrieben hatten who had written
Quartette quartets
[**das Quartett, die Quartette**]
die Trompete the trumpet (2)
die Trommel the drum (2)
selbst ans Werk zu gehen to go to work themselves
[**das Werk, die Werke** the work (3)]
der Montag Monday
der Dienstag Tuesday
der Mittwoch Wednesday
verschieden different (2)
die Teile the parts
[**der Teil, die Teile** the part (3)]
ihrer Quartette of their quartets
[**das Quartett, die Quartette** the quartet (2)]
ihre besondere Aufgabe their special assignments
[**besonder** special (3)]
[**die Aufgabe, die Aufgaben** the assignment, task, lesson (3)]
die . . . Instrumente the . . . instruments
[**das Instrument, die Instrumente** the instrument (3)]
verfassen to compose, to write
der Text the text
[**der Text, die Texte**]
dichten to write
[**dichten** to write poetry]
die Reime the rhymes
[**der Reim, die Reime**]

das Futter, das er zu Haus von seiner Herrin bekommen hatte. Das Trinken stellte kein Problem dar: die Fässer im Keller waren alle voll.

Unsere vier Freunde hatten es gut. Sie konnten ein schönes, bequemes Heim ihr eigen nennen und lebten glücklich und zufrieden. Als sie sich nach einiger Zeit zu langweilen begannen, kamen sie auf den Gedanken, einen Musikverein zu bilden. „Was ist das Leben ohne die Kunst?" sagten sie sich; und sie hatten recht. Es war natürlich schwierig, ja unmöglich, die richtige Musik zu finden, denn damals, als diese Geschichte passiert ist, gab es noch keine Musiker, die Quartette für Trompete, Trommel, Katze und Hahn geschrieben hatten. Sie waren also gezwungen, selbst ans Werk zu gehen. In der ersten Hälfte der Woche, am Montag, Dienstag und Mittwoch arbeitete jeder in seinem eigenen Zimmer an den verschiedenen Teilen ihrer Quartette, denn alle hatten ihre besondere Aufgabe: der Esel und der Hund schrieben die Musik für die zwei Instrumente, die Katze verfaßte den Text und dichtete die Reime, und der Hahn setzte den vollendeten Text in Musik. Donnerstag war der Tag, an dem jeder prüfte, was die anderen gemacht hatten; sie lehrten und förderten einander, indem jeder dem anderen seine Fehler zeigte. Am Freitag und Sonnabend übten sie dann mit großem Eifer die einzelnen Teile in

---

vollendet completed
[**vollenden** to finish, to complete]
der Donnerstag Thursday
prüfte examined
[**prüfen** to check, to examine (3)]
lehren to teach (2)
fördern to encourage
[**fördern** to promote, to encourage (2)]
indem jeder . . . zeigte by each one showing
seine Fehler his mistakes
[**der Fehler, die Fehler** the error, mistake (3)]
der Freitag Friday (2)
der Sonnabend Saturday (3)
üben to practice (3)
der Eifer the zeal (3)

der Sonntag Sunday (3)
ihre Pulte their music stands
[**das Pult, die Pulte** the desk (2)]
das Konzert the concert
[**das Konzert, die Konzerte**]
klang sounded
[**klingen, klang, hat geklungen** to sound (2)]
freilich to be sure (2)
musikalisch musical (3)
Regeln rules
[**die Regel, die Regeln**]
immer noch still
trotzdem nevertheless (3)
diese Konzerte these concerts
[**das Konzert, die Konzerte** (2)]
gerade precisely
sie genossen they enjoyed
[**genießen, genoß, hat genossen** to enjoy]
modern modern (2)

an dem Haus vorbei past the house
[**vorbei-kommen** to come past, to pass]
die Reime the rhymes
[**der Reim, die Reime** (2)]
dichten to write
[**dichten** to write poetry (2)]
sahen . . . aus looked
die Fachleute the experts
[**der Fachmann, die Fachleute** the expert]
[**das Fach, die Fächer** the subject, line of work, profession (2)]
sandte sent
[**senden, sandte, hat gesandt** to send (3)]
studieren to study (3)
vollständig completely (3)
erfinden to invent
[**erfinden, erfand, hat erfunden** to invent]
wovon of which
bisher up to that time (3)
nur zu träumen gewagt hatte had only dared to dream
[**träumen** to dream (3)]
[**wagen** to dare, to risk (3)]
sie hatten . . . erfunden they had invented
[**erfinden, erfand, hat erfunden** to invent (2)]
die Zukunft the future (3)
die Geschichte the history
als die Erfinder as the inventors
[**der Erfinder, die Erfinder** the inventor]
die Dreizehntonmusik the thirteen-tone music
bekannt known (3)

der Küche, und am Sonntag trugen sie ihre Pulte in das Wohnzimmer und gaben ein großes Konzert. Was sie spielten, klang freilich manchmal etwas falsch, weil sie nicht alle musikalischen Regeln kannten und deshalb immer noch eine Menge Fehler gemacht hatten. Aber ihre Musik gefiel ihnen trotzdem, und für diese Konzerte war das Haus auch gerade der richtige Ort: sie genossen ihre Kunst allein und hatten keine Nachbarn, die über ihre moderne Musik klagen konnten.

Als die vier Freunde nach einem langen und glücklichen Leben gestorben waren, kam jemand aus Zufall an dem Haus vorbei und fand die Musik, die sie für ihre Sonntagskonzerte geschrieben hatten. Er nahm sie mit und brachte sie nach Bremen. Die Musik und die Reime, welche die Katze gedichtet hatte, sahen so interessant aus, daß man sie an die besten Fachleute Deutschlands sandte, welche die Quartette sofort mit großem Eifer studierten und untersuchten. Man fand, daß es unseren Freunden gelungen war, etwas vollständig Neues zu erfinden, wovon die musikalische Welt bisher nur zu träumen gewagt hatte: sie hatten die Musik der Zukunft erfunden. In der Geschichte der Musik sind sie heute als die Erfinder der Dreizehntonmusik bekannt und berühmt.

FRAU PIEPENBRINK HAT EINE IDEE

[6B]

NOTES

REVIEW OF STRONG AND IRREGULAR VERBS USED IN STORY 6A

beißen		biß	gebissen	*to bite*
empfinden		empfand	empfunden	*to feel*
entstehen		entstand	ist entstanden	*to originate*
erfinden		erfand	erfunden	*to invent*
erschrecken	erschrickt	erschrak	ist erschrocken	*to frighten*
fliegen		flog	ist geflogen	*to fly*
fliehen		floh	ist geflohen	*to flee*
fressen	frißt	fraß	gefressen	*to eat (of beasts)*
genießen		genoß	genossen	*to enjoy*
gießen		goß	gegossen	*to pour*
stechen	sticht	stach	gestochen	*to sting, stab*

IDIOMS FOR REVIEW

von Anfang an from the beginning
allerlei Gemüse all sorts of vegetables
keinerlei Schulden no debts of any kind, no debts whatever
sie hatte es sich zur Regel gemacht she had made it a rule
sie ließ sich die Sache durch den Kopf gehen she thought about the matter
ein gutes Geschäft machen to strike a good bargain, to make a good deal

der Philosoph the philosopher
Wesen creatures
Haare hair
[**das Haar, die Haare** the hair (3)]
ihn bewegt haben mögen may have induced him
[**bewegen** to move; to induce (3)]
. . . zu urteilen to judge
[**urteilen** to judge]
die Art the way
[**die Art, die Arten** the way, manner (3)]
menschlich human (2)
beweisen to prove (2)
im Fall in the case
brav good
die Hafenstadt the harbor town
[**der Hafen, die Häfen** the port, harbor]
der Nord(en) the north(2)

vor mehreren Jahren several years ago
der Papagei the parrot
das Häuschen the little house (2)
dicht am Hafen close by the harbor
[**dicht** dense, thick; near, close (3)]
[**der Hafen, die Häfen** the port, harbor (2)]
bei einer Baufirma with a construction company
[**der Bau, die Bauten** the construction, building]
[**die Firma, die Firmen** the firm (2)]
um . . . leben zu können to be able to live
von Anfang an from the beginning
[**der Anfang, die Anfänge** the beginning, start (2)]
daß sie . . . hatten haben können that they had been able to have
das Dienstmädchen the maid
[**das Dienstmädchen, die Dienstmädchen**]
[**der Dienst, die Dienste** the service (2)]
war das anders geworden things had changed
[**anders** different (2)]
besaß owned
[**besitzen, besaß, hat besessen** to own, to possess (3)]
keinerlei Schulden no debts of any sort
die Pension the pension
reichte gerade was just sufficient
an Vergnügen of pleasures

[6 B]

(THREE PARTS)

Frau Piepenbrink hat eine Idee

1.

Der berühmte deutsche Philosoph Schopenhauer hat einmal gesagt: „Frauen sind Wesen mit langen Haaren und kurzen Ideen." Es ist nicht unsere Aufgabe, zu untersuchen, welche Gründe ihn bewegt haben mögen, in dieser bösen Art über die bessere Hälfte der menschlichen Gesellschaft zu urteilen. Die folgende Geschichte will nur beweisen, daß er nicht immer recht hatte; wenigstens nicht im Fall der braven Frau Piepenbrink aus Cuxhaven, einer kleinen deutschen Hafenstadt im Norden von Hamburg.

Frau Piepenbrink, deren Mann vor mehreren Jahren gestorben war, lebte ganz allein mit ihrem Papagei in einem kleinen Häuschen dicht am Hafen. Ihr Mann hatte als Buchhalter bei einer Baufirma gearbeitet und genug verdient, um mit seiner Frau ohne Sorgen leben zu können. Die Firma hatte den jungen Mann von Anfang an gefördert, und es war ihnen später so gut gegangen, daß sie sogar ein Dienstmädchen hatten haben können. Nach Herrn Piepenbrinks plötzlichem Tod war das anders geworden. Frau Piepenbrink besaß zwar noch das Häuschen, auch hatte sie keinerlei Schulden; aber was jetzt immer fehlte, war Geld. Die geringe Pension, die ihr die Baufirma jeden Monat schickte, reichte gerade für die Lebensmittel, ein paar Kleider und die Gas- und Lichtrechnung; wenn sie die bezahlt hatte, war das Geld zu Ende. An Vergnügen, die etwas kosteten, konnte sie nicht denken, und eine

die Ferienreise the vacation trip (2)
[**die Ferien** the vacation (3)]
[**die Reise, die Reisen** the trip, voyage (3)]
kam jetzt überhaupt nicht mehr in Frage was now entirely out of the question
[**das kommt nicht in Frage** that is out of the question]

unzufrieden dissatisfied
unglücklich unhappy (2)
Tausende thousands
solange as long as (3)
die Hauptsache the main thing (3)
das Dienstmädchen the maid
[**das Dienstmädchen, die Dienstmädchen** (2)]
hatte sie . . . gleich gehen lassen müssen she had been obliged to let go right away
[**gleich = sogleich** at once (3)]
der Papagei the parrot (2)
grün green
gelb yellow (3)
die Federn the feathers
[**die Feder, die Federn** the feather; pen; spring (2)]
glänzen to shine (2)
vom Westen from the west
[**der West(en)** the west]
drang penetrated
[**dringen, drang, ist gedrungen** to penetrate; enter; urge, press (3)]
fern distant
fremd foreign (3)
die Jugend the youth (2)
Bilder pictures
[**das Bild, die Bilder** the picture (3)]
der Frühling the spring
der Sommer the summer (2)
der Herbst the autumn, fall (2)
geliebt beloved
[**lieben** to love (2)]
gleich hinter right behind
und an dessen einem Ende and at whose one end
die Südwand the south wall
[**der Süd(en)** the south]
[**die Wand, die Wände** the wall (3)]
bedecken to cover
zog sie she grew
Erbsen peas
[**die Erbse, die Erbsen** the pea (2)]
Bohnen beans
[**die Bohne, die Bohnen** the bean]
allerlei all sorts of (2)

kleine Ferienreise kam jetzt überhaupt nicht mehr in Frage.

Trotzdem war Frau Piepenbrink nicht unzufrieden oder unglücklich. „Gibt es nicht Tausende von Menschen, denen es schlechter geht als mir?" sagte sie sich oft; „solange ich in meinem Häuschen wohnen kann und genug zu tun habe, kann ich nicht klagen. Die Hauptsache ist, daß ich mich nicht langweile." Im Haus gab es jetzt genug Arbeit, denn das letzte Dienstmädchen hatte sie natürlich gleich gehen lassen müssen. Wenn sie mit der Hausarbeit fertig war, spielte sie mit ihrem Papagei mit den grünen und gelben Federn, die so schön glänzten, wenn die Sonne vom Westen in das Wohnzimmer drang. Sie lehrte ihn deutsche Wörter und kleine Sätze sprechen und dachte an die fernen, fremden Länder, in denen er in seiner Jugend gewesen sein mußte und die sie leider nur aus Büchern und Bildern kannte. Im Frühling, Sommer und Herbst hatte sie ihren geliebten Garten, der gleich hinter dem Häuschen lag und an dessen einem Ende die herrlichsten Rosen die ganze Südwand des Hauses bedeckten. Im Garten zog sie Erbsen und Bohnen und allerlei anderes Gemüse, das sie in der Küche brauchte. Weiter hinten wuchsen Erdbeeren, und in der Ecke stand ein mächtiger Apfelbaum, in dessen Zweigen ein paar Vögel sich ihre Nester gebaut hatten und unter dem sie sich ausruhen konnte, wenn die Arbeit sie müde gemacht hatte.

---

das Gemüse the vegetable(s)
weiter hinten farther back
wuchsen grew
[**wachsen, er wächst, wuchs, ist gewachsen** to grow (3)]
Erdbeeren strawberries
[**die Erdbeere, die Erdbeeren** the strawberry]
mächtig mighty (2)
der Apfelbaum the apple tree (2)
[**der Apfel, die Äpfel** the apple (3)]
in dessen Zweigen in whose branches
sich . . . gebaut hatten had built
[**bauen** to build]
ihre Nester their nests
[**das Nest, die Nester** the nest; small town, village (2)]
sich aus-ruhen to rest (2)

ärgern to annoy
[**sich ärgern** to be annoyed (3)]
änderte sich das alles all that changed
[**ändern** to change (3)]

die Überraschung the surprise
[**die Überraschung, die Überraschungen** (2)]
ungewöhnlich unusually
rieb rubbed
[**reiben, rieb, hat gerieben** to rub (2)]
es waren they were
Arbeiter workers
[**der Arbeiter, die Arbeiter** the worker]
irgend etwas something
bauen to build (2)
sie zog sich . . . an she got dressed
man unterrichtete sie she was told
[**unterrichten** to instruct, to inform (2)]
die Schiffahrtsgesellschaft the shipping company
[**das Schiff, die Schiffe** the ship, boat]
vor kurzem a short time ago (2)
das Lagerhaus the warehouse
[**das Lagerhaus, die Lagerhäuser**]
[**das Lager, die Lager** the store; camp]
darauf on it
die Treppe the steps
[**die Treppe, die Treppen** the stairs, steps, staircase (3)]
und . . . hinausgeblickt and had looked out
[**hinaus-blicken** to look out]
blau blue (2)
das Meer the sea
[**das Meer, die Meere** the sea, ocean (2)]
die Schiffe the ships
[**das Schiff, die Schiffe** the ship (2)]
sie . . . mitgefahren war she had traveled
[**mit-fahren** to go along]
das Mädchen the girl
[**das Mädchen, die Mädchen** (4)]
auf so einem Schiff on such a ship
die Heirat the marriage
hatten . . . bleiben müssen had had to remain
ihre Wünsche her wishes
[**der Wunsch, die Wünsche** the wish, desire (4)]
Träume dreams
[**der Traum, die Träume** the dream]
die Ehe the marriage
[**die Ehe, die Ehen** the marriage, married life (2)]
das Gehalt the salary
[**das Gehalt, die Gehälter** the salary (3)]

So war ein Jahr dem anderen gefolgt, und Frau Piepenbrink hatte keinen Grund gehabt, über ihr Leben zu klagen. Sie langweilte sich nicht, und es gab niemanden, der sie ärgerte. Eines Morgens jedoch änderte sich das alles. Frau Piepenbrink begann sich zu ärgern.

Als sie aufwachte und aus dem Fenster blickte, sah sie zu ihrer großen Überraschung eine ungewöhnlich große Menge von Menschen auf der anderen Seite der Straße. Sie rieb sich die Augen. War es möglich? Ja, es waren Arbeiter, die eben angefangen hatten, irgend etwas zu bauen. Sie zog sich schnell an und lief über die Straße. Man unterrichtete sie, daß eine Schiffahrtsgesellschaft vor kurzem den Platz gekauft und begonnen hatte, ein großes Lagerhaus darauf zu bauen. Frau Piepenbrink war außer sich. Wie oft hatte sie nicht an ihrem Fenster gestanden oder auf der Treppe vor ihrem Häuschen gesessen und auf den Hafen und das blaue Meer hinausgeblickt, auf dem die großen Schiffe kamen und gingen und mit denen sie oft in Gedanken mitgefahren war! Wie oft hatte sie nicht als junges Mädchen gewünscht, auch einmal auf so einem Schiff sein zu können und die weite Welt zu sehen! Nach ihrer Heirat hatten ihre Wünsche Träume bleiben müssen. Ihre Ehe war zwar sehr glücklich gewesen; aber das Gehalt, das ihr Mann damals bekam, hatte nicht für große Reisen gereicht. Wenn sie sich manchmal Sommerferien genommen hatten, so waren sie immer so kurz gewesen, daß sie und ihr Mann nie sehr weit hatten fortgehen können.

Und jetzt baute man direkt vor ihrem Haus dieses große Gebäude, und sie sollte ihr geliebtes Meer nicht mehr sehen dürfen!

---

hatte nicht . . . gereicht had not been sufficient
Sommerferien summer vacation
hatten fortgehen können had been able to go away

direkt directly (3)
das Gebäude the building
[**das Gebäude, die Gebäude** (2)]
und sie sollte . . . nicht mehr sehen dürfen! and she should no longer be allowed to see . . .!

wie sie . . . haßte! how she hated!
[**hassen** to hate]
das Lagerhaus the warehouse
[**das Lagerhaus, die Lagerhäuser** (2)]
die Schiffahrtsgesellschaft the shipping company (2)

der Bau the construction
[**der Bau, die Bauten** the construction, the building (2)]
vollendet completed
[**vollenden** to complete, to finish (2)]
klingeln to ring (the bell) (3)
der Besucher the visitor
[**der Besucher, die Besucher** the visitor]
elegant elegant (3)
niemand anders als none other but
der Direktor the director
Atlantica und Co. Atlantica and Company
ein-treten to enter (3)
der Boden, worauf the land on which
bereit prepared
[**bereit** ready, prepared]
bieten to offer
wert worth (3)
dazu to that
versucht tempted
sie hatte es sich zur Regel gemacht she had made it a rule
[**die Regel, die Regeln** the rule (2)]
Entscheidungen decisions
[**die Entscheidung, die Entscheidungen** the decision]
überlegen to think over
[**überlegen** to think, to think over (2)]

vor vielen Jahren many years ago
hatte . . . kaufen wollen had wanted to buy
zwölftausend twelve thousand
geboten offered
[**bieten, bot, hat geboten** to offer (3)]
war es ihnen gut gegangen they had been doing well
sich . . . zu trennen to part
[**trennen** to separate, to part]
sie sich entschied she decided
[**(sich) entscheiden** to decide]
[**entscheiden, entschied, hat entschieden**]
Vorteile advantages
[**der Vorteil, die Vorteile** the advantage (2)]
der Verkauf the sale (3)
das Schreibpult the writing desk

2.

Nach einigen Wochen war draußen der Keller fertig; dann kamen die Wände. Je höher das Gebäude wurde, desto mehr wuchs Frau Piepenbrinks Ärger und Zorn. Wie sie das Lagerhaus und die Schiffahrtsgesellschaft haßte! Aber was konnte sie tun?

Ein paar Monate später, als der Bau schon vollendet war, klingelte jemand an ihrer Haustür. Der Besucher, ein eleganter Herr, reichte ihr seine Karte. Es war niemand anders als der Direktor der Schiffahrtsgesellschaft „Atlantica und Co.“, der gleichen Gesellschaft, die das Lagerhaus gebaut hatte. Frau Piepenbrink bat den Herrn, einzutreten. „Ich bin gekommen, Frau Piepenbrink“, sagte er, „um Sie im Namen meiner Firma zu fragen, ob Sie uns nicht Ihr Haus verkaufen möchten. Was uns interessiert, ist natürlich nicht das Haus selbst, sondern der Boden, worauf es steht. Unsere Firma wird von Jahr zu Jahr größer, wir brauchen Platz und haben die Absicht, neben dem ersten Lagerhaus ein zweites zu bauen. Die Firma ist bereit, Ihnen einen guten Preis zu bieten. Das Haus ist, wie wir erfahren haben, jetzt etwa fünfzehntausend Mark wert. Wir bieten Ihnen zwanzigtausend. Was sagen Sie dazu?“—„Zwanzigtausend Mark!“ dachte Frau Piepenbrink. Sie war versucht, sofort ja zu sagen. Aber sie hatte es sich zur Regel gemacht, wichtige Entscheidungen lange zu überlegen. So sagte sie zunächst nichts und bat dann den Herrn, am nächsten Tag wiederzukommen.

Vor vielen Jahren, als ihr Mann noch lebte, hatte einmal jemand das Haus kaufen wollen und hatte zwölftausend Mark geboten. Aber damals war es ihnen gut gegangen, und sie hatten nicht daran gedacht, sich von ihrem Häuschen und dem Garten zu trennen. Diesmal war die Sache jedoch anders. Sie brauchte Geld; aber bevor sie sich entschied, ihr Heim für immer zu verlassen, mußte sie gut überlegen, welche anderen Vorteile der Verkauf des Hauses ihr vielleicht bieten konnte. Am Abend ging Frau Piepenbrink zu dem hohen Schreibpult

holte . . . hervor took out
[**hervor** out (3)]
das Heft the notebook
[**das Heft, die Hefte** (3)]
die Feder the pen
[**die Feder, die Federn** the feather; pen; spring (3)]
der Armstuhl the armchair
[**der Stuhl, die Stühle** the chair (2)]
die Tischlampe the table lamp
[**die Lampe, die Lampen** the lamp (2)]

der Direktor the director (2)
haben Sie sich . . . durch den Kopf gehen lassen? have you thought . . . over?
wie vor einer Minute as a minute ago
hören Sie gut zu! listen closely!
[**zu-hören** to listen (3)]
ist mir ein Geheimnis is a mystery to me
[**das Geheimnis, die Geheimnisse** the secret, mystery]
direkt davorsteht stands directly in front of it
Sehen Sie you see
während while
die Pension the pension (2)
werden behalten können will be able to keep
ohne Schulden zu machen without going into debt
[**Schulden machen** to go into debt]
sich . . . zu leihen to borrow
[**leihen** to lend (3)]
heutzutage nowadays
praktisch in a practical manner
[**praktisch** practical]
heute morgen this morning
erlauben to allow (3)
fordern demand (3)
ich werde wohl . . . zufrieden sein müssen I suppose I shall have to be satisfied
die Gunst the favor
wie früher as before
empfohlen recommended
[**empfehlen, er empfiehlt, empfahl, hat empfohlen** to recommend]
die Seereise the ocean voyage
[**die See, die Seen** the sea, ocean]
[**der See, die Seen** the lake (3)]
zwei freie Schiffskarten two free boat tickets
[**die Schiffskarte** the boat ticket]
wenn ich Lust haben sollte if I should feel like
irgendwohin somewhere
begleiten to accompany
als ältere Dame as an elderly lady

ihres Mannes und holte ein Heft, Feder und Tinte hervor. Dann setzte sie sich in ihren bequemen Armstuhl, zündete die kleine Tischlampe an und begann zu rechnen.

„Nun, liebe Frau Piepenbrink", sagte der Direktor, als er am nächsten Morgen wieder erschien, „haben Sie sich die Sache durch den Kopf gehen lassen?"–„Ich glaube", entgegnete Frau Piepenbrink, „daß das Haus ein bißchen mehr wert ist, als Sie gestern sagten. Ich sollte vielleicht dreißigtausend Mark verlangen."–„Meine liebe Frau", erwiderte der Direktor, dessen Stimme jetzt nicht mehr so freundlich war wie vor einer Minute, „hören Sie gut zu! Wie Sie je für Ihr kleines Haus dreißigtausend Mark bekommen wollen, ist mir ein Geheimnis; besonders wenn unser Lagerhaus jetzt direkt davorsteht. Lassen Sie mich Ihnen einen guten Rat geben: denken Sie an Ihr Alter und Ihre Zukunft! Sehen Sie, die Preise steigen jedes Jahr, während Ihre Pension die gleiche bleibt. Ich weiß nicht, ob Sie Ihr Haus werden behalten können, ohne Schulden zu machen. Dann werden Sie gezwungen sein, sich Geld zu leihen; aber das ist heutzutage nicht so einfach. Sie müssen praktisch denken. Glauben Sie mir; je eher Sie das Haus verkaufen, desto besser wird es sein. Ein schneller Verkauf kann nur zu Ihrem Vorteil sein. Meine Firma hat mir heute morgen erlaubt, Ihnen fünfundzwanzigtausend Mark zu bieten. Mehr können Sie nicht fordern."–„Vielleicht haben Sie recht", sagte Frau Piepenbrink nach einer kurzen Pause; „ich werde wohl mit fünfundzwanzigtausend Mark zufrieden sein müssen. Nur möchte ich Sie in diesem Fall um eine kleine Gunst bitten. Sehen Sie, ich bin nicht mehr so gesund wie früher, und mein Arzt hat mir empfohlen, mir von Zeit zu Zeit Ferien zu nehmen. ‚Das Beste für Sie, Frau Piepenbrink', hat er gesagt, ‚ist eine kleine Seereise.' Glauben Sie, Herr Direktor, daß es Ihrer Firma möglich sein wird, mir jedesmal zwei freie Schiffskarten zu geben, wenn ich Lust haben sollte, irgendwohin zu fahren? Der Grund, warum ich um zwei Karten bitte, ist, daß ich jemanden brauche, der mich begleitet. Sie werden verstehen, daß ich als ältere Dame nicht gern allein fahren möchte.–Und dann noch eine

die Gunst the favor (2)
noch einen Monat one more month
auf diese Art in this way
die Schiffskarten the boat tickets
[**die Schiffskarte** the boat ticket (2)]
fast bestimmt almost certainly
der Gefallen the favor (2)
ich freue mich I am glad
[**sich freuen** to be glad, happy (3)]
der Scheck the check
[**der Scheck, die Schecks** the check (3)]
ich persönlich I personally
[**persönlich** personal]
die Erlaubnis the permission (3)
zu jeder Zeit at all times
die Person the person
[**die Person, die Personen** the person (3)]
unserer Linie of our line
[**die Linie, die Linien** the line]
erster Klasse first class
[**die Klasse, die Klassen** the class]
als nötig war than was necessary
[**nötig** necessary]

rieb rubbed
[**reiben, rieb, hat gerieben** to rub (3)]
der Wert the value
[**der Wert, die Werte** the worth, value (3)]
wird uns nicht weh tun will not hurt us
[**weh tun** to hurt (3)]
Seereisen ocean voyages
[**die Seereise, die Seereisen** the ocean voyage (2)]
[**die See, die Seen** the sea, ocean (2)]
irgendwo somewhere
ausgegeben spent
[**aus-geben** to spend]
denn sie wird ja auch . . . bezahlen müssen for she will, after all, also have to pay
die Kosten the expenses (3)
die . . . hinzukommen which will be added
[**hinzu** in addition, besides; near, close (to)]
reichen to last

nachdem Frau P. . . . empfangen hatte after Mrs. P. had received
[**empfangen, er empfängt, empfing, hat empfangen** to receive]
versprochen promised
[**versprechen, er verspricht, versprach, hat versprochen** to promise (3)]
ließ sie . . . erscheinen she had . . . appear

letzte Gunst, bitte. Wollen Sie mir gestatten, noch einen Monat in meinem Haus zu bleiben?"—„Aber natürlich können Sie noch einige Wochen bleiben", sagte der Direktor. „Es wird mir und meiner Firma ein Vergnügen sein, Ihnen auf diese Art ein wenig zu helfen. Und die zwei Schiffskarten, um die Sie bitten, kann ich Ihnen fast bestimmt versprechen. Das ist ein Gefallen, den wir Ihnen gern tun werden. Ich freue mich, daß Sie meinem Rat gefolgt sind. Den Scheck für das Haus bekommen Sie in den nächsten paar Tagen. Und ich persönlich bringe Ihnen morgen den Brief mit der Erlaubnis, daß Sie zu jeder Zeit mit einer anderen Person auf den Schiffen unserer Linie reisen dürfen—sogar erster Klasse, weil Sie uns die Sache mit dem Haus nicht schwieriger gemacht haben, als nötig war."

3.

Der Direktor verließ das Haus und rieb sich draußen die Hände. „Das Haus hat dieser Tage einen Wert von wenigstens vierzigtausend Mark", dachte er. „Die Sache mit den zwei freien Schiffskarten wird uns nicht weh tun. Die gute Frau Piepenbrink hat jetzt freilich Geld; aber wenn sie Seereisen macht und irgendwo bleiben will, sind die fünfundzwanzigtausend Mark bald ausgegeben—eigentlich doppelt so schnell, denn sie wird ja auch die Kosten bezahlen müssen, die durch die zweite Person hinzukommen. Zwei, drei Reisen werden wahrscheinlich alles sein; länger wird das Geld nicht reichen. Aber das ist i h r e Sache, nicht meine. M e i n Problem, das Haus so billig wie möglich zu kaufen, ist auf jeden Fall gelöst."

Nachdem Frau Piepenbrink die versprochene Erlaubnis und den Scheck für das Haus empfangen hatte, ließ sie die folgende Annonce in den Zeitungen von Hamburg und Bremen erscheinen: „Welches junge, gebildete Mädchen möchte eine

---

die Annonce the ad
[**die Annonce, die Annoncen** the advertisement, ad]
gebildet educated (2)

möchte . . . begleiten would like to accompany
[**begleiten** to accompany (2)]
erster Klasse first class
[**die Klasse, die Klassen** the class (2)]
keinerlei Pflichten no duties of any sort
[**die Pflicht, die Pflichten** the duty (3)]
die Schiffahrtslinie the shipping line
[**die Linie, the Linien** the line (2)]

die . . . Antworten the . . . replies
[**die Antwort, die Antworten** the answer, reply (3)]
auf diese Annonce to this ad
[**die Annonce, die Annoncen** the ad (2)]
von Studentinnen from students
[**die Studentin, die Studentinnen** the (female) university student]
die schon lange . . . hatten fahren wollen who had long wanted to travel
denen es aber but for whom
unter among
wählte sie das she chose the one
[**wählen** to choose (2)]
am besten best (2)
packen to pack

das Datum the date
[**das Datum, die Daten** (3)]
die Abfahrt the departure (2)
zugleich at the same time (2)
scheiden to part
sich . . . trösten console herself
[**trösten** to console (3)]
keinerlei Sorgen no worries of any kind

hatte bezahlen müssen had had to pay
das Hotel the hotel
[**das Hotel, die Hotels**]
ehe before
indem sie . . . übersetzen ließ by having . . . translated
[**übersetzen** to translate]
ähnlich similar
sie . . . nur hatte träumen können she had only been able to dream
[**träumen** to dream (4)]

auf diese Art und Weise in this way (and manner)
England England
Italien Italy
Südamerika South America
[**der Süd(en)** the south (2)]
auf Kosten at the expense

ältere Dame für halben Preis erster Klasse nach New York begleiten? Keinerlei Pflichten. Schiffahrtslinie: Atlantica und Co.“

Die vielen Antworten, die Frau Piepenbrink auf diese Annonce bekam, werden niemanden überraschen. Sie kamen besonders von Studentinnen, die schon lange einmal nach Amerika hatten fahren wollen, denen es aber bisher unmöglich gewesen war, den vollen Preis für die teure Reise zu bezahlen. Unter den jungen Mädchen, die Frau Piepenbrink schrieben, wählte sie das, welches ihr am besten gefiel. Dann verkaufte sie alle ihre Sachen und packte ihre Koffer. Den Papagei nahm sie mit.

Das Datum der Abfahrt des Schiffes war zugleich der Tag, an dem Frau Piepenbrink von ihrem Häuschen und Garten für immer scheiden mußte. Das Herz war ihr etwas schwer, aber sie konnte sich jetzt mit dem Gedanken trösten, daß von nun an ihre Zukunft sicher war und daß sie sich keinerlei Sorgen zu machen brauchte.

Der halbe Preis, den das junge Mädchen ihr im voraus hatte bezahlen müssen, machte es Frau Piepenbrink möglich, in New York in einem besseren Hotel zu wohnen und durch kleine Reisen ein wenig das Land kennenzulernen. Ehe das Geld zu Ende ging, suchte sie ein anderes junges Mädchen, indem sie eine ähnliche Annonce übersetzen ließ und in eine New Yorker Zeitung setzte. Von New York fuhr sie dann in eines der vielen anderen Länder, von denen sie in ihrer Jugend nur hatte träumen können.

Auf diese Art und Weise macht Frau Piepenbrink seit Jahren Reisen nach England, nach Italien, nach Südamerika. Es gibt fast kein Land der Welt mehr, das sie nicht kennt. Und alles auf Kosten der Firma Atlantica und Co., die ihr jedesmal zwei neue Schiffskarten geben muß und absolut nichts dagegen tun kann. Was sie sonst braucht, bekommt sie von den jungen Mädchen,

---

absolut absolutely (2)
dagegen against it
was sie sonst braucht what else she needs

es kam manchmal vor it happened sometimes
[**vor-kommen** to happen (2)]
besuchen to visit (2)
geholfen hatte had helped
[**helfen, er hilft, half, hat geholfen** to help (3)]
ihre Besuche her visits
[**der Besuch, die Besuche** the visit (2)]
da sie merkte since she noticed
die Gegenwart the presence
[**die Gegenwart** the present; the presence]
zuckersüß as sweetly (as sugar)
das Geschäft the deal

praktisch practical (2)
getan hatte had put
immer noch still
hat es . . . bestimmt has designated it
[**bestimmen** to determine, to set, to destine, to designate, to intend (2)]
ihre Erben her heirs
[**der Erbe, die Erben** the heir]
der Vetter the cousin
[**der Vetter, die Vetter** the (male) cousin]
die Nichte the niece
[**die Nichte, die Nichten**]
die ihr früher . . . getan hatten who had previously . . . done her

die sie begleiten und ihr gern den halben Preis einer guten Schiffskarte bezahlen, mit der sie billig eine lange Reise machen können.

Es kam manchmal vor, daß Frau Piepenbrink auch nach Cuxhaven zurückkehrte. Während der ersten Jahre vergaß sie dann nie, dort den Direktor zu besuchen, der ihr damals geholfen hatte, das Haus zu einem so guten Preis zu verkaufen. Ihre Besuche hörten jedoch bald auf, da sie merkte, daß ihre Gegenwart dem Direktor nicht sehr angenehm war. Wenn er sie sah, lächelte er nicht mehr so zuckersüß wie damals, als er glaubte, ein solch gutes Geschäft gemacht zu haben.

Die fünfundzwanzigtausend Mark, welche die praktische Frau Piepenbrink auf die Bank getan hatte, liegen immer noch dort. Sie braucht das Geld nicht und hat es deshalb für ihre Erben, einen Vetter und eine Nichte, bestimmt, die ihr früher, in den schlechten alten Tagen, oft einen kleinen Gefallen getan hatten.

LEBEN UND TOD DES SEBASTIAN TAMUSCHAT

[7A]

NOTES

I. 1. When an action is exerted upon the subject (person or thing) by an agent (personal or impersonal, means, or instrument), the passive voice is used both in English and German. English forms the passive by using the past participle and the auxiliary *to be;* German combines the past participle of a verb of action with the proper tense, person, and number of the auxiliary verb **werden.** In the compound tenses, the past participle **geworden** is reduced to **worden.** It comes directly after the past participle, and its presence always indicates a passive voice construction.

Das Warenhaus *wird* neben Frau Piepenbrinks Häuschen *gebaut.* . . . is being built . . .

Die Handschuhe *wurden* für hundertfünfundsechzig Mark *gekauft.* . . . were bought . . .

„Ich *bin* ins Bein *gestochen worden!*", rief der Räuber. "I have been stabbed . . ."

Der Räuber *war* die ganze Zeit *beobachtet worden.* . . . had been observed . . .

2. a. The present infinitive of the passive is formed by combining the past participle of the verb of action with the infinitive **werden.**

„Der Mord wird sicher nicht *entdeckt werden*", dachte Herr Müller. . . . will certainly not be discovered . . .

„Warum muß i c h zu dem Haus *geschickt werden?*", sagte sich der Räuber. . . . must *I* be sent . . .

b. The past infinitive of the passive combines the past participle of the verb of action with **worden sein.** All three always stand together, in that order.

„Der Mann muß aus dem Zug *geworfen worden sein*", dachte der intelligente Polizeiinspektor. . . . must have been thrown . . .

3. English *by* is usually expressed by **von. Durch** is used when the accent is on the cause, means, or instrument by which the action is brought about.

Der junge Mann wurde *von* Herrn Müller aus dem Zug geworfen.

Der Schatz war *von* Jans und Jens gestohlen worden.

Der Mörder wurde *durch* die Karte entdeckt, die der junge Mann im Ärmel hatte.

***Durch* den Brief, der ihm *von* Bolte geschickt worden war, war Meierbach auf den Gedanken gebracht worden, ihn zu ermorden.**

4. If the German verb of action governs the *dative* case in the *active* voice, the dative must be retained in the passive construction.

   Kein Arzt konnte *ihm* helfen.—*Ihm* konnte von keinem Arzt *geholfen werden.* He could not be helped . . .

   Der alte Dieb hatte *dem* König geraten . . .—*Dem König war* von dem alten Dieb *geraten worden* . . . The king had been advised by . . .

5. While English passives must have a subject, German passives can do without one if the subject is considered unnecessary or obvious from the context. In this case, the impersonal **es** is used as the "subject" if it introduces the sentence. It is omitted if the sentence begins with another word. This so-called impersonal passive must be paraphrased in English.

   Nun *wurde* im Haus der Räuber nach Herzenslust *gegessen, getrunken* und *getanzt.* *They* (= the four friends) now ate, drank, and danced . . .

   ***Es wurde gelacht,* aber so leise, daß die Prinzessin nichts hören konnte.** *They* (= the ladies) laughed, but . . .

   Examples of passive voice constructions from Story 7A:

   (1) **Die Geschichte, die Ihnen heute *erzählt wird* . . .** . . . which is being told to you today . . . (= which we are telling you today)

   (2) **An diesem Tage *wurde* er von einem Freund *besucht,* der . . .** . . . he was visited by a friend who . . .

   (3) **Der Kaufmann *ist* heute früh in seinem Zimmer *gefunden worden.*** . . . was found this morning . . .

   (4) **Der Freund *war* von der Tante *gebeten worden* . . .** . . . had been asked by the aunt . . .

   (5) **Das Haus, das sein Onkel besaß, sollte *verkauft werden.*** . . . was to be sold.

   Dann wirst du *freigelassen werden.* Then you will be set free.

   Er mußte durch etwas *geweckt worden sein,* was . . . He must have been awakened by something which . . .

   Der Kaufmann konnte nur von Sebastian *ermordet*

worden sein. . . . could only have been murdered by Sebastian.

(6) **Als *ihm* das Messer *gezeigt wurde* . . .** When he was shown the knife; when the knife was shown to to him . . .

Das Buch, das *ihm geschenkt worden war* . . . . . . that he had been given; that had been given to him . . .

(7) **Von der Polizei *wurde* nach Zeugen *gesucht.*** Witnesses were being sought by the police; the police looked for witnesses.

***Wurde* gestern nicht *gesagt* . . .?** Was it not said yesterday; did not someone say yesterday . . .?

Während *gefragt* und *geantwortet wurde* . . . While questions were (being) asked and answered . . .

Als der Brief ankam, in dem *befohlen wurde* . . . . . . in which the order was given; which contained the order . . .

II. 1. When *two* past participles in a compound tense take the *same auxiliary* form, only *one* of the auxiliaries need be expressed.

Er sah sich von mehreren Soldaten umgeben, die kurz nach ihm angekommen (waren) und von ihren Pferden gesprungen waren. He saw himself surrounded by several soldiers who had arrived shortly after him and had jumped from their horses.

2. A *single* auxiliary in a compound tense is sometimes omitted in *dependent* clauses when the auxiliary is clearly understood.

. . . wie er für etwas litt, was er nicht getan (hatte), und wie er starb. . . . how he suffered for something that he had not done, and how he died.

Er sah die kleine Schule, wo er erzogen worden (war), sein Heim und seine Frau . . . . . . where he had been educated, his home and his wife . . .

Er sah die zwei Knaben, auf die er so stolz gewesen (war) . . . . . . of whom he had been so proud . . .

REVIEW OF STRONG AND IRREGULAR VERBS USED IN STORY 6B

bieten		bot	geboten	*to offer*
empfangen	empfängt	empfing	empfangen	*to receive*
empfehlen	empfiehlt	empfahl	empfohlen	*to recommend*
entscheiden		entschied	entschieden	*to decide*

IDIOMS FOR REVIEW

in Geschäften on business
bis zum Morgen until morning
gegen Mittag toward noon
von außen from the outside
bis auf den letzten Pfennig down to the last penny
es gibt keinen Zweifel there is no doubt
Hoffnung (Mut) machen to give hope (courage)
gern haben to like
  sie hatten ihn gern they liked him
zu Fuß on foot
vor langer Zeit a long time ago
was für Sünden what kind of sins
zur Seite nehmen to take aside
laß mich in Frieden! leave me alone!
eines Nachts one night
zu so früher Stunde at such an early hour
vor dem Tode retten to save from death
um . . . willen for the sake of, for . . . sake
  um Gottes willen! for Heaven's sake!
es wurde ihm leicht ums Herz his heart grew light

Sebastian Tamuschat name of the principal character

die Ihnen . . . erzählt wird which you are being told
  [*literally:* which is being told to you]
 etwas anderer Art of a somewhat different kind
 als diejenigen than those
  [**derjenige, diejenige, dasjenige** the one]
brav upright
  [**brav** good, well behaved; honest, upright (2)]
 von dem Gipfel from the peak
  [**der Gipfel, die Gipfel** the summit, peak, top (2)]
 in das bitterste Unglück into the most bitter misfortune
  [**bitter** bitter (3)]
  [**das Unglück** the misfortune]
 gestürzt wurde was plunged
 der stets nach dem Rechten gestrebt hatte who had always striven for what was right

(FIVE PARTS)

Leben und Tod des Sebastian Tamuschat

1.

Die Geschichte, die Ihnen heute erzählt wird, ist etwas anderer Art als diejenigen, die Sie bis jetzt gehört haben. Sie berichtet, wie ein braver, einfacher Mann eines Tages von dem Gipfel seines Glückes in das bitterste Unglück gestürzt wurde; wie er, der stets nach dem Rechten gestrebt hatte, für etwas litt, was er nicht getan, und wie er starb.

Um die Mitte der zweiten Hälfte des achtzehnten Jahrhunderts lebte in Kosel, einer kleinen Stadt im Südosten des Königreiches Preußen, ein junger Kaufmann namens Sebastian Tamuschat. Das Leben hatte alle seine Wünsche erfüllt. Seine

---

[**stets** always (2)]
[**streben** to strive]
was er nicht getan what he had not done

um die Mitte toward the middle
achtzehnt eighteenth
das Jahrhundert the century
[**das Jahrhundert, die Jahrhunderte** the century (2)]
im Südosten in the southeast
[**der Süd(en)** the south (3)]
[**der Ost(en)** the east]
das Königreich the kingdom (3)
Preußen Prussia
namens by the name of
erfüllen to fulfill (4)

die Ehe the marriage (3)
blühen flourish
[**blühen** to bloom, to blossom, to flourish (3)]
lieben to love (3)
da er since he
und man . . . rechnen konnte and one could . . . count
auf seine Hilfe on his help
[**die Hilfe** the help]
und von den anderen and by the others
wurde er . . . geachtet und gerühmt he was respected and praised
[**achten** to respect, to esteem]
[**achten auf** to pay attention to, to take care of]
[**rühmen** to praise]
gerade upright
der Charakter the character (2)

das Unglück the misfortune (2)
traf struck
[**treffen, er trifft, traf, hat getroffen** to meet, encounter; to hit, strike (3)]
wurde er . . . besucht he was visited
[**besuchen** to visit (3)]
von einem Freund by a friend
die Provinzhauptstadt the provincial capital
[**die Provinz, die Provinzen** the province]
[**die Haupstadt, die Hauptstädte** the capital (2)]
in Geschäften on business
ein naher Verwandter a close relative
[**der Verwandte, die Verwandten** the relative]
[**verwandt** related]
ein Onkel an uncle
[**der Onkel, die Onkel** the uncle]
verkauft werden sollte was to be sold
die Tante the aunt
[**die Tante, die Tanten**]
sich . . . befand found herself
[**sich befinden** to be, to find oneself (3)]
die Not the need
[**die Not** the need, distress, misery, necessity, want (3)]
der Freund war . . . gebeten worden the friend had been asked
von der Tante by the aunt
[**die Tante, die Tanten** the aunt (2)]
Sebastian zu berichten to tell Sebastian
die Hilfe the help (2)
gebraucht wurde was needed

Ehe war glücklich, sein Geschäft blühte, und er lebte mit Gott und der Welt in Frieden. Seine Freunde und Nachbarn liebten ihn, da er stets freundlich war und man immer auf seine Hilfe rechnen konnte; und von den anderen, die ihn kannten oder von ihm gehört hatten, wurde er wegen seines geraden Charakters geachtet und gerühmt.

An dem Tage, an dem ihn das Unglück traf, wurde er von einem Freund besucht, der in der Provinzhauptstadt wohnte und in Geschäften nach Kosel gekommen war. Von ihm erfuhr Sebastian, daß ein naher Verwandter, ein Onkel, gestorben war, daß das Häuschen, das er besaß, verkauft werden sollte, um Schulden zu bezahlen, und daß seine Tante sich mit ihrer Familie in großer Not befand. Der Freund war von der Tante gebeten worden, Sebastian zu berichten, daß schnelle Hilfe gebraucht wurde. Sebastian, der wohl wußte, daß er der einzige war, durch den seine Verwandten vor noch größerem Unglück gerettet werden konnten, hielt es für seine Pflicht, alles zu tun, was in seiner Macht stand. Er beschloß, sogleich mit einer großen Summe Geldes in die Hauptstadt zu eilen. Sein Wagen stand bereit, die Pferde waren schon aus dem Stall geführt worden, Sebastian hatte eben seine Kinder geküßt, als seine Frau ihm plötzlich um den Hals fiel und sagte: „Warte bis morgen, Sebastian! Fahre nicht jetzt, denn ich habe einen bösen Traum gehabt."—„Was für einen Traum?" entgegnete Seba-

---

durch den seine Verwandten . . . gerettet werden konnten through whom his relatives could be saved
[**der Verwandte, die Verwandten** the relative (2)]
[**verwandt** related (2)]
[**retten** to save, to rescue, to salvage (3)]
vor noch größerem Unglück from a still greater misfortune
hielt es für considered it
[**halten für** to consider, to believe to be (3)]
die Macht the power
bereit ready (2)
waren . . . geführt worden had been led
der Stall the stable (3)
küssen to kiss (3)
ihm . . . um den Hals fiel embraced him
der Traum the dream
[**der Traum, die Träume** (2)]

der Hut the hat (3)
grau gray (2)
das Zeichen the sign
[**das Zeichen, die Zeichen** (3)]
weise wise (2)
darauf thereupon
machte er sich auf den Weg he set out on his way

unterwegs on the way (3)
ebenfalls likewise
in Geschäften on business (2)
reisen to travel (3)
das Gasthaus the inn (3)
das . . . empfohlen worden war that had been recommended
[**empfehlen, er empfiehlt, empfahl, hat empfohlen** to recommend (2)]
wo ihnen . . . gegeben wurden where they were given
von dem Wirt by the innkeeper
[**der Wirt, die Wirte** the innkeeper (3)]
zu Abend gegessen hatten had eaten supper
[**zu Abend essen** to have supper]
der Schlaf the sleep (3)

er mußte . . . durch etwas geweckt worden sein he must have been awakened by something
das Nebenzimmer the adjoining room
wurde . . . nicht wieder gestört was not disturbed again
[**stören** to disturb (3)]

er reiste gern he liked to travel
kühl cool (2)
und da er and since he
der Reisesack the traveling bag
[**der Sack, die Säcke** the sack, bag (4)]
der Schlüssel the key (4)
der ihm . . . gegeben worden war which had been given to him
und machte sich auf den Weg and set out on his way

gegen Mittag around noon
um sich auszuruhen to rest
[**sich aus-ruhen** to rest (3)]
fressen to eat (of beasts)
[**fressen, er frißt, fraß, hat gefressen** (3)]
sah er sich . . . umgeben he saw himself surrounded
[**umgeben, er umgibt, umgab, hat umgeben** (3)]
der Polizeioffizier the police officer
[**der Offizier, die Offiziere** the officer]
er wurde . . . geführt he was led

stian lächelnd.–„Ich habe geträumt, daß es lange dauern wird, bis du zurückkommst", sagte die Frau; „ich sah dich zurückkehren; doch als du ankamst und den Hut vom Kopfe nahmst, hattest du graue Haare."–„Das ist ein gutes Zeichen", erwiderte Sebastian und lachte; „es bedeutet, daß ich in wenigen Tagen viel weiser geworden bin." Darauf machte er sich auf den Weg.

Unterwegs traf er einen anderen Kaufmann, den er kannte und der ebenfalls in Geschäften in die Hauptstadt fuhr. Sie reisten zusammen und hielten am Abend an einem Gasthaus, das dem anderen Kaufmann empfohlen worden war und wo ihnen von dem Wirt zwei Zimmer für die Nacht gegeben wurden. Nachdem beide zu Abend gegessen hatten, bezahlte Sebastian seine Rechnung und ging in sein Zimmer, wo er sogleich in einen tiefen Schlaf fiel.

Plötzlich wachte er auf. Er mußte, so schien es ihm, durch etwas geweckt worden sein, was im Nebenzimmer zu Boden gefallen war. Aber er hatte wahrscheinlich nur geträumt, dachte er, denn jetzt war alles wieder still. Er schlief bald wieder ein, und seine Ruhe wurde bis zum Morgen nicht wieder gestört.

Er reiste gern, solange das Wetter noch kühl war, und da er die Absicht hatte, so schnell wie möglich die Hauptstadt zu erreichen, stand er früh auf, nahm seinen Reisesack, öffnete die Haustür mit dem Schlüssel, der ihm am Abend von dem Wirt gegeben worden war, holte die Pferde aus dem Stall und machte sich auf den Weg.

Gegen Mittag hielt er an einem Gasthaus, um sich auszuruhen und seinen Pferden zu fressen zu geben. Während er noch bei seinem Wagen im Hof stand, sah er sich plötzlich von mehreren Soldaten und einem Polizeioffizier umgeben, die kurz nach ihm angekommen und von ihren Pferden gesprungen waren. Er wurde in ein leeres Zimmer geführt, und nun begann der Polizeioffizier ihn zu fragen: War er gestern allein gereist oder mit jemand anderem? Mit einem Kaufmann? Wie hieß der Kaufmann? Hatte er ihn heute morgen noch

---

wie hieß der Kaufmann? what was the merchant's name?
[**heißen, hieß, hat geheißen** to be called (2)]
heute morgen this morning (3)

noch einmal once more
zu so früher Stunde at such an early hour

daß er . . . gefragt wurde that he was being questioned
auf diese Weise in this manner
die Wahrheit the truth (3)
beschrieb genau described exactly
[**beschreiben, beschrieb, hat beschrieben** to describe]
warum werde ich gefragt und behandelt why am I being questioned and treated
[**behandeln** to treat]
ist etwas gestohlen worden? has anything been stolen?
[**stehlen, er stiehlt, stahl, hat gestohlen** to steal (3)]

mit dem du . . . gesehen wurdest with whom you were seen
streng stern
[**streng** severe, stern, strict (3)]
ist . . . gefunden worden was found
heute früh this morning
mit durchschnittener Kehle with his throat cut
[**durch-schneiden** (or **durchschneiden**) to cut through]
[**schneiden, schnitt, hat geschnitten** to cut (3)]
[**die Kehle, die Kehlen** the throat (2)]
bis du gerufen wirst until you will be called

um sprechen zu können to be able to speak
wurde . . . abgeschlossen was locked
[**ab-schließen** to lock]
[**schließen, schloß, hat geschlossen** to close, shut, lock; to conclude (3)]
von außen from the outside
[**außen** outside (2)]
wurde den Soldaten befohlen the soldiers were ordered
[**befehlen, er befiehlt, befahl, hat befohlen** to order, to command (3)]
zu suchen to search
der Reisesack the traveling bag (2)
zog etwas hervor pulled something out
[**hervor-ziehen** to pull out, to draw out (2)]
Sebastian wurde gerufen und . . . geführt Sebastian was called and taken
als ihm . . . gezeigt wurde when he was shown
blutbedeckt blood-covered
[**bedecken** to cover (2)]
das . . . entdeckt worden war which had been discovered
von dem Soldaten by the soldier
erschrak er he became frightened
[**erschrecken, er erschrickt, erschrak, ist erschrocken** to be frightened (3)]

einmal gesehen? Warum hatte er das Gasthaus zu so früher Stunde verlassen?

2.

Sebastian wunderte sich, daß er auf diese Weise gefragt wurde; aber er antwortete, sagte die Wahrheit und beschrieb genau, was geschehen war, seit er den Kaufmann gestern getroffen hatte. „Aber", so fragte er schließlich, als er fertig war, „warum werde ich gefragt und behandelt wie jemand, der etwas Böses getan hat? Bin ich ein Dieb? Ist etwas gestohlen worden? Was ist geschehen?"

„Der Kaufmann, mit dem du gestern gereist bist und mit dem du gesehen wurdest", antwortete der Polizeioffizier mit strenger Stimme, „ist heute früh mit durchschnittener Kehle in seinem Zimmer gefunden worden. Ich kann dich nicht weiterfahren lassen; du mußt hierbleiben und warten, bis du gerufen wirst."

Sebastian war zu überrascht, um sprechen zu können. Die Tür wurde von außen abgeschlossen; er war allein. Draußen wurde den Soldaten befohlen, in Sebastians Sachen zu suchen, die im Wagen lagen. Einer öffnete den Reisesack, zog etwas hervor und reichte es dem Offizier. Sebastian wurde gerufen und zu dem Wagen geführt. Als ihm das blutbedeckte Messer gezeigt wurde, das von dem Soldaten entdeckt worden war, erschrak er und wurde bleich. Die einzigen Worte, die er über die Lippen bringen konnte, waren: „Es gehört nicht mir."

Die Soldaten suchten weiter. In Sebastians Taschen wurden die achttausend Mark gefunden, die für die Familie seiner Tante bestimmt waren. Alles Geld, das der tote Kaufmann bei

---

bleich pale (3)

wurden . . . gefunden were found
bestimmt waren were meant

bei sich on him
war . . . gestohlen worden had been stolen
bis auf down to
in dessen Gesellschaft in whose company
gesehen worden war had been seen
darum therefore
wurde verhaftet was arrested
[**verhaften** to arrest (2)]
bei sich on him
wurde ihm weggenommen was taken away from him
[**weg-nehmen** to take away (3)]
banden tied
[**binden, band, hat gebunden** to bind, to tie (2)]
er wurde . . . geworfen he was thrown
und . . . gebracht and taken

an dem er . . . geführt werden sollte on which he was to be taken
wurde . . . nach Zeugen gesucht witnesses were sought
[**der Zeuge, die Zeugen** the witness]
von denen by whom
beobachtet worden sein mochte might have been observed
man fand zwar keine one did not find any, to be sure
die Schuld the guilt
auch ohne Zeugen even without witnesses
[**der Zeuge, die Zeugen** the witness (2)]
beweisen zu können to be able to prove
[**beweisen, bewies, hat bewiesen** (3)]
schwor swore
[**schwören, schwor, hat geschworen** to swear]
von ihm persönlich by him personally
[**persönlich** personal (2)]
abgeschlossen worden war had been locked
[**ab-schließen** to lock (2)]
dem Richter . . . gezeigt wurden were shown to the judge
von Sebastian ermordet worden sein konnte could . . . have been murdered by Sebastian
[**ermorden** to murder (2)]
wurde . . . verurteilt was sentenced
[**verurteilen** to sentence]
lebenslänglich lifelong
und . . . bestimmt and assigned
die Strafkolonie the penal colony
im Osten des Reiches in the eastern part of the kingdom
[**der Ost(en)** the east (2)]
[**das Reich, die Reiche** the realm, kingdom, empire (4)]

waren ihm . . . Briefe geschickt worden letters had been sent to him
von mehreren Freunden by several friends

sich getragen hatte, war bis auf den letzten Pfennig gestohlen worden, und Sebastian war die einzige Person, in dessen Gesellschaft der Kaufmann gesehen worden war. Der Polizeioffizier glaubte darum, den Mörder gefangen zu haben. Sebastian wurde verhaftet. Was er bei sich hatte, wurde ihm weggenommen. Die Soldaten banden ihn, er wurde in den Wagen geworfen und am gleichen Tage in die nächste Stadt gebracht.

Während er im Gefängnis Hunger und Durst litt und auf den Tag wartete, an dem er vor den Richter geführt werden sollte, wurde von der Polizei nach Zeugen gesucht, von denen Sebastian in jener Nacht im Gasthaus beobachtet worden sein mochte. Man fand zwar keine, aber man glaubte, Sebastians Schuld auch ohne Zeugen beweisen zu können. Außer ihm waren nur der Wirt und der Kaufmann im Gasthaus gewesen; der Wirt schwor, daß die Haustür am Abend von ihm persönlich abgeschlossen worden war, und als schließlich dem Richter das Messer und das Geld gezeigt wurden, da gab es keinen Zweifel mehr, daß der Kaufmann nur von Sebastian ermordet worden sein konnte. Sebastian wurde zu lebenslänglichem Gefängnis verurteilt und für eine Strafkolonie im Osten des Reiches bestimmt.

Während er noch im Gefängnis gelegen hatte, waren ihm von mehreren Freunden Briefe geschickt worden. Sie hatten versucht, ihn zu trösten und ihm Hoffnung und Mut zu machen; aber Sebastian fühlte, daß er auch in ihren Augen der Mörder war. Der schwerste Schlag traf ihn jedoch, als er eines Tages von seiner Frau besucht wurde, der es gelungen war, Erlaubnis zu bekommen, einige Minuten mit ihm zu

---

und ihm Hoffnung und Mut zu machen and to give him hope and courage
  [**die Hoffnung** the hope (3)]
  [**der Mut** the courage (2)]
 der Mörder the murderer (3)
der Schlag the blow
  [**der Schlag, die Schläge** the blow, stroke (3)]
 traf ihn struck him
 als er . . . besucht wurde when he was visited

ob du es warst whether it was you
fortgegangen war had left
[**fort-gehen** to go away, to leave (3)]
weinen to weep (4)
verzweifeln an to despair of (2)
menschlich human (3)
die Gerechtigkeit the justice (3)
auf ihn muß ich trauen in Him must I trust

wurde er . . . gebracht he was taken
die Provinzhauptstadt the provincial capital
[**die Provinz, die Provinzen** the province (2)]
Gefangene prisoners
[**der Gefangene, die Gefangenen** the prisoner]
die . . . bestimmt worden waren who had been assigned
die Strafkolonie the penal colony (2)
wurden alle . . . geführt all were led
der Gefängnishof the prison courtyard
bis ihnen die Hände . . . gebunden wurden until their hands were tied
von Soldaten begleitet accompanied by soldiers
[**begleiten** to accompany (3)]
wurden sie . . . getrieben they were driven
[**treiben, trieb, hat getrieben** to drive (3)]
wie eine Herde Vieh like a herd of cattle
[**die Herde, die Herden** the herd (3)]
[**das Vieh** the cattle]
der Marsch the march
währen to last
einsam isolated (2)
das Ziel the destination
[**das Ziel, die Ziele** the goal, aim, target, destination (3)]

der Ort the place (3)
die Wohnung the habitation
[**die Wohnung, die Wohnungen** the apartment, lodging, habitation (3)]
die Außenwelt the outside world (2)
vollkommen completely
abgeschnitten cut off
[**ab-schneiden** to cut off (2)]
der Schnee the snow
der Verlust the loss
die Freiheit the freedom (2)
empfand felt
[**empfinden, empfand, hat empfunden** to feel (3)]
der Gram um alles, was his grief for all that
[**der Gram** the grief, sorrow]
verwandeln to change (2)
früher formerly

sprechen. Als sie ihn bat, ihr die Wahrheit zu sagen und ihn fragte: „Sag mir, deiner Frau, ob du es warst, der es getan hat!", da wußte er, daß es für ihn auf dieser Welt keine Hoffnung mehr gab. Als seine Frau fortgegangen war, weinte er bittere Tränen und verzweifelte an der menschlichen Gerechtigkeit. „Jetzt weiß nur Gott allein, daß ich ohne Schuld bin", sagte er sich; „auf ihn muß ich trauen."

Nach einiger Zeit wurde er in ein Gefängnis der Provinzhauptstadt gebracht, in dem sich schon andere Gefangene befanden, die für die gleiche Strafkolonie bestimmt worden waren wie er. Eines Nachts wurden alle in den Gefängnishof geführt. Dort mußten sie warten, bis ihnen die Hände auf den Rücken gebunden wurden. Dann, von Soldaten begleitet, wurden sie wie eine Herde Vieh durch die Stadt getrieben. Nach einem Marsch, der mehrere Tage währte und sie durch weite, einsame Wälder führte, erreichten sie endlich ihr Ziel. Hier, an der Grenze des Reiches, befand sich die Strafkolonie.

3.

An diesem Orte, fern von jeder menschlichen Wohnung und von der Außenwelt vollkommen abgeschnitten, blieb Sebastian sechsundzwanzig Jahre. Sein Haar wurde grau und schließlich weiß wie Schnee. Der Verlust der Freiheit, den er tief empfand, und der Gram um alles, was er besessen und geliebt hatte, verwandelten ihn in einen anderen Menschen. Er, der früher froh und lustig gewesen war, lachte nicht mehr und sprach jetzt nur, wenn er es für nötig hielt. Wenn seine Lippen sich bewegten, so war es, um zu beten. Abends, wenn er mit den anderen von der schweren Arbeit im Wald zurück-

---

froh gay (4)
lustig cheerful (3)
wenn er es für nötig hielt if he considered it necessary
[**nötig** necessary (2)]
beten to pray
abends in the evening (3)

das Tageslicht the light of day
im „Leben der Heiligen" in the *Lives of the Saints*
[**der Heilige, die Heiligen** the saint]
[**heilig** holy]
das ihm . . . geschenkt worden war that had been given to him
[**schenken** to give (as a present)]
von einem Gefangenen by a prisoner
[**der Gefangene, die Gefangenen** the prisoner (2)]
kurz vor dessen Tod shortly before the latter's death

hatten ihn gern liked him
[**gern haben** to like]
loben to praise
still quiet (4)
friedliebend peace-loving (2)
das Wesen the nature (3)
warum er . . . geachtet wurde why he was respected
von den anderen Gefangenen by the other prisoners
Onkel uncle
[**der Onkel, die Onkel** the uncle (2)]
wurde irgend etwas gebraucht if something was needed
das Gefängnisleben the prison life
weniger hart less hard
[**hart** hard (3)]
der . . . geschickt wurde who was sent
ein paar Wolldecken a few woolen blankets (2)
[**die Wolle** the wool (2)]
[**die Decke, die Decken** the blanket; ceiling (3)]
die Kranken the sick
[**der Kranke, die Kranken** the sick man; the sick (people)]
[**krank** sick, ill (3)]
und wenn es vorkam and when it happened
[**vor-kommen** to happen, to occur (3)]
sich stritten quarreled
[**streiten, stritt, hat gestritten** to fight, to quarrel]
wenn Situationen entstanden when situations arose
[**entstehen, entstand, ist entstanden** to originate, to come about, to arise (2)]
die . . . geheimgehalten werden mußten which had to be kept secret
[**geheim-halten** to keep secret (2)]
[**geheim** secret (3)]
vor den Beamten from the officials
der gebeten wurde who was asked
zu entscheiden to decide
[**entscheiden, entschied, hat entschieden** to decide (2)]
was getan werden sollte what was to be done

nicht einmal not even

kehrte, las er, solange das Tageslicht noch durch die kleinen Fenster drang, im „Leben der Heiligen", das ihm von einem Gefangenen kurz vor dessen Tod geschenkt worden war.

Die Soldaten hatten ihn gern und lobten ihn, weil er den anderen ein gutes Beispiel gab, und die Offiziere trauten ihm wegen seiner stillen, ruhigen Art. Sein friedliebendes Wesen war auch der Grund, warum er von den anderen Gefangenen geachtet wurde. Sie nannten ihn „Onkel". Wurde irgend etwas gebraucht, um das Gefängnisleben weniger hart zu machen, dann war es jedesmal „Onkel" Sebastian, der zu den Beamten geschickt wurde, um für sie alle zu sprechen und um etwas Brot und Kartoffeln zu bitten oder ein paar Wolldecken für die Kranken zu verlangen. Und wenn es vorkam, daß die Gefangenen sich stritten, oder wenn Situationen entstanden, die vor den Beamten geheimgehalten werden mußten, so war es stets wieder Sebastian, der gebeten wurde, zu entscheiden, was getan werden sollte.

So kamen und gingen die Monate, ein Jahr folgte dem anderen, und Sebastian wußte nicht einmal, ob seine Frau und Kinder noch lebten, denn den Gefangenen wurde nicht erlaubt, Briefe zu empfangen. Was draußen geschah, erfuhr man nur durch neue Gefangene, die von Zeit zu Zeit an Stelle derer geschickt wurden, die inzwischen in der Strafkolonie gestorben waren. An solchen Tagen sammelten sich alle am Abend nach der Arbeit um die neuen Gefangenen. Jeder wurde gefragt, aus welcher Stadt oder welchem Dorf er kam und warum er verurteilt worden war. Während gefragt und geantwortet wurde, saß

---

den Gefangenen wurde nicht erlaubt the prisoners were not permitted
empfangen to receive
[**empfangen, er empfängt, empfing, hat empfangen** to receive (2)]
die . . . an Stelle derer geschickt wurden who were sent . . . in the place of those
inzwischen in the meantime (3)
sammeln to gather (3)
jeder wurde gefragt each one was asked
er verurteilt worden war he had been sentenced
[**verurteilen** to sentence (2)]
während gefragt und geantwortet wurde while questions were asked and answered

mit stumpfem Blick with a dull gaze
[**stumpf** dull, blunt]
die Bank the bench
[**die Bank, die Bänke** the bench (2)]
hörte schweigend zu listened silently
unter among

einst aber once, however
[**einst** once, once upon a time (2)]
der Winter the winter (3)
als wieder einmal when once again
gebracht wurden were brought

breit broad (3)
hervorstehend protruding
Backenknochen cheekbones
[**die Backe, die Backen** the cheek (3)]
[**der Knochen, die Knochen** the bone (3)]
um verurteilt zu werden to be sentenced
urteilt selbst judge for yourselves
[**urteilen** to judge (2)]

der Vetter the cousin
[**der Vetter, die Vetter** the (male) cousin (2)]
der Heimweg the way home
zu Fuß on foot
auf einmal suddenly
einige Schritte a few paces
[**der Schritt, die Schritte** the step, pace (3)]
schreiten to step
[**schreiten, schritt, ist geschritten** to go, to step, to walk]
es mußte . . . gebunden worden sein it must have been tied
von jemandem by someone
der Baumstamm the trunk of a tree
[**der Stamm, die Stämme** the stem, trunk, stalk; the tribe (2)]
war dort stehengelassen worden had been left standing there
von wem? by whom?
ich fror I was cold
[**frieren, fror, ist/hat gefroren** to freeze, to be cold (3)]
ohne die geringste Absicht without the slightest intention
[**gering** small, little, slight (3)]
reiten to ride
ich wurde verhaftet I was arrested
so wurde mir gesagt so I was told
war . . . gestohlen worden had been stolen
das Nachbardorf the neighboring village
mußte ich . . . sein I had to be
war . . . beobachtet worden had . . . been observed

Sebastian mit stumpfem Blick auf einer Bank in der Ecke und hörte schweigend zu. Unter den neuen Gefangenen war bisher niemand gewesen, der aus Kosel kam oder dort jemanden kannte.

Einst aber, im Winter des sechsundzwanzigsten Jahres, als wieder einmal Gefangene in die Strafkolonie gebracht wurden, befand sich unter ihnen ein Mann aus Kosel. Sein Name war Barnabas Kralik.

Barnabas war ein großer, starker Mann von etwa sechzig Jahren, mit breiten Schultern, einem roten Bart und hervorstehenden Backenknochen. „Ihr fragt", sagte er mit lauter Stimme, „was ich getan habe? Nicht genug, sage ich euch, um verurteilt zu werden, mein ganzes Leben in diesem Loch zu bleiben. Hört zu und urteilt selbst!

„Letzten Winter besuchte ich einen Verwandten, einen Vetter, der in der nächsten Stadt wohnte. Auf dem Heimweg kam ich durch einen Wald. Ich war zu Fuß. Auf einmal sehe ich einige Schritte vor mir ein Pferd stehen. Ich schreite näher. Das Pferd ist allein. Es mußte von jemandem an den Baumstamm gebunden worden sein und war dort stehengelassen worden. Aber von wem? Ich rufe. Keine Antwort. Es war bitterkalt, ich fror und war müde. Warum nimmst du nicht das Pferd, denke ich, und versuchst später, zu erfahren, wem es gehört? Ich steige also auf das Pferd, ohne die geringste Absicht, es zu behalten, und will nach Haus reiten. Kaum habe ich jedoch den Wald verlassen, da höre ich Stimmen und Pferde hinter mir. Es ist die Polizei. Ich wurde verhaftet. Das Pferd, so wurde mir gesagt, war in einem Nachbardof gestohlen worden, und weil ich es hatte, mußte ich der Dieb sein. Der wirkliche Dieb, denke ich, war vielleicht von irgendeinem Bauern beobachtet worden, hatte das Pferd im Wald versteckt und war geflohen. Ich wurde verurteilt und hierhergebracht.—So, jetzt

---

von irgendeinem Bauern by some peasant
[**der Bauer, die Bauern** the farmer, peasant (3)]
war geflohen had fled
[**fliehen, floh, ist geflohen** to flee (2)]

behaupten to claim
  [**behaupten** to assert, to maintain, to claim (2)]
vor langer Zeit a long time ago
bin ich . . . nicht entdeckt worden I was not discovered

woher where . . . from
die Nähe the vicinity (3)
heiraten to marry (3)
 reich rich (4)
 ist . . . geworden became
 vor zwei Jahren two years ago
 das Rathaus the city hall
 obwohl although (2)
 gewesen sein soll is said to have been
stumpf dully
  [**stumpf** dull, blunt (2)]

gebeten wurden were asked
 ihre Lebensgeschichte the story of their lives
 schütteln to shake (4)
 er liebte es nicht he did not like
und habe . . . wohl verdient and have probably deserved
 wegen meiner Sünden because of my sins
  [**die Sünde, die Sünden** the sin]
und einer wissen wollte and someone wanted to know
 was für Sünden what (kind of) sins
  [**die Sünde, die Sünden** (2)]
 erklärte einer one . . . explained
  [**erklären** to explain; to declare (3)]
 was Sebastian geschehen war what had happened to Sebastian
wiederholen to repeat (4)
 der . . . gefunden worden war who had been found
 mit durchschnittener Kehle with his throat cut
 das . . . entdeckt wurde which was discovered
 und . . . gesteckt worden sein mußte and must have been put
während while
 erzählt wurde was being told
 hörten alle . . . zu all listened
 das Interesse the interest
 scharf anzusehen to look sharply at
  [**scharf** sharp (3)]
  [**an-sehen** to look at (2)]
 als ob as if
 sich an ihn zu erinnern to remember him
  [**sich erinnern (an)** to remember (3)]
  [**erinnern** to remind (3)]
genannt wurde was mentioned
 murmeln to murmur (2)

wißt ihr alle, warum ich hier bin. Wegen nichts. Wegen nichts, sage ich euch! Ich will nicht behaupten, daß ich nie in meinem Leben eine Strafe verdient habe. Ja, einmal, vor langer Zeit, habe ich etwas wirklich Böses getan. Nur bin ich damals nicht entdeckt worden."

„Woher kommst du?" fragte einer.–„Aus der Nähe von Kosel", antwortete Barnabas. Bei diesen Worten hob Sebastian den Kopf und fragte: „Kennst du die Familie Tamuschat?"– „Ob ich die Tamuschats kenne?" entgegnete Barnabas. „Aber natürlich! Die Frau ist seit langem tot. Den Kindern geht es gut. Das Mädchen hat gut geheiratet, der älteste Sohn ist der reichste Kaufmann der Stadt, und der andere ist vor zwei Jahren ein hoher Beamter im Rathaus geworden, obwohl der Vater ein Mörder gewesen sein soll. Doch warum fragst du? Kennst du die Leute?"–„Ja, ich kenne sie", antwortete Sebastian. Dann schwieg er und sah wieder stumpf zu Boden.

4.

Später, als auch die alten Gefangenen gebeten wurden, ihre Lebensgeschichte zu erzählen, schüttelte Sebastian nur den Kopf; er liebte es nicht, von seinem Unglück zu sprechen. Alles, was er sagte, war: „Ich bin schon sechsundzwanzig Jahre hier und habe meine Strafe wegen meiner Sünden wohl verdient." Als er nicht weitersprach und einer wissen wollte, was für Sünden er meinte, erklärte einer der alten Gefangenen, was Sebastian geschehen war. Er wiederholte die Geschichte von dem Kaufmann, der damals mit durchschnittener Kehle in dem Gasthaus gefunden worden war, und von dem blutbedeckten Messer, das später entdeckt wurde und von dem wirklichen Mörder in Sebastians Sachen gesteckt worden sein mußte. Während die Geschichte erzählt wurde, hörten alle mit großem Interesse zu; besonders aber Barnabas, der schon nach einigen Augenblicken begonnen hatte, Sebastian scharf anzusehen, als ob er versuchte, sich an ihn zu erinnern. Als Sebastians Name genannt wurde, erschrak er, wurde bleich und murmelte: „Gott

der Himmel the heaven
[**der Himmel** the sky, heaven (3)]
von denen by whom
er gehört worden war he had been heard
war er . . . begegnet had he met
[**begegnen** to meet, to encounter (2)]
schon einmal once before
gefragt wurde was asked

zur Seite aside
von wem by whom
wie hat jemand es tun können how could someone do it
wurde gestern nicht gesagt was it not said yesterday
erwähnen to mention
gefunden wurde was found

allein es gelang ihm nicht he did not succeed, however
[**allein** but, however (2)]
allerlei all sorts of
zogen an seinem Geist vorüber went through his mind
[**vorüber–ziehen** to go past]
die Großmutter the grandmother
gebacken baked
[**backen, er bäckt, backte (buk), hat gebacken** to bake]
der Kuchen the cake
[**der Kuchen, die Kuchen** the cake (2)]
die Schule the school
[**die Schule, die Schulen**]
wo er erzogen worden where he had been educated
[**erziehen, erzog, hat erzogen** to educate]
neugeboren newly born
[**geboren** born]
Knaben boys
[**der Knabe, die Knaben** the boy]
auf die er so stolz gewesen of whom he had been so proud
[**stolz** proud (2)]
feiern to celebrate (2)
er . . . gestürzt worden war he had been plunged
hassen to hate (2)
war . . . entzündet worden had been kindled
[**entzünden** to kindle, to light (2)]
die Seele the soul
[**die Seele, die Seelen** the soul (2)]
er nicht für möglich gehalten hatte he had not believed possible
beten to pray (2)

im Himmel! Und hier muß ich ihn endlich treffen, nach so langer Zeit!" Die anderen, von denen er gehört worden war, wunderten sich, daß die Geschichte von Sebastians Unglück ihn so überrascht hatte. Wo war er Sebastian schon einmal begegnet? Wußte er etwas über den Mord? Als Barnabas gefragt wurde, gab er keine Antwort.

Am nächsten Tag nahm Sebastian ihn zur Seite und sagte: „Du weißt mehr über den Mord, als du gestern sagen wolltest. Sage mir, was es ist!" Barnabas sah ihm nicht in die Augen. „Laß mich in Frieden!" rief er. „Wie soll ich wissen, von wem das Messer in deinen Reisesack gesteckt wurde? Und sage mir: wie hat jemand es tun können, ohne daß du es merktest? Wurde gestern nicht gesagt, daß der Sack unter deinem Kopf lag, während du schliefst?" Als Sebastian das hörte, schwieg er und ging fort. Niemand hatte gestern erwähnt, daß das Messer in dem Sack gefunden wurde, und außer ihm hatte bisher keiner gewußt, daß er damals auf dem Sack geschlafen hatte.

Während der Nacht fand Sebastian keine Ruhe. Er fühlte sich unglücklicher, als er je gewesen war. Er schloß die Augen und versuchte zu schlafen; allein es gelang ihm nicht. Allerlei Bilder zogen an seinem Geist vorüber. Er sah seine Eltern; die Großmutter, die ihm jedesmal das erste Stück vom frisch gebackenen Kuchen gegeben hatte; die kleine Schule, wo er erzogen worden; er sah sein Heim und seine Frau mit dem neugeborenen Kind im Arm; die zwei Knaben, auf die er so stolz gewesen; das kleine Mädchen; und wie er sie alle zum letzten Mal geküßt hatte. Er dachte an die Feste, die sie zusammen gefeiert hatten, und wie froh und ohne Sorgen das Leben damals gewesen war. Und dann erinnerte er sich an jenen Tag und diesen Mann, der nun einige Schritte neben ihm schlief und durch dessen Schuld er ins Unglück gestürzt worden war. Nie in seinem Leben hatte Sebastian einen Menschen gehaßt; jetzt aber war in seiner Seele ein Feuer entzündet worden, dessen Gewalt er nicht für möglich gehalten hatte. Er versuchte zu beten; aber während seine Lippen sich bewegten und den Namen Gottes riefen, dachte er immer nur an Barnabas und die

die Rache the vengeance
töten to kill (3)

abgeschlossen worden waren had been locked
ruhelos restlessly (2)
der Raum the room
[**der Raum, die Räume** (3)]
schwach weak (3)]
unter einem der Holzbetten from under one of the wooden beds
eine Handvoll a handful
herausgeworfen wurde was thrown out
sich rühren to move (2)
kroch . . . hervor crawled out
[**kriechen, kroch, ist gekrochen** to crawl, to creep (3)]
an-blicken to look at
er war . . . gemieden worden he had been shunned
[**meiden, mied, hat gemieden** to avoid, to shun]
von den anderen Gefangenen by the other prisoners
hatte sich entschlossen had decided
[**sich entschließen** to decide]
[**entschließen, entschloß, hat entschlossen** (2)]
das . . . gegraben worden war which had been dug
sollte ihm . . . öffnen was to open for him
getrieben wurden were driven
war . . . entdeckt worden had been discovered
der Plan the plan
[**der Plan, die Pläne** the plan (3)]

blickte sich um looked around
[**sich um-blicken** to look around (2)]
flüstern to whisper (3)
wenn dir dein Leben lieb ist if you love your life
werde ich totgeschlagen I shall be beaten to death
[**tot-schlagen** to beat to death (3)]
und einen Toten and a dead man

wurde . . . entdeckt was discovered
von einem Soldaten by a soldier
wurden . . . getrieben were driven
von wem by whom
gegraben worden war had been dug
war . . . hinausgebracht worden had been taken out
diejenigen, von denen those by whom
[**derjenige, diejenige, dasjenige** the one (2)]
beobachtet worden war had been observed

Rache, die er nehmen wollte. „Er muß sterben", sagte er schließlich; „ich werde ihn töten."

Seit diesem Augenblick fand Sebastian keinen Schlaf mehr. Eines Nachts, nachdem die Türen von außen abgeschlossen worden waren, wanderte er ruhelos durch den großen Raum, in dem die Gefangenen schliefen. Plötzlich blieb er stehen. In dem schwachen Licht des Mondes, das durch die engen Fenster drang, sah er, wie unter einem der Holzbetten eine Handvoll Erde herausgeworfen wurde. Sebastian rührte sich nicht. Nach einer Weile kroch jemand unter dem Bett hervor. Es war Barnabas, der ihn erschrocken anblickte. Er war seit dem ersten Tage von den anderen Gefangenen gemieden worden, er fürchtete für sein Leben und hatte sich entschlossen zu fliehen. Das Loch, das von ihm unter dem leeren Bett gegraben worden war, sollte ihm den Weg in die Freiheit öffnen. Die Erde hatte er jede Nacht in die Taschen gesteckt und während des Tages draußen weggeworfen, wenn die Gefangenen zur Arbeit getrieben wurden. Und jetzt war sein Plan entdeckt worden!

5.

Sebastian wollte weitergehen, aber Barnabas hielt ihn fest, blickte sich um und flüsterte: „Wenn dir dein Leben lieb ist, dann schweige! Du kannst mit mir fliehen, wenn das Loch fertig ist; aber halte geheim, was du weißt, denn wenn du etwas sagst, werde ich totgeschlagen. Bevor i c h jedoch sterben muß, werde ich dich töten."–„Ich will nicht von hier fliehen", antwortete Sebastian, „und einen Toten brauchst du nicht mehr zu töten, denn ich war tot, als ich vor sechsundzwanzig Jahren hierher kam, und du, Barnabas, hast mich getötet. Frage mich nicht, ob ich etwas sagen werde. Ich weiß es noch nicht."

Einige Tage später wurde das Loch von einem Soldaten entdeckt. Die Gefangenen wurden in den Hof getrieben. Wußte jemand, von wem das Loch gegraben worden war? Wie war die Erde hinausgebracht worden? Diejenigen, von denen Barnabas beobachtet worden war, sagten nichts; sie wußten, daß jeder,

totgeschlagen wurde was beaten to death
wurde . . . herbeigerufen was called
[**herbei** here]
war ihm die Macht in die Hand gegeben worden the power had been put into his hands
[**die Macht** the power (2)]
die Rache the vengeance, revenge (2)
vor dem Tode from death
durch den Sinn through his mind

donnernd thundering
[**donnern** to thunder (3)]

an-blicken to look at (2)

alle Mittel all means
[**das Mittel, die Mittel** the means (2)]
versucht worden waren had been tried
mußten die Dinge gelassen werden things had to be left

wurde . . . geweckt was awakened
an sein Bett to his bed
erkannte recognized
[**erkennen, erkannte, hat erkannt** to recognize (4)]
trotz in spite of (3)
die Dunkelheit the darkness (2)
gesunken war had sunk
[**sinken, sank, ist gesunken** to sink (3)]
flossen ran
[**fließen, floß, ist geflossen** to flow, to run, to pour (2)]
verzeihen to forgive (3)
wegen dessen because of which
du hierhergeschickt wurdest you were sent here
ich bin es it is I
ich hatte . . . töten wollen I had wanted to kill
war . . . geschlichen had crept
[**schleichen, schlich, ist geschlichen** to creep, to sneak, to crawl (3)]
und daher and therefore

der zu fliehen versuchte, wie ein Hund von den Soldaten totgeschlagen wurde. Schließlich wurde Sebastian herbeigerufen. „Du hast stets die Wahrheit gesagt“, sprach der Offizier; „sag uns, wer es getan hat!“ Sebastian stand da, seine Hände zitterten, er wollte sprechen; aber er brachte kein Wort über die Lippen. Endlich, dachte er, war ihm die Macht in die Hand gegeben worden, Rache zu nehmen für das, was er so lange gelitten hatte! Warum sollte er Barnabas vor dem Tode retten? Dann aber ging es ihm durch den Sinn, daß Barnabas vielleicht doch nicht der Mörder war. „Aber selbst wenn er es getan hat“, sagte er sich, „was hilft es mir, wenn er stirbt?“

„Nun, sprich!“ rief der Offizier mit donnernder Stimme, „und sage die Wahrheit!“

„Es ist nicht Gottes Wille, daß ich sage, wer es getan hat“, antwortete Sebastian, ohne Barnabas anzublicken. „Tut mit mir, was ihr wollt. Ich bin in eurer Gewalt. Ich kann nicht sprechen.“

Nachdem alle Mittel versucht worden waren, von ihm und den anderen Gefangenen die Wahrheit zu erfahren, mußten die Dinge gelassen werden, wie sie waren.

In derselben Nacht wurde Sebastian plötzlich geweckt. Jemand war an sein Bett getreten und hatte sich schweigend neben ihn gesetzt. Es war Barnabas. Sebastian erkannte ihn trotz der Dunkelheit. „Was willst du von mir?“ fragte er; „warum bist du gekommen?“ Als Barnabas nicht antwortete, wiederholte Sebastian seine Frage: „Was willst du von mir? Sprich oder gehe fort, sonst rufe ich die Soldaten!“ Da sah er, daß Barnabas' Kopf auf die Brust gesunken war und daß ihm die Tränen aus den Augen flossen, und er hörte ihn flüstern: „Verzeihe mir, Sebastian, verzeih mir!“—„Verzeihen?“ antwortete Sebastian. „Was soll ich dir verzeihen?“—„Den Mord, wegen dessen du hierhergeschickt wurdest“, entgegnete Barnabas. „Ich bin es, der den Kaufmann ermordet hat. Ich hatte damals auch dich töten wollen und war in dein Zimmer geschlichen; aber ich wurde durch etwas erschreckt, was ich draußen zu hören glaubte, und daher versteckte ich das Messer in deinem Sack, sprang durch das Fenster und floh.“

glitt slid
[**gleiten, glitt, ist geglitten** to glide, to slide]
ließ sich . . . nieder went down
die Knie the knees
[**das Knie, die Knie** the knee (3)]
dann wirst du freigelassen werden then you will be set free
[**frei-lassen** to set free, to release]
hohl hollow
mein Weib my wife
[**das Weib, die Weiber** the woman; the wife (3)]
von meinen Kindern by my children
bin ich . . . vergessen worden I have been forgotten
die Bahn the course (3)
vollendet completed
[**vollenden** to complete (3)]

um unseres Gottes willen for the sake of our God
[**um . . . willen** for the sake of]
der Sünder the sinner
[**der Sünder, die Sünder** the sinner]
wurde . . . gerührt was moved
ein noch größerer Sünder a still greater sinner
[**der Sünder, die Sünder** the sinner (2)]
bei diesen Worten at these words
wurde ihm leicht ums Herz his heart grew light
verlangte nicht mehr nach Haus no longer longed for home

obgleich although (2)
ihm von Sebastian verziehen worden war he had been forgiven by Sebastian
[**verzeihen, verzieh, hat verziehen** to forgive (3)]
dennoch nevertheless (3)
erklärte declared
öffentlich publicly (3)
der ungewöhnliche Fall the unusual case
[**ungewöhnlich** unusual (2)]
wurde geprüft was examined
dem König berichtet reported to the king
in dem befohlen wurde in which the order was given
daß dem Gefangenen Tamuschat die Freiheit wiedergegeben werden sollte that the prisoner Tamuschat was to be given back his freedom

Sebastian schwieg; er wußte nicht, was er sagen sollte. Da glitt Barnabas von dem Bett und ließ sich auf die Knie nieder. „Verzeihe mir, Sebastian! Ich werde morgen zu den Offizieren gehen und ihnen sagen, daß ich es war, der den Kaufmann getötet hat. Dann wirst du freigelassen werden und kannst nach Haus zurückkehren."–„Nach Haus?" wiederholte Sebastian mit hohler Stimme. „Wo soll ich jetzt hingehen? Ich habe kein Heim mehr. Mein Weib ist tot, und von meinen Kindern bin ich seit langem vergessen worden. Wie kann ich dir verzeihen? Sechsundzwanzig Jahre habe ich hier gelitten; für dich, Barnabas. Sechsundzwanzig Jahre. Die Bahn meines Lebens ist bald vollendet.–Nun stehe auf und gehe, Barnabas!"

Aber Barnabas stand nicht auf, sondern schlug mit dem Kopf auf die harte Erde und rief: „Verzeihe mir, Sebastian! Um unseres Gottes willen, verzeih mir armem Sünder!" Da wurde auch Sebastian zu Tränen gerührt und er sprach: „Gott wird dir verzeihen, Barnabas. Vielleicht bin ich ein noch größerer Sünder als du. Nun geh in Frieden!" Bei diesen Worten wurde ihm leicht ums Herz, und seine Seele verlangte nicht mehr nach Haus. Er wünschte nicht mehr, das Gefängnis zu verlassen, sondern hoffte und wartete jetzt nur auf seine letzte Stunde.

Obgleich ihm von Sebastian verziehen worden war, ging Barnabas dennoch nach einiger Zeit zu den Offizieren und erklärte öffentlich, daß er der Mörder war. Der ungewöhnliche Fall wurde geprüft und schließlich dem König berichtet. Als aber der Brief ankam, in dem befohlen wurde, daß dem Gefangenen Tamuschat die Freiheit wiedergegeben werden sollte, war Sebastian schon gestorben.

WAR ES MORD?

[7B]

NOTES

REVIEW OF STRONG AND IRREGULAR VERBS USED IN STORY 7A

beschreiben	beschrieb	beschrieben	*to describe*
binden	band	gebunden	*to bind, tie*
erkennen	erkannte	erkannt	*to recognize*
(sich) entschließen	entschloß	entschlossen	*to decide*
erziehen	erzog	erzogen	*to educate, bring up*
gleiten	glitt	ist geglitten	*to glide, slide*
meiden	mied	gemieden	*to avoid, shun*
schreiten	schritt	ist geschritten	*to step, go*
schwören	schwor	geschworen	*to swear*

IDIOMS FOR REVIEW

vor Jahren years ago
im Sinn haben to have in mind, to intend (to do)
zu ebener Erde level with the ground
zu welchem Zweck? for what purpose?
zu diesem Zweck for this purpose
ich stehe zu Ihren Diensten I am at your service
etwas auf dem Herzen haben to have something on one's mind
heute nacht tonight *or* last night
seit langem for a long time
zum dritten Mal for the third time
urteilen nach to judge from
mit Absicht intentionally

das Nachtmahl the supper
[**das Mahl** the meal (3)]
die kleine Gesellschaft the small company
die . . . eingeladen worden war which had been invited
[**ein-laden, er lädt ein, lud ein, hat eingeladen** to invite]
von dem alten Fürsten Auersfeld by the old Prince Auersfeld
[**der Fürst, die Fürsten** the prince]
zur Fuchsjagd to the fox hunt
[**der Fuchs, die Füchse** the fox (3)]
[**die Jagd, die Jagden** the hunt, chase (3)]
das Landgut the country estate
[**das Gut, die Güter** the estate; the goods (2)]
hatte sich . . . begeben had gone
[**sich begeben** to go]
[**begeben, er begibt, begab, begeben**]
das Spielzimmer the game room
Gruppen groups
[**die Gruppe, die Gruppen** the group]
von einem der Gäste by one of the guests
[**der Gast, die Gäste** the guest (4)]
vorgeschlagen wurde it was suggested
[**vor-schlagen** to propose, to suggest (3)]
. . . zu unterhalten to entertain
[**unterhalten, er unterhält, unterhielt, hat unterhalten** to entertain]
[**sich unterhalten** to have a good time; to converse]
mit der Erzählung von Geschichten by telling stories
[**die Erzählung, die Erzählungen** the tale, story, narrative, narration (2)]
aus dem wirklichen Leben from real life
es war beschlossen worden it had been decided
verschieden different (3)
von jedem by everyone
berichtet werden sollte should be told
die ihm . . . begegnet war which had happened to him
[**begegnen** to meet, encounter; to happen (3)]

der Kamin the fireplace (3)
hell bright (3)
von den Dienern by the servants
[**der Diener, die Diener** the servant (4)]
wurde Wein gebracht wine was brought
mit Ungeduld impatiently
[**die Ungeduld** the impatience (2)]
der Fürst the prince (2)
er war . . . gerufen worden he had been called
und hatte . . . gefehlt and had . . . been absent
das Abendessen the supper (4)
bequem comfortable (3)

[7 B]

(THREE PARTS)

War es Mord?

I.

Das Nachtmahl war vorüber, und die kleine Gesellschaft, die von dem alten Fürsten Auersfeld zur Fuchsjagd auf sein Landgut eingeladen worden war, hatte sich in das Spielzimmer begeben. Während der ruhigen Abendstunden hatte man dort bisher in kleinen Gruppen Karten gespielt, bis von einem der Gäste vorgeschlagen wurde, die ganze Gesellschaft mit der Erzählung von Geschichten aus dem wirklichen Leben zu unterhalten. Die Idee hatte allen gefallen, und es war beschlossen worden, daß an verschiedenen Abenden von jedem die interessanteste und ungewöhnlichste Geschichte berichtet werden sollte, die ihm in seinem Leben begegnet war.

Die Gäste hatten sich gesetzt, in dem großen Kamin brannte ein helles Feuer, von den Dienern wurde Wein gebracht, und man wartete nun mit Ungeduld auf den Fürsten, der seine Erzählung für diesen Abend versprochen hatte. Er war am Morgen in wichtigen Geschäften in die Stadt gerufen worden und hatte noch während des Abendessens gefehlt. Schon fing man an, sich Sorgen zu machen, als der Fürst nach einer Weile eintrat. Ein bequemer Armstuhl wurde nahe ans Feuer geschoben, der Fürst setzte sich und begann seine Erzählung.

---

der Armstuhl the armchair (2)
  [**der Stuhl, die Stühle** the chair (3)]
wurde . . . geschoben was pushed
  [**schieben, schob, hat geschoben** to push, to shove (2)]

der Lauf the course
außerordentlich extraordinary
ich bin an sie erinnert worden I was reminded of it
vor zwei . . . Tagen two . . . days ago
von einem von Ihnen by one of you
unser Sieg in der Schlacht bei Waterloo our victory at the battle of Waterloo
[**der Sieg, die Siege** the victory]
[**die Schlacht, die Schlachten** the battle]
erwähnt wurde was mentioned
[**erwähnen** to mention (2)]
der Neffe the nephew
[**der Neffe, die Neffen** the nephew]
das Versprechen the promise
[**das Versprechen, die Versprechen** the promise]
davon of it
der Neffe the nephew (2)
er ist . . . gefallen he died
als Held as a hero
[**der Held, die Helden** the hero (2)]
das Volk the people
[**das Volk, die Völker** the people, the nation (3)]
daher therefore (2)
hindern to prevent (2)
meine Herren gentlemen
wie sie mir . . . berichtet wurde as it was told to me
vor Jahren years ago

der Graf the count
[**der Graf, die Grafen** the count]
der Feind the enemy (4)
französisch French (4)
der Baron the baron
aus dem Grunde from the bottom
der Ursprung the origin
der Haß the hatred
der Graf the count (2)
blutig bloody
schwören to swear
[**schwören, schwor, hat geschworen** to swear (2)]
genügen to be sufficient (3)
wogen weighed
[**wiegen, wog, hat gewogen** to weigh (2)]
bestimmen to determine
da er since he
zugleich at the same time (3)
sich selbst . . . zu schaden to hurt himself
[**schaden** to hurt (3)]

„Im Laufe meines Lebens", sprach er, „ist mir nie etwas so Außerordentliches vorgekommen wie die folgende Geschichte. Ich bin an sie erinnert worden, als vor zwei oder drei Tagen von einem von Ihnen unser Sieg in der Schlacht bei Waterloo erwähnt wurde. Es ist eine Geschichte, die nicht mir selbst, sondern einem Neffen von mir passiert ist. Er bat mich damals, sie für mich zu behalten, solange er lebte, und ich gab ihm mein Versprechen, niemandem etwas davon zu sagen. Dieser Neffe ist nun schon seit Jahren tot—er ist damals bei Waterloo als Held für unser Volk und unsere Freiheit gefallen—, und ich glaube daher, daß mich nun nichts mehr hindert, Ihnen, meine Herren, diese ungewöhnliche Geschichte mit denselben Worten zu erzählen, wie sie mir vor Jahren von meinem Neffen berichtet wurde.

„Dieser Neffe—ich will ihn hier Graf Friedrich nennen—hatte einen Feind, einen französischen Baron, den er aus dem Grunde seiner Seele haßte. Es ist nicht nötig, daß ich hier den Ursprung eines Hasses erkläre, der den Grafen bewegt hatte, dem Baron blutige Rache zu schwören. Es wird genügen, denke ich, wenn ich Ihnen sage, daß die Gründe für einen Mann von stolzem Charakter schwer genug wogen, um ihn zu bestimmen, den Baron zu töten. Da er jedoch zugleich nicht die geringste Absicht hatte, sich selbst in irgendeiner Weise zu schaden, hatte er darauf geachtet, daß kein Mensch von seinem Haß erfuhr. Keiner durfte wissen, was er im Sinn hatte; niemand sollte nach dem Tode des Barons auf den Gedanken kommen, daß er vielleicht der Mörder war. Ja, es war ihm sogar gelungen, seinen Haß vor dem Baron selbst geheimzuhalten. Er hatte beschlossen, mit Geduld auf den rechten Augenblick zu warten,

---

hatte er darauf geachtet he had seen to it
[**achten** to respect, to esteem; to pay attention (3)]
der Haß the hatred (2)
keiner durfte no one must
im Sinn in mind
ja indeed
die Geduld the patience (2)

lehren to teach (3)
wenn sie . . . trifft when it strikes
dem Blitze ähnlich similar to lightning
[**der Blitz, die Blitze** the lightning (3)]
unerwartet unexpectedly

befanden sich were
[**sich befinden** to be, find oneself]
[**befinden, befand, hat befunden** (3)]
Italien Italy (2)
war . . . geschickt worden had been sent
der Herbst the fall (3)
hinausritt rode out into
[**reiten, ritt, ist geritten** to ride]
die Schönheit the beauty (2)
gerühmt worden war had been praised
[**rühmen** to praise (2)]
ließ sich . . . leiten let himself be guided
der Nord(en) the north (3)
an . . . entlang along
[**entlang** along (4)]
das Ufer the bank
[**das Ufer, die Ufer** the shore, bank (3)]
der Strom the river
[**der Strom, die Ströme** the (large) river; stream, current (3)]
die Brücke the bridge
[**die Brücke, die Brücken** the bridge]
flach flat
bog turned
[**biegen, bog, hat/ist gebogen** to turn, to bend (3)]
der Berg the mountain
[**der Berg, die Berge** the mountain (3)]
an dessen Fuß . . . lag at whose foot lay
römisch Roman
Ruinen ruins
[**die Ruine, die Ruinen** the ruin (2)]
das Bauernhaus the farmhouse
gedeckt covered
[**decken** to cover (3)]
der Rauch the smoke (2)
Pflanzen plants
[**die Pflanze, die Pflanzen** the plant]
reif ripe
[**reif** ripe, mature (2)]
Früchte fruit
[**die Frucht, die Früchte** the fruit]
mächtig mighty (3)
der Birnbaum the pear tree
[**die Birne, die Birnen** the pear]

denn das Leben hatte ihn gelehrt—so sagte er mir damals—, daß die Rache am süßesten ist, wenn sie, dem Blitze ähnlich, den Feind schnell und unerwartet trifft.

„Der Graf und der Baron befanden sich damals in Italien. Der Baron war von seiner Familie in Geschäften nach Rom geschickt worden, und der Graf, den der Baron für seinen Freund hielt, war ihm dorthin gefolgt. Eines Tages im Herbst geschah es, daß der Graf aufs Land hinausritt, dessen Schönheit zu dieser Zeit des Jahres ihm von mehreren Freunden gerühmt worden war. Er hatte kein bestimmtes Ziel und ließ sich von seinem Pferd leiten. Die Straße führte ihn zunächst nach Norden, an dem Ufer des breiten Stromes entlang, dann über eine Brücke und schließlich auf das flache Land hinaus. Nach einer Weile bog der Weg nach rechts; das Pferd folgte ihm, bis sie zu einem Berg kamen, an dessen Fuß ein mit römischen Ruinen bedecktes Feld lag. Dicht an dem Berge stand ein Bauernhaus, in dem niemand zu wohnen schien, denn aus dem mit Stroh gedeckten Dach stieg kein Rauch. In einem Garten wuchsen wilde Pflanzen, und die reifen Früchte eines mächtigen Birnbaumes, die in Mengen auf der Erde lagen, zeigten dem Grafen, daß niemand gekommen war, sie zu sammeln. Er befand sich an einem Ort, der vielleicht schon seit Jahren von niemandem mehr besucht worden war. Plötzlich, so schien es ihm, wurde ihm von einer inneren Stimme befohlen, von seinem Pferd zu steigen. Während er das Tier an den Stamm des Birnbaumes band, erblickte er an der Seite des Berges eine offene Tür. Er trat ein und befand sich in einem

---

in Mengen in large quantities
besucht worden war had been visited
wurde ihm . . . befohlen he was commanded
inner inner
das Tier the animal
[**das Tier, die Tiere** the animal (2)]
band tied
[**binden, band, hat gebunden** to bind, to tie (3)]
der Birnbaum the pear tree
[**die Birne, die Birnen** the pear (2)]

der Gang the corridor
[**der Gang, die Gänge** the corridor; the walk]
der in . . . hineinführte which led into
der Felsen the rock
[**der Fels(en), die Felsen** the rock]
sich . . . teilte branched
[**teilen** to divide, to share (3)]
der Gang the corridor (2)
er schritt . . . weiter he walked on
[**schreiten, schritt, ist geschritten** to walk, to step (2)]
im Dunkeln in the dark
[**das Dunkel** the darkness]
auf einmal suddenly
stieß . . . auf encountered
[**stoßen, er stößt, stieß, hat/ist gestoßen** to push, to thrust; to encounter (3)]
seine ausgestreckte Hand his extended hand
[**aus-strecken** to stretch out, to extend (3)]

das Brett the board
[**das Brett, die Bretter**]
durch das by which
vorwärts forward (2)
trocken dry (3)
der Flammen of the flames
[**die Flamme, die Flammen** the flame (3)]
zu ebener Erde level with the ground
[**eben** flat, level]
römisch Roman (2)
der Brunnen the well
der Zustand the condition
[**der Zustand, die Zustände** the state, condition (3)]
hatte . . . gedient had served
[**dienen** to serve (4)]
von dem by whom
das Brett the board
[**das Brett, die Bretter** (2)]
der Brunnen the well (2)
gelegt worden war had been placed
Besucher visitors
[**der Besucher, die Besucher** the visitor (2)]
warnen to warn
um . . . hineinblicken zu können in order to be able to . . . look into it
lehnen to lean (3)
an das Brett against the board
waren nicht . . . festgemacht had not been fastened
mit Nägeln with nails
[**der Nagel, die Nägel** the nail (2)]
sondern . . . gelegt worden but had been placed

Gang, der in den Felsen hineinführte und sich nach ein paar Schritten in zwei teilte. Es war jetzt so dunkel geworden, daß der Graf ein Streichholz anzünden mußte, bevor er dem engen Gang nach rechts folgte. Das Streichholz ging aus; er schritt langsam im Dunkeln weiter. Auf einmal stieß seine ausgestreckte Hand auf etwas Hartes.

2.

„Es schien ein Brett zu sein, das von einer Wand zur anderen reichte und durch das er gehindert wurde, weiterzuschreiten. Sein Fuß, den er vorwärtsstreckte, fand keinen Boden. Der Graf ließ sich auf die Knie nieder, sammelte einige trockene Zweige, die auf der Erde lagen, und machte ein kleines Feuer. Im Licht der Flammen erkannte er die Gefahr, in der er gewesen war. Vor ihm, zu ebener Erde, öffnete sich ein schwarzes, rundes Loch. Es war ein alter römischer Brunnen. Er schien in gutem Zustand zu sein und hatte vielleicht noch dem letzten Bauern gedient, dem das Haus und der Garten gehört hatten. Wahrscheinlich war es auch dieser Bauer gewesen, von dem das Brett vor den Brunnen gelegt worden war, um mögliche Besucher vor der Gefahr zu warnen. Um besser von oben hineinblicken zu können, lehnte sich der Graf mit der Brust leicht an das Brett. Es fiel zu Boden. Die Enden waren nicht mit Nägeln festgemacht, sondern einfach auf zwei Felsstücke gelegt worden, die rechts und links aus der Wand hervorstanden. Wer es nicht wußte und sich auf das Brett lehnte, mußte in den Brunnen fallen. Der Graf kroch einen Schritt vorwärts und warf einen Stein hinein. Es währte einige Se-

---

Felsstücke pieces of rock
[**der Fels(en), die Felsen** the rock (2)]
die . . . hervorstanden which protruded
warf . . . hinein threw in
der Stein the stone
[**der Stein, die Steine** the stone (2)]
währen to last (2)

einige Sekunden a few seconds
[**die Sekunde, die Sekunden** the second (2)]
glatt smooth
hinauf-steigen to climb up
[**hinauf** up (2)]

in Gedanken versunken sunk in thought
[**versinken, versank, ist versunken** to sink]
von der ihm befohlen worden war by which he had been commanded
verlassen deserted
die Macht the power (2)
bin ich hierhergeführt worden have I been led here
zu meinem Heil for my benefit
[**das Heil** the salvation]
der Geist the spirit
der mich hierhergeleitet which led me here
[**leiten** to lead, to guide (2)]
ich . . . gerettet wurde I was saved
auf einmal suddenly
blitzen to flash (like lightning) (3)
ich hierhergebracht wurde I was brought here
welch ein . . .! what a . . .!
genau wie er exactly as he
ritt rode
[**reiten, ritt, ist geritten** to ride (2)]

wurde eine Teegesellschaft gegeben a tea party was given
eingeladen worden waren had been invited
[**ein-laden, lädt ein, lud ein, hat eingeladen** to invite (2)]
er hatte . . . wohl gewogen had weighed . . . well
[**wägen, wog, hat gewogen** to weigh]
das Für und Wider the advantages and disadvantages
[**wider** against (3)]
auszusehen to look
als ob as if
sich unterhielten conversed
[**sich unterhalten** converse (2)]
[**unterhalten, er unterhält, unterhielt, hat unterhalten** to entertain]
gesagt wurde was said
hörte er . . . nicht zu he did not listen
mit Absicht intentionally
wenn er gefragt wurde when he was asked a question
wie er as he
wurde er . . . zur Seite genommen he was taken aside
ich kenne Sie nicht wieder I do not recognize you
auf dem Herzen on your mind
zu teilen to share
zu Ihren Diensten at your service
[**der Dienst, die Dienste** the service (3)]

kunden, bis er ihn in das Wasser fallen hörte. Wer in diesen Brunnen stürzte, starb eines sicheren Todes. An diesen glatten Wänden konnte niemand hinaufsteigen.

„Lange stand der Graf da, in Gedanken versunken, und starrte in den Brunnen. Er dachte an die Stimme in seiner Brust, von der ihm befohlen worden war, an diesem verlassenen Ort zu halten. ‚Durch welche dunkle Macht', sagte er sich, ‚bin ich hierhergeführt worden? Zu welchem Zweck? Zu meinem Heil—oder um hier den Tod zu finden? Nein, nein, es kann nicht sein! Der Geist, der mich hierhergeleitet, es ist derselbe, durch den ich auch vor einem plötzlichen Tod gerettet wurde. Doch welche Absicht hatte dieser Geist, als er mir diesen Brunnen zeigte?—Oh Gott!' rief er auf einmal, und seine Augen blitzten; ‚ich weiß, warum ich hierhergebracht wurde! Ha, welch ein Plan!' Mit fester Hand legte er das Brett wieder auf die zwei Felsstücke, genau wie er es gefunden hatte, und ritt nach Rom zurück.

„Am folgenden Nachmittag wurde eine Teegesellschaft gegeben, zu der auch er und der Baron eingeladen worden waren. Der Graf erschien spät. Sein Plan war reif; er hatte das Für und Wider wohl gewogen. Die Stunde der Rache war gekommen. Es gelang ihm, auszusehen, als ob er sich nicht wohl fühlte. Während die Gäste sich unterhielten, schien er in Gedanken verloren; wenn etwas gesagt wurde, hörte er mit Absicht nicht zu; wenn er gefragt wurde, antwortete er kaum. Wie er gehofft hatte, wurde er von dem Baron nach einer Weile zur Seite genommen. ‚Ich kenne Sie nicht wieder, lieber Freund', begann der Baron; ‚Sie haben etwas auf dem Herzen. Wenn es möglich ist, so lassen Sie mich den Grund Ihrer Sorgen wissen, oder erlauben Sie mir, Ihren Schmerz zu teilen. Sie sind mein Freund; ich stehe zu Ihren Diensten.' Der Graf konnte zunächst durch nichts bewegt werden, etwas zu sagen. Als der Baron jedoch nicht aufhörte, weiter in ihn zu dringen, sprach er endlich: ‚Sie haben recht, lieber Baron. Sie, als mein Freund,

---

konnte . . . durch nichts bewegt werden could not be moved by anything
weiter in ihn zu dringen to press him further

der Eindruck the impression
    [**der Eindruck, die Eindrücke** the impression (3)]
  heute nacht last night
dem Grafen war bekannt it was known to the count
  abergläubisch superstitious (2)
er hatte . . . gerechnet he had counted
  und hatte sich nicht geirrt and had not been mistaken
    [**(sich) irren** to be wrong, to be mistaken (3)]
allerdings you are right
    [**allerdings** to be sure; that is correct, etc. (3)]
um mich for myself
inner inner (2)
warnen to warn (2)
erstaunt astonished (2)
  ja indeed

die Brücke the bridge
    [**die Brücke, die Brücken** the bridge (2)]
die Landschaft the landscape
  doch sah sie aus but it looked
  wie hier um Rom like here around Rome
flach flat (2)
worin in which
  Pflanzen plants
    [**die Pflanze, die Pflanzen** the plant (2)]
  daneben next to it
  Früchte fruit
    [**die Frucht, die Früchte** the fruit (2)]
dahinter behind it

drinnen inside
  die Hand . . . gestreckt your hand stretched
der Schrecken the terror
    [**der Schreck(en), die Schrecken** the terror, fright (2)]
es half nichts it was to no avail
Sie wurden . . . vorwärtsgetrieben you were driven forward
  von irgendeiner by some

haben erkannt, daß ich etwas auf dem Herzen habe. Ich stehe noch ganz unter dem Eindruck eines ungewöhnlichen Traumes, den ich heute nacht hatte.' Dem Grafen war bekannt, daß der Baron abergläubisch war. Er hatte auf diese schwache Seite seines Charakters gerechnet und hatte sich nicht geirrt. Sein Herz schlug schneller, als er den Baron jetzt fragen hörte: ‚Ein Traum, mein Freund? Erzählen Sie! Ich fürchte sehr, ein böser Traum, denn Ihr Gesicht ist bleich.'—‚Allerdings', entgegnete der Graf. ‚Ich bin in großer Sorge; doch nicht um mich, wie Sie vielleicht dachten. Nein, um Sie, Baron! Eine innere Stimme sagt mir, daß Sie in Gefahr sind. Ich muß Sie warnen, denn ich fürchte für Ihr Leben.'—‚Was sagen Sie?' rief der Baron erstaunt, ja fast erschreckt. ‚Ich in Gefahr? Lassen Sie mich wissen, was es ist! Erzählen Sie, ich bitte Sie!'

„‚Nun, hören Sie', sprach der Graf, ‚und urteilen Sie selbst! Ich sah im Traum, wie Sie aufs Land hinausritten, an einem Strom entlang und über eine Brücke. Die Landschaft war mir fremd, doch sah sie aus wie hier um Rom. Sie ritten weiter, über flache Felder, und kamen an ein Haus, in dem seit langem niemand mehr zu wohnen schien. Ein Garten, worin wilde Pflanzen wuchsen, lag daneben, und dort, am Ende, stand ein Baum—ein Birnbaum war's—voll reifer Früchte. Dahinter, am Fuße eines Berges, erblickte ich im Felsen eine Tür. Ich sah Sie halten und vom Pferde steigen. Ich rief: „Zurück, Baron, zurück!" Ob Sie mich hörten, weiß ich nicht. Sie gingen zu der Tür—Sie traten ein.

3.

„‚Obgleich es drinnen dunkel war, konnt' ich im Traume trotzdem sehen, wie Sie, die Hand nach rechts zur Wand gestreckt, langsam einem Gange folgten, der sich nach einigen Schritten teilte. Wieder begann ich zu rufen: „Zurück, Baron, von diesem Ort des Schreckens!" Jedoch es half nichts; Sie achteten nicht auf mich. Sie wurden, so schien es mir, von irgendeiner Macht vorwärtsgetrieben. Sie biegen in den Gang

Sie . . . getrennt werden you are separated
[**trennen** to separate, to part (2)]
herbeizueilen to hasten toward you
[**herbei** here, there (2)]
dritt third (3)
mit aller Kraft with all my strength
[**die Kraft, die Kräfte** the strength (2)]
halt! stop! (2)
statt instead (3)
noch rief ich Sie I was still calling you
um verstehen zu können to be able to understand
was Ihnen gesagt wurde what was said to you
nach dem Ausdruck Ihres Gesichtes zu urteilen to judge from the expression on your face
furchtbar terrible (2)
los-reißen tear away
[**reißen, riß, hat gerissen** to tear (3)]
da wurde ich . . . geschreckt then I was scared
[**schrecken** to scare, to frighten (2)]
an allen Gliedern zitternd trembling all over
[**das Glied, die Glieder** the limb, member (3)]

mit steigendem Interesse with rising interest
[**das Interesse** the interest (2)]
von der ich gewarnt wurde by which I was warned
was mir von ihr gesagt wurde what it said to me (*literally:* what was said to me by it)
selten rarely (3)
je eher the sooner
durchaus quite
[**durchaus** quite, by all means (2)]
die Pause the pause
[**die Pause, die Pausen** the pause (3)]

täglich daily (3)
wurde . . . erwähnt was . . . mentioned.
schlug . . . vor proposed
. . . zu genießen to enjoy
[**genießen, genoß, hat genossen** to enjoy (2)]
die Natur (the) nature (2)
zu diesem Zweck for this purpose
gegen Mittag toward noontime
bei einer . . . Mühle near a . . . mill
[**die Mühle, die Mühlen** the mill (2)]
der Bergsee the mountain lake
[**der See, die Seen** the lake (3)]

nach rechts und stehen nun vor einem Brett, durch das Sie von einem Brunnen getrennt werden, der zu Ihren Füßen liegt. Ich versuchte herbeizueilen, doch etwas hielt mich fest. Da rief ich Sie zum dritten Mal; ich bat Sie, stehenzubleiben; ich schrie mit aller Kraft: „Halt! Halt!, Baron!" Doch statt auf mich zu achten, lehnen Sie sich auf das Brett und blicken in den Brunnen. Noch rief ich Sie, als plötzlich eine Stimme aus dem Brunnen kam, die zu Ihnen zu sprechen schien. Ich war nicht nahe genug, um verstehen zu können, was Ihnen gesagt wurde. Nach dem Ausdruck Ihres Gesichtes zu urteilen, schien es jedoch etwas Wichtiges, ja etwas Furchtbares zu sein. Ich will mich losreißen, um näher zu schreiten—da wurde ich plötzlich aus dem Schlaf geschreckt. Der Traum war vorüber. An allen Gliedern zitternd, wachte ich auf.—Dies war der Traum. Und nun, Baron, gestatten Sie mir, daß ich Ihnen für die Geduld danke, mit der Sie mir zugehört haben. Die drückende Sorge, die auf meinem Herzen lag, ist jetzt verschwunden.'

„Der Baron hatte mit steigendem Interesse zugehört. ‚Und diese Stimme, Graf', rief er, ‚die Stimme, von der ich gewarnt wurde—Sie haben nicht verstanden, was mir von ihr gesagt wurde?'—‚Nein', erwiderte der Graf; ‚ich war zu weit vom Brunnen, um die Worte zu verstehen. Doch machen Sie sich keine Sorgen, lieber Baron! Es war ein Traum, und wer weiß nicht, daß Träume nur selten etwas bedeuten? Je eher Sie und ich ihn vergessen, desto besser wird es sein.'—‚Sie haben durchaus recht', entgegnete der Baron nach einer kurzen Pause. ‚Lassen Sie uns von etwas anderem sprechen!'

„Obwohl der Graf und der Baron von diesem Tage an einander fast täglich trafen, wurde der Traum nicht wieder erwähnt. Nach etwa einer Woche schlug der Graf vor, das angenehme Wetter und die Schönheit der Natur auf dem Lande zu genießen und zu diesem Zweck am folgenden Tage zusammen in die Berge hinauszureiten. Sie verließen Rom am frühen Morgen und erreichten gegen Mittag ihr Ziel. Nach einem einfachen Mahl bei einer alten Mühle am Ufer eines kleinen Bergsees empfahl der Graf, auf einem anderen Wege zur Stadt zurückzukehren. Der Weg, der ihm bekannt

und den er . . . gewählt hatte and which he had chosen
[**wählen** to choose (3)]
mit Absicht intentionally
der Lauf the course (2)
der Bach the brook
[**der Bach, die Bäche** the brook (2)]
mehrere Stunden lang for several hours
Täler valleys
[**das Tal, die Täler** the valley (2)]
der West(en) the west (3)
während while
stehengeblieben war had stopped
näherte sich approached
[**sich nähern** to come near, to approach (2)]
was fehlt Ihnen? what is the matter with you?
sich umwandte turned around
[**um-wenden** to turn (around) (2)]
er hatte seinen Zweck erreicht he had accomplished his purpose
die ihm . . . beschrieben worden war which had been described to him
[**beschreiben, beschrieb, hat beschrieben** (2)]
klang sounded
[**klingen, klang, hat geklungen** to sound (3)]
anders als sonst different than usual
und haben . . . nötig and need
[**nötig haben** to need]
wurde . . . kaum ein Wort gewechselt hardly a word was exchanged
von beiden by the two

der Ball the ball
[**der Ball, die Bälle** the ball (2)]
eingeladen worden war had been invited
ließ sich . . . entschuldigen asked to be excused
[**entschuldigen** to excuse, to pardon (3)]
die Kopfschmerzen the headache (2)
begab sich went
[**sich begeben** to go (2)]
mehrere Tage lang several days
wenn if
von ihm by him
nicht verlassen worden war had not been left

wurde er . . . besucht he was visited
außerordentlich extraordinary (2)
er war . . . beobachtet worden he had been observed
vor einigen Tagen a few days ago
von mehreren Personen by several persons
wie er as he
die Richtung the direction
[**die Richtung, die Richtungen**]

war und den er mit Absicht gewählt hatte, folgte dem Lauf eines Baches und führte sie mehrere Stunden lang durch kühle Wälder und frische Täler. Als die Sonne im Westen zu sinken begann, erreichten sie den Fuß des letzten Berges. Plötzlich sah der Baron den Grafen halten, der einige Schritte vor ihm ritt. Während er sich fragte, warum der Graf an dieser Stelle stehengeblieben war, hörte er ihn laut rufen: ,Oh Gott! Ist es möglich?' Der Baron näherte sich erstaunt. 'Was fehlt Ihnen, Graf?' rief er erschrocken, als der Graf sich umwandte. ,Sie sind krank, Ihr Gesicht ist bleich! Sie brauchen Ruhe. Kommen Sie, dort unter jenem Baum können Sie . . .'—,Es ist schon vorüber', sprach der Graf; ,schnell, lassen Sie uns weitereilen!' Er hatte seinen Zweck erreicht. Die wenigen Minuten hatten genügt, dem Baron zu zeigen, wo er sich befand. Er hatte das Bauernhaus und den Garten erblickt. Er wandte sich um. Ja, da war der Baum und dort die Tür, die in den Felsen führte; die gleiche Tür, die ihm von dem Grafen beschrieben worden war. ,Ja', sagte er, und seine Stimme klang anders als sonst, ,ja, lassen Sie uns in die Stadt zurückeilen! Sie fühlen sich nicht wohl und haben schnelle Hilfe nötig.'— Unterwegs wurde von beiden kaum ein Wort gewechselt.

„Der Graf, der an diesem Abend zu einem Ball eingeladen worden war, ließ sich durch einen Diener entschuldigen. Er klagte über starke Kopfschmerzen und begab sich zu Bett, wo er mehrere Tage lang blieb. Wenn es nötig sein sollte, konnten seine Diener schwören, daß das Haus von ihm während dieser Zeit nicht verlassen worden war.

„Während er noch zu Bett lag, wurde er von einem Freund besucht, der eine außerordentliche Geschichte zu erzählen hatte. Der Baron war verschwunden. Er war vor einigen Tagen von mehreren Personen beobachtet worden, wie er früh am Morgen in der Richtung der Berge aufs Land hinausritt. Als er am Abend nicht zurückkehrte und auch während der folgenden Tage nicht gesehen wurde, hatte man begonnen, ihn

---

nicht gesehen wurde was not seen

gefunden wurde was found
treu faithful
[**treu** faithful, loyal]
das man . . . hatte gehen sehen which one had seen going
seinen Herrn its master

es braucht nicht gesagt zu werden it need not be said
daß von dem Baron nie wieder etwas gehört wurde that nothing was ever heard of the Baron again
meine Herren gentlemen (2)
die Meinung the opinion
[**die Meinung, die Meinungen** the opinion (2)]

zu suchen. Alles, was jedoch schließlich gefunden wurde, war sein treues Pferd, das man langsam über ein mit Ruinen bedecktes Feld hatte gehen sehen. Es schien seinen Herrn zu suchen.

„Ich bin am Ende meiner Erzählung“, sprach der Fürst. „Es braucht nicht gesagt zu werden, denke ich, daß von dem Baron nie wieder etwas gehört wurde. Sie, meine Herren, wissen jetzt warum.—Und nun möchte ich Sie um Ihre Meinung fragen: War es Mord?“

DAS WEIZENFELD

[8A]

NOTES

1. German uses the subjunctive mood principally (a) to refer to hypothetical situations, (b) to report someone's words or opinions (indirect-discourse subjunctive, which will be introduced in Story 8B).
2. There are situations that we know are not really true, or which we do not expect to be true. Such contrary-to-fact situations can be imagined in present time or in past time. They are expressed in the subjunctive.

   Present Time: You ask me whether I am rich? No, I am not. But if *I were* rich, *I would do* a great many things that I cannot do now.

   Past Time: You want to know whether I knew about it. No, I didn't. But if *I had known* about it, *I would have done* something about it right away.

3. To express contrary-to-fact situations in present time, German uses the subjunctive forms *derived from the simple past tense of the indicative.* To express them in past time, it uses the subjunctive forms *derived from the past perfect.* (For the formation of the subjunctive, see 4 below.)

   These forms are used for both the *if*-clauses and the conclusion-clauses. In the conclusion-clauses, however, the present-time and past-time subjunctive can be replaced by the forms **würde** + the present or past infinitive (*would* + present or past infinitive).

   Note: The use of the **würde**-construction is discouraged in conclusion-clauses which contain a modal auxiliary.

   Examples of the present-time subjunctive adapted from Story 8A:

<table>
<tr><td rowspan="2">Wenn wir unseren eigenen Weizen hätten,</td><td>brauchten wir dem Ritter nicht unser weniges Geld zu geben.</td></tr>
<tr><td>würden wir dem Ritter nicht unser weniges Geld zu geben brauchen.</td></tr>
</table>

   If we had our own wheat, we would not need to give the knight what little money we have.

<table>
<tr><td rowspan="2">Wenn wir den schönen Acker besäßen,</td><td>so hätten wir unseren eigenen Weizen.</td></tr>
<tr><td>so würden wir unseren eigenen Weizen haben.</td></tr>
</table>

If we owned that beautiful field, we would have our own wheat.

Wenn jemand uns ein paar Schweine *gäbe,* dann *könnten* wir zu Weihnachten einen guten Schinken essen. If someone gave us a few pigs, we could eat a good ham at Christmas.

Examples of the past-time subjunctive adapted from Story 8A:

Wenn der Ritter Theobald nicht durch ein Versprechen gebunden *gewesen wäre,*
- ***hätte* er sich vielleicht von seinem Acker *getrennt.***
- ***würde* er sich vielleicht von seinem Acker *getrennt haben.***

If the knight Theobald had not been bound by a promise, he would perhaps have parted with his field.

Wenn die Mönche kein so träges Leben *geführt hätten,*
- ***wäre* das Kloster vielleicht reich *geworden.***
- ***würde* das Kloster vielleicht reich *geworden sein.***

If the monks had not led such a lazy life, the monastery would perhaps have become rich.

4. Formation of the Subjunctive.
   a. The subjunctive has just one set of personal endings: **–e, –est, –e; –en, –et, –en.**
   b. Weak verbs use the indicative forms of the simple past tense. The present-time subjunctive is, therefore, identical in form with the simple past tense.
   c. Strong verbs umlaut the stem vowel of the simple past tense if the stem vowel is **a, o,** or **u.**

Indicative:	**ich trug**	**du nahmst**	**er zog**	**ihr wart**
Subjunctive:	**ich trüge**	**du nähmest**	**er zöge**	**ihr wäret**

Note: A dozen or so strong verbs change their stem vowels entirely.

The following four are the most important of these:

stehen	**helfen**	**sterben**	**werfen**
ich stand	**ich half**	**er starb**	**ich warf**
ich stünde	**ich hülfe**	**er stürbe**	**ich würfe**

   d. (1) Most irregular verbs also umlaut the stem vowel, as is shown in the list on the opposite page.

Indicative	Subjunctive
hatte	**h*ä*tte**
wurde	**w*ü*rde**
mußte	**m*ü*ßte**
durfte	**d*ü*rfte**
konnte	**k*ö*nnte**
mochte	**m*ö*chte**
wußte	**w*ü*ßte**
dachte	**d*ä*chte**
brachte	**br*ä*chte**

(2) **wollen** and **sollen** do *not* have umlaut.

(3) Irregular verbs whose stem of the infinitive is **–end–** or **–enn–** retain the **e.**

senden	**sandte**	**s*e*ndete**	**kennen**	**kannte**	**k*e*nnte**
wenden	**wandte**	**w*e*ndete**	**nennen**	**nannte**	**n*e*nnte**
brennen	**brannte**	**br*e*nnte**	**rennen**	**rannte**	**r*e*nnte**

5. The **wenn** in *if*-clauses is often omitted. In this case, the finite verb stands first in the clause.

   Wenn **jemand uns ein paar Schweine** ***gäbe*** . . .
   Gäbe **uns jemand ein paar Schweine** . . .
   Wenn **die Mönche kein so träges Leben** ***geführt hätten*** . . .
   Hätten **die Mönche kein so träges Leben** ***geführt*** . . .

6. The conclusion-clause is often introduced by **so** or **dann.** Both can be translated by "then," but are best omitted altogether in English. **So** must never be translated by "so."

7. The forms of the present-time and past-time subjunctives are also used

   a. after **als ob** or **als wenn** ("as if").

   Der Abt sah aus, ***als ob*** **er hungrig** ***wäre.***
   Der Abt sah aus, ***als wenn*** **er nichts** ***gegessen hätte.***

   Note: The **ob** or **wenn** can be omitted. In this case, the finite verb must stand right after the **als.**

   Der Abt sah aus, ***als wäre*** **er hungrig.** . . . as if . . .
   Der Abt sah aus, ***als hätte*** **er nichts gegessen.** . . . as if . . .

   b. in wishes whose fulfillment is either impossible or improbable. These wishes often contain the words **nur** or **doch** ("only"), or both. Here, too, the **wenn** can be omitted.

   Ach, ***wenn wir*** **nur den schönen Acker** ***hätten!***
   Ach, ***hätten wir*** **doch den schönen Acker!**
   Wenn **es doch nur Erbsen** ***gewesen wären!***
   Wären **es doch nur Erbsen** ***gewesen!***

REVIEW OF STRONG AND IRREGULAR VERBS USED IN STORY 7B

(sich) begeben	begibt	begab	begeben	*to go*
ein-laden	lädt ein	lud ein	eingeladen	*to invite*
reiten		ritt	ist geritten	*to ride (horse)*
unterhalten	unterhält	unterhielt	unterhalten	*to entertain*
versinken		versank	ist versunken	*to sink*
wägen		wog	gewogen	*to weigh*
wiegen		wog	gewogen	*to weigh*

IDIOMS FOR REVIEW

das Feld war ihm ans Herz gewachsen the field had grown dear to his heart
sich freuen über to be happy about, to rejoice at
hin und her to and fro, back and forth
er meinte es ernst he meant it in earnest
in Stücke reißen to tear to pieces

---

das Weizenfeld the field of wheat
[**der Weizen** the wheat (2)]

die Schweiz Switzerland (3)
italienisch Italian
der Gipfel the peak
[**der Gipfel, die Gipfel** the peak, summit, top (3)]
die Ruinen the ruins
[**die Ruine, die Ruinen** the ruin (3)]
die Burg the castle
[**die Burg, die Burgen** the (fortified) castle]
vor mehreren Jahrhunderten several centuries ago
[**das Jahrhundert, die Jahrhunderte** the century (3)]
der Ritter the knight
[**der Ritter, die Ritter** the knight]
namens Theobald by the name of Theobald (2)
die Burg the castle (2)
war . . . gebaut worden had been built
von seinem Großvater by his grandfather
der . . . gestritten hatte who had fought
[**streiten, stritt, hat gestritten** to fight, to quarrel (3)]

[8 A]

(THREE PARTS)

Das Weizenfeld

1.

Im Süden der Schweiz, nicht weit von der italienischen Grenze, kann man noch heute auf dem Gipfel eines Berges die Ruinen einer mächtigen Burg sehen, in der vor mehreren Jahrhunderten ein Ritter namens Theobald wohnte. Die Burg war von seinem Großvater gebaut worden, der lange Jahre im Heer des Kaisers mit großem Mut wider die Feinde des Reiches gestritten hatte und dessen treue Dienste dadurch gelohnt worden waren, daß der Kaiser ihm eine Menge Felder, Wiesen und Wälder schenkte. Die Kosten des Baues waren jedoch so hoch gewesen, daß die meisten Wiesen und Felder verkauft

---

lange Jahre for many years
im Heer in the army
[**das Heer, die Heere** the army]
der Kaiser the emperor (3)
der Mut the courage (3)
wider against (4)
treu loyal (3)
dadurch gelohnt worden waren had been rewarded
[**lohnen** to reward (2)]
Wiesen meadows
[**die Wiese, die Wiesen** the meadow]
schenken to give (as a gift) (2)
der Bau the construction (3)
Wiesen meadows
[**die Wiese, die Wiesen** the meadow (2)]
verkauft werden mußten had to be sold

hatte behalten können had been able to keep
damit so that
für ewige Zeiten for all time
[**ewig** eternal]
hatte der einzige Erbe . . . versprechen müssen the only heir had had to promise
[**der Erbe, die Erben** the heir (2)]
sich nie . . . zu trennen never to part
[**trennen** to separate, to part (3)]
dessen the latter's
der Ritter the knight
[**der Ritter, die Ritter** the knight (2)]
als Knabe as a boy
[**der Knabe, die Knaben** the boy (2)]
schwören to swear
[**schwören, schwor, hat geschworen** to swear (3)]
heilig sacred
[**heilig** holy, sacred (2)]

dem braven Ritter Theobald waren die Wälder und Felder besonders ans Herz gewachsen the woods and fields had grown especially dear to the heart of the good knight Theobald
das Tal the valley
[**das Tal, die Täler** (3)]
seine Äcker his fields
[**der Acker, die Äcker** the (cultivated) field (2)]
freute sich über rejoiced at
die Schönheit the beauty (3)
ja mit Stolz in fact, with pride
[**der Stolz** the pride]
hing sein Auge his eye dwelt
der Sommer the summer (3)
hin und her to and fro

das Kloster the monastery
[**das Kloster, die Klöster** the monastery, convent]
Mönche monks
[**der Mönch, die Mönche** the monk]
träg(e) lazy (2)
Schafe sheep
[**das Schaf, die Schafe** the sheep]
das Gras the grass (3)
die Kühe the cows
[**die Kuh, die Kühe** the cow]
fett fat (3)
das Futter the food, feed (3)
wenn wir . . . hätten if we had
das Vieh the cattle (2)
der Abt the abbot

werden mußten und der alte Mann nur die besten hatte behalten können. Damit die Burg für ewige Zeiten in den Händen der Familie blieb, hatte der einzige Erbe dem alten Vater versprechen müssen, sich nie von den Feldern zu trennen. Und auch dessen Erbe, der Ritter Theobald, mußte schon als Knabe schwören, das Versprechen seiner Väter heilig zu halten.

Dem braven Ritter Theobald waren die Wälder und Felder besonders ans Herz gewachsen. Jeden Tag blickte er aus den Fenstern der Burg hinunter in das Tal auf seine Äcker und Wiesen, die den Berg umgaben, und freute sich über ihre Schönheit. Mit besonderer Freude jedoch, ja mit Stolz, hing sein Auge an dem letzten Acker, dem besten und größten, auf dem im Sommer ein leichter Wind den schweren gelben Weizen hin und her bewegte.

In dem gleichen Tal, ganz in der Nähe des Weizenfeldes, lag auch ein Kloster, dessen Mönche in früheren Jahren ein so träges Leben geführt hatten, daß das Kloster nie reich geworden war. Es besaß nur einige Wiesen, auf denen ein paar dünne Schafe nach Gras suchten, während einige Schritte weiter die dicken Kühe und fetten Schweine des Ritters auf ihren Wiesen das beste Futter fanden. „Wenn wir nur etwas Vieh hätten", sagte der Abt zu seinen Mönchen, „dann würden unsere Mahlzeiten ein wenig mehr Geschmack haben. Was essen wir jetzt, einen Tag nach dem anderen? Zu Mittag gibt's Gemüse mit Schafkäse und abends Schafkäse mit Gemüse, am Freitag ein paar Fische, und nur am Sonntag und an besonderen Festtagen

---

die Mönche the monks
[**der Mönch, die Mönche** the monk (2)]
würden . . . haben would have
die Mahlzeiten the meals
[**die Mahlzeit, die Mahlzeiten** the meal (2)]
der Geschmack the taste (3)
das Gemüse the vegetables (2)
der Schafkäse the sheep cheese
[**das Schaf, die Schafe** the sheep (2)]
[**der Käse, die Käse** the cheese]
der Freitag the Friday (3)

schwimmt . . . herum floats around
[**schwimmen, schwamm, ist geschwommen** to swim, to float (3)]
das Fleisch the meat (4)
der Suppenteller the soup plate
[**der Teller, die Teller** the plate (3)]
wenn jemand uns . . . gäbe if someone gave us
Kühe cows
[**die Kuh, die Kühe** the cow (2)]
dann hätten wir then we would have
die Sahne the cream (3)
käme would come
die Wurst the sausage
[**die Wurst, die Würste** the sausage (3)]
zu Weihnachten at Christmas (3)
könnten wir we could
in den Mund nehme pronounce
geliebte Brüder beloved brethren
daß wir . . . backen könnten that we could . . . bake
[**backen, er bäckt, backte (buk), hat gebacken** to bake (2)]
nicht einmal not even
der Kuchen the cake
[**der Kuchen, die Kuchen** (3)]
daß uns selbst das Notwendigste fehlt that we lack even the most necessary things
wenn wir nur . . . besäßen if we only owned
so hätten wir then we would have
und brauchten . . . nicht . . . zu geben and would not need to give

der Abt the abbot (2)
die Rede the speech
[**die Rede, die Reden** the speech, talk]
an dem er wieder . . . würde essen müssen on which he would have to eat again
Schafkäse sheep cheese
[**der Käse, die Käse** the cheese (2)]
trieb ihn so zur Verzweiflung drove him to such despair
[**die Verzweiflung** the despair]
reden to speak
[**reden** to talk, to speak (2)]

der Kamm the crest
[**der Kamm, die Kämme** the comb; the crest, top (3)]
der Tau the dew (2)
glänzen to glisten (3)
nachdem er . . . beschrieben hatte after he had described
[**beschreiben, beschrieb, hat beschrieben** to describe (3)]
traurig sad (3)
das Kloster the monastery
[**das Kloster, die Klöster** the monastery, convent (2)]

schwimmt etwas Fleisch im Suppenteller herum. Wenn jemand uns ein paar Schweine und Kühe gäbe, dann hätten wir wenigstens etwas Sahne und Butter; jeden Sonntag käme eine fette Wurst auf den Tisch, und zu Weihnachten könnten wir einen guten Schinken essen. Ach, wenn ich das Wort ‚Wurst' in den Mund nehme, kann ich kaum weitersprechen! Wißt ihr, geliebte Brüder, daß wir nicht einmal Brot oder für den Sonntag etwas Kuchen backen könnten, wenn uns der Ritter Theobald nicht jedes Jahr einen Teil seines Weizens verkaufte? So tief sind wir gesunken, daß uns selbst das Notwendigste fehlt! Ach, wenn wir nur den schönen Acker besäßen, der an der Grenze unserer Wiesen liegt, so hätten wir wenigstens unseren eigenen Weizen und brauchten unser weniges Geld nicht dem Ritter Theobald zu geben."

Der Abt war während dieser langen Rede so hungrig geworden, und der Gedanke an den nächsten Tag, an dem er wieder Gemüse und Schafkäse würde essen müssen, trieb ihn so zur Verzweiflung, daß er beschloß, am nächsten Morgen zur Burg zu gehen und mit dem Ritter zu reden.

2.

Früh am Morgen, als die Sonne gerade über den Kamm der Berge stieg und der Tau noch auf den Wiesen glänzte, erschien der Abt auf der Burg. Nachdem er dem Ritter die traurigen Zustände in seinem Kloster beschrieben hatte, sprach er: „Edler Herr! Vielleicht ist unsere große Armut eine Strafe, die uns der Himmel für unsere Sünden schon hier auf Erden gesandt hat. Möge Gott geben, daß wir dafür im nächsten Leben weniger zu leiden haben werden! Denn leiden müssen

---

edler Herr noble sir
[**edel** noble; precious (2)]
die Armut the poverty (2)
die Sünden the sins
[**die Sünde, die Sünden** the sin (3)]
möge Gott geben may God grant
dafür in exchange

der, welcher he who
zurück-lassen leave behind
der . . . betet who prays
[**beten** to pray (3)]
das Heil the salvation (2)
von uns Sündern of us sinners
[**der Sünder, die Sünder** the sinner (3)]
könnte could
die Hilfe the help (3)
von oben from above
wie wäre es how would it be
begännen began
ein Gut der Welt a wordly possession
[**das Gut, die Güter** the goods; the estate (2)]
an dem . . . hängt to which . . . is attached
ein Heide a heathen
[**der Heide, die Heiden** the heathen]
würden wir einander helfen we would help one another

die Überraschung the surprise (3)
die Rede the speech
[**die Rede, die Reden** the talk, speech (2)]
es tut mir leid I am sorry
höflich polite (4)
das Versprechen the promise
[**das Versprechen, die Versprechen** the promise (2)]
ich täte Ihnen gern I would gladly do you
der Gefallen the favor (3)

an dem Ton from the tone
[**der Ton, die Töne** the sound, tone (3)]
es ernst meinte meant it seriously
[**ernst** earnest, serious (3)]
ich könnte I could
murmeln to murmur (3)
die Würde the dignity (2)

noch schlechter als sonst even worse than usual
der Heimweg the way home (2)
der Punkt the point
[**der Punkt, die Punkte** the point; period]
die Geduld the patience (3)
schritt walked
[**schreiten, schritt, ist geschritten** to walk, to pace, to step (3)]
ruhelos restlessly (3)
hin und her to and fro (2)
überlegen to think (3)
konnte . . . doch noch gelöst werden could still be solved

wir auch dort, so hat man uns gelehrt. Wie glücklich ist dann der, welcher hier auf Erden jemanden zurücklassen kann, der für das Heil seiner Seele betet! Wer von uns Sündern könnte von sich sagen, daß er keine Hilfe von oben braucht? Keiner. Wie wäre es, edler Ritter, wenn meine Mönche und ich begännen, schon jetzt–und natürlich auch später nach Ihrem Tode–für Sie und das Heil Ihrer Seele zu beten, und wenn Sie uns das Weizenfeld schenkten, das neben unserem Kloster liegt? Was ist ein Feld, Herr Ritter? Ein Gut der Welt, an dem vielleicht ein Heide hängt, jedoch nicht wir. W i r müssen an den H i m m e l denken. Geben Sie uns das Feld! Auf diese Weise würden wir einander helfen, S i e uns in d i e s e m Leben, wir Ihnen im nächsten."

Zu seiner großen Überraschung schüttelte der gute Ritter Theobald am Ende dieser langen Rede nur den Kopf. „Es tut mir leid, Herr Abt", sagte er höflich, „aber ich kann Ihren Wunsch nicht erfüllen. Ich bin durch ein Versprechen gebunden, mich nie von meinem Land zu trennen. Ich täte Ihnen gern jeden anderen Gefallen; aber das Versprechen, das ich meinem Vater gab, muß ich heilig halten."

Der Abt erkannte an dem Ton der Stimme, daß der Ritter es ernst meinte. „Ich könnte den Mann in Stücke reißen", murmelte er zwischen den Zähnen. Aber er behielt seine Würde, grüßte höflich und ging.

Zu Mittag schmeckten ihm das Gemüse und der Käse noch schlechter als sonst, weil er auf dem Heimweg das fette Vieh des Ritters gesehen hatte und jetzt zu oft an Sahne, Butter und Wurst dachte. Er hatte den Punkt erreicht, wo seine Geduld zu Ende war. Während einer ganzen Woche schritt er ruhelos im Garten hin und her; in der Nacht schlief er nicht mehr. Er überlegte. Vielleicht konnte das Problem doch noch gelöst werden. Eines Nachts fiel ihm endlich etwas ein.

---

fiel ihm . . . ein occurred to him
[**ein-fallen** to occur (2)]

die Klosterbibliothek the monastery library
[**die Bibliothek, die Bibliotheken** the library]
der Bruder Bonifaz Brother Boniface
das Schreibpult the writing desk (2)
blau blue (3)
Buchstaben letters
[**der Buchstabe, die Buchstaben** the letter (2)]
unter among
richtig real
das Dokument the document
[**das Dokument, die Dokumente** the document]
geschenkt wurde was given

der Besuch the visit (3)
er wurde . . . empfangen he was received
[**empfangen, er empfängt, empfing, hat empfangen** to receive (3)]
gereizt irritated
[**reizen** to irritate; to attract]
auf dem Herzen on your mind
das Dokument the document
[**das Dokument, die Dokumente** the document (2)]
die Bibliothek the library
[**die Bibliothek, die Bibliotheken** the library (2)]
soll . . . geliehen haben is supposed to have lent
[**leihen, lieh, hat geliehen** to lend, to loan; to borrow]
der Großvater the grandfather (2)
so steht hier so it says here
dafür in exchange
ob whether
echt genuine
entscheiden to decide
[**entscheiden, entschied, hat entschieden** (3)]
es würde . . . führen it would lead
Gerichte courts of law
[**das Gericht, die Gerichte** the court, tribunal (3)]
geprüft werden are examined
wo . . . entschieden wird where it is decided
von dem Richter by the judge
echt genuine (2)
ich schlage vor I propose

Am Morgen ging er in die Klosterbibliothek, wo der Bruder Bonifaz an seinem hohen Schreibpult stand und mit roter und blauer Tinte schöne Buchstaben in ein großes Buch schrieb. „Hör gut zu, Bruder Bonifaz!“ sprach der Abt. „Ist es möglich, daß sich unter unseren vielen alten Papieren vielleicht eines befindet, in dem geschrieben steht, daß das schöne Weizenfeld neben dem Kloster uns gehört?“–„Sie meinen ein richtiges Dokument, welches beweist, daß der Acker dem Kloster einmal geschenkt wurde?“ entgegnete Bruder Bonifaz. „Ich will mein Bestes tun.“

Zwei Wochen nach seinem ersten Besuch erschien der Abt wieder auf der Burg. Er wurde zwar höflich empfangen, aber die Stimme des Ritters klang etwas gereizt, als er sagte: „Nun, Herr Abt, was führt Sie heute zu mir? Haben Sie etwas auf dem Herzen?“–„Nichts auf dem Herzen, edler Herr“, erwiderte der Abt lächelnd, “aber etwas in meiner Tasche. Ein altes Dokument, das gestern in unserer Bibliothek entdeckt wurde.“ Er zog es aus der Tasche und reichte es dem Ritter. Der las es schweigend. Dann blickte er auf, und seine Augen schossen Blitze und Flammen: „Sie wollen meinen Acker! Ihr Kloster soll meinem Großvater einmal eine große Summe Geld geliehen haben, so steht hier in großen Buchstaben, und dafür hat er dem Kloster den Acker und dieses Dokument gegeben. Das kann ich nicht glauben. Mein Großvater konnte nicht einmal schreiben! Das Dokument muß falsch sein.“–„Ob es falsch oder echt ist, können weder Sie noch ich entscheiden“, erwiderte der Abt. „Aber warum sollen wir uns streiten? Es würde zu nichts führen. Für solche Sachen gibt es Gerichte, wo Dokumente wie dieses hier geprüft werden und wo von dem Richter entschieden wird, ob sie echt sind. Ich schlage vor, daß wir i h n entscheiden lassen.“

bei sich to himself
  da stimmt etwas nicht there is something wrong there
    [**stimmen** to be correct, to be right (4)]
verfaßt hat wrote
    [**verfassen** to write, to be the author of (2)]
wenn es . . . wäre if it were
  von ihm by him
  so wüßte ich es I would know it
  wäre ich I would be
ich würde . . . gern I should like to
  wenn ich dächte if I thought
  daß es die Mühe lohnen würde that it would be worth the effort
    [**die Mühe, die Mühen** the effort, the pain (4)]
heutzutage nowadays (2)
da fiel ihm . . . ein then . . . occurred to him
friedliebend peace-loving (3)
wenn wir . . . brächten if we brought
  würde es . . . dauern it would last
  entschieden wird is decided
  selbst wenn ich verlöre even if I lost
  würde das Feld . . . gehören the field would . . . belong
würden Sie mir . . . erlauben would you allow me
  noch einmal once more
  ernten to harvest
wenn es . . . sein soll if it is to be
  so werden wir . . . gern gestatten we shall gladly allow
  noch einmal once more
  pflanzen to plant
  ernten to harvest (2)
  er . . . gewogen hatte he had weighed
    [**wägen, wog, hat gewogen** to weigh (2)]
notwendig necessary (4)
  hätte ich gern I should like to have
  darüber about it
sah ihn . . . an looked at him
    [**an-sehen** to look at (3)]
  erstaunt astonished (3)

der Frühling the Spring (2)
  grün green (2)
  war . . . nichts zu sehen als nothing was to be seen but
  braun brown (4)
darauf on it
  pflanzen to plant (2)
  erklärte declared
unterbrach interrupted
    [**unterbrechen, er unterbricht, unterbrach, hat unterbrochen** to interrupt (3)]

3.

Während der Abt redete, dachte der Ritter bei sich: „Da stimmt etwas nicht. Es ist unmöglich, daß mein Großvater dieses Dokument verfaßt hat. Wenn es von ihm wäre, so wüßte ich es von meinem Vater, und dann wäre ich sicher, daß es echt ist. Ich würde die Sache gern vor Gericht bringen, wenn ich dächte, daß es die Mühe lohnen würde. Aber wer weiß nicht, wie die Gerichte heutzutage sind? Wenn heute ein Abt mit einem geschriebenen Dokument zum Richter geht, verliere ich meinen Fall bestimmt." Da fiel ihm plötzlich etwas ein. „Herr Abt", sagte er, „streiten wir uns nicht! Ich bin ein friedliebender Mensch und möchte, daß wir gute Nachbarn bleiben. Nehmen Sie das Feld! Aber ich möchte Sie um einen kleinen Gefallen bitten. Sehen Sie, wenn wir die Sache vors Gericht brächten, würde es wenigstens ein Jahr dauern, bis der Fall entschieden wird, und selbst wenn ich verlöre, würde das Feld während dieser Zeit noch mir gehören. Würden Sie mir deshalb erlauben, im nachsten Jahr noch einmal auf dem Acker zu ernten? Sobald ich geerntet habe, gehört das Feld Ihnen."– „Wenn es nur e i n m a l sein soll, so werden wir Ihnen gern gestatten, noch einmal zu pflanzen und zu ernten", entgegnete der Abt nach einer kurzen Pause, während deren er die Worte des Ritters gewogen hatte. „Ich glaube, das ist das Wenigste, was wir für Sie tun können."–„Ich danke Ihnen", sprach der Ritter. „Aber da es heutzutage notwendig zu sein scheint, daß solche Dinge schwarz auf weiß auf einem Stück Papier stehen, hätte ich gern von Ihnen darüber ein kleines Dokument." Der Abt sah ihn erstaunt an. Dann aber tat er, was der Ritter verlangt hatte, und verfaßte das Dokument.

Im nächsten Frühling, als alle anderen Felder langsam grün wurden, war auf dem schönen Acker des Ritters nichts zu sehen als braune Erde. „Sie haben nichts darauf gepflanzt, Herr Ritter", erklärte der Abt; „der Acker gehört jetzt uns."–„Nicht so schnell, Herr Abt!" unterbrach ihn Ritter Theobald. „Sie

zart tender (2)
rotbraun reddish-brown
Pflänzchen little plants
[**die Pflanze, die Pflanzen** the plant (3)]
Erbsen peas
[**die Erbse, die Erbsen** the pea (3)]
Bohnen beans
[**die Bohne, die Bohnen** the bean (2)]
Unsinn! nonsense! (3)
der eben hinzugekommen war who had just come over
[**hinzu** in addition; there, to that place (2)]
Eichen oak trees
[**die Eiche, die Eichen** the oak]
bis die Frucht tragen until *they* bear fruit
[**die Frucht, die Früchte** the fruit (3)]

sauer sour (4)
von fern from afar (2)
was . . . kommen würde what would come
die Reihe the row
[**die Reihe, die Reihen** the row (2)]
es nichts anderes zu essen geben würde there would be nothing else to eat

die Eichen the oak trees
[**die Eiche, die Eichen** the oak (2)]
das Grab the grave
[**das Grab, die Gräber** the grave (4)]

irren sich. Was ich gepflanzt habe, braucht nur einige Zeit, bis es aus dem Boden kommt.“

Von nun an lief der Abt jeden Morgen mit seinen Mönchen durch die Wiesen zum Acker. Endlich kam etwas aus der Erde, zarte, rotbraune Pflänzchen. „Aha! Erbsen–oder vielleicht Bohnen!“ rief der Abt voller Freude. „Unsinn!“ murmelte Bruder Ignatius, der eben hinzugekommen war und etwas von Pflanzen verstand; „wenn das Erbsen oder Bohnen sind, dann ist mein Name nicht Ignatius. Das sind keine Erbsen, Herr Abt, sondern kleine Eichen, und bis d i e Frucht tragen, können wir alle lange warten!“

Mit saurem Gesicht ging der Abt mit seinen Mönchen langsam ins Kloster zurück. Schon von fern rochen sie die Gemüsesuppe, die auf sie wartete. Sie wußten genau, was nach der Suppe kommen würde. Schafkäse. Und vor ihnen lag eine lange, lange Reihe von Tagen, an denen es nichts anderes zu essen geben würde.

Die Eichen wuchsen, aber sie wuchsen langsam. Als sie zum ersten Mal Frucht trugen, lagen der Abt und Ritter Theobald schon lange im Grab.

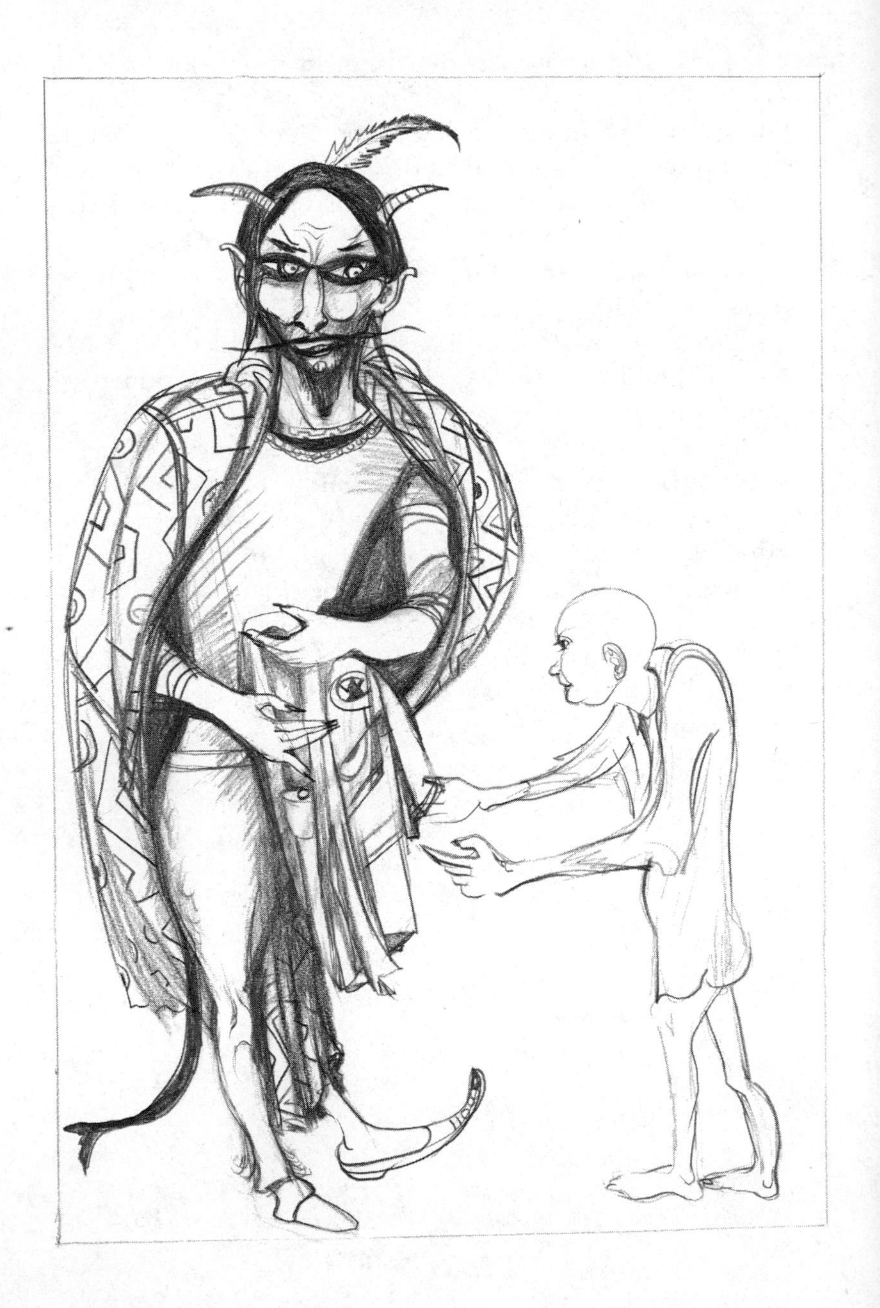

DER BÄRENHÄUTER

[8B]

NOTES

I. 1. By indirect discourse we understand the *re*statement of someone's words, thoughts, ideas, opinions. Such restatements are prefaced by a governing verb of saying, stating, reporting, thinking, believing, hoping, asking, and the like.

"I did not do it," he said.
He said (that) he had not done it.

2. In changing from direct discourse (a statement in quotation marks) to indirect discourse, German replaces the indicative by the subjunctive when the *governing verb,* which introduces the restatement, is in *a past tense.*

Note: There is a tendency to use the indicative in the indirect discourse when the governing verb is in the *present* tense. However, the subjunctive *can* be used.

3. If the *original statement* (as it would appear in quotation marks) is in the *present tense,* German, in changing to indirect discourse, uses
   a. the subjunctive forms derived from the indicative of the simple past; see Notes to Story 8A, 3. and 4.
   b. or a special set of subjunctive forms derived from the *infinitive* and formed by adding the personal subjunctive endings **–e, –est, –e; –en, –et, –en** to the stem of the infinitive.

ich habe	**werde**	**müsse**	**könne**
du habest	**werdest**	**müssest**	**könnest**
er habe	**werde**	**müsse**	**könne**
wir haben	**werden**	**müssen**	**können**
ihr habet	**werdet**	**müsset**	**könnet**
sie haben	**werden**	**müssen**	**können**
möge	**dürfe**	**wolle**	**solle**
mögest	**dürfest**	**wollest**	**sollest**
möge	**dürfe**	**wolle**	**solle**
mögen	**dürfen**	**wollen**	**sollen**
möget	**dürfet**	**wollet**	**sollet**
mögen	**dürfen**	**wollen**	**sollen**

wisse	**gehe**	**fahre**	**laufe**
wissest	**gehest**	**fahrest**	**laufest**
wisse	**gehe**	**fahre**	**laufe**
wissen	**gehen**	**fahren**	**laufen**
wisset	**gehet**	**fahret**	**laufet**
wissen	**gehen**	**fahren**	**laufen**

lese	**nehme**	**tue**	
lesest	**nehmest**	**tuest**	
lese	**nehme**	**tue**	
lesen	**nehmen**	**tuen**	
leset	**nehmet**	**tuet**	
lesen	**nehmen**	**tuen**	etc.

Only **sein** "to be" is irregular:

ich sei, du sei(e)st, er sei; wir seien, ihr seiet, sie seien

4. a. *Either form* can be used provided that it is *a clearly subjunctive form.*

Direct statement: He said: "I cannot come."
They said: "She is sick."

Indirect statement: He said that he could not (was not able to) come.
They said that she was sick.

Er sagte, daß er nicht kommen *könne/könnte.*

Sie sagten, daß sie krank *sei/wäre.*

Note: As in English, the conjunction **daß** which introduces the indirect discourse is frequently omitted. Without the **daß**, the clause is no longer a dependent clause, but becomes a main clause in which the finite verb stands immediately after the subject.

Er sagte, *er könne/könnte* nicht kommen.

Sie sagten, *sie sei/wäre* krank.

b. If one of the two forms is identical with the indicative (this applies to every first- and third-person plural except for **sein**), the other, clearly subjunctive form is used.

Er sagte, daß sie nicht kommen *könnten.*

Er sagte ihr, daß sie nicht zu kommen *brauche.*

Er dachte, sie *hätten* kein Geld.

c. If both forms are identical with the indicative, the one derived from the simple past is preferred.

Er sagte, daß sie nicht kommen *wollten.*

Er sagte ihnen, sie *brauchten* nicht zu kommen.

5. If the original statement is in *a past tense,* German, in changing to indirect discourse, uses the past participle with the subjunctive forms of **sein** or **haben,** depending on which of these two auxiliaries is required by the verb.

   ich sei/wäre, du sei(e)st/wärest, er sei/wäre, etc. + *past participle.*

   ich habe/hätte, du habest/hättest, er habe/hätte; wir hätten, ihr habet/hättet, sie hätten + *past participle.*

   Er sagte, daß sein Bruder letzte Woche krank *gewesen sei/wäre.*

   Er sagte, er *habe/hätte* ihn gestern *gesehen.*

6. To express the future in indirect discourse, the subjunctive forms **ich werde, du werdest, er werde,** etc., or **ich würde, du würdest, er würde,** etc. + *the infinitive* are used.

   Er sagte, daß er morgen nicht *kommen werde/würde.*

7. Indirect questions are like indirect statements and follow the same rules.

   Er öffnete die Tür, um zu sehen, wer *gekommen sei/wäre.*

   Er fragte sich, was der Herr in seinem armen Hause *wünsche.*

II. 1. All subjunctive forms can be used after **als ob, als wenn** ("as if").

   Er sah aus, als ob er hungrig *sei/wäre.*

   Er sah aus, als ob er nichts *gegessen habe/hätte.*

   Es sah aus, als ob er bald mit seiner Arbeit fertig *sein werde/würde.*

2. The subjunctive forms derived from the infinitive (see **I.3.b.** above) are also used for

   a. indirect commands **(sollen)** or requests **(mögen).**

      Er sagte ihm, er *solle* schnell kommen.

      Betet zu Gott, daß mir nichts geschehen *möge.*

   b. wishes whose fulfillment is possible.

      Lang *lebe* der König! Long live the king (= may the king live long)!

      Gott *sei* Dank! Thank God (= God be thanked)!

      Er *ruhe* in Frieden! May he rest in peace!

   c. to fill the role of a non-existent imperative in the first person plural.

      ***Laufen wir* schnell!** Let's run fast!

Komm, *gehen wir* nach Hause! Come, let's go home!

d. direct commands in the third person singular or plural.

Er *komme!* Let him come!
Man *nehme* zwölf Eier, ein Pfund Butter . . . Take twelve eggs, one pound of butter . . .

REVIEW OF STRONG VERB USED IN STORY 8A

leihen lieh geliehen *to lend, loan*

IDIOMS FOR REVIEW

ich weiß, was dir fehlt I know what your trouble is
was fehlt Ihnen? what's the trouble?
auf . . . zu toward
der Bär rannte auf ihn zu the bear ran toward him

---

der Bärenhäuter Mr. Bearskin

es war einmal there was once
die Schule the school
[**die Schule, die Schulen** the school (2)]
das Interesse the interest (3)
lernen to learn (4)
gemein common
[**gemein** mean; common (3)]
das Heer the army
[**das Heer, die Heere** the army (2)]
der Krieg the war (4)
gebrauchen to use (4)
das Gewehr the rifle
[**das Gewehr, die Gewehre** the rifle (3)]
gestritten hatte had fought
wurden . . . geschickt were sent
unserem jungen Mann to our young man
der Hauptmann the captain (3)

[8 B]

(FIVE PARTS)

Der Bärenhäuter

I.

Es war einmal ein junger Mann, der als Knabe für die Schule wenig Interesse gezeigt und deshalb nicht viel gelernt hatte. Als die Zeit kam, sich sein tägliches Brot zu verdienen, wußte er nicht, was er tun sollte, und so ging er und diente als gemeiner Soldat im Heere des Königs, denn damals war gerade Krieg und man konnte jeden gebrauchen, der stark genug war, ein Gewehr auf den Schultern zu tragen. Solange der Krieg dauerte, ging alles gut. Nachdem unser Soldat aber mit großem Mut gegen die Feinde des Königs gestritten hatte und der Friede endlich wieder ins Land gekommen war, wurden alle Soldaten nach Haus geschickt, und auch unserem jungen Mann erklärte sein Hauptmann, er könne jetzt gehen, denn der Krieg sei zu Ende und der König brauche keine Soldaten mehr.

So hatte unser junger Freund nun weder Arbeit noch Geld, und ein Heim besaß er auch nicht mehr, weil seine Eltern während des Krieges gestorben waren. In seiner Not hätte er nicht gewußt, was er tun sollte, wenn er nicht auf den Gedanken

---

er könne . . . gehen that he could go
sei zu Ende was over
brauche needed

hätte er nicht gewußt he would not have known
wenn er nicht auf den Gedanken gekommen wäre if it had not occurred to him

bis . . . wieder anfinge until . . . would start again
behaupteten asserted
[**behaupten** to maintain, to assert (3)]
sie seien that they were
hätten nicht einmal did not even have
nämlich namely
[**nämlich** you see; that is to say; namely (4)]

eben flat (2)
die Gruppe the group
[**die Gruppe, die Gruppen** the group (2)]
der Stein the stone
[**der Stein, die Steine** the stone (3)]
erstens first (2)
zweitens second(ly) (2)
drittens third(ly) (3)
werde ich . . . gebraucht I am . . . needed
ich . . . werde sterben müssen I shall have to die
versunken sunk
[**versinken, versank, ist versunken** to sink (2)]
obwohl although (3)
sich . . . umsah looked around
unbekannt unknown (3)
die Jacke the jacket
[**die Jacke, die Jacken** the jacket (3)]
anhatte had on
[**an-haben** to have on (2)]
die Hahnenfeder the rooster's feather
er sah ganz . . . aus he looked entirely
der Pferdefuß the hoof of a horse
was dir fehlt what you lack
der Fremde the stranger (4)
und dich vor nichts fürchtest and are not afraid of anything
[**sich fürchten vor** to be afraid of]
damit so that
ausgebe spend
[**aus-geben** to spend (2)]
die Furcht the fear (2)
mir hat . . . niemand Angst machen können no one has been able to make me be afraid

gekommen wäre, bei seinen Brüdern Hilfe zu suchen. Zu ihnen ging er nun und bat sie, ihn so lange bei sich wohnen zu lassen, bis der Krieg wieder anfinge. Die Brüder hatten jedoch ein hartes Herz und behaupteten, sie seien selbst arme Leute und hätten nicht einmal genug für ihre eigenen Familien. Da nahm unser Soldat alles, was er besaß, nämlich sein Gewehr, und machte sich auf den Weg in die weite Welt.

Kaum war er einige Stunden gegangen, als er auf ein weites, ebenes Feld kam, auf dem nichts zu sehen war als eine Gruppe von hohen Bäumen. Dort setzte er sich traurig auf einen Stein und überlegte, was nun aus ihm werden solle. „Erstens habe ich kein Geld", sagte er sich; „zweitens habe ich nichts gelernt, und drittens werde ich nicht mehr als Soldat gebraucht. Ich sehe, daß ich bald vor Hunger werde sterben müssen." Wie er so in die bittersten Gedanken versunken dasaß, erschrak er plötzlich, denn über ihm hatten sich die Blätter der Bäume bewegt, obwohl nicht der geringste Wind über das Feld blies. Als der Soldat sich erstaunt umsah, stand ein unbekannter Mann vor ihm, der eine grüne Jacke anhatte und an dessen Hut eine Hahnenfeder steckte. Er sah ganz wie andere Menschen aus; nur war unser Soldat etwas überrascht, als er dort, wo andere Leute ihre Füße haben, an dem einen Bein einen menschlichen Fuß, am anderen aber einen Pferdefuß erblickte. „Ich kenne deine Not und weiß, was dir fehlt", sprach der Fremde. „Du gefällst mir, und deshalb sollst du von mir alles bekommen, was du dir wünschst. Nur muß ich zunächst wissen, ob du Mut besitzt und dich vor nichts fürchtest, damit ich mein Geld nicht für die falsche Person ausgebe."–„Ein Soldat und Furcht!" rief unser Freund; „mach mich nicht lachen! Mir hat bis jetzt niemand Angst machen können. Aber du kannst es versuchen!"–„Nun", entgegnete der andere, „sieh hinter dich!"

sich um-blicken to look around (3)
der Bär the bear
[**der Bär, die Bären** the bear]
das Maul the mouth (of an animal) (2)
auf ihn zurannte was running toward him
als ob as if (3)
fressen to eat
[**fressen, er frißt, fraß, hat gefressen** to eat (of beasts) (3)]
der Bär the bear (2)
daß es dir nicht an Mut fehlt that you do not lack courage
erfüllt werden können can be fulfilled
gern gladly
dem langsam klar wurde to whom it was slowly becoming clear
[**klar** clear (4)]
im Laufe in the course
[**der Lauf** the course (3)]
die Gabel the fork
[**die Gabel, die Gabeln** the fork (3)]
der Löffel the spoon
[**der Löffel, die Löffel** the spoon (3)]
wäschst wash
[**waschen, er wäscht, wusch, hat gewaschen** to wash (3)]
die Fingernägel the fingernails
[**der Fingernagel, die Fingernägel** the fingernail (2)]
der Kamm the comb (4)
versprichst du das if you promise that
stirbst du if you die
solltest du aber but if you should
dazu in addition

wog weighed
[**wägen, wog, hat gewogen** to weigh (3)]
der so etwas verlange who demanded something like that
nur . . . sein könne could only be
nichts weniger als . . . bringen wolle wanted nothing less than to bring
und da er and since he
darauf thereupon
zog . . . aus took off
[**aus-ziehen** to take off (3)]
so wirst du you will
zog . . . ab removed
die Haut the skin (2)
darauf on it

2.

Wie unser Freund sich umblickte, sah er einen großen Bären, der mit offenem Maul auf ihn zurannte, als ob er ihn fressen wollte. „Oho!" rief er; „dir will ich gleich etwas zeigen!" Sprach es, nahm sein Gewehr und schoß, daß der Bär sofort tot niederfiel. „Daß es dir nicht an Mut fehlt, hast du bewiesen", sagte der Fremde; „aber du mußt mir noch etwas versprechen, bevor deine Wünsche erfüllt werden können."–„Das tue ich gern, wenn es meiner Seele nicht schadet", erwiderte der Soldat, dem langsam klar wurde, wen er vor sich hatte.–„Ob es deiner Seele schadet, wirst du erst im Laufe der Zeit sehen", sprach der Fremde. „Ich verlange, daß du während der nächsten sieben Jahre nicht mit Gabel und Löffel, sondern mit den Fingern ißt; daß du dich weder wäschst noch dir die Fingernägel schneidest; und daß du dir den Bart und die Haare wachsen läßt und keinen Kamm gebrauchst. Auch darfst du während dieser Zeit nicht zu Gott beten. Versprichst du das, so gebe ich dir eine Jacke und einen Mantel, den du die ganze Zeit lang tragen mußt. Stirbst du in diesen sieben Jahren, so gehörst du mir; solltest du aber am Ende dieser Zeit noch leben, dann bist du frei und dazu reich dein ganzes Leben lang."

Der Soldat wog jedes Wort, das der andere gesprochen hatte, und sagte sich, daß jemand, der so etwas verlange, wirklich nur der Teufel sein könne, und daß der Teufel nichts weniger als seine Seele in seine Gewalt bringen wolle. Dann aber dachte er auch an seine große Not, und da er während des Krieges so oft den Tod vor Augen gesehen hatte, wollte er auch jetzt sein Leben wagen und sagte schließlich zu allem ja. Darauf zog der Teufel–denn es war wirklich der Teufel!–seine grüne Jacke aus, reichte sie dem Soldaten und sagte: „Wenn du die anhast und in die Tasche greifst, so wirst du deine Hand immer voll Geld finden." Dann nahm er ein Messer, ging zum Bären, zog ihm die Haut ab und sagte: „Das soll von nun an dein Mantel sein und auch dein Bett, denn darauf mußt du schlafen,

die Kleidung the clothing (2)
Bärenhäuter Bearskin
damit with that

gesagt habe had told
voller Goldmünzen full of gold coins
[**die Münze, die Münzen** the coin]
das Bärenfell the bearskin
[**das Fell, die Felle** the fur, skin, hide]
ja . . . genug indeed enough

ziemlich rather (4)
sah . . . aus looked
schrecklich terrible (4)
die Krallen the claws
[**die Kralle, die Krallen** the claw]
der Löwe the lion
[**der Löwe, die Löwen** the lion]
schmutzig dirty (3)
die Stirn the forehead (4)
hinten in the back (3)
der Tannenbaum the fir tree
[**die Tanne, die Tannen** the fir tree]
er wurde . . . gemieden he was shunned
[**meiden, mied, hat gemieden** to avoid, to shun (2)]
weil er für . . . gehalten wurde because he was believed to be
der Heide the heathen
[**der Heide, die Heiden** the heathen (2)]
hatte ihn . . . gehen sehen had seen him go
die Kirche the church
[**die Kirche, die Kirchen**]
da er aber but since he
damit so that
nicht sterben möge might not die
so wurde er nicht fortgejagt he was not driven away
[**jagen** to hunt, to chase; to race (2)]

nicht einmal not even
Kühen cows
[**die Kuh, die Kühe** the cow (3)]
die Tiere the animals
[**das Tier, die Tiere** the animal (3)]
vor ihm Angst haben würden would be afraid of him
die Handvoll the handful (2)
Goldstücke gold coins
[**das Goldstück, die Goldstücke** the gold coin (2)]
nicht länger nein sagen zu können that he could no longer say no
hinterst farthest

und du darfst dich auf kein anderes Bett legen. Und wegen dieser Kleidung sollst du Bärenhäuter heißen." Damit verschwand er.

Um zu prüfen, ob der Teufel die Wahrheit gesagt habe, zog der Soldat die Jacke an und griff in die Tasche. Richtig, seine Hand war voller Goldmünzen! Zufrieden nahm er den Mantel, d.h. (das heißt) das Bärenfell, ging froh und lustig weiter und tat nun, was er wollte, denn Geld hatte er ja jetzt genug.

Im ersten Jahr ging alles noch ziemlich gut. Im zweiten jedoch sah unser Freund schon schrecklich aus. Seine Fingernägel waren so lang und scharf wie die Krallen eines Löwen, das dichte und schmutzige Haar fiel ihm über die Stirn tief ins Gesicht und bedeckte ihm hinten Hals und Rücken, und der Bart hing ihm bis auf die Brust und sah aus wie ein Tannenbaum sechs Wochen nach Weihnachten. Er wurde von allen gemieden, nicht nur, weil er so schrecklich aussah und mit den Fingern aß, anstatt Gabel und Löffel zu gebrauchen, sondern auch, weil er für einen Heiden gehalten wurde, denn niemand hatte ihn je in eine Kirche gehen sehen. Da er aber überall den armen Leuten Geld gab, damit sie für ihn zu Gott beteten, daß er vor dem Ende der sieben Jahre nicht sterben möge, und weil er auch immer alle seine Rechnungen bezahlte und nie Schulden machte, so wurde er nicht fortgejagt, wenn er abends in einem Gasthaus um ein Zimmer bat.

3.

Im vierten Jahr jedoch kam er zu einem Gasthaus, wo der Wirt ihm nicht einmal einen Platz im Stall bei den Pferden und Kühen geben wollte, weil er fürchtete, daß die Tiere vor ihm Angst haben würden. Doch als der Bärenhäuter eine Handvoll Goldstücke aus seiner Tasche holte, da glaubte der Wirt nicht länger nein sagen zu können und gab ihm ein Zimmer im hintersten Teil des Hauses. Vorher mußte der Bärenhäuter ihm

sich nicht sehen zu lassen not to let himself be seen
  damit niemand wisse so that no one would know
  was für Gäste what kind of guests
  habe had

die Verzweiflung the despair (2)
  vorüber wären would . . . be over
  das Nebenzimmer the adjoining room (2)
hinüber over
dieser the latter
ließ sich . . . dazu bewegen let himself be persuaded
getroffen habe had struck
  sein früherer Reichtum his former wealth
    [**der Reichtum** the wealth]
  geschwunden sei had disappeared
    [**schwinden, schwand, ist geschwunden** to disappear, to vanish]
  die Armut the poverty (3)
sei . . . gestorben had died
  vor kurzem a short while ago (3)
  geliebt beloved (2)
  die Krankheit the illness
  gekostet habe had cost
sei . . . zurückgekehrt had come back
  der Erfolg the success
    [**der Erfolg, die Erfolge** the success (2)]
  gemacht habe had made
  der Vetter the cousin
    [**der Vetter, die Vetter** the (male) cousin (3)]
werde er . . . ankommen he would arrive
  und . . . sagen müssen and would have to tell
nicht einmal not even
  werde . . . rufen would call
  und ihn . . . werfen lassen and have him thrown
  er erführe he would learn
  nicht bezahlen könne could not pay

wurde . . . gerührt was moved
    [**rühren** to move, to stir (3)]
konnte ihm nicht geholfen werden he could not be helped
etwas Mut zu machen to encourage . . . somewhat
  indem er ihm sagte by telling him
  werde . . . bezahlen would pay
ließ . . . kommen had . . . come

jedoch versprechen, sich nicht sehen zu lassen, damit niemand wisse, was für Gäste der Wirt in seinem Hause habe.

Als nun der Bärenhäuter abends allein in seinem Zimmer saß und in seiner Verzweiflung wünschte, daß die sieben Jahre bald vorüber wären, da hörte er im Nebenzimmer etwas, was klang, als ob ein Mensch laut klagte. Er öffnete seine Tür, ging hinüber und sah einen alten Mann, der so laut weinte, daß es dem Bärenhäuter ins Herz schnitt. Dieser trat näher. Wie der Alte ihn aber erblickte, sprang er auf und wollte fliehen. Doch als er an der Stimme hörte, daß der Fremde ein Mensch war, blieb er und ließ sich schließlich dazu bewegen, dem Bärenhäuter den Grund seiner Tränen zu erklären. Er erzählte, wie ihn seit Jahren ein Unglück nach dem anderen getroffen habe und wie sein früherer Reichtum langsam geschwunden sei, so daß er und seine Töchter jetzt in Armut lebten. Als ob all das noch nicht genug wäre, sagte er, sei vor kurzem auch seine geliebte Frau gestorben, deren Krankheit ihn sein letztes Geld gekostet habe. Er selbst sei eben ohne Erfolg von einer Reise zurückgekehrt, die er gemacht habe, um von einem Vetter seiner Frau etwas Geld zu leihen. Morgen werde er zu Haus ankommen und seinen Töchtern sagen müssen, daß sie nichts mehr zu essen hätten und nun alle Hunger leiden müßten. Aber würde er überhaupt nach Haus kommen? Wahrscheinlich nicht, denn er habe nicht einmal genug Geld, um sein Zimmer zu bezahlen, und der Wirt werde sicher die Polizei rufen und ihn ins Gefängnis werfen lassen, sobald er erführe, daß er seine Rechnung nicht bezahlen könne.

Der Bärenhäuter wurde von dieser traurigen Geschichte so gerührt, daß er zunächst nicht wußte, wie er den armen Alten trösten solle. Mit Worten allein konnte ihm nicht geholfen werden; was hier gebraucht wurde, war Geld. Es gelang ihm, dem Alten etwas Mut zu machen, indem er ihm sagte, er solle sich für die nächsten Tage keine Sorgen machen; er selbst werde dem Wirt bezahlen, was dieser verlange. Er ließ den Wirt sofort kommen und gab ihm, was er forderte. Dann steckte er dem unglücklichen Alten noch eine Handvoll Goldstücke in die Tasche. Der wußte nicht, wie er ihm danken

der Stolz the pride (2)
das Alter the old age
wird sie nicht nein sagen können she will not be able to say no
selbst wenn even if

maß measured, inspected
[**messen, er mißt, maß, hat gemessen** to measure]
vor Schreck with fright
[**der Schreck(en), die Schrecken** the fright, fear, terror, horror (3)]
um darauf zu sagen to say after that
eher heiraten würde would sooner marry
sie habe she had
der Marktplatz the market place
[**der Markt, die Märkte** the market (3)]
zahm tame
gewesen sei had been
die Offiziersuniform the officer's uniform
[**die Uniform, die Uniformen** the uniform]
und der and he
tausendmal a thousand times
und daher and therefore (3)

so würden alle . . . gesehen haben all would have seen
der Ausdruck the expression
[**der Ausdruck, die Ausdrücke** the expression (3)]
der Ring the ring
[**der Ring, die Ringe** the ring (3)]
brach broke
[**brechen, er bricht, brach, hat gebrochen** (2)]
komme ich nicht wieder if I do not come back
[**wieder-kommen** to come back, to return (3)]
geschehen möge may happen

die Braut the bride
[**die Braut, die Bräute** the bride, fiancée, betrothed]
der Bräutigam the bridegroom, the fiancé
wiederkommen werde would come back

könne. „Alles, was ich noch habe", sprach er, „ sind meine drei Töchter, der Stolz und die Freude meines Alters. Sie sind Wunder der Schönheit. Komm mit und wähle dir eine von ihnen zur Frau. Wenn sie hört, was du für mich getan hast, wird sie nicht nein sagen können, selbst wenn du ein wenig ungewöhnlich aussiehst." Dem Bärenhäuter gefiel das, und er ging mit.

4.

Als er in das Haus trat, maß ihn die älteste Tochter nur mit einem kurzen Blick; dann schrie sie vor Schreck und lief fort. Die zweite sah ihn etwas länger an, aber nur, um darauf zu sagen, daß sie einen wirklichen Bären eher heiraten würde als diesen wilden Heiden, der weder wie ein Mensch noch wie ein wirklicher Bär aussehe. Sie habe einmal auf dem Marktplatz einen zahmen Bären beobachtet, der viel schöner gewesen sei, weil er eine Offiziersuniform und weiße Handschuhe angehabt habe, und der, sagte sie, hätte ihr tausendmal besser gefallen. Die jüngste Tochter jedoch sprach: „Liebster Vater, jemand, der dir in der Not geholfen hat, muß ein guter Mensch sein, und daher werde ich tun, was du ihm versprochen hast."

Wenn die langen Haare und der dichte Bart nicht das ganze Gesicht des Bärenhäuters bedeckt hätten, so würden alle den Ausdruck der Freude gesehen haben, die er empfand, als er die Worte des Mädchens hörte. Er nahm einen Ring von seinem Finger, brach ihn in zwei Stücke und gab dem Mädchen die eine Hälfte. Die andere behielt er selbst. „Verliere deine Hälfte nicht", sprach er. „Ich muß noch drei Jahre fern von dir durch die Welt wandern. Komme ich nicht wieder, so bist du frei, weil ich dann tot bin. Bete aber zu Gott, daß mir während dieser Zeit nichts geschehen möge!"

Als er fortgegangen war, kamen der armen Braut die Tränen in die Augen. Sie hoffte, daß ihr Bräutigam wiederkommen werde; aber sie wagte kaum, es zu glauben. Von den wenigen Kleidern, die sie besaß, wählte sie eines, ein schwarzes,

die Schwestern the sisters
[**die Schwester, die Schwestern** the sister (3)]
warum um . . . trauern why grieve for
[**trauern** to mourn, to grieve (2)]
der Bräutigam the bridegroom, fiancé (2)
und darfst . . . nicht and must not
ebenfalls likewise (2)
aus Furcht for fear
. . . gern haben like
der Honig the honey (2)
macht er . . . auf he will open
auf einmal suddenly
du wirst gefressen you will be eaten
die Hochzeit the wedding
gewiß certainly (4)
konnte dazu nur schweigen could say nothing to that

obgleich although (3)
man ihn . . . rühmte people praised him
so wurde er . . . gemieden he was shunned
[**meiden, mied, hat gemieden** to avoid, to shun (3)]
von jedem Gasthaus from every inn
klopfen to knock (4)
da man . . . für zu gut . . . hielt since one considerd . . . as too good
der Schweinestall the pigsty (3)
Beeren berries
[**die Beere, die Beeren** the berry (3)]
Wurzeln roots
[**die Wurzel, die Wurzeln** the root (3)]
hohl hollow (2)
träg(e) lazy (3)
wenn er . . . danach strebte if he strove
[**streben** to strive, to endeavor (2)]

eben war die Sonne the sun had just
eben flat (3)
vor sieben Jahren seven years ago

das sie von nun an immer trug. Als ihre zwei Schwestern sie in dieser Kleidung erblickten, lachten sie nur. „Warum um deinen schönen Bräutigam trauern?" sagte die älteste. „Vielleicht kommt er zurück. Aber wenn er wieder hier ist, mußt du gut aufpassen und darfst ihm nicht die Hand geben. Du weißt, wie stark Bären sind und wie fest sie drücken." Die andere Schwester lachte ebenfalls, nur noch lauter als die erste. „Wenn er m e i n Bräutigam wäre, würde ich auch trauern und klagen", sagte sie; „aber nur aus Furcht, d a ß er zurückkommt. Vergiß nicht, daß Bären Honig und andere süße Dinge gern haben. Wenn du ihm gefällst, macht er auf einmal das Maul auf, und du wirst gefressen!—Aber die Hochzeit wird gewiß lustig sein, weil Bären so gut tanzen." Die arme Braut konnte dazu nur schweigen.

Indes zog der Bärenhäuter von einem Ort des Reiches zum anderen und tat Gutes, wo er konnte. Obgleich man ihn überall wegen seiner guten Werke rühmte, so wurde er doch jetzt von allen Menschen gemieden, weil er nun wirklich wie ein wildes Tier aussah. Von jedem Gasthaus, an dessen Tür er klopfte, wurde er fortgeschickt, da man jetzt sogar den schmutzigsten Schweinestall für zu gut für ihn hielt. So mußte der Bärenhäuter von den Beeren und Wurzeln des Waldes leben und in der Nacht in hohlen Bäumen schlafen. „Vielleicht ist dies die Strafe des Himmels für mein früheres träges Leben", dachte er. Aber, so hoffte er auch, wenn er nur immer danach strebte, jedem zu helfen, der sich in Not befand, dann würde Gott ihm vielleicht seine Sünden verzeihen und ihn vor dem Ende der sieben Jahre nicht sterben lassen.

5.

Endlich waren auch die letzten drei Jahre vorüber. Eben war die Sonne im Westen hinter den Gipfeln der Berge verschwunden, als der Bärenhäuter sein Ziel erreichte und zu dem weiten, ebenen Feld und der Gruppe von hohen Bäumen kam, wo er vor sieben Jahren gesessen hatte. Wieder setzte er

maß measured

[**messen, er mißt, maß, hat gemessen** to measure (2)]

zurückgebe should give back

gewaschen werden to be washed

die Goldmünzen the gold coins (2)

[**die Münze, die Münzen** the coin (2)]

mitgebracht brought along

[**mit-bringen** to bring along, to take along (3)]

die Uniform the uniform

[**die Uniform, die Uniformen** (2)]

ein so hoher Herr such a grand gentleman

er sei gekommen he had come

er . . . gehört habe he had heard

außerordentlich extraordinary (3)

und . . . bitten wolle and wanted to ask

noch vor wenigen Minuten only a few minutes ago

das Schlüsselloch the keyhole (3)

zur Frau as his wife

sich auf den Stein, wieder bewegten sich plötzlich die Blätter, und der Teufel stand vor ihm. Er maß den Bärenhäuter mit einem bösen Blick, warf ihm die alte Jacke vor die Füße und verlangte, daß er ihm seine grüne zurückgebe. „Nicht so schnell", meinte der Bärenhäuter; „erst will ich von dir gewaschen werden." Während der Teufel Wasser holen ging, zog der Bärenhäuter seine alte Jacke an und füllte schnell alle Taschen mit Goldmünzen. Dann ließ er sich von dem Teufel von Kopf bis zu Fuß waschen und die Fingernägel, die Haare und den Bart schneiden. Einen Kamm hatte er selbst mitgebracht. „So, jetzt kannst du auch deine grüne Jacke wiederhaben", sagte er. „Und nun fort mit dir!"

In der nächsten Stadt kaufte er sich eine herrliche Uniform, in der er wie ein Graf oder ein hoher Offizier aussah, und fuhr dann in einem Wagen mit vier Pferden und mehreren Dienern zum Haus seiner Braut. Dort wurde er von dem Vater empfangen, der ihn nicht erkannte, sondern ihn für einen Grafen oder den Fürsten eines fremden Landes hielt und sich fragte, was ein so hoher Herr in seinem armen Hause wünsche. Er sei gekommen, erklärte der Fremde, weil er von der außerordentlichen Schönheit seiner drei Töchter gehört habe und ihn um die Hand einer von ihnen bitten wolle. Der Vater war außer sich vor Freude und führte den fremden Herrn in das Zimmer, in dem seine drei Töchter noch vor wenigen Minuten gewesen waren. Aber die zwei ältesten, die durch das Schlüsselloch gesehen und alles gehört hatten, waren schnell fortgelaufen, um ihre besten Kleider anzuziehen. Nur die jüngste saß in ihrem schwarzen Kleid bei ihrer Arbeit, als der Fremde ins Zimmer trat. Sie blickte kurz auf, aber auch sie erkannte ihn nicht. Da schritt er näher, nahm die Hälfte seines Ringes und zeigte sie ihr schweigend. Und da wußte sie, daß ihr Bräutigam zurückgekommen war.

Während sie voller Glück einander in den Armen hielten, kamen die beiden Schwestern in ihren schönen Kleidern zurück; sie waren sicher, daß der hohe Herr eine von ihnen zur Frau wählen würde. Als sie aber sahen, daß der Fremde nicht s i e heiraten würde, sondern ihre jüngste Schwester gewählt hatte,

der Neid the envy (2)
die Brücke the bridge
[**die Brücke, die Brücken** (3)]

wer . . . gekommen sei who had come
zu so später Stunde at such a late hour
die Dunkelheit the darkness (3)
siehst du you see
dafür in exchange
statt einer instead of one

da liefen sie voll Neid und Zorn aus dem Haus und stürzten sich von der Brücke ins Wasser.

Am Abend klopfte jemand an die Tür. Als der Bärenhäuter sie öffnete, um zu sehen, wer zu so später Stunde gekommen sei, erblickte er draußen in der Dunkelheit eine Gestalt in einer grünen Jacke. „Ich wollte dir nur etwas sagen", lachte der Teufel, dessen lange Zähne weiß durch die Nacht schienen. „Siehst du, d i c h habe ich nicht in meine Gewalt bekommen, aber dafür habe ich jetzt zwei Seelen statt einer!"

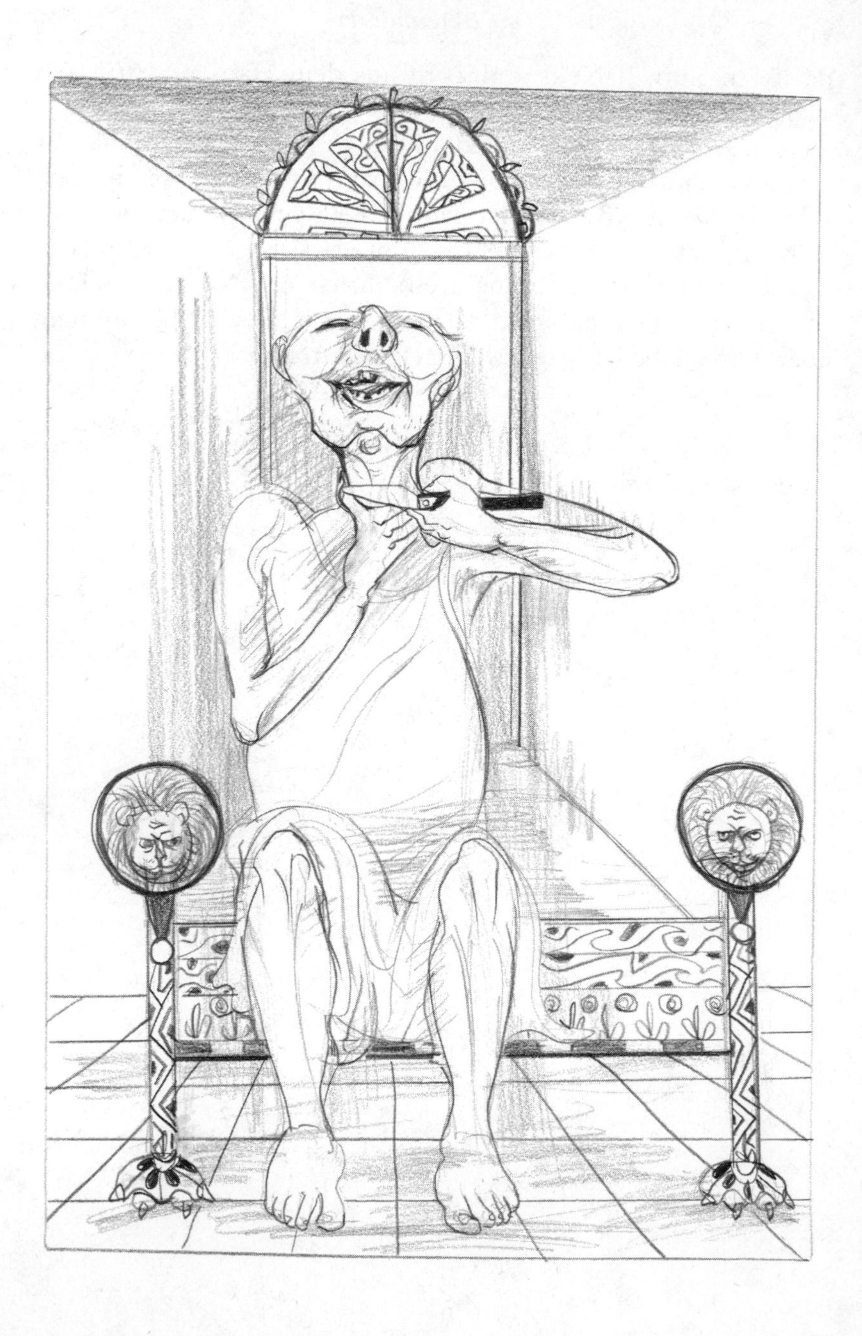

ZIMMER NUMMER 17

[9A]

NOTES

I. 1. The shift from direct to indirect discourse in the passive voice is made in a way similar to the one described for the active voice in the Notes to Story 8B.

2. If the *direct* statement is in the *present tense,* the subjunctive forms **du werdest, er, sie, es werde** or **würde, würdest, würde,** etc., + *past participle* are used in the indirect statement.

Note: Only **du werdest, er werde** should be used, as the remaining **werde**-forms are identical with the indicative.

Direct Statement: **„Die Sache wird natürlich untersucht", sagte der Inspektor.** . . . is, of course, being investigated . . .

Indirect Statement: **Die Sache *werde* natürlich *untersucht,* sagte der Inspektor.**

3. If the *direct* statement is in *a past tense,* the subjunctive forms for the change to indirect discourse are derived from the *present perfect or the past perfect of the passive construction.*

Direct statement:

„Die Sache wurde natürlich sofort untersucht"
„Die Sache ist natürlich sofort untersucht worden" } **, sagte**
„Die Sache war natürlich sofort untersucht worden"

Gustav Moser; „aber man weiß bis heute nicht",

fügte er hinzu, (he added), { **„ob Albert ermordet wurde. "** / **„ob Albert ermordet worden ist."** / **„ob Albert ermordet worden war."**

Indirect statement:

Die Sache *sei/wäre* natürlich sofort *untersucht worden,* sagte Gustav Moser; aber, so fügte er hinzu, man wisse/wüßte bis heute nicht, ob Albert *ermordet worden sei/wäre.*

4. If the *direct* statement is in the future, the subjunctive forms **werde/würde** + the *present infinitive of the passive* are used in the indirect statement.

Direct statement: **„Die Sache wird morgen noch einmal untersucht werden", sagte der Inspektor.**

Indirect statement: **Die Sache *werde* morgen noch einmal *untersucht werden,* sagte der Inspektor.**

Der Inspektor sagte, daß die Sache morgen noch einmal *untersucht werden würde.*

II. 1. The rules for the use of the subjunctive in contrary-to-fact situations in the active voice (see Notes to Story 8A) also apply to such situations in the passive voice.

2. Present time:

„Die Sache wird nicht von der Polizei untersucht, sagen Sie?"—„Nein. Aber wenn sie von der Polizei *untersucht würde,* dann . . ."

Wenn der Fall nicht klar wäre, *würde* er von der Polizei *untersucht* (*werden*).

3. Past Time:

Albert wurde im Hotelzimmer gefunden. Der Fall wurde von der Polizei untersucht.

Wenn Albert nicht im Hotelzimmer *gefunden worden wäre,* { ***wäre* der Fall von der Polizei nicht *untersucht worden.*** / ***würde* der Fall von der Polizei nicht *untersucht worden sein.*** }

REVIEW OF STRONG VERBS USED IN STORY 8B

aus-geben	gibt aus	gab aus	ausgegeben	*to spend (money)*
messen	mißt	maß	gemessen	*to measure*
schwinden		schwand	ist geschwunden	*to disappear*

IDIOMS FOR REVIEW

mitten in der Nacht in the middle of the night
es lohnt die Mühe it is worth the effort, it is worth the trouble
Glück haben to be lucky, to be fortunate
an Ihrer Stelle in your place, if I were you

Nummer number
[**die Nummer, die Nummern** the number (3)]
siebzehn seventeen

die Geistergeschichte the ghost story
soll . . . passiert sein is said to have happened
die Kleinstadt the small town (2)
verlassen deserted
der Kirchhof the churchyard
[**die Kirche, die Kirchen** the church (2)]
vor . . . Jahren . . . years ago
Hexen witches
[**die Hexe, die Hexen** the witch (3)]
das Hotel. the hotel
[**das Hotel, die Hotels** (2)]
Geschäftsreisende traveling salesmen
[**der Geschäftsreisende, die Geschäftsreisenden** the traveling salesman]
der Weltkrieg the World War (2)
zu einer Zeit at a time
modern modern (3)
genauso just as
daß man nicht . . . gern . . . gelesen oder gehört hätte that one would not have liked to read or listen to

Herr Mampe proper name
geschlossen concluded
die Kusine the cousin
[**die Kusine, die Kusinen** the (female) cousin]
habe sie . . . schreiten . . . sehen she had seen . . . walking
in Knabenkleidung in boys' clothing
[**der Knabe, die Knaben** the boy (3)]
[**die Kleidung** the clothing (3)]
anderer Geschäftsreisender of other traveling salesmen
[**der Geschäftsreisende, die Geschäftsreisenden** the traveling salesman (2)]
bei einem Glas over a glass
das Gastzimmer the lounge, taproom
„Zum Zahmen Löwen" at the sign of the "Tame Lion"
[**zahm** tame (2)]
[**der Löwe, die Löwen** the lion (2)]
sich . . . unterhielten entertained one another
[**unterhalten, er unterhält, unterhielt, hat unterhalten** to entertain (3)]
mit der Erzählung von Geschichten by telling stories
verschiedenster Art of all kinds
der November the November
die Rathausuhr the city hall clock
[**das Rathaus, die Rathäuser** the city hall (2)]

[9 A]

(FOUR PARTS)

Zimmer Nummer 17

I.

Die folgende Geschichte, eine Art Geistergeschichte, soll in einer deutschen Kleinstadt passiert sein; aber nicht in irgendeinem verlassenen Haus oder auf einem Kirchhof vor mehreren hundert Jahren, als die ganze Welt sich noch vor Hexen und Geistern fürchtete, sondern in einem Hotel für Geschäftsreisende kurz nach dem Ersten Weltkrieg–zu einer Zeit also, in der die Menschen schon ziemlich modern geworden waren und genauso wenig an Geister glaubten wie die meisten von uns heute. Man war aber trotzdem noch nicht so modern geworden, daß man nicht in einer ruhigen Stunde gern eine Geistergeschichte gelesen oder gehört hätte.

In dem Augenblick, in dem unsere Erzählung anfängt, hatte ein gewisser Herr Mampe gerade eine solche Geistergeschichte erzählt und mit den folgenden Worten geschlossen: „. . . und dann, sagte meine Kusine, habe sie eine weiße Gestalt durch das Zimmer schreiten und plötzlich verschwinden sehen." Herr Mampe reiste in Knabenkleidung und befand sich in der Gesellschaft anderer Geschäftsreisender, die nach dem Abendessen bei einem Glas Bier unten in dem großen Gastzimmer des Hotels „Zum Zahmen Löwen" zusammen saßen und sich mit der Erzählung von Geschichten verschiedenster Art unterhielten. Es war eine bitterkalte Novembernacht, und die Rathausuhr hatte eben zehn geschlagen. „Ich selbst", fuhr

fuhr . . . fort continued
[**fort-fahren** to go away, to drive away; to continue]
reden to speak (3)
die Kusine the cousin
[**die Kusine, die Kusinen** the (female) cousin (2)]
sie . . . nicht erzählt hätte she would . . . not have told
erschienen wäre had not appeared

der Satz the sentence (4)
vor zehn Minuten ten minutes ago
der Koffer the suitcase (4)
der Armstuhl the armchair (3)
[**der Stuhl, die Stühle** the chair (4)]
realistisch realistic
ich . . . hätte . . . gern gewußt I . . . should . . . have liked to know
die Nichte the niece
[**die Nichte, die Nichten** (2)]
nachher afterwards (4)
und so weiter (usw.) and so forth
das Schlafzimmer the bedroom (3)
kommen vor happen
interessanter gewesen wäre would have been more interesting
der Realismus the realism
mit anderen Worten in other words
realistisch realistic (2)
die Erklärung the explanation
[**die Erklärung, die Erklärungen** the explanation, declaration]
dessen, was of what
der Skeptiker the skeptic
ich persönlich I personally (3)
die Großmutter the grandmother (2)
hat mir genügt was enough for me
wäre ich heute I would be today
ich würde . . . erklären I would declare
rein pure
[**rein** clean, pure (2)]
davon of that
langweilen to bore
fortzufahren to continue
[**fort-fahren** to continue (2)]

die Pfeife the pipe (4)

Herr Mampe fort, „lächle immer, wenn ich jemanden von Geistern reden höre; aber ich muß in diesem Falle erklären, daß meine Kusine eine Frau ist, die gewöhnlich die Wahrheit sagt, und daß sie die Geschichte bestimmt nicht erzählt hätte, wenn die weiße Gestalt ihr nicht wirklich erschienen wäre."

Die Pause, die diesem Satz folgte, wurde von einem älteren Herrn unterbrochen, der vor zehn Minuten mit Koffer und Mantel in das Zimmer getreten war und sich still in einen Armstuhl gesetzt hatte. „Keine schlechte Geschichte", sagte er; „nur ist sie nach meinem Geschmack nicht realistisch genug. Ich für meinen Teil hätte zum Beispiel gern gewußt, w a r u m die weiße Gestalt Ihrer Kusine oder Nichte erschienen ist; w e r die Gestalt war; was nachher geschehen ist usw. (und so weiter). Verstehen Sie mich bitte nicht falsch! Ich habe nichts gegen Kusinen oder Nichten, die mitten in der Nacht plötzlich aufwachen und etwas Weißes in ihrem Schlafzimmer sehen. Solche Dinge kommen vor. Ich will nur sagen, daß die Geschichte interessanter gewesen wäre, wenn Sie oder Ihre Kusine alles viel genauer beschrieben hätten. Mehr Realismus, mit anderen Worten, und eine realistische Erklärung dessen, was wir nicht zu verstehen scheinen. Sie halten mich vielleicht für einen Skeptiker. Sie irren sich. Ich persönlich glaube an Geister. Warum? Nicht weil einmal ein Geist meiner alten Großmutter erschienen ist, sondern weil ich selbst einmal einen wirklichen Geist mit eigenen Augen gesehen habe. Aber dieses eine Mal hat mir genügt, sage ich Ihnen! Wenn die Sache mir damals nicht fast das Leben gekostet hätte, wäre ich heute wahrscheinlich wie die meisten von Ihnen: ich würde alle Geistergeschichten als reinen Unsinn erklären. Aber genug davon! Ich will Sie hier nicht mit persönlichen Dingen langweilen."—Die anderen baten ihn natürlich, fortzufahren.

2.

„Nun", sagte er, während er seine Pfeife füllte, „es ist eine lange Geschichte, und ich muß um Ihre Geduld bitten, weil es

die Vergangenheit the past
vor . . . Jahren . . . years ago
führten mich took me
der Bekannte the acquaintance
[**der Bekannte, die Bekannten** the acquaintance]
ebenfalls likewise (3)
wäre . . . gefunden worden had been found
mit durchschnittener Kehle with his throat cut
habe noch . . . gehalten had still held
das Rasiermesser the straight-edge razor
woraus man hätte schließen können from which one could have concluded
sei . . . untersucht worden had been investigated
man wüßte . . . nicht one did not know
oder ermordet worden sei or had been murdered
mein Bekannter my acquaintance
[**der Bekannte, die Bekannten** the acquaintance (2)]
ja er beschrieb in fact, he described
außer daß except that
an dessen Enden at whose ends
vier Löwenköpfe four lions' heads
es stellte . . . dar it represented
[**dar-stellen** to present, to represent (3)]
der Weihnachtsmann Santa Claus
und . . . schenkt and gives
[**schenken** to give (as a present) (3)]
Nüsse nuts
[**die Nuß, die Nüsse** the nut (3)]
Apfelsinen oranges
[**die Apfelsine, die Apfelsinen** the orange (3)]
manchmal sometimes
blitzend flashing
der Backenbart the whiskers

notwendig ist, daß ich etwas in die Vergangenheit zurückgehe. —Ich bin, wie wir alle in diesem Hotel, Geschäftsreisender. Was das bedeutet, wissen wir: jeden Tag in einer anderen Stadt, jede Nacht in einem anderen Bett. Vor etwa zehn Jahren führten mich meine Geschäfte nach Hannover, wo ich einen alten Bekannten traf, den ich seit langem nicht gesehen hatte. Moser war der Name, Gustav Moser. Sie wissen, wie es ist: bei einem Glas Bier spricht man von alten Zeiten, man fragt nach dieser oder jener Person, die man gekannt hat, und so fragte ich auch nach seinem Bruder Albert, der ebenfalls Geschäftsreisender war und von dem ich seit einiger Zeit nichts mehr gehört hatte. ‚Mein Gott, wissen Sie denn nicht, was passiert ist?' sagte Gustav Moser mit einer Stimme, die keinen Zweifel darüber ließ, daß sein Bruder nicht mehr lebte. Albert, so erzählte er mir dann, wäre eines Morgens in seinem Blute schwimmend auf dem Bett seines Hotelzimmers mit durchschnittener Kehle gefunden worden; seine kalte Hand habe noch das blutbedeckte Rasiermesser gehalten. Kein Brief, nichts, woraus man hätte schließen können, was geschehen war. Die Sache sei natürlich von der Polizei untersucht worden, aber man wüßte bis heute nicht, ob Albert sich das Leben genommen habe oder ermordet worden sei.—Ich wollte wissen, wo es passiert war. Mein Bekannter nannte mir die Stadt, ja er beschrieb sogar das Zimmer: groß und bequem, in keiner Weise verschieden von anderen Hotelzimmern, außer daß ein Bett darin stand, an dessen Enden sich vier Löwenköpfe befanden, und daß ein Bild über dem Bett hing, das etwas mit Weihnachten zu tun hatte; ich glaube, es stellte einen Weihnachtsmann dar, der einen großen Sack aufmacht und ein paar Kindern Äpfel, Nüsse und Apfelsinen schenkt.—Ja, bitte?" Der Herr im Armstuhl wandte sich an Herrn Mampe, der eben den Mund aufgemacht hatte, als ob er etwas sagen wollte. Aber Herr Mampe schüttelte nur den Kopf und schwieg. Der Herr im Armstuhl fuhr in seiner Erzählung fort. „Das war alles", sagte er. „Ich hatte Albert Moser gut gekannt, und es war natürlich, daß ich nun manchmal an ihn dachte, wie er vorher gewesen war: ein Bild des blühenden Lebens, mit seinen blitzenden Augen, seinem vollen Haar und dem schwarzen Backenbart.

vor zwei Jahren two years ago
bestellen reserved
[**bestellen** to order (4)]
blickte ein Herr . . . mich . . . an a gentleman . . . looked at me
[**an-blicken** to look at (3)]
er zog mich he drew me
wenn ich mich . . . mische if I meddle
[**mischen** to mix; to shuffle (cards); to mingle; to interfere, to meddle (3)]
womit with which
an Ihrer Stelle in your place
würde ich es mir . . . überlegen I would think it over
bevor ich . . . schliefe before I would sleep

so erinnerte ich mich when I remembered
ließ mir den Schlüssel geben asked for the key (*literally:* had the key given to me)
erwähnen to mention (3)
von Natur by nature
der leicht Angst hat who is easily afraid
daß ich . . . vorgezogen hätte that I would have preferred
[**vor-ziehen** to prefer (3)]
ich rief . . . an I called
[**an-rufen** to call, to telephone (4)]
genau thoroughly
ja ich sah in fact, I looked
sich irgendwo versteckt hätte had hidden somewhere
würde ich . . . gefunden haben I would have found
die Lampe the lamp
[**die Lampe, die Lampen** the lamp (3)]
der Nachttisch the bedside table

Aber die Sorgen des Lebens lassen den Menschen vieles vergessen, und so vergaß ich auch im Laufe der Zeit, was Gustav Moser mir von Alberts traurigem Ende erzählt hatte.—Vor zwei Jahren—es war im November, wie heute—führten mich meine Geschäfte in jene Stadt, wo Albert Moser sich das Leben genommen hatte oder, wie manche Leute glaubten, auf so schreckliche Weise ermordet worden war. Ich ging in das Hotel, wo ich ein Zimmer bestellt hatte. In dem Augenblick, in dem ich nach der Nummer meines Zimmers fragte und um meinen Schlüssel bat, blickte ein Herr, der neben mir stand, mich überrascht, ja fast erschrocken an. Er zog mich zur Seite. ‚Ich hoffe, Sie werden mir verzeihen', sagte er, ‚wenn ich mich in etwas mische, womit ich persönlich nichts zu tun habe—aber wollen Sie wirklich in d e m Zimmer schlafen? Es ist das Zimmer, in dem sich bis jetzt drei Menschen die Kehle durchgeschnitten haben. Erst ein gewisser Moser, und die beiden anderen waren auch Geschäftsreisende. An Ihrer Stelle würde ich es mir zweimal überlegen, bevor ich in dem Zimmer schliefe.'

3.

„Kaum hatte er das gesagt, so erinnerte ich mich, daß ich in demselben Hotel war, dessen Namen mir Gustav Moser damals genannt hatte. Ich dankte dem Herrn, ließ mir den Schlüssel geben und ging hinauf. Ich erkannte das Zimmer sofort. Das gleiche Bett mit den Löwenköpfen, das gleiche Bild.—Ich möchte erwähnen, meine Herren, daß ich von Natur kein Mensch bin, der leicht Angst hat; aber Sie werden verstehen, daß ich ein anderes Zimmer vorgezogen hätte. Es gelang mir jedoch nicht, eins zu bekommen. Ich rief mehrere Hotels an, aber sie waren alle voll. Ich mußte das Zimmer behalten. Um sicher zu sein, daß sich niemand darin versteckt hielt, untersuchte ich es genau; ja ich sah sogar unter das Bett. Wenn jemand sich irgendwo versteckt hätte, würde ich ihn gefunden haben. Ich ging zu Bett, ließ die kleine Lampe an, die neben mir auf dem Nachttisch stand, und schlief ein. Die Tür hatte

abgeschlossen locked
 [**ab-schließen** to lock (3)]

das Dienstmädchen the maid
 [**das Dienstmädchen, die Dienstmädchen** (3)]
da mein Zug . . . ging since my train left

ich halte nicht viel davon I do not think much of it
 [**halten von** to think of, to have an opinion of]

eigentlich actually (4)
nicht . . . gewesen wäre had not been
 hätte ich . . . gerufen I would have called
ich mich . . . würde rasieren müssen I would have to shave
 [**sich rasieren** to shave]
 bei meinem starken Bart with my strong beard
vor Kälte zitternd shivering with cold
 [**die Kälte** the cold (3)]
 der Waschtisch the wash stand
 mich zu rasieren to shave
 [**sich rasieren** to shave (2)]
ober upper
 das Kinn the chin (2)
 um . . . sehen zu können in order to be able to see
 der Spiegel the mirror
 [**der Spiegel, die Spiegel** the mirror]
wäre mir das Herz stillgestanden my heart would have stood still
 [**still-stehen** to stand still, to stop]
der Spiegel the mirror
 [**der Spiegel, die Spiegel** the mirror (2)]
 das Hemd the shirt (4)
 die Hosen the trousers
 [**die Hose, die Hosen** the trousers, pants (4)]
 der Backenbart the whiskers (2)
um ihn nicht sofort wiederzuerkennen not to recognize him at once
 [**wieder-erkennen** to recognize]
die Verzweiflung the despair (3)
 die Furcht the fear (3)
auf einmal suddenly
 blitzt etwas something flashes
 mit dem Daumen . . . streicht runs his thumb
 [**der Daumen, die Daumen** the thumb]
 [**streichen, strich, hat gestrichen** to stroke (3)]
 das Rasiermesser the straight-edge razor (2)

ich abgeschlossen und den Schlüssel in meine Tasche gesteckt.

„Plötzlich wachte ich auf. Jemand hatte leise an die Tür geklopft. Ich stand auf, ging zur Tür und flüsterte: ‚Wer ist da?' Eine Stimme antwortete: ‚Sechs Uhr.' Es war das Dienstmädchen. Da mein Zug um sieben Uhr ging, hatte ich gebeten, daß man mich um sechs Uhr wecken solle."

„Ihre Geschichte ist vielleicht sehr realistisch", sagte Herr Mampe, „aber ich halte nicht viel davon."

„Sie fängt eigentlich jetzt erst an", antwortete der Herr im Armstuhl.—„Draußen war es noch ganz dunkel. Ich begann mich anzuziehen. In der Hoffnung, daß das Dienstmädchen auch warmes Wasser gebracht hatte, ging ich zur Tür, machte sie auf und sah hinaus. Kein warmes Wasser! Das dumme Ding mußte es vergessen haben. Wenn das Haus nicht so still gewesen wäre, hätte ich laut gerufen; aber ich wollte niemanden wecken und ging ins Zimmer zurück. Nun, es war nicht das erste Mal, daß ich mich mit kaltem Wasser würde rasieren müssen; nur würde es bei meinem starken Bart länger dauern, und ich hatte wenig Zeit. Vor Kälte zitternd, nahm ich die Lampe, stellte sie neben den Waschtisch und fing an, mich zu rasieren. Ich war mit dem oberen Teil des Gesichtes fertig und hob gerade das Kinn, um im Spiegel den Hals besser sehen zu können, als ich sah, daß sich im Zimmer etwas bewegte. Das heißt, ich sah im S p i e g e l, daß jemand hinter mir im Zimmer war. Wenn ich damals an Geister geglaubt hätte, wäre mir das Herz stillgestanden, sage ich Ihnen! Vor mir im Spiegel erblickte ich das Bett, und auf dem Bett saß ein Mann in Hemd und Hosen, mit schwarzem Haar und Backenbart. Ich hatte Albert Moser zu oft gesehen, um ihn nicht sofort wiederzuerkennen. Auf seinem Gesicht lag ein Ausdruck der tiefsten Verzweiflung und Furcht, wie ich ihn in meinem ganzen Leben nie wieder gesehen habe. Ich konnte mich vor Schreck nicht bewegen; ich starrte nur in den Spiegel. Plötzlich fing der Mann zu lachen an; das heißt, ich h ö r t e es nicht, ich s a h nur den offenen Mund und die Zähne und wie der Bart sich bewegte. Auf einmal blitzt etwas in seiner Hand—ich sehe, wie der Mann mit dem Daumen leicht über das Rasiermesser in seiner Hand streicht, als ob er prüfen

wie scharf es sei how sharp it was
wie das Hemd aussah what the shirt looked like
will ich lieber . . . I would rather
das Bettuch the sheet (3)

drehte ich mich um I turned around
[**um-drehen** to turn (around)]
es war there was
wie zuvor as before
außer daß except that (2)
während sie sich rasierten while shaving
genauso wie ich just as I had
furchtbar terrible (3)
ausglitt slipped
[**aus-gleiten** to slip]
[**gleiten, glitt, ist geglitten** to slide, to glide (2)]
die Westentasche the vest pocket
[**die Weste, die Westen** the vest, waistcoat (3)]
erst zwei Uhr only 2 o'clock
interessieren to interest (4)
erfunden invented
[**erfinden, erfand, hat erfunden** to invent (3)]
nichts leichter wäre nothing would be easier
glauben Sie do you think
am dreißigsten November on November thirtieth
vor genau zwei Jahren exactly two years ago
ist . . . abgeschlossen worden was closed up
auf jeden Fall at any rate
der Direktor the director
[**der Direktor, die Direktoren** the director (3)

blaß pale (4)

wollte, wie scharf es sei–und im nächsten Augenblick hatte er sich vor meinen Augen die Kehle durchgeschnitten, von einem Ohr zum anderen. Wie das Hemd aussah, will ich lieber nicht beschreiben. Und auch das Bettuch war vorher ganz weiß gewesen." Der Herr im Armstuhl schwieg und hielt sich die Hände vors Gesicht.

4.

„Sobald ich konnte", fuhr er nach einer kurzen Pause fort, „drehte ich mich um. Es war niemand im Zimmer, und das Bett war so weiß wie zuvor.–Nun, das ist alles, außer daß ich jetzt wußte, was den beiden anderen Geschäftsreisenden das Leben gekostet hatte. Während sie sich rasierten, hatten sie, genauso wie ich, im Spiegel die furchtbare Gestalt auf dem Bett gesehen. Es muß ein solcher Schreck gewesen sein, daß die Hand, die das Rasiermesser hielt, ausglitt und das Messer die Kehle durchschnitt, bevor sie wußten, was ihnen geschah.–Das ist das Ende meiner Geschichte. Als ich etwas später meine Uhr aus der Westentasche zog, sah ich zu meiner Überraschung, daß es erst zwei Uhr war. Den Teil mit dem Dienstmädchen muß ich geträumt haben; aber was folgte, war kein Traum.–Ich kann von Ihnen nicht verlangen, daß Sie mir die Geschichte glauben, und es interessiert mich auch nicht besonders, wenn einer von Ihnen denken sollte, daß ich sie erfunden habe–obwohl wirklich nichts leichter wäre, als sie zu untersuchen. Warum, glauben Sie, habe ich die Geschichte gerade heute, am 30. (dreißigsten) November erzählt, und warum hier in diesem Hotel? Weil sie heute vor genau zwei Jahren hier im „Zahmen Löwen" passiert ist! Das Zimmer ist natürlich sofort abgeschlossen worden. Auf jeden Fall bat ich damals den Hoteldirektor, nie wieder einen Gast darin schlafen zu lassen."

Herr Mampe war plötzlich blaß geworden. „Darf ich fragen, welche Nummer es war?" sagte er.–„Nummer 17 (siebzehn)", antwortete der Herr im Armstuhl.–„Mein Gott!" rief

darüber over it

fest firmly
vor kurzem a short while ago
gebraucht wird is needed
es tut mir schrecklich leid I am terribly sorry
wäre . . . kein Wort über meine Lippen gekommen I would not have said a word
an Ihrer Stelle in your place
indem er sich . . . wischte while wiping
[**wischen** to wipe (4)]
der Schweiß the perspiration (4)

wetten to bet (3)
versucht jetzt is now going to try
und da and since
wenn er sich entschließt if he decides
[**sich entschließen** to decide]
[**entschließen, entschloß, hat entschlossen** (3)]
da geht er schon there he goes
ich täte . . . dasselbe I would . . . do the same thing

da stimmt irgend etwas nicht there is something wrong
wie kommt es dann how is it, then
indem er . . . hob while picking up
einen von diesen one of those
der Rasierapparat the safety razor
[**der Apparat, die Apparate** the apparatus]
die damals gerade erfunden worden waren which had just been invented then
vor der Nase from under my nose

Herr Mampe; „dann ist es das Zimmer, das ich jetzt habe. Number 17, mit dem Bett und dem Bild darüber."

Der Herr im Armstuhl sah überrascht aus. „Das verstehe ich nicht", sagte er. „Der Direktor hatte mir fest versprochen, das Zimmer für immer abzuschließen. Wahrscheinlich hat er es vor kurzem wieder aufgemacht, weil dieser Tage alle Hotels voll sind und jeder Raum gebraucht wird. Es tut mir schrecklich leid. Wenn ich das gewußt hätte, wäre natürlich kein Wort über meine Lippen gekommen. Aber an Ihrer Stelle würde ich nicht weiter an die Sache denken. Erstens ist sie schon zwei Jahre alt, und dann glauben Sie nicht an Geister. Ich bin sicher, daß Ihnen nichts passieren kann."—„Vielleicht nicht", sagte Herr Mampe, indem er sich den Schweiß von der Stirn wischte. Dann stand er auf und verließ das Zimmer.

„Ich wette, Mampe versucht jetzt, ein anderes Zimmer zu bekommen", sagte einer. „Und da das Hotel voll ist, würde ich mich nicht wundern, wenn er sich entschließt, mitten in der Nacht von einem Hotel zum anderen zu wandern, bis er ein Zimmer findet.—Sehen Sie? Was habe ich gesagt? Da geht er schon, mit Koffer, Hut und Mantel! Nun, ich täte wahrscheinlich dasselbe, wenn ich an seiner Stelle wäre."

Der Herr im Armstuhl war mit seinem Bier fertig und wollte gerade aufstehen, als jemand plötzlich rief: „Sagen Sie! Da stimmt irgend etwas nicht mit Ihrer Geschichte. Wenn der Geist den beiden anderen das Leben gekostet hat, während sie sich rasierten, wie kommt es dann, daß S i e sich damals nicht die Kehle durchgeschnitten haben?"—„Nun", antwortete der Herr, indem er seinen Koffer vom Boden hob, „ich hatte einen von diesen neuen Rasierapparaten, die damals gerade erfunden worden waren.—Aber Sie müssen mich jetzt entschuldigen. Nummer 17 ist eben frei geworden, und ich möchte nicht, daß jemand inzwischen kommt und mir das Zimmer vor der Nase wegnimmt. Es ist das beste Zimmer im Hotel, mit dem bequemsten Bett. Sehen Sie, jedesmal, wenn ich spät abends hier ankomme und erfahre, daß Nummer 17 nicht mehr frei ist,

daß es die Mühe lohnt that it is worth the effort
[**lohnen** to reward (3)]
Glück haben to be lucky

habe ich immer gefunden, daß es die Mühe lohnt, meine alte Geistergeschichte mit dem Rasiermesser zu erzählen. Bis jetzt habe ich immer Glück gehabt.–Keine schlechte Geschichte, denke ich. Gute Nacht, meine Herren!“

BURG FRANKENSTEIN

[9B]

NOTES

IDIOMS FOR REVIEW

seine Zukunft steht auf dem Spiel his future is at stake
zu Anfang des Frühlings at the beginning of Spring
ins Freie into the open
  im Freien in the open
die Tür war auf the door was open
  die Tür war zu the door was closed
die Nägel taten ihr weh the nails hurt her
bis zur Decke up to the ceiling
an + *dative* + **vorbei/vorüber** past . . .
  sie ging an ihr vorbei she went past her
  sie lief an ihm vorüber she ran past him
nach dem Licht zu urteilen to judge from the light

die Examen the examinations
[**das Examen, die Examen** the examination]
noch eine one more
die Klasse the class
[**die Klasse, die Klassen** the class (3)]
ob alle . . . bestanden hatten whether all (of them) had passed
[**bestehen, bestand, hat bestanden** to pass (an examination)]
die Reihe the series
[**die Reihe, dic Reihen** the row, series (3)]
von . . . Schlußprüfungen of . . . final examinations
[**der Schluß** the end, conclusion]
[**die Prüfung, die Prüfungen** the examination, test]
vom Direktor from the director, principal
[**der Direktor, die Direktoren** the director (4)]
das Gymnasium the *Gymnasium* (German secondary school)
[**das Gymnasium, die Gymnasien**]
zuerst first
die Zensuren the grades
[**die Zensur, die Zensuren** the grade, mark]
die Fächer the subjects
[**das Fach, die Fächer** the subject, line of work; drawer, compartment (3)]
ganz am Schluß at the very end
[**der Schluß** the end, conclusion (2)]
würde man . . . lesen können one would be able to read
die lobenden Worte the words of praise
[**lobend** praising]
[**loben** to praise (2)]
die Zukunft the future (4)
denn erst hier erfuhr man for only here did one find out
das Gymnasium the *Gymnasium* (2)
als richtiger Student as a real student
[**der Student, die Studenten** the (male university) student]
auf die Universität gehen durfte could go to the university
[**die Universität, die Universitäten** the university]

sich vor . . . zu fürchten to be afraid of
[**sich fürchten vor** to be afraid of]
Zensuren grades
[**die Zensur, die Zensuren** the grade, mark (2)]
um Lisel for Lisel
hatten alle etwas Angst all were a little bit afraid
[**Angst haben** to be afraid]
in ihrem Fall in her case
der Erfolg the success
[**der Erfolg, die Erfolge** the success (3)]
durchaus nicht by no means
[**durchaus** by all means; thoroughly, absolutely (3)]

[9 B]

(FOUR PARTS)

Burg Frankenstein

I.

Endlich waren die Examen vorüber. Noch eine Woche, dann würde die ganze Klasse wissen, ob alle die lange Reihe von schweren Schlußprüfungen bestanden hatten. Nächsten Freitag würde jeder von ihnen vom Direktor des Gymnasiums einen Brief bekommen, in dem zuerst die Zensuren für die verschiedenen Fächer standen. Und ganz am Schluß des Briefes, so hoffte jeder, würde man die lobenden Worte des Direktors und seine Wünsche für die Zukunft lesen können, denn erst hier erfuhr man, ob man sein Ziel erreicht hatte: ob man mit dem Gymnasium fertig war und nun als richtiger Student auf die Universität gehen durfte.

Nun, es war eine gute Klasse gewesen. Jeder hatte schwer gearbeitet, besonders in den letzten paar Wochen, und keiner glaubte Grund zu haben, sich vor schlechten Zensuren zu fürchten. Nur um Lisel hatten alle etwas Angst. In ihrem Fall war der Erfolg durchaus nicht so sicher. Sie war lange krank gewesen und hatte auf den Rat des Doktors oft zu Haus

---

hatte . . . bleiben müssen had had to stay
  auf den Rat at the advice
    [**der Rat, die Ratschläge** the advice, counsel (3)]
  der Doktor the doctor
    [**der Doktor, die Doktoren** the doctor (3)]

es gab keinen there was no one
der sie . . . nicht gern hatte who did not like her
[**gern haben** to like (2)]
Ehrensache a matter of honor
[**die Ehre, die Ehren** the honor]
bei den Schularbeiten with her schoolwork
[**die Schularbeit** the schoolwork]
[**die Schule, die Schulen** the school (3)]
der eine one
das Heft the notebook
[**das Heft, die Hefte** the notebook (4)]
worin in which
was . . . behandelt worden war what had been covered
[**behandeln** to treat (2)]
hatte . . . übersetzt had translated
[**übersetzen** to translate (2)]
ins Französische into French
von einem dritten by a third
die Bibliothek the library
[**die Bibliothek, die Bibliotheken** the library (3)]
Schwierigkeiten difficulties
[**die Schwierigkeit, die Schwierigkeiten** the difficulty]
die Schlußprüfungen the final examinations
[**die Prüfung, die Prüfungen** the examination, test (2)]
bestehen to pass (2)
das Gefühl the feeling
[**das Gefühl, die Gefühle**]
die Ehre the honor (2)
ein wenig auf dem Spiel stünden were a little bit at stake
[**auf dem Spiel stehen** to be at stake]
der Samstag the Saturday
war . . . bestimmt worden had been decided upon
die Fahrräder the bicycles
[**das Fahrrad, die Fahrräder** the bicycle]
[**das Rad, die Räder** the wheel; the bicycle]
das Picknick the picnic
die Fahrt the trip, ride
vorgeschlagen suggested
vor . . . Jahrhunderten . . . centuries ago
der Dreißigjährige Krieg the Thirty Years' War (1618–1648]
kaiserlich imperial (2)
das Heer the army
[**das Heer, die Heere**(3)]
blutig bloody (2)
der Kampf the battle
[**der Kampf, die Kämpfe** the fight, struggle, battle (2)]
war . . . niedergebrannt worden had been burned down
[**nieder-brennen** to burn down]

bleiben müssen. Es gab keinen in der Klasse, der sie wegen ihres freundlichen und stets lustigen Wesens nicht gern hatte, und so war es für alle siebzehn Ehrensache gewesen, ihr bei den Schularbeiten zu helfen. Der eine hatte ihr jeden Tag ein Heft gebracht, worin alles stand, was am Morgen in der Klasse behandelt worden war; der andere hatte mit ihr schwere Sätze ins Französische übersetzt; von einem dritten waren ihr Bücher aus der Bibliothek gebracht worden. Jeder hatte getan, was er konnte, und nun hofften alle, daß es Lisel trotz aller Schwierigkeiten gelungen war, die Schlußprüfungen zu bestehen. Jeder hatte das Gefühl, als ob seine eigene Ehre und Zukunft ein wenig auf dem Spiel stünden. Nun, am Samstag würde man erfahren, ob Lisel bestanden hatte, denn der Samstag war von allen als der Tag bestimmt worden, an dem sie sich mit ihren Fahrrädern auf dem Marktplatz treffen würden, um zusammen zu einem Picknick aufs Land zu fahren. Als Ziel der Fahrt hatte jemand die Burg Frankenstein vorgeschlagen, eine mächtige Ruine, die vor mehreren Jahrhunderten einem Grafen Hugo von Frankenstein gehört hatte. Die Burg war während des Dreißigjährigen Krieges in die Hände eines kaiserlichen Heeres gefallen, die ganze Familie hatte in dem blutigen Kampf um die Burg das Leben verloren, und die Burg selbst war einige Monate später niedergebrannt worden, als die kaiserlichen Truppen sich vor dem großen Schwedenkönig auf seinem Marsch nach Süden hatten zurückziehen müssen. Jetzt, zu Anfang des Frühlings, wo die Erde schon grün war und die Obstbäume so herrlich blühten, war die alte Ruine besonders

---

die . . . Truppen the . . . troops
  [**die Truppe, die Truppen** the troop, troupe]
sich . . . hatten zurückziehen müssen had had to withdraw
  [**zurück-ziehen** to draw back, to withdraw]
der Schwedenkönig the King of the Swedes
der Marsch the march
  [**der Marsch, die Märsche** the march (3)]
zu Anfang at the beginning
  [**der Anfang, die Anfänge** the start, beginning (3)]
der Frühling the spring (3)
die Obstbäume the fruit trees
  [**das Obst** the fruit (3)]

romantisch romantic
das Picknick the picnic (2)
dort würde man, ohne gestört zu werden . . . feiern können there, without being disturbed, they would be able to celebrate
[**feiern** to celebrate (3)]
und den der anderen and that of the others
nach Herzenslust to their hearts' desire (3)
die Gruppe the group
[**die Gruppe, die Gruppen** (3)]

der Samstag the Saturday (2)
die Treppe steps
[**die Treppe, die Treppen** the stairs, steps; stairway (4)]
das Rathaus the city hall (3)
mit Rädern with bicycles
[**das Rad, die Räder** the bicycle; wheel (2)]
die Examen the examinations
[**das Examen, die Examen** the examination (2)]
fehlte noch still had not come
einer der Jungen one of the boys
[**der Junge, die Jungen** the boy (2)]
ist sie durchgefallen she has failed
[**durch-fallen** to fail, to "flunk"]
ließ left
darüber about the fact
das Armband the bracelet
[**das Armband, die Armbänder** the bracelet]
die Freundin the friend
[**die Freundin, die Freundinnen** the (girl) friend]
hübsch pretty (4)
das Glöckchen the little bell
daran on it
der Stolz the pride (3)
echt real
[**echt** real, genuine (3)]
das Armband the bracelet (2)
hatte . . . gebacken had baked
[**backen, er bäckt, backte (buk), hat gebacken** to bake (3)]

die Vergangenheit the past (2)
man genoß one enjoyed
[**genießen, genoß, hat genossen** to enjoy (3)]
die Gegenwart the present (2)
sang sang
[**singen, sang, hat gesungen** to sing (3)]
Lieder songs
[**das Lied, die Lieder** the song (3)]
gegen Mittag around noon
wurden . . . aufgemacht were opened

romantisch. Gerade der richtige Ort für ein lustiges Picknick. Dort würde man, ohne gestört zu werden, seinen eigenen Erfolg und den der anderen nach Herzenslust feiern können. Vielleicht würde die kleine Gruppe zum letzten Mal zusammen sein, denn wer konnte sagen, wo sie alle im nächsten Jahr sein würden?

Am Samstag morgen füllte sich der kleine Platz neben der Treppe des Rathauses langsam mit Rädern. Alle hatten ihre Examen bestanden, einer schüttelte dem anderen die Hand. Nur Lisel fehlte noch. „Mein Gott!" sagte einer der Jungen; „vielleicht ist sie durchgefallen und deshalb kommt sie jetzt nicht. Das arme Ding!"—„Nein, da ist sie!" rief ein anderer. Die Freude auf Lisels Gesicht ließ keinen Zweifel darüber, daß auch sie bestanden hatte. Man wünschte ihr Glück und schüttelte ihr die Hand. „Oh, ein neues Armband!" sagte eine Freundin. „Wie hübsch! Besonders mit dem Glöckchen daran." —„Ja", erwiderte Lisel voller Stolz; „echt Silber. Als gestern morgen der Brief vom Direktor ankam, konnten meine Eltern es kaum glauben, und am Abend hab' ich das Armband auf meinem Teller gefunden. Kling-kling! Schön, was?—Und für das Picknick heute hatte meine Mutter schon einen Kuchen gebacken!"

Jeder stieg auf sein Rad. Nach etwa zwei Stunden erreichte die kleine Gesellschaft die Burg. Die Examen waren vergessen; sie gehörten der Vergangenheit. Man genoß die Gegenwart, man sprach über die Zukunft, man sang frohe Lieder. Gegen Mittag wurden die Picknickkörbe aufgemacht. Nach dem Essen wollten die Mädchen Ball spielen. „Wie wär's, wenn wir alle zusammen Verstecken spielten?" schlug einer der Jungen vor; „einen besseren Ort findet man wohl so leicht nicht wieder, mit

---

die Picknickkörbe the picnic baskets
[**der Korb, die Körbe** the basket]
der Ball the ball
[**der Ball, die Bälle** (3)]
wie wär's how would it be
Verstecken spielen to play hide-and-seek
schlug . . . vor suggested
findet man wohl one probably could . . . find

Mauern walls
[die Mauer, die Mauern the wall (4)]
Keller cellars
[der Keller, die Keller the cellar, basement (3)]
dafür for it
zählen to count (4)
liefen . . . davon ran away
in allen Richtungen in all directions
[die Richtung, die Richtungen the direction (2)]
die gesucht . . . werden würde who would be sought
das Glöckchen the little bell (2)
der Lauf the run
geklingelt hatte had jingled
[klingeln to ring (4)]
. . . fassend seizing . . .
[fassen to seize, to grasp (3)]
ins Dunkle into the darkness
[das Dunkel the darkness (2)]
der Gang the corridor
[der Gang, die Gänge the corridor (3)]
näherten sich came closer
[sich nähern to approach (3)]
aus Furcht for fear
gesehen zu werden to be seen
rückwärts backward
an . . . stieß encountered
vollkommen completely (2)
sich . . . etwas geschlossen hätte something had closed
vor ihr in front of her
würde sie niemand finden no one would find her

nervös nervous (3)
hier unten down here
kühl cool (3)
glatt smooth (2)
sie faßte nach hinten she reached behind her
erst als only when

all den Bäumen und den alten Mauern und Kellern in der Burg.“ Alle waren dafür. Einer blieb zurück und zählte langsam und laut bis zwanzig; die anderen liefen in allen Richtungen davon. Als Lisel „zwanzig“ hörte, verschwand sie gerade durch eine Tür, die in einen Keller zu führen schien. Vielleicht würde sie die erste sein, dachte sie, die gesucht und gefunden werden würde, weil das Glöckchen während ihres schnellen Laufes die ganze Zeit geklingelt hatte. Richtig, schon hörte sie Schritte hinter sich. Das Armband mit der rechten Hand fassend und festhaltend, ging sie leise weiter ins Dunkle hinein. Die Wände wurden enger; sie mußte sich in einem Gang befinden. Plötzlich ging es nicht mehr weiter. Die Schritte näherten sich. Aus Furcht, in ihrem hellen Kleid gesehen zu werden, drückte sie sich mit dem Rücken fest an die Wand. Was war das? Hatte die Mauer sich plötzlich bewegt, oder befand sich hinter ihr ein anderer Gang? Sie schritt rückwärts, bis sie an eine Wand stieß. Dort blieb sie stehen und wartete. Die Schritte hatten aufgehört; alles war vollkommen still. Es schien ihr, als ob sich vor ihr etwas geschlossen hätte, als ob sie allein wäre. Gut. Hier würde sie niemand finden.

2.

Nach einigen Minuten wurde Lisel nervös. Sie hörte nichts, sie sah nichts, und hier unten war es so kühl, ja kalt, daß sie in ihrem leichten Sommerkleid zu frieren begann. Wenn sie nur Streichhölzer hätte und etwas sehen könnte! Sie schritt vorwärts, in der Richtung, aus der sie gekommen war. Ihre ausgestreckten Hände stießen gegen die scharfen Steine einer Mauer, aber sie fanden keine Tür. War sie von dem Gang abgeschnitten? Zu ihrer Rechten fühlte sie eine glatte Wand. Sie faßte nach hinten; aber da war die Mauer, gegen die sie vor einigen Minuten mit dem Rücken gestoßen war. Erst als sie nach links schritt, schien der Raum weiterzugehen. Es mußte ein anderer Gang sein; er war viel enger als der erste. Sie folgte der Wand auf ihrer linken Seite; das Glöckchen an ihrem Arm

beinahe almost (2)
auf einmal suddenly
das Eisen the iron (3)
Gott sei Dank! thank God!
irgendwie somehow
ins Freie into the open
die Kraft the strength
[**die Kraft, die Kräfte** (3)]
schob pushed
[**schieben, schob, hat geschoben** to push, to thrust, to shove (3)]
der Körper the body (4)
die Eisennägel the iron nails
[**der Nagel, die Nägel** the nail (3)]
taten ihr weh hurt her
[**weh tun** to hurt (4)]
im Freien in the open

einst at one time
[**einst** once, at one time (3)]
bis zur Decke up to the ceiling
[**die Decke, die Decken** the blanket; the ceiling (4)]
ober upper (2)
wo . . . her? where . . . from?
die Bücherreihe the row of books
durch das Halbdunkel zu dringen to penetrate the semidarkness
einzeln individual
[**einzeln** single, individual (4)]
Gegenstände objects
[**der Gegenstand, die Gegenstände** the object; subject, topic, matter (3)]
Waffen weapons
[**die Waffe, die Waffen** the weapon (2)]
verschiedener Art of different types
die Kerze the candle
[**die Kerze, die Kerzen** the candle (4)]
darauf on it
am dunkelsten darkest
eine Sekunde lang for a second
[**die Sekunde, die Sekunden** the second (3)]
deren Haupt whose head
[**das Haupt, die Häupter** the head (4)]
das Kopftuch the kerchief
hätte . . . geschrien could . . . have shouted
die Freundin the friend
[**die Freundin, die Freundinnen** the (girl) friend (2)]
ich bin's it's me
davon of it
das Kinn the chin (3)

stieß an die Steine und klingelte so laut, daß sie beinahe erschrak. Auf einmal fühlte ihre ausgestreckte rechte Hand etwas Kaltes. Kaltes Eisen und Holz. Gott sei Dank! Eine Tür. Sie mußte irgendwie ins Freie führen. Lisel brauchte all ihre Kraft, um die schwere Tür zu bewegen. Sie schob mit dem ganzen Körper. Die dicken Köpfe der mächtigen Eisennägel drückten sie in die Seite und taten ihr weh. Die Tür war seit langem nicht geöffnet worden, soviel war sicher. Ah, endlich bewegte sie sich—jetzt war sie auf. Lisel war nicht mehr im Dunkeln. Aber sie war nicht im Freien.

Vor ihr lag ein großer Raum. Dies mußte einst eine Bibliothek gewesen sein, denn die ganze Wand, ja alle Wände waren bis zur Decke mit Büchern bedeckt. Das Licht war so schwach, daß Lisel zunächst nur den oberen Teil des Zimmers erkennen konnte. Wo kam es her? Ah, dort! Durch ein kleines, rundes Loch über der letzten Bücherreihe gerade unter der Decke. Lisels Augen folgten dem Licht und versuchten, durch das Halbdunkel zu dringen und die einzelnen Gegenstände zu erkennen, die sich im Zimmer befanden: einige Gewehre und Waffen verschiedener Art, die an einer Wand lehnten, zwei Stühle, ein großer Tisch mit einer Kerze darauf, die zur Hälfte niedergebrannt war, und hinter dem Tisch, dort, wo es am dunkelsten war, ein hoher Armstuhl. Lisels Herz stand eine Sekunde lang still. Im Armstuhl saß jemand! Eine Gestalt, deren Haupt von einem Kopftuch bedeckt war. Nach dem ersten Schreck hätte Lisel beinahe vor Freude geschrien: sie war nicht mehr allein! Es war eine Freundin, die den Weg in dasselbe Zimmer durch eine andere Tür gefunden hatte. Jetzt saß sie da und rührte sich nicht, weil sie nicht entdeckt werden wollte. „Du", flüsterte Lisel, „ich bin's, Lisel!" Keine Antwort. Lisel ging langsam näher. Das Gesicht der Person schien ganz weiß zu sein, aber Lisel konnte wenig davon sehen, weil das Kinn so tief auf die Brust gesunken war. Auf den Knien lag ein großes, offenes Buch, aber die Hände, die es hielten . . . Oh Gott! Das waren keine Hände! Aus den Ärmeln des Kleides

---

die Ärmel the sleeves
[der Ärmel, die Ärmel (4)]

Knochen bones
[**der Knochen, die Knochen** the bone (4)]
das Skelett the skeleton
die Bibel the Bible
noch jetzt even now
der Trost the solace
[**der Trost** the consolation, solace]
wer immer whoever
ewig eternal (2)
eben noch just now
schwinden to disappear
[**schwinden, schwand, ist geschwunden** to disappear, to vanish (2)]
wie immer in whatever way
verzweifeln to despair (3)
die Würde the dignity (3)
fleischlos fleshless
die Farbe the color
[**die Farbe, die Farben** the color, paint (3)]
der Stoff the material
[**der Stoff, die Stoffe** the matter, material, substance (2)]
die Form the shape
[**die Form, die Formen** the form, shape]
der Eichentisch the oak table
[**die Eiche, die Eichen** the oak, oak tree (3)]
das Tintenfaß the inkwell
[**das Faß, die Fässer** the cask, barrel, keg (3)]
die Gänsefeder the goose quill
[**die Gans, die Gänse** the goose (3)]
daneben next to them
die Gegenwart the presence
fest firm
die Buchstaben the letters
[**der Buchstabe, die Buchstaben** the letter (3)]
wie die, welche like those which
die Sprache the language
[**die Sprache, die Sprachen** the language, speech]
das Datum the date
[**das Datum, die Daten** (4)]
sechzehnhunderteinunddreißig 1631

des Heils of grace
[**das Heil** the salvation (3)]

der zehnte the tenth
schweigen schon seit Tagen have been silent for days
zu mir dringen reach me
es sind nicht eure they are not yours

steckten Knochen, an einem weißen Finger hing ein Ring. Lisel wollte schreien, aber sie brachte kein Wort über die Lippen. Vor ihr saß ein Skelett, dessen hohle Augen die Bibel vor sich nicht mehr sahen, die aber noch jetzt im Worte Gottes Trost zu suchen schienen. Wer immer die Gestalt war, um sie lag ewige Ruhe und ein solcher Friede, daß die Furcht, die eben noch Lisels Herz erfüllt hatte, zu schwinden begann. Wie immer diese Frau, dieses Mädchen in den Tod gegangen war, für sie hatte dieser Raum keine Schrecken mehr besessen. Sie hatte vielleicht verzweifelt, aber sie war mit Würde und im Frieden mit der Welt gestorben. Wie lange mochte sie schon tot sein? Die Kleider, die auf dem fleischlosen Körper hingen, zeigten keine Farbe mehr, aber der Stoff schien noch in ziemlich gutem Zustand zu sein. Der Ring war alt und von einer Form, die Lisel noch nie gesehen hatte. Ihr Blick suchte weiter. Ihre Augen fielen auf das glatte Holz des schweren Eichentisches. In einem Tintenfaß steckte eine Gänsefeder; daneben lagen mehrere Blätter Papier. Es war ein Brief. „Wenn ich doch nur ein Streichholz für die Kerze hätte!" dachte Lisel; in der Gegenwart des Todes wagte sie nicht zu sprechen. Sie nahm den Brief und brachte ihn ans Licht. Die Hand, die ihn geschrieben, war fest und ruhig; man konnte die Buchstaben ohne Mühe lesen, obwohl sie nicht so aussahen wie die, welche man heute gebrauchte. Aber die Sprache war so alt, daß Lisel fast übersetzen mußte. Sie begann zu lesen. Oben stand ein Datum. Es war das Jahr 1631 (sechzehnhunderteinunddreißig).

3.

„Burg Frankenstein, im Jahre des Heils 1631.

„Dies ist der zehnte Tag, und noch ist niemand gekommen. Der blutige Kampf ist nun vorüber, die Waffen, die ich klingen hörte, schweigen schon seit Tagen. Draußen ist es still geworden, und alle Hoffnung ist geschwunden. Der Ton der Stimmen, die schweren Schritte, die von oben zu mir dringen, es sind nicht eure. Oh Vater, meine Brüder, und du, mein

wäret ihr gekommen you would have come
und mit euch mich freuen and rejoice with you
ihr habt gestritten you fought
[**streiten, stritt, hat gestritten** to fight, to quarrel (3)]
wie die Helden like heroes
[**der Held, die Helden** the hero (3)]
die Löwin the lioness
ihre Jungen her young
[**das Junge, die Jungen** the young (of animals)]
selbst even
die Jugend the youth (3)
zu brauchen to use
geboren had born
[**geboren** born (2)]
der Gram the grief (2)
hätt' sie getötet would have killed her
als dessen Weib mein Vater mich bestimmte my father had meant me to be your wife (*literally:* as whose wife my father had destined me)

die Lebensmittel the food (4)
reichen to last
schrecken to frighten (3)
mögen . . . may . . .
auf den geheimen Knopf on the secret button
[**der Knopf, die Knöpfe** the button (2)]
ich fiele I would fall
daran zu denken to think of it
hassen to hate (3)
die Ehre the honor (3)
wäre schlimmer would be worse
[**schlimm** bad (3)]
ich ziehe vor I prefer

drehte es um turned it
[**um-drehen** to turn (around) (2)]

grau gray (3)
versucht tempted
nicht einmal not even
schwer heavy
scheiden to part
[**scheiden, schied, ist geschieden** to part (2)]
der Haß the hatred (3)
empfehlen to recommend
[**empfehlen, er empfiehlt, empfahl, hat empfohlen** to recommend (3)]
nur noch einen just one more

Waldemar! Wenn ihr noch lebtet, wäret ihr gekommen, mir zu sagen, daß ihr den Kampf gewonnen; ich würde frei sein und mit euch mich freuen. Ich weiß, ihr habt gestritten wie die Helden, wie eine Löwin, die für ihre Jungen stirbt. Jetzt seid ihr tot; der wilde Feind hat euch getötet. Selbst eure zarte Jugend, meine Brüder, hat ihn nicht gehindert, die scharfe Waffe gegen euch zu brauchen. Ihr wart noch Knaben, das Leben lag vor euch, die Zukunft stand euch offen. Wie gut, daß unsere Mutter starb, als sie das letzte Kind geboren! Wie gut, daß sie nicht hier ist! Der Gram um euch hätt' sie getötet.– Und du, mein Waldemar, als dessen Weib mein Vater mich bestimmte, auch du bist tot, und ohne dich will ich nicht leben.

„Die Lebensmittel, die ich brachte, sind fast zu Ende; sie werden nicht mehr lange reichen. Wie lange?–Was hindert mich, diesen Raum zu verlassen? Ist es die Gefahr, die mich schreckt? Nein. Mögen Hunger und Verzweiflung mich nicht dazu treiben, auf den geheimen Knopf in der Mauer zu drücken, der mir die Freiheit zu versprechen scheint! Die Freiheit? Nein. Ich fiele in die Hände des Feindes, und dann . . . Ich wage nicht, daran zu denken. Ich würde hassen, wie ich nie gehaßt, und ein Leben ohne Ehre wäre schlimmer als der Tod. Noch kann ich wählen. Ich ziehe vor, zu sterben."

Lisels Augen füllten sich mit Tränen. Das Blatt war zu Ende. Sie drehte es um; der Brief ging weiter.

„Zwanzig Tage! Das graue Licht eines neuen Morgens dringt langsam in mein Zimmer. Es wird der letzte sein. Gestern war ich versucht, zu fliehen. Ich kam nicht einmal bis zur Wand, zum Wege, der ins Freie führt. Ich habe versucht, die Zimmertür zu öffnen, die mich von dem rettenden Knopf trennt; sie war zu schwer. Meine Kraft ist zu Ende, ich kann nicht mehr. Dies Gefängnis, das ich mir selbst gewählt, ist nun mein Grab. Es ist besser so. Die Welt, von der ich scheide, bedeutet mir nichts mehr. Ich sterbe in Frieden, nicht in Verzweiflung, ohne Haß. Was Gott tut, ist wohl getan. In seine Hände empfehle ich meine Seele. Bevor ich scheide, habe ich nur noch einen

möge may
wer whoever
der Leib the body (3)

Amalie Amalia
die Gräfin the countess
ihres Stammes of her family
[**der Stamm, die Stämme** the trunk, stem, stalk; race, tribe (3)]

über . . . sehend looking over
der Toten of the dead girl
[**die Tote** the dead girl (woman)]
die Stelle the passage
auf die at which
deuten to point (3)
der Herr the Lord
sei gelobt be praised

in einem jener in one of those
wurden . . . geschickt were sent
in . . . zu dringen in getting into
von Daumen . . . zu fließen to flow from her thumbs
[**der Daumen, die Daumen** the thumb (2)]
[**fließen, floß, ist geflossen** to flow, to run (3)]
wie schwer . . . wog how much . . . weighed
[**wiegen, wog, hat gewogen** to weigh (3)]
darauf on it
hätte sie . . . geschrien she could . . . have cried
so weh taten ihr die Finger so much did her fingers hurt her
Feldblumen field flowers
[**die Blume, die Blumen** the flower (4)]
Erdbeeren strawberries
[**die Erdbeere, die Erdbeeren** the strawberry (2)]
umgeben zu sein to be surrounded
in den . . . niemand getreten sein konnte which no one could have entered
der Steinhaufen the pile of stones
[**der Haufe(n), die Haufen** the heap, pile, lot; crowd (4)]
eingefallen war had collapsed
[**ein-fallen** to fall in, to collapse]
nach außen zu dringen to reach outside
Fliegen flies
[**die Fliege, die Fliegen** the fly]
Bienen bees
[**die Biene, die Bienen** the bee (2)]
die Fliegen the flies (2)
flogen flew
[**fliegen, flog, ist geflogen** to fly (2)]
die Außenwelt the outside world (3)

Wunsch: möge, wer mich hier findet, meinen Leib zur letzten Ruhe bringen!

Amalie, Gräfin von Frankenstein,
die letzte ihres Stammes."

Lisel blickte auf und ging hinüber zum Armstuhl. Über die Schulter der Toten sehend, las sie die Stelle, auf die der weiße Finger deutete: „Der Herr hat gegeben, der Herr hat genommen, der Name des Herrn sei gelobt!"

Lisel wußte nun, wo sie war. Sie befand sich in einem jener geheimen Räume, von denen sie gelesen und in der Schule gehört hatte. In früheren Zeiten wurden die Frauen in solche Zimmer geschickt, wenn es dem Feind gelungen war, in die Burg zu dringen.–Der Brief erwähnte einen geheimen Knopf in der Mauer. Lisel lief in den dunklen Gang zurück und suchte mit beiden Händen. Die scharfen Steine rissen ihr ins Fleisch; das Blut begann, ihr von Daumen und Fingern zu fließen. Sie konnte nichts mehr fühlen. Zurück ins Zimmer. Vielleicht gab es noch einen anderen Weg ins Freie. Wie schwer der Tisch wog! Mit großer Mühe schob sie ihn zur Wand unter das Loch. Als sie den Stuhl darauf stellte, hätte sie vor Schmerz fast geschrien, so weh taten ihr die Finger. Sie stieg hinauf und blickte durch das Loch; es war zu klein, um den Kopf durchzustecken. Was sie vor sich sah, war ein kleiner Hof, in dem Feldblumen und wilde Erdbeeren wuchsen; er schien auf allen Seiten von Mauern umgeben zu sein. In seiner Mitte stand ein Brunnen. Es mußte ein Hof sein, in den seit Jahrhunderten niemand getreten sein konnte, denn vor der einzigen Tür, die in ihn führte, lag ein großer Steinhaufen, ein Teil der Mauer, die eingefallen war, als die Burg niedergebrannt wurde. Lisel begann zu rufen. Keine Antwort. Ihre Stimme schien nicht nach außen zu dringen. Sie hörte nichts, nur einige Fliegen und Bienen, die in der Nachmittagssonne spielten. Lisel schrie, bis sie nicht mehr konnte. Niemand rief zurück. Die Fliegen spielten weiter, die Bienen flogen von Blume zu Blume. Sie war von der Außenwelt abgeschnitten.

der Toten gegenüberstand stood opposite the dead girl
    [**die Tote** the dead girl (woman) (2)]
    [**gegenüber** opposite (3)]
das Wichtigste the most important thing
  die Ordnung the order (4)
  zu gleicher Zeit at the same time
gefangen trapped
wenn if
  die Gräfin the countess (2)
  und klaren Sinnen and with a clear mind
  so konnte sie es auch then she could do it, too
würde sterben müssen would have to die
  wollte sie . . . blicken können she wanted to be able to look

noch einmal once more
hatte das keinen Sinn it made no sense
selbst wenn even if
  würde sie . . . nicht fühlen können she would not be able to feel
es hatte keinen Zweck there was no point
  noch einmal once more
Durst bekommen become thirsty
  nicht einmal not even
  waren . . . gestört worden had been disturbed
  bei ihrem Spiel at their play
drehten sich . . . herum turned around
  das Mühlrad the mill wheel
    [**die Mühle, die Mühlen** the mill (3)]
käme would come
heiß hot (4)
  rollen to roll (3)
  die Wangen the cheeks
    [**die Wange, die Wangen** the cheek]

trocknen to dry (4)
die Wolke the cloud
    [**die Wolke, die Wolken** (4)]
die Bücherreihe the row of books (2)
an-blicken to look at (3)
der Satz the leap

4.

Lisel stieg vom Tisch und setzte sich auf den Stuhl, der der Toten gegenüberstand. Das Wichtigste war, daß sie jetzt nicht den Kopf verlor und Ordnung in die tausend Gedanken brachte, die alle zu gleicher Zeit durch ihren Kopf zu gehen schienen. Klar denken, so hatte die Schule sie immer gelehrt, klar denken, Lisel! Hier waren klare Gedanken notwendiger als je; nicht weil sie glaubte, daß sie aus diesem Gefängnis fliehen könne, sondern weil sie fürchtete, in wilder Verzweiflung zu sterben, wie ein gefangenes Tier. Wenn die junge Gräfin mit Würde und klaren Sinnen gestorben war, so konnte sie es auch. Sie fühlte, daß sie würde sterben müssen; nur wollte sie dem Tode mit Mut ins Auge blicken können.

Hatte sie alles versucht, sollte sie noch einmal nach dem Knopf suchen? In dem Zustand, in dem sich ihre Finger befanden, hatte das keinen Sinn. Selbst wenn sie die Stelle fände, würde sie den Knopf nicht fühlen können. Und es hatte keinen Zweck, noch einmal durch das Loch hinauszuschreien. Sie würde nur Durst bekommen, und nicht einmal die Fliegen waren bei ihrem Spiel von ihrer Stimme gestört worden. Und nun kamen wieder die tausend Gedanken und drehten sich wie ein Mühlrad in ihrem Kopf herum. Nein, sie konnte nicht mehr klar denken. Sie legte das müde Haupt auf den Tisch und fing an zu weinen. Mein Gott, wenn nur das Ende bald käme! Heiße Tränen rollten ihr über die Wangen und wollten nicht aufhören.

Wie lange sie so da gesessen hatte, wußte sie nicht. Wie spät mochte es sein? Sie blickte auf und trocknete sich die Augen. Es war dunkel. War es so schnell Abend geworden, oder hatte nur eine schwarze Wolke den Himmel bedeckt? Aber warum wurde es dann gleich wieder hell? Sie sah zum Loch hinauf. Auf der letzten Bücherreihe stand eine Katze, die sie mit ihren grauen Augen erstaunt anblickte. Lisel sprang auf. Im nächsten Augenblick war die Katze mit einem einzigen Satz auf den

an ihr vorbei past her
die Zimmerecke the corner of the room
miauend miaowing
der Korb the basket
[**der Korb, die Körbe** (2)]
Kätzchen kittens
[**das Kätzchen, die Kätzchen** the kitten (3)]
sie . . . geboren worden sein konnten they could have been born
erst vor wenigen Tagen only a few days ago
nach Milch verlangend clamoring for milk
sicher safe
die Jungen the young
[**das Junge, die Jungen** the young (of animals) (2)]
das Futter the food (4)
mußte . . . wieder hinaus would have to go out again
Vögel birds
[**der Vogel, die Vögel** the bird (4)]
jagen to hunt (3)
ein Zeichen a sign
nach dem Licht zu urteilen to judge from the light
[**urteilen** to judge (3)]
noch immer still
sie stürzte she rushed
sollte sie auch . . . zeichnen she should also draw
[**zeichnen** to draw (2)]
hätte . . . schreien können could have cried
womit with which
der Bleistift the pencil (4)
die Handtasche the handbag (2)
aber die but that
freundlich affectionately
los-werden to get rid of (2)
ärgerlich annoyed (3)
der Steinhaufen the pile of stones (2)

noch immer still
hielten Rat held counsel

Tisch gesprungen, von da auf den Boden. Dann ging sie, ohne auf Lisel zu achten, an ihr vorbei. Aus der dunklen Zimmerecke kamen schwache, miauende Töne. Lisel ging leise näher. In einem Korb, hinter den Waffen, die an der Wand lehnten, lagen mehrere Kätzchen, so süß, so klein, daß sie erst vor wenigen Tagen geboren worden sein konnten. Hungrig und nach Milch verlangend, sammelten sie sich um die Mutter, die ihnen jetzt zu trinken gab und sie dann wusch. Welch ein sicherer Ort für die Jungen! Hier konnten sie ohne Gefahr auf die Mutter warten, wenn sie fortging, um draußen für sich selbst nach Futter zu suchen. Wie ein Blitz fuhr es Lisel durch den Kopf: früher oder später mußte die Katze wieder hinaus, um nach Mäusen oder Vögeln zu jagen; aber sie würde auch wieder zu ihren Jungen zurückkehren! Oh Gott, wenn sie mit der Katze ihren Freunden ein Zeichen hinausschicken könnte! Nach dem Licht zu urteilen, war es noch nicht zu spät; ihre Freunde waren vielleicht noch nicht fortgegangen und suchten sie noch immer. Sie stürzte zum Tisch. Schnell! Ein Stück Papier, einige Worte, um zu beschreiben, wo sie war; vielleicht sollte sie auch einen einfachen Plan von dem kleinen Hof mit dem Brunnen zeichnen, damit man sie besser finden konnte. Lisel hätte vor Verzweiflung schreien können. Sie fand nichts, womit sie schreiben konnte. Sie hatte immer einen Bleistift in der Handtasche, aber die war draußen in ihrem Picknickkorb. Klar denken, Lisel, klar denken! Klar denk . . . Ah, das Armband! Sie nahm es ab, ging zum Korb hinüber und strich der Katze freundlich über den Rücken. Mit zitternden Händen band sie ihr das Armband um den Hals. So! Das Tier miaute und schüttelte mit dem Kopf. Lisel wartete. Die Katze versuchte noch immer, den fremden Gegenstand loszuwerden. Als es ihr nicht gelang, lief sie ärgerlich im Zimmer herum. Dann sprang sie auf den Tisch, von dort zur letzten Bücherreihe, und kroch durch das Loch ins Freie. Lisel folgte ihr mit den Augen und sah, wie sie durch die Erdbeeren lief und hinter dem Steinhaufen verschwand.

Draußen suchten die anderen noch immer. Sie riefen, sie schrien, sie hielten Rat; sie wußten nicht mehr, was sie nach

hinzugetreten waren had come up
[**hinzu** there; to that place; besides; in addition (3)]
irgendwo somewhere
nicht herauskann cannot get out

von dem klingelnden Glöckchen geleitet guided by the jingling little bell
gegen . . . stieß touched
gab es there was
silberhell silvery (*literally:* clear as silver)

all diesen Stunden noch tun sollten. „Habt ihr das gehört?" rief plötzlich eines der Mädchen. „Das war Lisels Glöckchen, dort hinter der Mauer!–Lisel! L-i-s-e-l!" Keine Antwort. Nur eine Katze mit einem Armband um den Hals schlich langsam um die Ecke und schüttelte immer mit dem Kopf. „Ruhe! Stört sie nicht!", flüsterte einer der Jungen, als die anderen hinzugetreten waren. „Das Armband kann nur ein Zeichen sein, daß Lisel irgendwo ist und nicht herauskann. Kommt, wir müssen sehen, wo die Katze hingeht. Sie wird uns zu Lisel führen."

Sie waren ruhig und beobachteten die Katze, die bald wieder hinter der Mauer verschwand. Sie sahen sie nicht mehr, aber sie folgten ihr, von dem klingelnden Glöckchen geleitet, denn jedesmal, wenn das Glöckchen gegen das Gras oder die Steine stieß, gab es einen silberhellen Ton. Es war ein Ton der Freude.

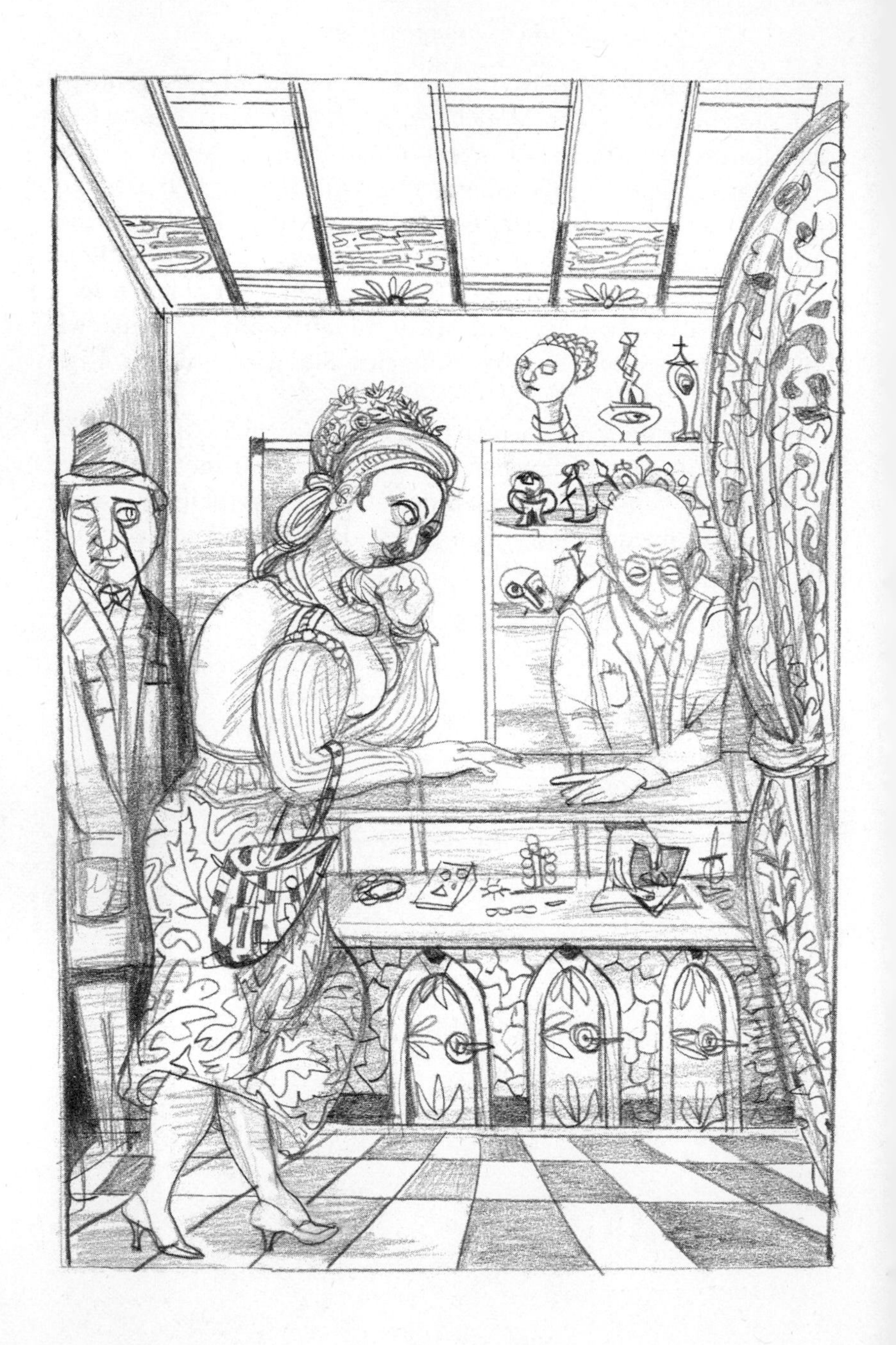

DIE PERLENKETTE

[10A]

NOTES

1. You are familiar with the so-called "double infinitive" construction. For example:

   Er *hatte* nicht früher *kommen können.* He had not been able to come sooner.

   Wie *hatte* so etwas *geschehen können?* How could something like that have happened?

   Warum *hatte* sie nicht *fortgehen wollen?* Why hadn't she wanted to leave?

   Er wußte nicht, warum er sie nicht *hatte sehen dürfen.* He did not know why he had not been allowed to see her.

   Wann *hatte* Frau Piepenbrink ihr Häuschen *verlassen müssen?* When had Mrs. Piepenbrink been obliged to leave her little house?

2. The *pattern* of this construction remains the same when it is used in the subjunctive. The only change occurs in the *forms* of the *finite verb,* **hatte,** which becomes:

   a. **habe, habest, habe,** etc./**hätte, hättest, hätte,** etc., in the indirect discourse subjunctive.

      Er sagte mir, daß er nicht früher *habe/hätte kommen können.*

      Er fragte sich, wie so etwas *habe/hätte geschehen können.*

      Er wolle wissen, sagte er mir, warum sie nicht *habe/hätte fortgehen wollen.*

      Endlich, so erzählte er mir, habe/hätte er sie gefragt, warum er sie nicht *habe/hätte sehen dürfen.*

      Er habe wissen wollen, sagte er mir, wann Frau Piepenbrink ihr Häuschen *habe/hätte verlassen müssen.*

   b. **hätte, hättest, hätte,** etc., wherever else the use of the subjunctive is required.

      Wenn er *hätte kommen können,* würde er uns geschrieben haben. If he had been able to come (or: if he could have come) . . .

      Wenn sie *hätte gehen wollen, hätte* sie es leicht *tun können.* If she had wanted to go, she could easily have done so.

      Wenn s i e nicht gegangen wäre, *hätte* i c h *gehen müssen.* If *she* had not gone, then *I* would have had to go.

Wenn er die ganze Arbeit *hätte machen müssen*, hätte er nein gesagt. If he had had to do *all* the work, he would have said no.

Ach, wenn ich sie nur noch einmal *hätte sehen dürfen!* Oh, if I had only been allowed to see her once more!

Wenn er etwas älter gewesen wäre, *hätte* er mit uns *gehen dürfen*. If he had been a little older, he would have been allowed to go with us.

Es war schon sehr spät, und ich *hätte* eigentlich nach Hause *gehen sollen*. It was already very late, and I really ought to have gone home.

Sie *hätten* das nicht *tun sollen*. You shouldn't have done that.

REVIEW OF STRONG VERBS USED IN STORY 9B

durch-fallen	fällt durch	fiel durch	ist durchgefallen	*to fail (an examination)*
(sich) zurück-ziehen		zog zurück	zurückgezogen	*to withdraw*

IDIOMS FOR REVIEW

offen gesagt . . . frankly . . .
in der Regel as a rule
ich mache es mir zur Regel I make it a rule
zur Zeit at the present time
auf die Seite legen to lay aside
das geht nicht that won't do, that won't work
es lohnt sich it is worth the effort, it is worth the trouble
aus diesem Grunde for this reason
wie kommt es, daß . . . how is it that . . .

die Perlenkette the pearl necklace
[**die Perle, die Perlen** the pearl]
[**die Kette, die Ketten** the chain; the necklace]

der Taxichauffeur the taxi chauffeur
[**das Taxi/die Taxe, die Taxen** the taxi]
[**der Chauffeur, die Chauffeure** the chauffeur]
elegant elegant (4)
das Taxi the taxi (2)
der Chauffeur the chauffeur (2)
stieg aus got out
[**aus-steigen** to get out, to climb out (3)]
der Fahrstuhl the elevator
der Stock the floor
[**der Stock, die Stöcke** the stick, cane; floor (of a building) (4)]
die Fahrstuhltür the elevator door
[**der Fahrstuhl** the elevator (2)]
das Wartezimmer the waiting room
der Psychiater the psychiatrist
die Krankenschwester the nurse

das Wartezimmer the waiting room (2)
biß bit
[**beißen, biß, hat gebissen** to bite (2)]
ein älterer Herr an elderly gentleman
so offen so openly
die Zeitschrift the magazine
[**die Zeitschrift, die Zeitschriften** the magazine (3)]
auswendig by heart (2)
würde sie . . . warten müssen she would have to wait
der Arzt the doctor
[**der Arzt, die Ärzte** the doctor (3)]
als ob sie as if she
nichts anderes nothing else

das Sprechzimmer the consulting room
woraus die Dame schloß from which the lady concluded
seine Patienten his patients
[**der Patient, die Patienten** the patient]
hinausließ let out
starrend staring

wenn ich bitten darf if you please
die Krankenschwester the nurse (2)

[10 A]

(THREE PARTS)

Die Perlenkette

I.

„Welche Nummer sagten Sie?“ fragte der Taxichauffeur. „Nummer 15 (fünfzehn)“, antwortete die elegante Dame. Das Taxi hielt, die Dame bezahlte den Chauffeur und stieg aus. Im Fahrstuhl drückte sie auf den Knopf, neben dem „2. (zweiter) Stock“ stand. Schon durch die Fahrstuhltür konnte sie den Namen sehen, der in großen Buchstaben an der Tür des Wartezimmers glänzte: „Prof. Dr. Siegfried Freudenberg, Psychiater.“ Sie klingelte. Eine Krankenschwester machte auf und bat um den Namen. „Ich komme nicht wegen mir“, sagte die Dame. „Die Sache ist so persönlich, daß ich lieber warten möchte, bis ich mit dem Herrn Doktor selbst gesprochen habe.“

Im Wartezimmer saßen zwei Herren. Ein junger Mensch, der sich die ganze Zeit in die Lippen biß, und ein älterer Herr, der schon nach einer Minute so offen auf die Dame starrte, daß sie nervös wurde und anfing, in einer alten Zeitschrift zu lesen, die sie selbst zu Haus hatte und fast auswendig kannte. Wie lange würde sie noch warten müssen, bis der Arzt mit diesen beiden fertig war? Als ob sie nichts anderes zu tun hätte!

Endlich wurde auch der zweite Herr ins Sprechzimmer gerufen. Der erste war nicht wieder herausgekommen, woraus die Dame schloß, daß der Doktor seine Patienten durch eine andere Tür hinausließ. Gut. Dann würde auch der zweite Herr nicht wiederkommen, der sie mit seinem starrenden Blick nervös gemacht hatte.

„Wenn ich bitten darf . . .“, sagte die Krankenschwester

das Sprechzimmer the consulting room (2)
trat ein entered
[**ein-treten** to go in(to), to enter (4)]
Platz nehmen to take a seat
die Ehre the honor
[**die Ehre, die Ehren** the honor (3)]
ich hätte . . . geben sollen I should have given
das Recht the right (4)
eine Formsache a formality, a matter of form
[**die Form, die Formen** the form, shape (2)]
diplomatisch diplomatic
erführe found out
der Psychiater the psychiatrist (2)
hätte ich . . . kommen sollen I should have come
irgendwie somehow
unruhig restlessly
einige Minuten lang for a few minutes
die Luft the air (3)
stünde stood
den er wegstoßen möchte whom he would like to push away
gegenüberliegend opposite
auf jeden Fall at any rate
die Perlenkette the pearl necklace (2)
wäre . . . nicht would not be
davon of it
öffentlich publicly (4)
wovon er eigentlich redet what he is actually talking about
die Stellung the position
[**die Stellung, die Stellungen** the position, job (3)]
diplomatisch diplomatic (2)
offen gesagt frankly speaking
darum therefore (4)

und öffnete die Tür zum Sprechzimmer. Die Dame trat ein. Der Doktor bat sie, Platz zu nehmen. „Mit wem habe ich die Ehre?“ begann er.—„Ich weiß, ich hätte der Krankenschwester meinen Namen geben sollen“, entgegnete die Dame, „und Sie haben natürlich das Recht, zu wissen, wer ich bin; aber die Sache ist wirklich so persönlich, daß ich . . .“—„Es braucht nicht jetzt zu sein“, unterbrach sie der Arzt; „der Name ist eine Formsache, die warten kann. Vielleicht ist es besser, wenn Sie mir zuerst sagen, was Sie zu mir bringt.“—„Ich komme wegen meines Mannes“, begann die Dame. „Mein Mann ist im diplomatischen Dienst, und Sie werden daher verstehen, wie sehr es ihm schaden könnte, wenn jemand erführe, daß ich wegen ihm zu einem Psychiater gegangen bin. Vielleicht hätte ich schon viel früher kommen sollen. Nun, ich kann jetzt nur hoffen, daß es nicht zu spät ist und daß Sie ihm irgendwie helfen können. Seit einigen Wochen schläft mein Mann so unruhig, daß ich fast jede Nacht aufwache. Nachdem er sich einige Minuten lang von einer Seite auf die andere gedreht hat, wirft er plötzlich die Decke von sich, streckt die Beine in die Luft, als ob jemand vor ihm stünde, den er wegstoßen möchte, und starrt auf die gegenüberliegende Wand mit einem Blick, den ich nicht beschreiben kann. Seine Augen sind offen; aber er schläft! Auf jeden Fall erinnert er sich am Morgen an nichts. Er selbst erwähnt nichts, und ich habe bis jetzt nichts gesagt. Aber das ist noch nicht alles. Wenn er so daliegt, fängt er plötzlich an zu murmeln. Dann wird die Stimme stärker, bis er schließlich laut schreit: ‚Die Perlenkette! Die Perlenkette!‘ Nur zwei Worte, und immer dieselben. Nun, all das wäre vielleicht nicht so schlimm, solange die Nachbarn nichts hören und ich die einzige Person bin, die etwas davon weiß. Aber seit etwa einer Woche spricht er auch während des Tages von einer Perlenkette, und zwar in einer Weise, daß ich nicht weiß, was er meint. Wenn er nun öffentlich von Perlenketten zu sprechen anfängt, ohne daß man versteht, wovon er eigentlich redet, dann fürchte ich, daß es nicht lange dauern wird, bis er seine Stellung im diplomatischen Dienst verliert. Offen gesagt, ich habe Angst. Ich weiß nicht, was ich machen soll, und darum

irgendeine some
die Krankheit the illness
[**die Krankheit, die Krankheiten** the sickness, illness (2)]
eine Geisteskrankheit a mental illness
er . . . bleiben müßte he would have to stay
das Krankenhaus the hospital (2)
die Großmutter the grandmother (3)
von der er . . . erzogen wurde by whom he was raised
[**erziehen, erzog, hat erzogen** to educate; to bring up, to raise (2)]
hat an . . . gelitten suffered from
der Ursprung the origin (2)
kompliziert complicated (3)
irgendein some
der Punkt the spot
[**der Punkt, die Punkte** the point; period (2)]
die Vergangenheit the past (3)
behandelt werden muß must be treated
[**behandeln** to treat (3)]
die Aufgabe the responsibility
[**die Aufgabe, die Aufgaben** the task, lesson, assignment (4)]
gnädige Frau Madam
ihn dazu zu bewegen to induce him
könnte ich mir ein besseres Bild darüber machen I could form a better picture
entstanden ist has come about
[**entstehen, entstand, ist entstanden** to originate, to come about (3)]
wie wäre es how would it be
Folgendes the following
vorschlüge proposed
daß er sich . . . von mir behandeln läßt him to (let himself) be treated by me
begleiten to accompany (4)
dagegen against it
es wäre besser it would be better
der Donnerstag the Thursday (2)
sagen wir let's say
der Honig the honey (3)
darin in it
darauf zu achten to see to it
das Bad the bath
[**das Bad, die Bäder** the bath (4)]
der Patient the patient
[**der Patient, die Patienten** the patient (2)]
etwas geschadet done any harm
die Nerven the nerves
. . . also . . . then

das Juweliergeschäft the jewelry store
der Geschäftsleiter the manager

habe ich mich entschlossen, zu Ihnen zu kommen. Es muß irgendeine Krankheit sein. Mein Gott, wenn ich daran denke, daß es eine Geisteskrankheit sein könnte und daß er vielleicht lange in einem Krankenhaus bleiben müßte, dann . . . Seine Großmutter, von der er nach dem Tode seiner Eltern erzogen wurde, hat an einer solchen Krankheit gelitten. Ich frage mich, ob der Ursprung der Krankheit vielleicht da . . ."–„Kein leichter Fall", unterbrach sie Dr. Freudenberg. „Sogar sehr kompliziert, würde ich sagen. Wir wissen leider immer noch nicht genug über den Ursprung solcher Krankheiten. Im Falle Ihres Mannes ist es wahrscheinlich irgendein dunkler Punkt in seiner Vergangenheit. Daß er behandelt werden muß, ist klar. Ich muß ihn natürlich persönlich sehen. Es ist Ihre Aufgabe, gnädige Frau, ihm das klarzumachen. Sehen Sie, wenn es mir gelänge, ihn dazu zu bewegen, mir ganz offen von seiner Vergangenheit zu erzählen, wie er erzogen wurde usw., dann könnte ich mir ein besseres Bild darüber machen, wie diese Krankheit entstanden ist. Wie wäre es, wenn ich Folgendes vorschlüge: Sie sagen Ihrem Mann, daß Sie ganz offen mit mir gesprochen haben. Sie möchten, daß er sich in seinem und Ihrem Interesse von mir behandeln läßt. Versuchen Sie Ihr Bestes. Begleiten Sie ihn, wenn er nichts dagegen hat. Ich glaube, es wäre besser, wenn Sie das erste Mal mit ihm zusammen kämen. Könnten Sie nächsten Donnerstag kommen? Gut. Sagen wir um vier Uhr. Inzwischen geben Sie Ihrem Mann jeden Abend ein Glas warme Milch mit etwas Honig darin. Und vergessen Sie nicht, darauf zu achten, daß er stets ein heißes Bad nimmt, bevor er zu Bett geht. Warme Milch und ein heißes Bad haben noch keinem Patienten etwas geschadet, was? Gut für die Nerven. Bis nächsten Donnerstag also!"

2.

Am Donnerstag um drei Uhr fünfzehn trat die elegante Dame in das beste Juweliergeschäft der Stadt. Der Geschäfts-

hatte es sich zur Regel gemacht had made it a rule
[**die Regel, die Regeln** the rule (3)]
der Laden the store
[**der Laden, die Läden**]
gemessen hatte had measured
[**messen, maß, hat gemessen** to measure (3)]
darüber about the fact
die Gesellschaft the society
die Handtasche the handbag (3)
italienisch Italian (2)
womit kann ich dienen? what can I do for you? (*literally:* with what can I serve (you)?
gnädige Frau Madam (2)
nach etwas Bestimmten for something in particular
je . . . desto the . . . the
der Juwelier the jeweler
der Kasten the case
[**der Kasten, die Kästen** the box, case (3)]
Linien lines
[**die Linie, die Linien** the line (3)]
wäre es it would be
der Geschäftsleiter the manager (2)
der Laden the store
[**der Laden, die Läden** (2)]
der Stoff the cloth
[**der Stoff, die Stoffe** the material, fabric, cloth, matter (3)]
dar Tau the dew (3)
sprachlos speechless
[**die Sprache, die Sprachen** the language, speech (2)]
der Juwelier the jeweler (2)
war . . . herbeigeeilt had . . . rushed over (to her)
[**herbei** here, over (3)]
[**eilen** to hurry, to hasten, to rush (3)]
schließlich after all
damit sie verkauft wurde in order to be sold
zur Zeit at present
gehören schließlich zu meinem Beruf are, after all, part of my business
[**der Beruf, die Berufe** the profession, job (2)]
selten rare (4)
bisher up to now (4)
rein pure
[**rein** clean, pure (3)]
die Art, wie the way in which
ein wahres Kunstwerk a true work of art
[**wahr** true (4)]
billig cheap (4)
der Wert the value (4)
das Doppelte the double
[**doppelt** double (4)]

leiter hatte es sich zur Regel gemacht, sich an jeden zu erinnern, der einmal im Laden gewesen war. Er kannte die Dame nicht. Aber der kurze Blick, mit dem er sie sofort gemessen hatte, ließ keinen Zweifel darüber, daß sie zu der besten Gesellschaft gehörte; der teure Mantel, die feine Handtasche, die italienischen Schuhe: alles zeigte, daß die Person Geld und Geschmack hatte. „Womit kann ich dienen, gnädige Frau?" fragte er. „Suchen Sie nach etwas Bestimmtem?"—„Ja", erwiderte die Dame, „ich möchte gern ein Armband. Etwas Modernes und Einfaches. Je einfacher in der Form, desto besser. In Silber, bitte."—„Hier, bitte", sagte der Juwelier; „wenn ich Ihnen zeigen darf, was wir haben . . ." Er schob das Glas von einem Kasten zurück, in dem ein Armband neben dem anderen lag. „Ah!" rief die Dame, „das ist genau das, was ich suche: moderne Form und einfache Linien. Nur ist es etwas zu eng, wie Sie sehen. Wenn Sie das gleiche Armband eine Nummer größer hätten, wäre es gerade richtig." Der Geschäftsleiter öffnete einen anderen Kasten, fand, was er suchte, und reichte ihr das Armband. Die Dame dankte, bezahlte und wandte sich zum Gehen. Auf dem Weg zur Tür blieb sie plötzlich stehen. In der Mitte des Ladens stand ein kleiner Tisch, auf dem unter schwerem Glas eine Perlenkette lag. Auf dem dunkelblauen Stoff glänzten die Perlen wie frischer Tau. Die Dame schien sprachlos zu sein. Der Juwelier war inzwischen herbeigeeilt. Man konnte nie wissen; schließlich lag die Kette dort, damit sie verkauft wurde. „So etwas Schönes habe ich seit langem nicht gesehen", sagte die Dame.—„Es ist das Beste, was wir zur Zeit im Laden haben", erwiderte der Juwelier. „Italienische Arbeit. Perlen gehören schließlich zu meinem Beruf, aber ich muß sagen, daß mir eine Kette von solch seltener Schönheit bisher noch nicht unter die Augen gekommen ist. Jede einzelne Perle von genau der gleichen, reinen Farbe, und die Art, wie die ganze Kette zusammengesetzt ist, ist ein wahres Kunstwerk."—„Darf ich fragen, wie teuer sie ist?" sagte die Dame.—„Jetzt nach Weihnachten verkaufen wir sie besonders billig", antwortete der Juwelier. „Nur 60 000 (sechzigtausend) Mark. Der wirkliche Wert ist etwa das Doppelte."—„Ich dachte, vielleicht

selbst so viel even that much
  dafür ausgeben spend for it
    [**aus-geben** to spend (3)]

das Geburtstagsgeschenk the birthday present
ein bißchen a little bit (4)
würde ich fast vorziehen I would almost prefer
  fahren zu lassen to let . . . go
Vorteile advantages
    [**der Vorteil, die Vorteile** the advantage (3)]
und das and that
  behaupten say
dazu bewegen könnte could induce
  müßte ich . . . irgendwie zeigen können I would somehow have to show
genau so überrascht sein würde wie ich would be just as surprised as I was
ich lege . . . gern auf die Seite I'll gladly lay . . . aside
das wird nicht gehen that will not be possible
wie wäre es how would it be
  hinführen went to see him

würde . . . sich ärgern would be annoyed
    [**sich ärgern** to be annoyed (4)]
ihre Meinung their minds
    [**die Meinung, die Meinungen** the opinion (3)]
  ändern to change (4)
der bekannteste the best-known
auf jeden Fall in any case

30 000 (dreißigtausend)", sagte die Dame; „aber selbst so viel könnte ich nicht dafür ausgeben. Das kann ich von meinem Mann nicht verlangen."

Eine solche Antwort war für den Geschäftsleiter nichts Neues. Es war eine Geschichte, die er auswendig kannte. „Vielleicht als Geburtstagsgeschenk?" meinte er laut.—„Ich weiß nicht", antwortete die Dame; „dafür ist die Kette ein bißchen zu teuer. Aber ich denke eben daran, daß mir mein Mann für nächstes Jahr eine Reise nach Italien versprochen hat. Wenn ich nun diese Kette sehe, würde ich fast vorziehen, die Reise fahren zu lassen."—„Ich will nichts gegen Reisen sagen", meinte der Juwelier; „aber so eine Kette hat doch ihre Vorteile. Man hat sie für das ganze Leben, und das kann man von einer Reise wohl kaum behaupten."—„Ich glaube fast", sagte die Dame, „daß ich meinen Mann dazu bewegen könnte, mir die Perlen zu schenken; nur müßte ich sie ihm irgendwie zeigen können. Ich bin sicher, daß er von ihrer außerordentlichen Schönheit genau so überrascht sein würde wie ich, und dann . . ."—„Nun, ich lege die Kette gern auf die Seite, bis er kommt", unterbrach sie der Juwelier. „Wenn Sie mir sagen könnten, ob Sie vielleicht morgen mit ihm . . ."—„Nein, das wird nicht gehen", entgegnete die Dame. „Mein Mann—Dr. Freudenberg—Sie kennen wahrscheinlich den Namen—mein Mann würde den Fuß in kein Geschäft setzen, in dem ich etwas kaufen möchte, was 60 000 Mark kostet. Wenn er aber die Perlen sähe, ohne zu wissen, wie teuer sie sind, dann . . . Ah, warten Sie! Ich habe eine Idee. Wie wäre es, wenn Sie und ich hinführen, wenn Sie die Kette mitnähmen und wir meinen Mann damit überraschten? Ich glaube, er würde nicht nein sagen können.—Natürlich nur, wenn es Ihnen möglich ist, meine ich."

Der Geschäftsleiter überlegte schnell. Wenn er nein sagte, würde Frau Freudenberg sich ärgern. Vielleicht würde sie die Kette überhaupt nicht mehr haben wollen. Er wußte, wie schnell Frauen ihre Meinung ändern können. Daß Dr. Freudenberg jeden Preis bezahlen konnte, war sicher; er war schließlich der bekannteste Psychiater der Stadt. Man sollte es auf jeden Fall versuchen.

in der Regel as a rule
das Vergnügen the pleasure (4)
das Kästchen the little case
  die Brusttasche the breast pocket (3)
indem er . . . öffnete while opening

um Punkt vier Uhr at four o'clock sharp
  das Gebäude the building
    [**das Gebäude, die Gebäude** (3)]
breit wide
    [**breit** broad, wide (4)]
  der Stock the floor (2)
voraus ahead (4)
  rufe . . . herein will . . . call you in
    [**herein-rufen** to call in]
das Gefühl the feeling
    [**das Gefühl, die Gefühle** the feeling (2)]
hereingerufen habe called . . . in
  das Nebenzimmer the adjoining room (3)
lieber rather

das Kästchen the little case (2)
das Tischchen the little table
erwarten to expect
herein! come in!

höchste Zeit high time
irgend etwas something

die Daumen the thumbs
    [**der Daumen, die Daumen** the thumb (3)]
die Sache richtig anfing started things properly
  müßte eigentlich alles gut gehen everything would simply have to go well

„In der Regel tun wir das nicht, gnädige Frau", sagte er nach einer kurzen Pause; „aber ich sehe, daß es in diesem Fall notwendig ist. Es wird mir ein Vergnügen sein, Sie zu begleiten." Er legte die Perlen in ein kleines Kästchen, steckte sie in die Brusttasche und zog den Mantel an. „Gestatten Sie!" sagte er, indem er die rechte Tür seines Autos öffnete, das vor dem Geschäft stand. „Wohin, bitte?" fragte er dann.—„Lindenstraße 15", antwortete die elegante Dame.

3.

Um Punkt vier Uhr hielt das Auto vor dem Gebäude. Der Fahrstuhl war nicht frei. Während sie die breiten Treppen zum 2. Stock hinaufstiegen, sagte die Dame: „Ich schlage vor, Sie geben mir die Perlen und bleiben im Wartezimmer. Ich gehe voraus, spreche mit meinem Mann, zeige ihm die Perlen und rufe Sie dann herein. Ich habe das bestimmte Gefühl, daß alles gut gehen wird. Wenn ich Sie hereingerufen habe, gehe ich ins Nebenzimmer und warte. Über den Preis sollten Sie mit meinem Mann vielleicht lieber allein sprechen. Wenn Sie beide fertig sind, kann mein Mann mich dann hereinrufen."

Sie steckte das Kästchen in ihre Handtasche und trat mit dem Juwelier ins Wartezimmer. Die Krankenschwester, die an einem Tischchen saß und Rechnungen schrieb, blickte auf und lächelte freundlich: „Guten Tag, gnädige Frau! Der Herr Doktor erwartet Sie. Wenn Sie gleich hineingehen wollen . . ." Die Dame klopfte, man hörte ein lautes „Herein!". Sie trat ein.

„Ich habe ihn mitgebracht, Herr Doktor", flüsterte sie. „Ich glaube, es ist höchste Zeit. Die Krankheit ist inzwischen noch schlimmer geworden. Statt nur von Perlen zu sprechen, redet mein Mann jetzt auch von Geld und Preisen. Irgend etwas, was 60 000 Mark kostet. Wahrscheinlich meint er die Perlen."— „Nun, wir werden sehen", sagte der Doktor.

Indessen saß der Geschäftsleiter draußen und drehte die Daumen. Wenn Frau Freudenberg die Sache richtig anfing, müßte eigentlich alles gut gehen. Die Frau wußte, was sie

würde er . . . sein müssen he would have to be
rechnen to do some figuring
selbst wenn even if
  er . . . bekäme he got
  wäre das . . . immer noch it would still be
  der Verlust the loss
    [**der Verlust, die Verluste** the loss (2)]
die Hauptsache the main thing (4)
  loswurde got rid of
    [**los-werden** to get rid of (3)]
sie hätte . . . verkauft werden sollen it should have been sold
  wäre er nicht gezwungen gewesen he would not have been forced
  herunter-gehen to go down
aber selbst but even
  der Profit the profit (3)
nicken to nod (3)
es hatte sich also gelohnt it had then been worth the trouble

miteinander with each other (2)
fordert Ihr Beruf von Ihnen your profession requires from you
  aus diplomatischen Gründen for diplomatic reasons
  geheimgehalten werden müssen must be kept secret
    [**geheim-halten** to keep secret (3)]
das Gleiche gilt the same is true
    [**gelten, er gilt, galt, hat gegolten** to be worth; to be valid; to be considered]

vollkommen perfectly
    [**vollkommen** complete; perfect (3)]
die Diskretion the discretion
  die Pflicht the duty (4)
der höheren Gesellschaft of the higher society
  erfahren dürfe must find out
  bestimmt war was meant

kosten soll is supposed to cost

etwas gereizt somewhat irritated
    [**reizen** to irritate; to charm (2)]
  überhaupt davon of it at all
deshalb bin ich ja schließlich hier that's why I am here, after all

hat recht is right
absolut absolutely (3)

wollte. Vielleicht würde er mit 55 000 (fünfundfünfzigtausend) Mark zufrieden sein müssen. Er nahm seinen Bleistift und rechnete. Selbst wenn er 5 000 (fünftausend) Mark weniger bekäme, wäre das natürlich immer noch kein Verlust. Die Hauptsache war, daß er die Kette endlich loswurde. Sie hätte schon vor Weihnachten verkauft werden sollen; dann wäre er nicht gezwungen gewesen, mit dem Preis herunterzugehen. Aber selbst ein kleiner Profit war besser als . . . Die Tür zum Sprechzimmer öffnete sich, die Dame steckte den Kopf heraus, nickte und gab ihm ein Zeichen. Es hatte sich also gelohnt, persönlich gekommen zu sein. Er trat ein.

„Vielleicht ist es besser, wenn ich Sie beide jetzt verlasse", sagte die Dame lächelnd. „Ich werde im Nebenzimmer warten."

Die beiden Männer waren allein. „Ich glaube, wir sollten als Männer ganz offen miteinander reden", begann Dr. Freudenberg. „Wenn ich mich nicht irre, fordert Ihr Beruf von Ihnen, daß gewisse Dinge aus diplomatischen Gründen geheimgehalten werden müssen. Das Gleiche gilt von meinem Beruf. Die Liste meiner Patienten und ihre Krankheiten sind geheim."

„Ich verstehe Sie vollkommen", antwortete der Juwelier. „Diskretion ist unsere erste Pflicht." Er dachte an die vielen Herren der höheren Gesellschaft, die jedes Jahr in sein Geschäft kamen und verlangten, daß niemand erfahren dürfe, für wen dieser Ring oder jenes Armband bestimmt war.

„Gut, dann verstehen wir uns vollkommen", fuhr der Doktor fort. „Sagen Sie mir: was, glauben Sie, würde passieren, wenn man Sie oder jemanden in Ihrem Beruf von einer Perlenkette reden hörte, die 60 000 Mark kosten soll? Ich denke, es würde . . ."

„Aber wer redet denn öffentlich von solchen Dingen, Herr Doktor?" unterbrach ihn der Juwelier etwas gereizt. „Wenn ich überhaupt davon spreche, dann nur mit Ihnen! Deshalb bin ich ja schließlich hier."

„Ein interessanter Fall", dachte der Doktor. „Die Frau hat recht. Der Mann scheint in zwei verschiedenen Welten zu leben.—Ganz richtig", entgegnete er; "ich wollte nur absolut

wozu Indiskretionen führen können what indiscretions can lead to
[**die Indiskretion** thc indiscretion]

hätte sich . . . gerieben could . . . have rubbed
die Furcht vor the fear of
praktisch practically (3)
von den Perlen selbst of the pearls themselves
es Ihnen recht ist it is all right with you
[**es ist mir recht** it is all right with me]
man soll nicht . . . loben one should not praise
[**loben** to praise (3)]
seine eigene Ware his own wares

ernster more serious

jahrelang for years
bis man . . . fände before finding
etwas Ähnliches something like it

der Narr the fool
[**der Narr, die Narren** the fool (3)]
wie kommt es how is it

weil sie . . . gehören because they are part of
auf sie stolz sein wird will be proud of it
[**stolz auf** proud of (3)]
wäre ich schließlich nicht . . . gekommen I would, after all, not have come

die Unterhaltung the conversation
[**die Unterhaltung, die Unterhaltungen**]

die Kette ist doch but the necklace is
doch eben gezeigt just shown . . . after all

zur Zeit at present

kreideweiß white as chalk (3)
stottern to stutter (3)
als er die Sprache wiedergefunden hatte when he could speak again

sicher sein, daß Sie verstehen, wozu Indiskretionen führen können."

Der Juwelier hätte sich vor Freude fast die Hände gerieben. Wenn die Furcht vor einer Indiskretion Dr. Freudenbergs einzige Sorge war, dann war die Kette praktisch verkauft. „Könnten wir vielleicht jetzt von den Perlen selbst reden, wenn es Ihnen recht ist?" sagte er. "Ich weiß, man soll nicht seine eigene Ware loben, aber ich kann wirklich sagen, daß ich eine Kette von solcher Schönheit bisher nur selten gesehen habe. Jede einzelne Perle ist gleich rein, die Form ist so vollkommen, daß . . ."

„Der Fall ist wirklich ernster, als ich geglaubt hatte", dachte der Arzt.

„. . . so vollkommen", fuhr der Juwelier fort, „daß man jahrelang suchen könnte, bis man etwas Ähnliches fände."

„Der arme Narr", dachte Dr. Freudenberg und sagte laut: „Wie kommt es, daß diese Perlen Ihnen so viel bedeuten?"

„Was für eine Frage, Herr Doktor!" rief der Juwelier überrascht. „Die Perlen bedeuten mir etwas, weil sie zu meinem Beruf gehören, und ich dachte, daß die Kette vielleicht auch I h n e n etwas bedeuten würde, weil ich weiß, daß Ihre Frau auf sie stolz sein wird. Wenn die Kette Ihrer Frau nicht so gefallen hätte, wäre ich schließlich nicht hierher gekommen. Für den Preis, den ich genannt habe, 60 000 Mark . . ."

„Darf ich fragen, was Ihre Kette mit meiner Frau zu tun hat?" unterbrach ihn der Doktor. Die Unterhaltung fing an, ihm ein wenig auf die Nerven zu gehen.

Auch der Juwelier war jetzt etwas nervös geworden. „Die Kette ist doch für Ihre Frau bestimmt, Herr Doktor!" sagte er. „Ihre Frau hat Ihnen die Perlen doch eben gezeigt!"

Jetzt hatte Dr. Freudenberg genug. „Meine Frau, mein lieber Herr", entgegnete er, "ist zur Zeit in England."

Der Juwelier war plötzlich kreideweiß geworden. „E-E-England", stotterte er endlich, als er die Sprache wiedergefunden hatte.

es wäre gut it would be good
riß . . . auf tore . . . open
[**auf-reißen** to tear open (2)]

„Ich glaube, es wäre gut, wenn ich die Krankenschwester und Ihre Frau rufe“, sagte der Doktor und riß die Tür zum Nebenzimmer auf.

Aber die elegante Dame war verschwunden–und mit ihr die Perlenkette.

DER SCHNEESTURM

[10B]

NOTES

REVIEW OF STRONG VERB USED IN STORIES 10A AND 10B

gelten gilt galt gegolten *to be worth, to be considered (as)*

IDIOMS FOR REVIEW

er war den ganzen Tag unterwegs he was busy ("on the go") all day
heute früh this morning
den Mund halten to keep one's mouth shut
mit der Zeit in time
es fehlte nicht an Männern there was no lack of men

der Schneesturm the snowstorm
[**der Schnee** the snow (2)]
[**der Sturm, die Stürme** the storm (3)]

ganz Europa all of Europe
die Provinz Ostpreußen the province of East Prussia
[**der Ost(en)** the east (3)]
[**Preußen** Prussia (2)]
siebzehnjährig seventeen-year-old
waren . . . vorübergegangen had bypassed
[**vorüber-gehen** to pass by, to bypass (2)]
an den fern von der Hauptstadt gelegenen Gütern des Grafen the count's estates, which were situated far from the capital
[**die Hauptstadt** the capital (3)]
[**das Gut, die Güter** the estate; the goods (4)]
und selbst and even
hatten . . . gemieden had avoided
der Marsch the march (3)
Rußland Russia
die Truppen the troops
[**die Truppe, die Truppen** the troop, troupe (2)]
einsam lonely
[**einsam** solitary, lonely, isolated, secluded (3)]
und . . . gestört and disturbed
die Dörfer the villages
[**das Dorf, die Dörfer** the village (4)]
Bekannte acquaintances
[**der Bekannte, die Bekannten** the acquaintance (3)]
hätten . . . aufgehört would have ceased
vollständig completely (4)
schlank slender (3)
Züge features
die Gräfin the countess (3)
Besucher visitors
[**der Besucher, die Besucher** the visitor (3)]
. . . denkend thinking
wären überglücklich gewesen would have been overjoyed
hätte Maria Gabriele . . . gewählt if Maria Gabriele had chosen
wenn auch even though, although
die sich . . . nicht erklären konnten who could not explain (to themselves)
unnatürlich unnatural
die Kälte the coolness
sie zu bewegen to induce her
sich für einen . . . zu entscheiden to make up her mind (to marry) one
gereizt irritated
[**reizen** to irritate, to annoy; to charm (3)]

[10 B]

(FIVE PARTS)

Der Schneesturm

I.

Am Anfang des neunzehnten Jahrhunderts, als ganz Europa vor den Heeren Napoleons zitterte, lebte in der Provinz Ostpreußen ein reicher Graf mit seiner Frau und Tochter, der siebzehnjährigen Maria Gabriele. Die langen Kriege waren an den fern von der Hauptstadt gelegenen Gütern des Grafen vorübergegangen, und selbst auf ihrem Marsch nach Rußland hatten die Truppen des großen Kaisers die weiten, einsamen Wälder gemieden und weder die Ruhe der wenigen Dörfer noch den Frieden des kleinen Schlosses gestört, in dem der Graf mit seiner Familie wohnte. Die Besuche von Freunden und Bekannten, die schon in früheren Jahren ziemlich selten gewesen waren, hätten während der Kriegszeit fast vollständig aufgehört, wenn nicht die außerordentliche Schönheit, die schlanke Gestalt und die feinen, blassen Züge der jungen Gräfin mehr Besucher als je auf das Schloß ihres Vaters gebracht hätte. Der Graf und die Mutter, an die Zukunft ihrer einzigen Tochter denkend, wären überglücklich gewesen, hätte Maria Gabriele einen unter den jungen Fürsten und Grafen gewählt, die sich jetzt um sie sammelten. Aber das junge Mädchen, wenn auch freundlich und höflich zu allen, hatte für keinen der Gäste besonderes Interesse gezeigt. Die Eltern, die sich die unnatürliche Kälte ihrer Tochter nicht erklären konnten, versuchten alles, sie zu bewegen, sich für einen der jungen Herren zu entscheiden. Schließlich, gereizt durch

das Schweigen the silence
war . . . in sie gedrungen had pressed her (to confide in her)
das Geheimnis the secret
[**das Geheimnis, die Geheimnisse** (2)]

ihrer Mutter to her mother
die Liebe the love (2)
der Leutnant the lieutenant
namens by the name of (3)
den Eltern to the parents
er galt als he was believed to be
[**gelten, er gilt, galt, hat gegolten** to be considered; to be worth, valid (2)]
die Heirat the marriage
nicht in Frage kommen konnte was out of the question
Reden speeches
[**die Rede, die Reden** the speech, talk (3)]
guter Rat good advice
verbot forbade
[**verbieten, verbot, hat verboten** to forbid, to prohibit (2)]
der Geliebte the beloved
daß er damit . . . würde ändern können that he could thereby change
romantisch romantic (2)
der Sinn the temperament
so hatte er sich geirrt he had been mistaken
irgendwo somewhere
außerhalb outside (3)
wechseln to exchange
[**wechseln** to change, to exchange (2)]
die Trennung the separation
ewig everlasting (3)
einander . . . treu zu bleiben to remain true to each other
[**treu** loyal, faithful, true (3)]
Schwierigkeiten difficulties
[**die Schwierigkeit, die Schwierigkeiten** the difficulty (2)]
gestellt würden would be put

währen to last (3)
Maria Gabriele to Maria Gabriele
die Last the burden
[**die Last, die Lasten** the burden]
die Geliebte the beloved
ohne deren Gegenwart without whose presence
atmen to breathe (4)
die Trennung the separation (2)
ich wäre nur zu bereit I would be only too ready
[**bereit** ready, prepared (3)]
damit erreichen accomplish with that
sie dazu bewegen induce them

Gabrieles Schweigen, war die Mutter in sie gedrungen, um das Geheimnis zu erfahren, das dem Glück ihrer Tochter im Wege stand.

Ihrer Mutter öffnete Maria Gabriele endlich ihr Herz. Zu ihrem Schrecken erfuhren die Eltern, daß die Liebe ihrer Tochter einem jungen Leutnant namens Rupert gehöre und daß sie, so hatte sie gesagt, nie jemand anderen würde lieben und heiraten können als ihn. Den Eltern war der Name und die Familie des Leutnants bekannt. Er galt als so arm, daß eine Heirat zwischen den beiden nicht in Frage kommen konnte. Der Graf, wohl wissend, daß lange Reden und guter Rat zu nichts führen würden, verbot darauf seiner Tochter, ihren Geliebten je wiederzusehen. Wenn er jedoch geglaubt hatte, daß er damit den romantischen Sinn des jungen Mädchens würde ändern können, so hatte er sich geirrt. Anstatt sich irgendwo außerhalb des Schlosses zu treffen, wie sie es früher getan hatten, wechselten die beiden nun Briefe, in denen sie von bitterer Trennung, ewiger Liebe usw. sprachen und schworen, einander trotz aller Schwierigkeiten treu zu bleiben, die ihnen in den Weg gestellt würden.

Das währte einige Zeit, bis eines Tages Maria Gabriele durch ihr Dienstmädchen ein Brief von Rupert gebracht wurde, worin dieser schrieb: „Der Gedanke, noch länger von dir getrennt sein zu müssen, ist eine Last, die zu tragen meinem Herzen nicht länger möglich ist. Du, Geliebte, ohne deren Gegenwart ich nicht atmen und leben kann, du weißt, daß ich seit Wochen daran gedacht haben muß, unserer Trennung ein Ende zu machen. Ich wäre nur zu bereit, mit dir deinen Eltern zu Füßen zu fallen; aber was würden wir damit erreichen? Wenn wir sie bäten, uns zu verzeihen, so würden sie vielleicht unsere Liebe mit unserer Jugend entschuldigen; nie jedoch könnten wir sie dazu bewegen, dir eine Heirat mit einem Manne zu erlauben, der so arm ist wie ich. Da nun ihr harter Wille durch nichts gebrochen werden kann, müssen wir selbst

---

da nun since, then, . . .
gebrochen werden kann can be broken

bestimmen decide
das Wissen the knowledge
ungerührt unmoved
als verheiratetes Paar as a married couple
[**verheiraten** to marry (3)]
[**das Paar, die Paare** the couple, the pair (4)]
würden sie nicht . . . müssen would they not have to
entwickeln to develop (2)
unterrichten to inform
[**unterrichten** to teach; to inform (3)]
die Absicht the intention (3)
packen to pack (3)
du . . . nötig haben wirst you will need
[**nötig** necessary (4)]
[**nötig haben** to need]
begib dich go
[**sich begeben** to go (3)]
das Nachtmahl the supper (2)
[**das Mahl** the meal (4)]
gegen zehn around ten
die Hintertür the back door (3)
der Schlitten the sleigh
[**der Schlitten, die Schlitten** the sleigh, sled]
erwarten to expect, to wait for (2)
die Kirche the church
[**die Kirche, die Kirchen** (3)]
die Trauung the wedding (ceremony)
um Mitternacht at midnight (4)
stattfinden to take place
[**statt-finden, fand statt, hat stattgefunden** to take place (3)]
der Pfarrer the priest
[**der Pfarrer, die Pfarrer** the priest, pastor, clergyman, parson]
die Trauzeugen the marriage witnesses
[**der Zeuge, die Zeugen** the witness (3)]

hätte . . . klingen können could have sounded
das Schreibpult the writing desk (3)
schneien to snow
selbst wenn even if
hinaus-blicken to look out (2)
begegnen to meet (4)
das Mädchen = das Dienstmädchen
der Schlitten the sleigh
[**der Schlitten, die Schlitten** the sleigh, sled (2)]
darauf afterwards

den Lauf unseres Lebens bestimmen. Laß uns heiraten o h n e ihr Wissen! Glaubst du, daß das Herz deiner Eltern ungerührt bleiben könnte, wenn wir als verheiratetes Paar, als Mann und Frau vor sie träten? Würden sie nicht rufen müssen: ‚Kinder, kommt in unsere Arme!'? Laß mich dir meinen Plan entwickeln! Unterrichte dein Dienstmädchen über unsere Absicht, laß sie packen, was du während der nächsten Tage nötig haben wirst, und halte dich mit ihr für morgen nacht bereit. Begib dich nach dem Nachtmahl in dein Zimmer, bleibe dort bis gegen zehn Uhr und verlasse dann das Schloß durch die Hintertür. Mein treuer Diener Johann, den du kennst, wird euch mit einem Schlitten hinter dem Garten erwarten und von da zur Kirche nach Ostrau bringen, wo die Trauung um Mitternacht stattfinden wird. Ich werde dort mit dem Pfarrer und den Trauzeugen auf dich warten."

Keine Musik des Himmels hätte in Maria Gabrieles Ohren süßer klingen können als diese Worte. Liebe und Glück sprachen aus der kurzen Antwort, die sie sogleich zurücksandte. Von nun an wurden ihr die Minuten zu Stunden. Am folgenden Tag schloß sie sich abends in ihr Zimmer und bat in einem langen Brief ihre Eltern, ihr zu verzeihen; den Brief legte sie auf ihr Schreibpult, wo man ihn am nächsten Tage finden würde. Draußen hatte es inzwischen zu schneien begonnen. „Gut", sagte sie. Selbst wenn später jemand in den Garten hinausblickte, könnte man sie nicht sehen, und niemand würde ihnen bei diesem Wetter auf den Straßen begegnen oder sie erkennen. Um zehn Uhr verließ sie mit ihrem Mädchen das stille Schloß. Der Schlitten stand bereit und war kurz darauf in der weißen Nacht verschwunden.

unterwegs busy (*literally:* on his way) (4)
war er . . . geritten he had ridden
[**reiten, ritt, ist geritten** to ride (3)]
der Pfarrer the priest (2)
dazu zu bewegen to induce
sich . . . zu erklären to declare himself
die Trauung the wedding ceremony (2)
als Trauzeugen as marriage witnesses (2)
zuvor before
schneien to snow (2)
die Wohnung the lodging
[**die Wohnung, die Wohnungen** the apartment, residence, lodging (4)]
geliehen hatte had lent
[**leihen, lieh, hat geliehen** to lend, to loan; to borrow (3)]
jagte . . . entlang raced along
sich beeilen to hurry (2)

sich zum Sturm entwickelte developed into a storm
flach flat (3)
glitt was gliding
[**gleiten, glitt, ist geglitten** to slide, to glide (3)]
beißend biting, piercing
[**beißen, biß, hat gebissen** to bite (3)]
selbst wenn even if
wäre es . . . nicht möglich gewesen it would not have been possible
die Landschaft the landscape
[**die Landschaft, die Landschaften** the landscape (2)]
hatte sich in . . . verwandelt had turned into
[**verwandeln** to change, to transform (3)]
das Meer the sea (4)
unter-gehen to perish
das Ufer the shore (4)
als wäre er as if he had been
nicht einmal not even

2.

Rupert war den ganzen Tag unterwegs gewesen. Schon am frühen Morgen war er nach Ostrau geritten, wo es ihm nur mit der größten Mühe gelang, den alten Pfarrer dazu zu bewegen, sich zu der Trauung bereit zu erklären. Als er das kleine Dorf verließ, war es schon Mittag. Von den zwei Freunden, die er als Trauzeugen brauchen würde, fand er den ersten zu Haus. Der zweite, der in einem Nachbardorf lebte, war am Tage zuvor in die Hauptstadt gereist und würde erst nächste Woche zurückkehren. Um einen Bekannten zu finden, der ihm versprach, als Trauzeuge in Ostrau zu erscheinen, brauchte er mehrere Stunden. Auf dem Weg nach Haus, wohin er zurückritt, um seine Sachen zu holen, begann es zu schneien. Als er in seiner Wohnung ankam, fand er sie leer: sein Diener Johann war schon seit einer Stunde unterwegs. In wenigen Minuten hatte Rupert gepackt. Er warf sich in den kleinen Schlitten, den ihm ein Nachbar für heute geliehen hatte, und jagte einen Augenblick später die Straße nach Ostrau entlang. Wenn er sich beeilte, würde er nicht mehr als zwei oder drei Stunden brauchen, um das Dorf noch vor Mitternacht zu erreichen.

Kaum hatte er jedoch das Haus verlassen, als der Wind stärker zu werden begann und sich zum Sturm entwickelte. Der Schnee fiel in solch dichten Mengen, daß Rupert schon nach kurzer Zeit nicht mehr sicher war, ob der Schlitten noch der Straße folgte oder nun über die flachen Felder glitt. Der beißende Nordwind schnitt Rupert ins Gesicht. Selbst wenn der Schmerz ihn nicht gezwungen hätte, die Augen zu schließen, wäre es ihm nicht möglich gewesen, die Landschaft zu erkennen. Die Welt hatte sich in ein weißes Meer verwandelt, in dem er untergehen würde, wenn sich nicht bald ein rettendes Ufer zeigte. Wie lange konnte er schon gefahren sein? Es schien ihm, als wäre er schon seit Stunden unterwegs. Nicht einmal ein Haus hatte er gesehen, in dem er nach dem rechten Wege

er . . . hätte fragen können he could have inquired
die Richtung the direction (3)
selbst wenn even if

stechend stinging
[**stechen, er sticht, stach, hat gestochen** to sting, to stab, to prick (3)]
der Tannenzweig the branch of a fir tree
[**die Tanne, die Tannen** the fir tree (2)]
[**der Zweig, die Zweige** the branch (4)]
auf dessen on whose
am Ziel sein würden would . . . be at their destination
würde sich . . . ausruhen können would be able to rest
[**sich aus-ruhen** to rest (4)]
er trieb . . . an he urged . . . on
[**an-treiben** to drive on, to urge on]
es kam Rupert vor it seemed to Rupert
[**vor-kommen** to happen, to occur; to seem, to appear (4)]
sah sie . . . nur anders aus it only looked different
schneebedeckt snow-covered
[**der Schnee** the snow (3)]
das Dach the roof
[**das Dach, die Dächer** the roof (4)]

Glieder limbs
[**das Glied, die Glieder** the member, limb (4)]
an-treiben to urge on (2)
zog er he pulled

hätte fragen können. Führte ihn sein müdes Pferd jetzt nach Norden oder Süden? Wo war Osten, wo war Westen? Rupert wußte es nicht. Er konnte nur hoffen, daß er die Richtung nach Ostrau nicht ganz verloren hatte. Aber selbst wenn er auf dem falschen Wege war, jetzt mußte er weiter; er mußte wissen, wo er war.

Plötzlich fühlte er einen stechenden Schmerz. Er blickte auf. Es war ein Tannenzweig, der ihm ins Gesicht geschlagen war. Dies mußte der Wald sein, auf dessen anderer Seite Ostrau lag. Warum ging das Pferd nicht schneller? Wußte es nicht, daß sie beide bald am Ziel sein würden? Nun, es konnte jetzt nicht mehr weit sein . . . Der Wind wurde schwächer, und es hörte auf zu schneien. „Gut“, dachte er; das Pferd würde sich ein wenig ausruhen können. Rupert wurde ruhiger. Die Tannen waren jetzt weniger dicht als zuvor. Dies mußte das Ende des Waldes sein. Richtig, er hatte sich nicht geirrt. Zwischen den schwarzen Stämmen der Bäume konnte Rupert ein Dorf erkennen, das im reinen Weiß des frisch gefallenen Schnees vor ihm lag. Er trieb das Pferd an, das mit seiner letzten Kraft zu laufen begann. Sie waren jetzt so nahe, daß er die Formen der einzelnen Häuser sehen konnte. Wo war die Kirche? Ah, dort! Aber war das die gleiche Kirche, in der er noch heute früh so lange mit dem alten Pfarrer gesprochen hatte? Es kam Rupert vor, als ob dies eine andere Kirche wäre; aber vielleicht sah sie mit ihrem schneebedeckten Dach und in der Nacht nur anders aus.

Plötzlich blieb das Pferd stehen. Sein Körper war mit Schweiß bedeckt, und es zitterte an allen Gliedern. Rupert sprang aus dem Schlitten und versuchte, das arme Tier mit guten Worten anzutreiben; aber es wollte nicht weiter. Da zog er es, und das Pferd begann ihm zu folgen. Das Dorf war jetzt ganz nahe. Nein, das war nicht die Kirche von Ostrau! Nun, dann konnte es nur ein Nachbardorf sein. Schwer atmend erreichte Rupert das erste Haus und klopfte an ein Fenster, durch das er das gelbe Licht einer Kerze erblickte. „Wie weit ist Ostrau?“–„Ostrau?“ fragte die erstaunte Stimme eines

schlug gerade die Kirchuhr the church clock was just striking
hell clear
das Pfarrhaus the parsonage, rectory
der Ofen the stove
[**der Ofen, die Öfen** the stove, oven (4)]

die Hähne the roosters
krähen to crow (2)
Schläge blows
[**der Schlag, die Schläge** the blow, stroke, slap (4)]
schrecken to frighten (4)

das Frühstück the breakfast (4)
die sich . . . darüber gewundert hatte, daß had wondered why
irgend etwas anything
das Fräulein the young lady
berichten to report (4)
kurz danach shortly thereafter
die Kopfschmerzen the headache (3)
schweigend silently
nach oben upstairs
wieder einmal once again
der Rauch the smoke (3)
heute nacht last night

mußte . . . gerufen werden had to be called
das Fieber the fever, temperature (2)
trocken dry (4)
gefährlich dangerous (2)

Bauern, dessen Gesicht im Fenster erschienen war. „Nicht sehr weit; etwa eine Stunde von hier, bei gutem Wetter."

Rupert war der Verzweiflung nahe. Er bat um ein Pferd, das er morgen zurückschicken würde. Als man das Tier aus dem Stall holte, schlug gerade die Kirchuhr. Vier kurze, helle Töne, dann zwei lange. Zwei Uhr! Gabriele, der Pfarrer und seine Freunde waren schon seit langem in Ostrau und mußten sich Sorgen machen; aber sie würden warten. Wahrscheinlich saßen sie jetzt im Pfarrhaus am warmen Ofen.

Die Hähne krähten, und es begann hell zu werden, als er die dunkle Kirche von Ostrau erreichte. Er stürzte zum Pfarrhaus, wo er mit lauten Schlägen auf die geschlossene Tür den alten Pfarrer aus dem Schlaf schreckte. Von ihm erfuhr er, was geschehen war.

3.

Am Morgen erschien Maria Gabriele nicht zum Frühstück. Die Mutter, die sich schon am Abend zuvor darüber gewundert hatte, daß ihre Tochter viel früher als gewöhnlich zu Bett gegangen war, schickte das Dienstmädchen hinauf, um zu erfahren, ob Maria Gabriele sich nicht wohl fühle und irgend etwas brauche. Das Fräulein würde bald kommen, berichtete das Mädchen. Kurz danach hörte man Maria Gabriele langsam die Treppe herunterschreiten. Sie trat ein, wünschte ihren Eltern einen guten Morgen, klagte über furchtbare Kopfschmerzen und setzte sich schweigend an den Tisch. Nach einigen Minuten legte sie Messer und Gabel nieder, entschuldigte sich und begab sich wieder nach oben. „Wahrscheinlich hat der Wind wieder einmal den Rauch aus dem Ofen in ihr Zimmer getrieben", meinte der Graf; „kein Wunder bei dem Wetter heute nacht!"

Am Abend mußte ein Arzt gerufen werden. Maria Gabriele lag in hohem Fieber; ihre Augen glänzten, die trockenen Lippen verlangten zu trinken, sie verstand nicht, was man ihr sagte. Der Arzt erkannte sofort, daß dies ein ernster Fall eines ge-

das Nervenfieber the nerve fever
riet advised
[**raten, er rät, riet, hat geraten** to advise, to counsel]
gerettet werden könne could be saved

von dem, was . . . geschehen of what had happened
daß sie nur . . . kommen würden that they would only get
hielt weise den Mund wisely kept his mouth shut
da der Verlust since the loss
die Stelle the job
wenn auch nur ein einziges Wort über seine Lippen kam if only so much as a single word escaped him

der Kranken of the patient
wurde . . . geschreckt was frightened
die Wolldecken the woolen blankets
[**die Wolle** the wool (3)]
. . . sitzend sitting

hielten . . . Rat held counsel
waren der Meinung were of the opinion
hoffnungslos hopeless
gerettet werden könne could be saved
. . . stünden stood
Rupert kommen zu lassen to have Rupert come

die Einladung the invitation
[**die Einladung, die Einladungen**]
er erklärte he declared
konnten sich nicht erklären could not explain to themselves

fährlichen Nervenfiebers war. Er empfahl absolute Ruhe und riet, die Kranke keinen Augenblick allein zu lassen. Die nächsten zwei Wochen würden entscheiden, ob ihr Leben gerettet werden könne.

Von dem, was während der Nacht geschehen, wußte niemand im Schloß außer dem Dienstmädchen, das aber aus Furcht vor dem Zorn des Grafen und der Gräfin nichts zu sagen wagte. Der Pfarrer und die zwei Trauzeugen wußten, daß sie nur in große Schwierigkeiten kommen würden, wenn jemand durch sie von dem Geheimnis erführe, und Ruperts Diener hielt weise den Mund, da der Verlust seiner Stelle gewiß war, wenn auch nur ein einziges Wort über seine Lippen kam.

Der Zustand der Kranken wurde schlimmer. Das hohe Fieber wollte nicht aufhören, so daß man fürchtete, daß Maria Gabriele bald dem Tode nahe sein würde, wenn nicht ein Wunder geschähe. Eines Nachts wurde die Mutter, die jetzt im Krankenzimmer schlief, plötzlich aus dem Schlaf geschreckt. Maria Gabriele war aufgewacht. Sie hatte das Bettuch und die Wolldecken auf den Boden geworfen und streckte, mit wild rollenden Augen im Bette sitzend, die Arme nach jemandem aus, den sie zu sehen schien, während sie mit lauter Stimme, in der die tiefste Verzweiflung lag, mehrere Male den Namen „Rupert“ rief.

Am nächsten Morgen hielten die Eltern Rat. Beide waren der Meinung, daß Maria Gabrieles hoffnungslose Liebe zu Rupert wahrscheinlich der Grund für ihre Krankheit sei und daß ihr Leben vielleicht gerettet werden könne, wenn sie, die Eltern, dem Glück ihrer Tochter nicht länger im Wege stünden. Sie beschlossen, Rupert kommen zu lassen.

Anstatt jedoch der Einladung mit Freude zu folgen, wie man erwartet hatte, sandte Rupert nur einen kurzen Brief, der die Eltern wie ein Schlag traf. Er erklärte, daß er seinen Fuß niemals wieder in ihr Haus setzen könne und bat, daß man ihn, dessen einzige Hoffnung der Tod sei, so bald wie möglich vergessen möge. Die unglücklichen Eltern konnten sich nicht erklären, welche Gründe ihn zu einer solchen Antwort ge-

getrieben haben mochten might have driven
das Regiment the regiment
[**das Regiment, die Regimenter** the regiment]

erklärte declared
die Kranke the patient (2)
außer Gefahr out of danger
die Wangen the cheeks
[**die Wange, die Wangen** the cheek (2)]
stumpf dull
[**stumpf** dull, blunt (3)]
aber wenn auch but even though
der Sieg dem Leben gehört hatte life had been victorious (*literally:* victory had belonged to life)
[**der Sieg, die Siege** the victory (2)]
der Gram the grief (3)
die Zeitung the newspaper (4)
die Schlacht bei Leipzig the Battle of Leipzig (1813)
[**die Schlacht, die Schlachten** the battle (2)]
gefallen sei had died
wechselte . . . die Farbe turned pale (*literally:* changed her color)
bleich pale (4)
ließ . . . fürchten caused . . . to fear
an der sie . . . gelitten from which she had suffered
von neuem anew, again
was sie an Rupert erinnerte that reminded her of Rupert
heilig sacred (3)
ihr von ihm geschenkt worden waren had been given her by him
die Bildchen the little pictures
zeichnen to draw (3)
die Heftchen the little notebooks
die Verse the verses
[**der Vers, die Verse** the verse]
die er gedichtet which he had written
[**dichten** to write poetry (3)]
in ihrem Schmerz in her sorrow, grief

wurde . . . getroffen was struck
hätte es vorgezogen would have preferred
still für sich quietly to herself
allein but
drang in sie urged her
die Hochzeit the marriage (2)
die Lebensweise the way of life
bot offered
[**bieten, bot, hat geboten** to offer (4)]
ihrer Tochter gut tun (würde) would do her daughter good
mit der Zeit in time

trieben haben mochten. Sie schrieben zurück und erfuhren, daß Rupert mit seinem Regiment die Stadt verlassen habe.

Am Anfang der dritten Woche erklärte der Arzt die Kranke außer Gefahr. Langsam kehrte die Farbe in die blassen Wangen zurück, in die stumpfen Augen kam wieder Leben. Aber wenn auch nach langem Kampfe der Sieg dem Leben gehört hatte, so war Maria Gabriele nicht mehr die gleiche. Ein tiefer Gram schien an ihrem Herzen zu fressen. Von Rupert wagten die Eltern nicht zu sprechen, und Maria Gabriele hatte seit ihrer Krankheit seinen Namen nicht mehr erwähnt. Als eines Tages die Zeitung berichtete, daß Rupert in der Schlacht bei Leipzig gefallen sei, wechselte Maria Gabriele die Farbe. Ihr bleiches Gesicht ließ die Eltern fürchten, daß die Krankheit, an der sie so lange gelitten, von neuem anfangen würde. Das böse Fieber kehrte jedoch nicht zurück; nur wurde Maria Gabriele jetzt noch stiller und ernster als zuvor. Alles, was sie an Rupert erinnerte, schien sie heilig zu halten: die Bücher, die ihr von ihm geschenkt worden waren, die Bildchen, die er von ihr gezeichnet, die kleinen blauen Heftchen mit den Versen, die er gedichtet und ihr von Zeit zu Zeit gesandt hatte. Maria Gabriele schien in ihrem Schmerz glücklich zu sein.

Bald darauf wurde die Familie von einem anderen Schlag getroffen. Der Graf starb. Maria Gabriele hätte es vorgezogen, nach dem Tode ihres Vaters still für sich weiter auf dem Lande zu leben. Allein ihre Mutter drang in sie, das Gut zu verlassen, weil sie selbst, so behauptete sie, sich nun in dem Schlosse sehr einsam fühle, in dem sie seit ihrer Hochzeit mit ihrem Mann gelebt habe. Der wahre Grund war jedoch ihre Hoffnung, daß eine andere Lebensweise und die Vergnügen, die eine große Stadt bot, ihrer Tochter gut tun und vielleicht mit der Zeit ihren ernsten Sinn ändern würden. Maria Gabriele hatte geschworen, sich niemals von ihrer Mutter zu trennen, und so zogen die beiden Frauen in die Provinzhauptstadt, wo die Familie ein großes Haus besaß.

---

ihren ernsten Sinn her serious disposition
zogen moved

hatte . . . bestimmt had named
die Erbin the heiress
das Vermögen the fortune (3)
darum therefore
die . . . galt who was considered
. . . darstellte represented
da since
der Reichtum the wealth (2)
fehlte es nicht an there was no lack of
die danach strebten who strove
[**streben** to strive, to endeavor (3)]
ihre her
melancholisch melancholy (3)
die Züge the features
zart delicate
[**zart** tender, delicate (3)]
die Haut the skin (3)
die . . . gegolten hätten which would have been considered
inner inner (3)
in den Augen aller in the eyes of all
nur um so reizender all the more charming
da sie since she
niemand . . . hatte erfahren können no one had been able to learn
das Geringste the slightest bit
der Neid the envy (3)
die Erbin the heiress (2)
auf ihre Seite zu bringen to bring over to her side
die Einladung the invitation (2)
wechselten alternated
Hauskonzerte private concerts
man machte Besuche one paid visits
und gab Feste and gave parties
[**das Fest, die Feste** the feast, celebration, festival (4)]
die Ungeduld the impatience (3)

allein but
sie machte keinem she gave no one

war . . . geschlagen worden had been defeated
von Preußen by Prussia
im Verein mit in alliance with
[**der Verein, die Vereine** the association, club (2)]
die Macht the power
[**die Macht, die Mächte** the power (3)]
unter denen, die among those who
ostpreußisch East Prussian
ein Artilleriehauptmann an artillery captain
[**die Artillerie** the artillery (2)]
[**der Hauptmann, die Hauptleute** the captain (4)]

4.

Der Graf hatte Maria Gabriele als Erbin seines großen Vermögens bestimmt. Es war darum kein Wunder, daß sie, die als das reichste Mädchen der Provinz galt, in kurzer Zeit das Ziel der Wünsche aller Mütter der höheren Gesellschaft darstellte, die ihre Söhne gut verheiratet sehen wollten. Da Maria Gabriele außer ihrem Reichtum noch jung und schön war, fehlte es nicht an Männern, die danach strebten, ihr zu gefallen und sie als ihre Frau in ein neues Heim zu führen. Ihre ernsten, melancholischen Züge und die zarte, blasse Farbe ihrer Haut, die bei anderen Mädchen als Zeichen einer inneren Krankheit gegolten hätten, machten Maria Gabriele in den Augen aller nur um so reizender und interessanter, da sie in ihrem Herzen ein Geheimnis zu tragen schien, von dem bisher niemand das Geringste hatte erfahren können. Voller Hoffnung und Neid entwickelte jede der Mütter ihren eigenen Plan, die reiche Erbin auf ihre Seite zu bringen. Eine Einladung folgte der anderen, Bälle wechselten mit Hauskonzerten, man machte Besuche und gab Feste. Jeder beobachtete den anderen und erwartete mit Ungeduld den Helden, dem es gelingen würde, das Herz der schönen Maria Gabriele für sich zu gewinnen.

Allein es geschah nichts. Maria Gabriele konnte niemanden hindern, sie zu lieben; aber sie machte keinem die geringste Hoffnung. Die Mutter versuchte manchmal, mit ihr zu reden und ihren Sinn zu ändern; doch Maria Gabriele schüttelte nur schweigend den Kopf.

So gingen zwei Jahre vorüber. Nach all seinen Siegen war Napoleon endlich von Preußen im Verein mit Wellingtons Truppen bei Waterloo geschlagen worden, die Macht des großen Kaisers war gebrochen, ganz Europa atmete wieder frei, die Soldaten wurden nach Haus geschickt. Unter denen, die in die ostpreußische Hauptstadt zurückkehrten, befand sich auch ein gewisser Graf Burkhard, ein Artilleriehauptmann, den

der Onkel the uncle (3)
die Tante the aunt (3)
eingeladen hatten had invited
[**ein-laden, er lädt ein, lud ein, hat eingeladen** to invite (3)]
er sich . . . zurückzöge he withdrew
[**zurück-ziehen** to withdraw (2)]

fort away
zum Gegenstand the topic
die Unterhaltung the conversation (2)
er habe he had
man sie kaum mehr hätte zählen können one could no longer have counted them
kurz in short
ein Gegenstand an object
stundenlang for hours
gemischt mixed
was immer whatever
im Verein mit in combination with
das Wesen the character
zum Ziel the object
manches Mädchenherzens of many a girl's heart
wären nicht bereit gewesen would not have been ready
Fehler failings
[**der Fehler, die Fehler** the mistake, error (4)]
er . . . zugewandt hätte had turned . . . to
[**zu-wenden** to turn to]
allein but
ihm zu Ehren in his honor
die Gegenwart the presence
die Art the manner
waren . . . lange . . . spazierengegangen had . . . taken a long walk
[**spazieren-gehen** to go for a walk (3)]
entzünden to kindle (3)
reif mature
[**reif** ripe, mature (3)]
erfahren genug experienced enough
[**erfahren** experienced]
um zu merken to notice (4)
die Gunst the favor (3)
seit langem for a long time

sein Onkel und seine Tante, eine alte Freundin von Maria Gabrieles Mutter, eingeladen hatten, als ihr Gast einige Wochen bei ihnen zu wohnen und die Vergnügen der Hauptstadt zu genießen, bevor er sich auf sein in der Nähe gelegenes Gut zurückzöge.

Obgleich Graf Burkhard einige Jahre fort gewesen war, hatte ihn doch niemand vergessen. Das wilde Leben, das er in seiner Jugend geführt, hatte ihn damals zum Gegenstand mancher Unterhaltung gemacht; er habe, so sagte man, so viele Herzen gebrochen, daß man sie kaum mehr hätte zählen können. Kurz, in der Person des Grafen war nun ein Gegenstand des Interesses in die Stadt gekommen, über den besonders die jungen Damen der höheren Gesellschaft stundenlang flüstern konnten, während die Eltern, an seine wilde Jugend denkend, ihn mit gemischten Gefühlen beobachteten und in Sorge um ihre Töchter lebten. Was immer man jedoch von seiner Vergangenheit erzählte, schien ihm in den Augen der Mädchen nicht zu schaden. Sein früheres Leben im Verein mit seinem jetzt so ernsten Wesen, seine melancholischen braunen Augen, in denen noch das alte Feuer brannte: all dies machte ihn zum Ziel der geheimen Wünsche manches Mädchenherzens. Wie viele von ihnen wären nicht bereit gewesen, ihm seine früheren Fehler zu verzeihen, wenn er nur sein Interesse i h n e n zugewandt hätte! Allein Graf Burkhard schien nur Augen für Maria Gabriele zu haben. Sie waren einander bei einem Ball begegnet, den sein Onkel und seine Tante ihm zu Ehren gegeben hatten. In seiner Gegenwart hatte Maria Gabriele viel von ihrer ernsten Art verloren; sie hatten getanzt und waren später lange im Garten spazierengegangen. Was Maria Gabriele von da an sagte oder tat—Graf Burkhard ließ sie nicht aus den Augen. Daß sie in seinem Herzen eine Liebe entzündet hatte, die echt und reif war, darüber konnte es für Maria Gabriele bald keinen Zweifel mehr geben. Und auch er, das fühlte sie, war erfahren genug, um zu merken, daß er mehr als ihre Gunst gewonnen hatte. Mußte er nicht gehört haben, daß er der einzige war, für den sie seit langem ein so außerordentliches Interesse gezeigt hatte? Aber wenn er sie liebte,

aus welchem Grunde for what reason
erklären to dcclare
welcher Art sie auch sein mögen of whatever kind they may be
die Last the burden
[**die Last, die Lasten** the burden (2)]
das Frauenherz a woman's heart

den gewünschten Erfolg the desired effect
die Entscheidung the decision
die Erklärung the declaration
[**die Erklärung, die Erklärungen** the explanation; the declaration (2)]

das Wohnzimmer the drawing room

fand Maria Gabriele . . . sitzend found Marie Gabriele sitting
die Bank the bench
[**die Bank, die Bänke** the bench (3]
der Apfelbaum the apple tree (3)
die Sterne the stars
[**der Stern, die Sterne** the star (3)]
der Mond the moon (4)
goß poured
[**gießen, goß, hat gegossen** to pour, to shed (3)]
wie ein Wesen like a being
in Gedanken versunken sunk in thoughts
[**versinken, versank, ist versunken** to sink (3)]
küssen to kiss (4)
sie zog sie nicht zurück she did not withdraw it

warum hatte er dann bisher geschwiegen? Aus welchem Grunde hatte sie ihn noch nicht zu ihren Füßen gesehen? Was hielt ihn zurück, ihr seine Liebe zu erklären? Stolz? Ein dunkles Geheimnis? Sie mußte erfahren, warum Burkhard schwieg. Geheimnisse, welcher Art sie auch sein mögen, sind eine Last, die lange zu tragen einem Frauenherzen nicht möglich ist.

Maria Gabriele überlegte lange und beschloß, Burkhard noch mehr als zuvor zu zeigen, wie sehr er ihr gefiel, und ihn auf diese Weise vielleicht zu zwingen, sich zu erklären. Ihr Plan schien den gewünschten Erfolg zu haben. Burkhards Augen begannen, ihr mit einem solchen Feuer zu folgen, daß sie endlich vor dem Augenblick der Entscheidung zu stehen glaubte. Mit Ungeduld erwartete sie die romantische Erklärung seiner Liebe, die nun jeden Augenblick kommen mußte.

Sie hatte sich nicht geirrt. Eines Abends, als die Mutter im Wohnzimmer saß und Briefe schrieb, trat Burkhard ein und fragte sofort nach Maria Gabriele. „Sie ist draußen im Garten", antwortete die Alte; „gehen Sie zu ihr, ich werde Sie hier erwarten." Burkhard ging hinaus. „Endlich!" murmelte die alte Gräfin.

5.

Burkhard fand Maria Gabriele auf einer Bank unter dem blühenden Apfelbaum sitzend. Ein leichter Wind bewegte die Blätter, die Sterne glänzten, der Mond goß sein blasses Licht durch die Zweige und ließ die zarte Gestalt des Mädchens in Burkhards Augen wie ein Wesen aus einer anderen Welt erscheinen. Das Buch, in dem sie gelesen hatte, lag offen auf ihren Knien; in Gedanken versunken, schien sie die Ruhe und die kühle Luft des Abends zu genießen. Als sie Burkhards Schritte hörte, öffnete sie die Augen. Er stand schweigend vor ihr; sie gab ihm ein Zeichen, sich zu setzen. Er nahm ihre Hand und küßte sie; sie zog sie nicht zurück.

„Ich muß Ihnen mein Herz öffnen", begann er. „Ich liebe Sie, wie ich nie zuvor jemanden geliebt habe . . ."

ich hätte es nicht tun sollen I should not have done it

ich werde . . . müssen I shall have to
  Ihr geliebtes Bild your beloved image
zugleich at the same time
bleibt mir noch there remains for me
  das . . . bildet which forms
    [**bilden** to form; to educate (4)]
  voneinander from each other

war schon immer da has always existed
  nie hätte ich . . . werden können I could never have become

der Trost the consolation (2)
daß Sie bereit gewesen wären that you would have been prepared

um Gottes willen for heaven's sake

Sie . . . geworden wären you would have become
  die Meine mine

fahren Sie fort continue
    [**fort-fahren** to continue; to go away, to drive away (3)]
der Gefallen the favor (4)
  sprechen Sie weiter continue

achtzehnhundertzwölf 1812
Tilsit Tilsit (city in East Prussia)
  das Regiment the regiment (2)
das Nest the village
    [**das Nest, die Nester** the nest; small town, small village (3)]

Ein zartes Rot bedeckte Maria Gabrieles Wangen. Sie unterbrach ihn. „Es war nicht recht von mir, daß ich Ihnen erlaubte, mich so oft zu sehen“, sagte sie; „ich hätte es nicht tun sollen . . .“

„Es ist zu spät“, erwiderte er; „ich kann nicht länger schweigen. Seit ich Sie kenne, habe ich nur für Sie gelebt. Ich werde fortgehen müssen, aber ich weiß, daß Ihr geliebtes Bild mir überallhin folgen wird. Der Gedanke an Sie wird für immer der tiefste Schmerz und zugleich die einzige Freude meines Lebens sein. Doch ehe ich Sie verlasse, bleibt mir noch eine schwere Pflicht: Sie müssen das schreckliche Geheimnis erfahren, das zwischen Ihnen und mir eine Mauer bildet, die uns ewig voneinander trennen muß. Ach, ich bin . . .“

„Diese Mauer war schon immer da“, unterbrach ihn Maria Gabriele; „nie hätte ich Ihre Frau werden können, denn . . .“

„Ich weiß“, antwortete Burkhard leise; „ich weiß, daß Sie geliebt haben, aber ich dachte, daß sein Tod und die lange Zeit, die inzwischen . . . Oh, nehmen Sie mir nicht meinen letzten Trost! Lassen Sie mich glauben, daß Sie bereit gewesen wären, mich glücklich zu machen, wenn ich Sie gebeten hätte, meine Frau zu werden! Lassen Sie mich . . .“

„Schweigen Sie, um Gottes willen, schweigen Sie!“ rief Maria Gabriele. „Sie brechen mir das Herz!“

„Ja, ich weiß es“, erwiderte Burkhard, „ich fühle es, daß Sie die Meine geworden wären, aber ich, der unglücklichste aller Menschen, ich bin–schon verheiratet.“

Maria Gabriele sah ihn erstaunt an.

„Ja, verheiratet“, sagte er; „aber ich weiß nicht, mit wem. Ich kenne meine Frau nicht, ich weiß nicht, wo sie ist und ob ich sie je wiedersehen werde.“

„Was sagen Sie da?“ rief Maria Gabriele. „Wie ist das möglich? Aber fahren Sie fort, ich werde Ihnen dann nachher erzählen . . . Tun Sie mir den Gefallen, sprechen Sie weiter!“

„Es war im Winter des Jahres 1812 (achtzehnhundertzwölf)“, erzählte Burkhard. „Ich befand mich auf dem Wege nach Tilsit, wo mein Regiment stand. Eines Abends kam ich spät in irgendeinem Nest auf dem Lande an. Ich durfte keine Zeit

die Poststation the stagecoach station
[**die Post** the post, post office]
der Postmeister the postmaster
[**der Meister, die Meister** the master (3)]
rieten mir advised me
[**raten, er rät, riet, hat geraten** to advise, to counsel (2)]
allein but
unruhig restless (2)
mir schien it seemed to me
mich vorwärtsstieße were pushing me forward
man warnte mich I was warned
[**warnen** to warn (3)]
ich befahl I gave the order
[**befehlen, er befiehlt, befahl, hat befohlen** to order, to command (4)]
das Eis the ice (3)
gefroren frozen
der Bach the brook
[**der Bach, die Bäche** the brook (3)]
bog turned
[**biegen, bog, hat/ist gebogen** to bend, to turn (4)]
wir . . . hätten hinauffahren müssen we would have had to go up
unbekannt unknown
und vor der and in front of which
hin und her to and fro (3)
wo sind Sie . . . geblieben? where have you been . . .?
Gott sei Dank! thank God!
unser Fräulein our young lady
wäre beinahe gestorben could almost have died
[**beinahe** almost (3)]
die Braut the bride (3)
der Altar the altar
[**der Altar, die Altäre**]
ich stellte mich I took my place
wandte . . . zu turned . . . to
[**zu-wenden** to turn to (2)]
erschrocken in shock

verlieren und hatte eben auf der Poststation frische Pferde bestellt, um sofort weiterzureisen, als es dicht zu schneien begann. Der Postmeister und seine Leute rieten mir, bis zum Morgen zu warten. Allein ich konnte mich nicht entschließen, dem Rate zu folgen. Ich war unruhig; mir schien, als ob eine geheime Macht mich vorwärtsstieße. Der furchtbare Sturm hörte nicht auf, man warnte mich, aber ich befahl, die Pferde zu wechseln und weiterzufahren. Mein Diener verlor bald die Richtung. Die Straße war von hohem Schnee bedeckt. Nach kurzer Zeit wußten wir, daß wir sie verlassen haben mußten, ohne es gemerkt zu haben. Wir beschlossen, auf dem Eis eines gefrorenen Baches zu fahren, dessen Lauf mein Diener zu kennen schien. Er hatte sich geirrt. Der Bach bog plötzlich in eine andere Richtung; wir fanden die Stelle nicht, wo wir wieder auf die Straße hätten hinauffahren müssen. So kamen wir in eine unbekannte Landschaft. Der Sturm hörte nicht auf. Da erblickte ich plötzlich ein schwaches Licht. Ich befahl, ihm zu folgen. Es leitete uns in ein Dorf. Das Licht kam aus der Kirche, deren Tür offenstand und vor der einige Schlitten warteten. Zwei Männer liefen hin und her. ‚Hierher! Hierher!' rief eine Stimme. Ich stieg aus. ‚Wo sind Sie so lange geblieben?' fragte mich jemand; ‚der Pfarrer weiß nicht, was er tun soll. Wir wollten schon zurückfahren. Beeilen Sie sich!' Von Kopf bis zu Fuß mit Schnee bedeckt, trat ich in die Kirche, in der nur zwei oder drei Kerzen brannten. ‚Gott sei Dank, daß Sie endlich gekommen sind', sagte eine junge Person in der Kleidung eines Dienstmädchens; ‚unser Fräulein wäre beinahe gestorben.'— ‚Soll ich anfangen?' fragte mich der Pfarrer.—‚Fangen Sie an!' entgegnete ich. Zwei Männer halfen der Braut und führten sie zum Altar. Sie schien so schwach zu sein, daß man sie halten mußte. Ich stellte mich neben sie. Die Trauung begann, der Pfarrer beeilte sich, wir wurden Mann und Weib. ‚Küssen Sie sich jetzt!' sagte der Pfarrer. Meine Frau wandte mir ihr blasses Gesicht zu. Es schien hübsch zu sein. Ich wollte sie küssen. ‚Oh Gott, das ist er ja gar nicht!' schrie sie und fiel wie tot zu Boden. Die Zeugen blickten mich erschrocken an. Ich drehte mich um, stürzte aus der Kirche und warf mich in

fahr los! drive away!

[**los-fahren** to drive away, to drive off]

jagte . . . hinaus raced out

die Poststation the stagecoach station (2)

[**die Post** the post, post office (2)]

ich abgefahren war I had left

[**ab-fahren** to leave, to depart (2)]

zu jener Zeit at that time

so wenig ernst so lightly

[**etwas ernst nehmen** to take something seriously]

bald danach soon after that

Sie sind es also gewesen so it was you

den Schlitten. ‚Fahr los!' rief ich, und mein Diener jagte die Pferde in die Nacht hinaus."

„Mein Gott!" flüsterte Maria Gabriele. „Und Sie wissen nicht, was aus Ihrer armen Frau geworden ist?"

„Nein, ich weiß es nicht", antwortete Burkhard. „Ich weiß nicht, wie das Dorf hieß, und ich erinnere mich nicht, von welcher Poststation ich abgefahren war. Zu jener Zeit nahm ich mein Leben so wenig ernst, daß ich einschlief, nachdem ich die Kirche verlassen hatte. Erst am Morgen wachte ich wieder auf. Mein Diener, der mich damals begleitete, ist bald danach in der Schlacht gefallen, so daß ich nicht hoffen kann, je zu erfahren, mit wem . . ."

„Mein Gott, mein Gott", sagte Maria Gabriele; „Sie sind es also gewesen! Und Sie erkennen mich nicht?"

Questions

QUESTIONS FOR 1A

Directions: Give simple German answers in complete sentences and, if possible, in main clauses. Take your basic answers directly from the text.

Caution: Do not use "because" clauses in Questions 4, 19, and 26.

PART (1). 1. Wo steht der Igel? 2. Was raucht er? 3. Ist der Morgen auch wunderbar für seine Frau? 4. Warum nicht? 5. Wie lange arbeitet der Igel? 6. Was braucht ein Mann am Sonntag nicht zu tun? 7. Wer (*who*) ist auch auf dem Felde? 8. Was macht der Hase auf dem Felde? 9. Was denkt der Hase? 10. Wie grüßt der Igel den Hasen?

PART (2) 11. Ist der Hase höflich zu dem Igel? 12. Was sagt er so unfreundlich zu dem Igel? (*Three answers*) 13. Was will der Igel auf dem Feld sehen? 14. Was macht den Igel so böse? 15. Was glaubt der Igel? 16. Was antwortet der Hase? 17. Worum (*for what*) will der Hase wetten? („Er will um _____ wetten.") 18. Trinkt der Igel Wein? 19. Warum wettet er nicht um Alkohol? („Er ist _____.") 20. Um wieviel will er wetten? 21. Ist das dem Hasen zu viel?

PART (3). 22. Kann der Igel sofort anfangen? 23. Wann wird seine Frau böse? 24. Was will sie immer wissen? 25. Ohne was kann der Igel nicht wetten? 26. Warum will der Hase nach Hause laufen? („Er will _____ holen.") 27. Was sagt der Igel zu seiner Frau, wie (*when*) er nach Hause kommt? (*Two answers*) 28. Was erzählt der Igel unterwegs seiner Frau? 29. Wohin führt der Igel seine Frau? 30. Wie lange wartet der Hase schon? 31. Wer läuft rechts, und wer läuft links?

PART (4). 32. Wie schnell rennt der Hase? 33. Wie viele (*how many*) Schritte läuft der Igel vorwärts? 34. Was tut er dann? 35. Was ruft die Frau des Igels? 36. Was glaubt der Hase? 37. Wo bleibt die Frau des Igels? 38. Was schreit der Hase ganz laut? 39. Wievielmal (*how many times*) rennt der Hase? (*Count:* „Er rennt einmal, zweimal, ____.") 40. Wie weit (*far*) kommt er beim zwölften Mal? 41. Wieviel Mark hat der Igel jetzt? 42. Was sagt der Igel zufrieden zu seiner Frau?

QUESTIONS FOR 1B

PART (1). 1. Wo steht der Esel? 2. Warum ist er schwach und müde? 3. Warum kann er zu Hause nicht mehr arbeiten? 4. Wie alt ist er schon? 5. Was sieht der Esel sofort, als (*when*) der Hund kommt? 6. Warum geht der Hund ganz langsam? 7. Was muß der Hund tun, wenn jemand kommt? 8. Was hat der Herr des Hundes im Haus? 9. Ist die Nase des Hundes noch gut? Und wie ist seine Stimme? 10. Gibt sein Herr ihm genug zu essen? 11. Was tut der Schmied vielleicht, wenn Diebe oder Räuber sein Geld stehlen? 12. Was für einen (*what kind of*) Wunsch hat der Hund? („Er sagt: ‚Ich möchte ____.' ") 13. Was hofft der Esel zu finden?

PART (2). 14. Wen (*whom*) sehen die zwei Freunde am Wege sitzen? 15. Was für ein (*what kind of*) Gesicht macht die Katze? 16. Was antwortet die Katze dem Esel zuerst? 17. Warum kann sie keine Mäuse mehr fangen? 18. Sie ist müde. Was möchte sie tun? („Ich möchte ____.") 19. Warum will ihre Herrin sie nicht länger behalten? 20. Was ist die Katze von Natur, und was tut sie gern? 21. Was weiß jeder, wenn die Katze den Mund aufmacht? 22. Was ist bitter? 23. Was weiß jeder von (*about*) Katzen? 24. Wann möchte die Katze lachen? („Wenn sie ____ denkt.") 25. Was will sie nicht zeigen? 26. Warum müssen die zwei Freunde weitergehen?

PART (3). 27. Was hören und sehen die drei Freunde nach einer Weile? 28. Wo sitzt der Hahn? 29. Was macht er dort? 30. Was singt er? 31. Wie alt ist der Hahn? 32. Was will seine Herrin mit ihm tun? 33. Gefällt ihm das? 34. Was möchte er tun, bevor er sterben muß? („Er möchte ____.") 35. Was wissen die drei Freunde sofort? 36. Was für eine (*what kind of*) Stimme hat der Hahn? 37. Warum schreit der Hahn „Herrlich!"?

PART (4). 38. Wohin kommen die vier Freunde? 39. Wie lange müssen sie dort warten? 40. (a) Was tun der Esel und der Hund? (b) Was tut die Katze? (c) Was tut der Hahn? 41. Was sieht der Hahn zwischen den Bäumen? 42. Woher (*from where*) kommt das Licht?

43. Was für (*what kind of*) Menschen leben allein in einem großen Wald? 44. Der Esel geht zur Tür. Was tut er dort? 45. Was steht im Zimmer? 46. Was liegt mitten auf dem Tisch? 47. Was tun die Männer? 48. Was liegt vor ihnen auf dem Tisch? 49. Was sagen die anderen drei Freunde? 50. Was tun die vier Freunde dann? (a) der Esel, (b) der Hund, (c) die Katze, (d) der Hahn. 51. Was zeigen sie nun? 52. Wohin fallen sie alle zusammen? 53. Was glauben die Räuber? 54. Wie schnell rennen sie?

QUESTIONS FOR 2A

PART (1). 1. Aus welcher Zeit ist die Erzählung? 2. Was machen die drei jungen Männer im Gasthaus? 3. Wo findet sie die Morgensonne jeden Tag? 4. Was hören sie draußen auf der Straße? 5. Wer folgt dem Leichenwagen? 6. Wer ist der Tote? 7. Was liegt jetzt vor den Frauen? 8. Was möchte der zweite junge Mann die ganze Zeit tun? 9. Was will der dritte junge Mann mit dem Tod tun? 10. Was beschließen die drei jungen Leute?

PART (2). 11. Was sagt der Wirt, als die drei das Gasthaus verlassen? 12. Wann treffen sie den alten Mann? 13. Beschreiben Sie (*describe*) den alten Mann! 14. Was fragt der erste den alten Mann? 15. Worum (*for what*) bittet der alte Mann den Tod? 16. Warum will der Tod den Alten nicht nehmen? 17. Warum—so denkt der dritte—läßt der Tod den alten Mann so lange leben? 18. Was wollen die drei mit dem Alten tun, wenn er ihnen nicht sogleich sagt, wo der Tod ist? 19. Wo werden die drei jungen Leute den Tod finden? 20. Was macht der Tod dort?

PART (3). 21. Wie schnell laufen die drei? 22. Was sehen sie von fern? 23. Warum gehen sie langsam und leise? 24. Was finden sie statt des Todes? 25. Wovon (*of what*) träumen sie? 26. Was werden die Leute glauben, wenn sie die drei mit dem Geld in die Stadt gehen sehen? 27. Was müssen sie tun, damit (*so that*) niemand sie sieht? 28. Warum sollen zwei bei dem Schatz bleiben? 29. Was soll der dritte in der Stadt machen? 30. Wer soll in die Stadt gehen?

PART (4). 31. Was bekommt jeder, wenn sie das Geld in drei gleiche Teile teilen? 32. Was versteht der andere nicht? 33. Was soll der zweite tun, wenn der Freund aus der Stadt zurückkehrt? 34. Was soll der älteste dann tun? 35. Was wiegt schwerer als die Liebe zum Freund? 36. Was beschließen beide? 37. Was verlangt der jüngste in der Apotheke? 38. Was macht er mit dem Gift? 39. Was macht er mit der dritten Flasche? 40. Was beschließen die zwei Freunde, bevor sie an die Arbeit gehen? 41. Worauf (*on what*) scheint das Licht der Sonne am nächsten Morgen?

QUESTIONS FOR 2B

PART (1). 1. Für wen kaufen wir Geschenke im Ausland? 2. Warum sind Dinge, die wir im Ausland kaufen, gut als (*as*) Geschenke? 3. Wieviel Geld haben wir am Ende der Ferien in unseren Taschen? 4. Was wartet auf uns an der Grenze? 5. Was macht die Polizei an der Grenze? 6. Was fragen uns die Zollbeamten? 7. Was müssen wir für die Zollbeamten oft aufmachen? 8. Wann müssen wir Zoll bezahlen? 9. Wie wissen die Zollbeamten, wieviel eine gewisse Ware wert ist? 10. Was kann geschehen, wenn wir falsche Preise nennen?

PART (2). 11. Wie sind die Preise in Europa um das Jahr achtzehnhundertfünfzehn? 12. Wann ist eine Liste zwecklos? 13. Ist das Zollsystem damals genau und kompliziert? 14. Was muß ein deutscher Geschäftsmann an der deutschen Grenze erklären? 15. Warum gelten Papiere oder Rechnungen nicht? 16. Wann geht alles gut? 17. Welches Recht hat der Beamte, wenn ein Kaufmann einen falschen Preis nennt? 18. Was darf der Kaufmann verlangen, wenn der Beamte seine Waren kauft? 19. Was tun die Beamten mit den Waren, die sie so billig kaufen? 20. Wer verliert bei diesem System?

PART (3). 21. Welchen Wert haben die zwei Kästen Handschuhe? 22. Wohin fährt der schlaue Kaufmann? 23. Wie lange arbeitet der Kaufmann in seinem Zimmer? 24. Wovon (*of what*) träumt der Kaufmann? 25. Wohin fährt der Kaufmann mit dem Kasten? 26. Was sieht der Beamte gleich? 27. Wieviel bezahlt der Beamte dem Kaufmann für die Handschuhe? 28. Was zeigt das Gesicht des Kaufmanns nicht? 29. Was macht der Kaufmann, als (*when*) er ins Gasthaus zurückkommt? 30. Was geschieht, als (*when*) er mit dem zweiten Kasten zur Grenze kommt? 31. Was zählen die beiden Beamten schon im voraus?

PART (4). 32. Warum geht der Kaufmann nicht selbst zum Verkauf? 33. Warum liegen die Waren offen auf dem Tisch? 34. Warum hält der Beamte ein Paar Handschuhe hoch? 35. Was stimmt nicht mit den Handschuhen, die der Zollbeamte verkaufen will? 36. Wieviel bietet der Freund des Kaufmanns für die Handschuhe? 37. Wem wird er sie vielleicht verkaufen? 38. Wieviel bezahlt der Freund für den zweiten Kasten im zweiten Zollamt? 39. Wann und wo trifft der

Kaufmann seinen Freund wieder? 40. Was macht der Kaufmann mit den Handschuhen in den zwei Kästen? 41. Wieviel Profit macht der Kaufmann?

QUESTIONS FOR 3A

PART (1). 1. Wie klein war das Königreich des Prinzen? 2. Wofür (*for what*) war sein Königreich groß genug? 3. Wen möchte der Prinz heiraten? 4. Wann blühte der Rosenbusch des Prinzen? 5. Wie wunderbar war die Rose? 6. Wie schön sang die Nachtigall? 7. Was machte die Prinzessin, als der Wagen in den Hof fuhr? 8. Warum wollte die Prinzessin die Rose nicht haben? 9. Woran (*of what*) erinnerte die Stimme der Nachtigall den Kaiser? 10. Was gestattete die Prinzessin dem Prinzen nicht?

PART (2). 11. Was tat der Prinz mit seinem Gesicht? 12. Was zog er an? 13. Was fragte er den Kaiser? 14. Wo war das Zimmer des Prinzen? 15. Was machte der Prinz in der Nacht? 16. Beschreiben Sie (*describe*) den Topf! 17. Was konnte man riechen, wenn man den Finger in den Topf hielt? 18. Worauf (*on what*) und wie spielte die Prinzessin das Liedchen? 19. Was verlangte der Schweinehirt für den Topf? 20. Was machten die Hofdamen, als die Prinzessin dem Prinzen die zehn Küsse gab?

PART (3). 21. Was wußte man nun von jeder Wohnung in der Stadt? 22. Was sagte die Prinzessin plötzlich zu den Hofdamen? 23. Was für ein Instrument machte der Schweinehirt diesmal? 24. Was tat jeder, der die Walzer und Polkas hörte? 25. Was verlangte der Prinz für die Pfeife? 26. Welche Aufgabe hatte die Prinzessin als Tochter des Kaisers? 27. Was wollte sie für die Pfeife geben? 28. Warum müssen die Hofdamen tun, was die Prinzessin ihnen befiehlt? 29. Wie lachten die Hofdamen? 30. Warum wurden die Hofdamen so müde?

PART (4). 31. Wovon (*of what*) träumte der Kaiser? 32. Was war das größte Vergnügen des Kaisers? 33. Was zog der Kaiser an? 34. Warum merkten die Hofdamen nicht, daß der Kaiser plötzlich hinter ihnen stand? 35. Warum wurde er rot vor Zorn? 36. In welchem Augenblick schlug der Kaiser den Prinzen und die Prinzessin an den Kopf? 37. Was befahl der Kaiser seinen Soldaten? 38. Worüber (*about what*) klagte die Prinzessin? 39. Was machte der Schweinehirt hinter dem Baum? 40. Was konnte die Prinzessin jetzt draußen im Regen tun?

QUESTIONS FOR 3B

PART (1). 1. Für wen hielt man Tobias Puff? 2. Warum fand Tobias Puff es nicht schwer, sein tägliches Brot zu verdienen? 3. Was für Leute brauchte Tobias Puff? 4. Warum war Tobias Puff einem Buchhalter ähnlich? 5. Wie lange ging es Tobias Puff ganz gut? 6. Wie lange saß er auf Kosten des Staates im Gefängnis? 7. Wie bildete Tobias Puff seinen Geist im Gefängnis? 8. Warum war Tobias Puff selbst im Gefängnis nie ohne Geld? 9. Was konnte man im Gefängnis nicht werden? 10. Was war Tobias Puffs Motto?

PART (2). 11. Was war Tobias Puff, als diese Geschichte anfängt? 12. Was meinte Tobias Puff, wenn er von Geld sprach? 13. Wieviel Geld hatte er für sich selbst? 14. Wann ging Tobias Puff nach Hause? 15. Warum schien die Gestalt ein Freund zu sein? 16. Was konnte Tobias Puff von dem alten Mann sehen? 17. Was gab Tobias Puff dem alten Mann? 18. Was wollte der Alte Tobias Puff verkaufen? 19. Warum war es eine ungewöhnliche Zeitung? 20. Warum wagte Tobias Puff nicht zu laufen?

PART (3). 21. Wie wußte Tobias Puff, daß das Datum der Zeitung stimmte? 22. Wohin ging Tobias Puff? 23. Wie lange wartete er dort, bevor er die Zeitung öffnete? 24. Warum sollte Tobias Puff keinen Alkohol trinken? 25. Was sollte er statt Alkohol trinken? 26. Was tat Tobias Puff, als der Kellner kam? 27. Welche Rennen zählten wirklich? 28. Wie konnte er noch größere Summen setzen, wenn er wollte? 29. Wovon (*of what*) träumte Tobias Puff? 30. Welche Worte wiederholte die Stimme immer wieder?

PART (4). 31. Wie fühlte sich Tobias Puff am Morgen? 32. Wohin schrieb Tobias Puff die Telephonnummern? 33. Was für einen Platz fand Tobias Puff? 34. Was tat Tobias Puff nach dem ersten Rennen? 35. Was mochten die Buchmacher in der Stadt machen, und warum? 36. Warum interessierten Tobias Puff die anderen Rennen nicht? 37. Was beobachtete er während der anderen Rennen? 38. Was wußte Tobias Puff nach dem letzten Rennen? 39. Warum hatte er keine Lust, mit den anderen Leuten im Zug zu sprechen? 40. Wie versuchten seine Nachbarn ihm zu helfen?

QUESTIONS FOR 4A

PART (1). 1. Wo lebte Jans? 2. Warum wollte Jans Jens kennenlernen? 3. Wo trafen sich Jans und Jens? 4. Wann entdeckte Jans, daß seine Uhr fehlte? 5. Wann entdeckte Jens, daß seine Brieftasche fort war? 6. Was hatte Jans mehr als einmal gewünscht? 7. Warum sollte Jens in das Land fahren, in dem Jans lebte? 8. Was nahmen Jans und Jens mit, bevor sie das Gasthaus verließen? 9. Was taten sie, als sie in die Hauptstadt kamen? 10. Auf welche Weise gelang es ihnen, in das Schatzhaus zu dringen?

PART (2). 11. Wann wurde der König rot vor Zorn und Ärger? 12. Was konnten die Soldaten dem König nicht sagen? 13. Was soll der König befehlen, um die Diebe zu fangen? 14. Was konnten die Bürger am nächsten Tag kaufen? 15. Warum konnte die Marktpolizei den Mann nicht fangen? 16. Warum machte der alte Dieb gewisse Zeichen an die Türen? 17. Was hatte Jens in Jans' Haus getan? 18. Was tat Jens, als er das Zeichen an der Haustür sah? 19. Was wußten die Soldaten am Morgen nicht?

PART (3). 20. Was taten Jans und Jens, als sie kein Geld mehr hatten? 21. Was geschah mit Jans? 22. Was sah Jens, als er zu dem Loch kam? 23. Warum schnitt er Jans den Kopf ab? 24. Warum nahm er den Kopf mit? 25. Was erblickte der König, als er an das Loch trat? 26. Wie wird man wissen, wo die Frau des Toten wohnt? 27. Was sah die Frau, als sie ans Fenster trat? 28. Was wußte Jens sofort, als er die Frau laut um ihren Mann klagen hörte? 29. Was machte er mit den Tassen und Tellern? 30. Was beschloß der König zu tun?

PART (4). 31. Wie wollte der König das Problem in dieser Nacht lösen? 32. Was tat er, bevor er sich ins Bett legte? 33. Wie lange wartete Jens? 34. Was tat er dann? 35. Was erschien um Mitternacht draußen am Fenster? 36. Wer mußte es sein? 37. Warum mußte der Mann tot sein? 38. Warum will der König hinuntergehen? 39. Was hatte er im Garten gefunden? 40. Was sah er, als er wieder heraufkam? 41. Was tat der König, als Jens mit dem Bettuch erschien? 42. Was konnte der König nicht wissen? 43. Was geschah mit dem Geld, wenn Jens es jetzt stehlen sollte?

QUESTIONS FOR 4B

PART (1). 1. Was hatte Herrn Meierbach einige Mühe gekostet? 2. Auf welchen Gedanken sollte niemand kommen? 3. Wo war Bruno Boltes Kopf? 4. Warum hatte Bolte nicht viele Freunde? 5. Wie hatte Meierbach Bolte das Schlafmittel gegeben? 6. Was tat Meierbach, bevor er anfing, die Briefe zu suchen? 7. Worüber (*about what*) hatte Meierbach sich gewundert, als er und Bolte vor dem Richter standen? 8. Wann hatte Meierbach endlich den wahren Grund dafür (*for that*) erfahren? 9. Warum hatte Bolte es vorgezogen, die Briefe zu behalten?

Part (2). 10. Wieviel hatte Bolte für jeden Brief gefordert? 11. Was war das Beste, was Meierbach tun konnte? 12. Worum (*for what*) hatte Meierbach Bolte gebeten? 13. Was war Herrn Bolte nicht eingefallen? 14. (a) Was fand Meierbach im Schreibtisch? (b) Was fand Meierbach in dem alten Pult? 15. Was fand er in der Jacke? 16. Wo suchte er dann? 17. Warum konnte Meierbach die Briefe nicht finden? 18. Was sollte das Blatt Papier auf dem Schreibtisch beweisen? 19. Was hatte Meierbach sofort gesehen, als er Boltes Brief las?

Part (3). 20. Was machte Meierbach mit seinem Glas? 21. Warum wollte er die fast leere Flasche auf dem Tisch stehen lassen? 22. Was hatte er fast vergessen? 23. Womit (*with what*) hatte das erste Blatt von Boltes Brief zu tun? 24. Was hatte Bolte nicht gewußt? 25. Wohin legte er das zweite Blatt? 26. Warum schloß er das halboffene Fenster? 27. Was hatte Meierbach sofort getan, nachdem Bolte eingeschlafen war? 28. Was tat er, nachdem er das Gas angedreht hatte? 29. Warum wollte er zuerst Boltes Regenschirm nehmen?

Part (4). 30. Warum hatte Meierbach mit Absicht einige Lampen in seinem Haus angelassen? 31. Was tat er, bevor er ins Bett ging? 32. Was interessierte ihn heute in der Abendzeitung? 33. Wie kam ihm das Frühstück vor? 34. Warum war jetzt jeder Tag für ihn ein Festtag? 35. Wozu (*to what*) zwang er sich, bevor er die Tür aufmachte? 36. Warum entschuldigte sich der Milchmann? 37. Was geschah, als der Milchmann gerade die Rechnung unter Boltes Tür schieben wollte? 38. In welchem Augenblick sah er, daß Bolte sich bewegte? 39. Was tat Bolte, nachdem er aufgestanden war? 40. Warum wollte er die Gasgesellschaft anrufen? 41. Was konnte der Milchmann nicht verstehen?

QUESTIONS FOR 5A

Part (1). 1. Beschreiben Sie (*describe*) den Schmuggel in guten und in schlechten Zeiten! 2. Wann war eine Zeit der Not in Deutschland? 3. Warum sollen Sie diese schrecklichen Zustände kennenlernen? 4. Warum gab es nicht genug Häuser? 5. Warum waren die Zimmer kalt? 6. Warum ist der Junge froh, daß sein Bruder gestorben ist? 7. Was suchten die Menschen in den Wäldern und auf den Landstraßen? 8. Was war mit dem berühmten deutschen Bier geschehen? 9. Was konnte man in den Geschäften nicht kaufen? 10. Warum war es nicht so schlimm, zwei oder drei Monate im Gefängnis zu sitzen? 11. Warum ging es der Schweiz damals ziemlich gut?

Part (2). 12. Beschreiben Sie (*describe*) das Gepäck der jungen Dame! 13. Was wollte der Herr mit der Hutschachtel der jungen Dame machen? 14. Was dachten die anderen Reisenden, als die junge Dame die Hutschachtel bei sich behalten wollte? 15. Wohin stellte das Fräulein die Schachtel? 16. Beschreiben Sie (*describe*) den dicken Herrn! 17. Was machte er mit seinem Taschentuch? 18. Wie wußte jeder, daß jemand im Abteil Kaffee hatte? 19. Wann hatte es begonnen, nach Kaffee zu riechen? 20. Wo hatte die Dame den Kaffee versteckt? 21. Wem hatte die Dame den Kaffee versprochen?

Part (3). 22. Was zeigte die klare, laute Stimme des Zollbeamten? 23. Was sagte der Herr mit dem Ziegenbart zu dem Zollbeamten? 24. Welches Recht hat der Zollbeamte? 25. Warum ist der Zollbeamte nicht so streng, wie er eigentlich sein sollte? 26. Wieviel Zoll mußte die junge Dame zahlen? 27. Wie versuchte ihr Nachbar, sie zu trösten, als sie zu weinen begann? 28. Warum gibt der Herr mit dem Ziegenbart der Dame Kaffee? 29. Was gibt er ihr noch außer dem Kaffee? 30. Wann bekommt immer jeder Herr im Abteil von ihm eine Zigarre?

QUESTIONS FOR 5B

Part (1). 1. Was wußte Herr Müller noch nicht, als er auf den Zug sprang? 2. Wo arbeitete Herr Müller und als was? 3. Wo wohnte Herr Müller? 4. Was hatte Herr Müller im Zug gemacht, bevor er die drei Herren kennenlernte? 5. Was machten die vier Herren während der Fahrt? 6. An welchem Abend wurde Herr Müller zum Mörder? 7. Warum war Herr Müller zur Bank gegangen? 8. Warum hatte es auf der Bank so lange gedauert? 9. Was hatte er im Bahnhofsrestaurant gegessen? 10. Beschreiben Sie (*describe*) den anderen Mann im Abteil!

Part (2). 11. Um wieviel spielten sie? 12. Warum hatte Herr Müller keine Angst, um so viel zu spielen? 13. Wie lange dauerte jedes Spiel? 14. Wieviel hatte Herr Müller nach zehn Minuten verloren? 15. Was hatte Herr Müller in der Tasche? 16. Was hatten Diebe mehrere Male versucht? 17. Warum hatte Herr Müller den Revolver für seine Frau gekauft? 18. Was machte der andere Mann, nachdem Herr Müller sein ganzes Geld verloren hatte? 19. Worum (*for what*) bat Herr Müller den jungen Mann? 20. Wann schoß Herr Müller?

Part (3). 21. Was beschloß Herr Müller mit der Leiche zu tun? 22. Was machte er mit der Uhr des Toten? 23. Was mußte die Polizei glauben, wenn sie die Leiche und die Uhr fand? 24. Was nahm er aus der Brieftasche des Toten? 25. Warum konnte niemand

Herrn Müller sehen, als er die Leiche hinauswarf? 26. Bis wann wartete Herr Müller, als der Zug die Stadt erreichte? 27. Was erfährt man gewöhnlich aus der Zeitung? 28. Was stimmte nicht mit den Karten? 29. Welche Karte fehlte? 30. Wo hatte der Polizeiinspektor die Karte gefunden?

QUESTIONS FOR 6A

PART (1). 1. Wann waren die vier müde geworden? 2. Warum konnte der Esel nicht in dem Bett schlafen? 3. Wohin ging er dann? 4. Worüber (*about what*) klagte der Hund? 5. Warum zog der Hund eine Wolldecke über sich? 6. Was tat die Katze, damit kein Feuer entstand? 7. Warum schlief der Hahn in der Linde? 8. Beschreiben Sie (*describe*) das Wetter draußen im Wald! 9. Was hatten die Räuber im Haus gelassen? 10. Was tut der Räuber nicht gern um Mitternacht?

PART (2). 11. Was glaubte der Räuber zu sehen? 12. Warum entzündeten sich die Streichhölzer nicht? 13. Was waren die Kohlen, die der Räuber sah? 14. Was machte die Katze? 15. Warum stand der Hund nicht auf? 16. Was für einen Schlag gab der Esel dem Räuber? 17. Was berichtete der Räuber seinem Hauptmann (a) über die Katze? (b) über den Hund? (c) über den Esel? 18. Was wußten die vier Freunde, als niemand in der nächsten Nacht ihren Schlaf störte? 19. Was machten sie während der ersten Tage nach dem Essen?

PART (3). 20. Warum wollten die vier Freunde nicht mehr nach Bremen gehen? 21. Was fand der Esel vor dem Haus und im Wald? 22. Was fraß der Hund? 23. Worauf (*to what*) mußte die Katze aufpassen, wenn sie Honig suchte? 24. Wo fand der Hahn sein Futter? 25. Wann bildeten sie einen Musikverein? 26. Warum konnten sie nicht die richtige Musik finden? 27. Was machten sie in der ersten Hälfte der Woche? 28. Was machten sie am Sonntag? 29. Warum war das Haus gerade der richtige Ort für diese Konzerte? 30. Was geschah mit der Musik, als der Mann sie nach Bremen brachte? 31. Was hatten die vier Freunde erfunden?

QUESTIONS FOR 6B

PART (1). 1. Was hat Schopenhauer über Frauen gesagt? 2. Was will die folgende Geschichte beweisen? 3. Wo lebte Frau Piepenbrink? 4. Wie gut war es den Piepenbrinks früher gegangen? 5. Was fehlte Frau Piepenbrink nach dem Tode ihres Mannes? 6. Wozu (*for what*) genügte ihre Pension? 7. Was lehrte Frau Piepenbrink ihren Papagei? 8. Was zog sie in ihrem Garten? 9. Wo hatte man begonnen, ein Lagerhaus zu bauen? 10. Was hatte Frau Piepenbrink als junges Mädchen gewünscht?

PART (2). 11. Wann klingelte der Besucher an ihrer Tür? 12. Wer war der Besucher? 13. Warum war er gekommen? 14. Warum wollte seine Firma Frau Piepenbrinks Haus kaufen? 15. Wieviel wollte der Direktor für das Haus bieten? 16. Warum hatten die Piepenbrinks das Haus früher nicht verkaufen wollen? 17. Was machte Frau Piepenbrink am Abend? 18. Wieviel verlangte Frau Piepenbrink für das Haus am nächsten Tag? 19. Was hatte ihr der Arzt empfohlen? 20. Um welche Gunst bat Frau Piepenbrink zuerst? 21. Warum bat Frau Piepenbrink um z w e i Schiffskarten?

PART (3). 22. Wieviel war das Haus wirklich wert? 23. Was für eine Annonce ließ Frau Piepenbrink in der Zeitung erscheinen? 24. Von wem bekam sie viele Antworten? 25. Welches Mädchen wählte Frau Piepenbrink? 26. Was machte sie, nachdem sie ein junges Mädchen gefunden hatte? 27. Was konnte sie mit dem Geld machen, das sie von dem jungen Mädchen bekommen hatte? 28. Wen besuchte Frau Piepenbrink, wenn sie nach Cuxhaven zurückkehrte? 29. Warum hörten ihre Besuche jedoch bald auf? 30. Für wen hatte Frau Piepenbrink die fünfundzwanzigtausend Mark bestimmt?

QUESTIONS FOR 7A

PART (1). 1. Was berichtet diese Geschichte? 2. Wann lebte dieser Kaufmann? 3. Wie hatte das Leben alle seine Wünsche erfüllt? 4. Von wem wurde Sebastian besucht? 5. Was erfuhr Sebastian von seinem Freund? 6. Worum (*for what*) hatte Sebastians Tante den Freund gebeten? 7. Was hielt Sebastian für seine Pflicht? 8. Warum wollte seine Frau, daß er bis zum nächsten Tag wartete? 9. An was für einem Gasthaus hielten Sebastian und der Kaufmann? 10. Was tat Sebastian nach dem Abendessen? 11. Warum verließ Sebastian das Gasthaus so früh? 12. Was war Sebastian am Abend gegeben worden? 13. Wo und warum hielt er gegen Mittag? 14. Wohin wurde er von dem Polizeioffizier geführt?

PART (2). 15. Worüber (*about what*) wunderte sich Sebastian? 16. Was wurde den Soldaten befohlen? 17. Was wurde von einem Soldaten in Sebastians Reisesack entdeckt? 18. Was war mit dem Geld des toten Kaufmanns geschehen? 19. Wohin wurde Sebastian gebracht? 20. Auf welchen Tag wartete Sebastian, während er im Gefängnis lag? 21. Was schwor der Wirt? 22. Von wem wurde

Sebastian im Gefängnis besucht? 23. Wohin wurde er nach einiger Zeit gebracht? 24. Wohin wurden alle Gefangenen geführt? 25. Wann erreichten die Gefangenen die Strafkolonie?

PART (3). 26. Was verwandelte Sebastian in einen anderen Menschen? 27. Was war ihm von einem Gefangenen geschenkt worden? 28. Warum hatten ihn die Soldaten gern? 29. Warum wurde „Onkel" Sebastian zu den Beamten geschickt? 30. Warum wußte Sebastian nicht, ob seine Frau und Kinder noch lebten? 31. Wie erfuhr man, was draußen geschah? 32. Was wurde jeder neue Gefangene gefragt? 33. Beschreiben Sie (*describe*) Barnabas! 34. Warum hatte der wirkliche Dieb das Pferd im Wald versteckt? 35. Was erzählte Barnabas von Sebastians Familie?

PART (4). 36. Was sagte Sebastian, als er gebeten wurde, seine Lebensgeschichte zu erzählen? 37. Was machte Barnabas, während Sebastians Geschichte erzählt wurde? 38. Was sagte Barnabas, als Sebastians Name genannt wurde? 39. Wie wußte Sebastian, daß Barnabas etwas mit dem Mord zu tun gehabt hatte? 40. Woran dachte Sebastian in der Nacht? 41. Woran dachte Sebastian, als er zu beten versuchte? 42. Was sah Sebastian in dem Licht des Mondes? 43. Was war von Barnabas mit der Erde getan worden?

PART (5). 44. Warum brauchte Barnabas Sebastian nicht zu töten? 45. Warum sagten die Gefangenen nichts von dem Loch? 46. Warum sagte Sebastian nichts? 47. Wann mußten die Dinge so gelassen werden, wie sie waren? 48. Von wem war der Kaufmann wirklich ermordet worden? 49. Warum hatte Barnabas Sebastian nicht getötet? 50. Warum wollte Sebastian nicht mehr nach Hause gehen? 51. Was tat Barnabas nach einiger Zeit? 52. Was wurde mit dem ungewöhnlichen Fall getan? 53. Was wurde in dem Brief befohlen?

QUESTIONS FOR 7B

PART (1). 1. Was hatten die Gäste bisher am Abend gemacht? 2. Was wurde von einem der Gäste vorgeschlagen? 3. Was für eine Geschichte sollte von jedem berichtet werden? 4. Warum fehlte der Fürst während des Abendessens? 5. Wann wurde der Fürst an seine Geschichte erinnert? 6. Warum durfte der Fürst seine Geschichte endlich öffentlich erzählen? 7. Warum hatte der Graf darauf geachtet, daß niemand von seinem Haß erfuhr? 8. Wann ist die Rache am süßesten? 9. Warum war der Baron in Italien? 10. Beschreiben Sie (*describe*) das Bauernhaus! 11. Was wurde dem Grafen von einer inneren Stimme befohlen?

PART (2). 12. Wie machte der Graf ein Feuer? 13. In welcher Gefahr war er gewesen? 14. Warum war das Brett vor den Brunnen gelegt worden? 15.Warum konnte niemand aus dem Brunnen heraussteigen? 16. Von wem war der Graf zum Brunnen geführt worden? 17. Wie sah er aus, als er bei der Teegesellschaft erschien? 18. Was tat der Baron nach einer Weile? 19. Was wußte der Graf von dem Baron? 20. Warum dachte der Baron, daß der Traum des Grafen ein böser Traum war? 21. Was sah der Graf im Traum? 22. Was wußte der Graf nicht, nachdem er den Baron gerufen hatte?

PART (3). 23. Wie ging der Baron im Traum den Gang entlang? 24. Was tat der Baron, als der Graf zum dritten Mal rief? 25. Was hörte der Graf aus dem Brunnen kommen? 26. Warum konnte der Graf die Worte der Stimme nicht verstehen? 27. Was geschah, als der Graf näher schreiten wollte? 28. Was schlug der Graf nach einer Woche vor? 29. Wo aßen sie zu Mittag? 30. Welchen Zweck hatte der Graf erreicht? 31. Was machte der Graf an diesem Abend? 32. Was konnten seine Diener tun, wenn es nötig sein sollte? 33. Wann wurde der Baron zum letzten Mal gesehen? 34. Was wurde gefunden, als man nach dem Baron suchte? 35. Was brauchte von dem Fürsten nicht gesagt zu werden?

QUESTIONS FOR 8A

PART (1). 1. Wo kann man heute noch die Ruinen einer mächtigen Burg sehen? 2. Wie waren die treuen Dienste des Großvaters von dem Kaiser gelohnt worden? 3. Warum hatten die meisten Wiesen und Felder verkauft werden müssen? 4. Was hatte der einzige Erbe dem Vater versprechen müssen? 5. Warum hatte er das tun müssen? 6. Worauf (*at what*) blickte der Ritter Theobald immer mit besonderer Freude? 7. Warum war das Kloster nie reich geworden? 8. Wann würden die Mahlzeiten der Mönche ein wenig mehr Geschmack haben? 9. Was würden die Mönche wenigstens haben, wenn sie den Acker des Ritters besäßen? 10. Was trieb den Abt zur Verzweiflung?

PART (2). 11. Wann erschien der Abt auf der Burg? 12. Was hatte der Abt dem Ritter beschrieben? 13. Was kann kein Sünder von sich sagen? 14. Was wollen der Abt und seine Mönche für den Ritter tun? 15. Was soll der Ritter für das Kloster tun? 16. Was würden beide auf diese Weise für einander tun? 17. Warum konnte der Ritter den Wunsch des Abtes nicht erfüllen? 18. Warum schmeckte das Mittagessen dem Abt noch schlechter als sonst? 19.

Was tat Bruder Bonifaz in der Bibliothek, als der Abt eintrat? 20. Was für ein Papier wollte der Abt gern finden? 21. Was trug der Abt in der Tasche, als er wieder auf der Burg erschien? 22. Warum glaubte der Ritter Theobald, daß das Dokument nicht echt war?

PART (3). 23. Warum beschloß der Ritter, die Sache nicht vor Gericht zu bringen? 24. Was würde mit dem Feld geschehen, solange der Fall von dem Richter nicht entschieden war? 25. Was soll der Abt dem Ritter deshalb erlauben? 26. Was hatte der Abt während der kurzen Pause getan? 27. Warum wollte der Ritter von dem Abt gern ein kleines Dokument? 28. Wann war auf dem Acker des Ritters noch nichts zu sehen? 29. Was tat der Abt von nun an? 30. Was wuchs endlich auf dem Acker? 31. Was würden die Mönche von nun an wieder essen müssen? 32. Wann trugen die Eichen zum ersten Mal Frucht?

QUESTIONS FOR 8B

PART (1). 1. Was hatte der junge Mann als Knabe in der Schule getan? 2. Wen konnte man in dem Heer des Königs brauchen? 3. Was erklärte der Hauptmann dem jungen Mann? 4. Warum besaß der junge Mann kein Heim mehr? 5. Warum ließen seine Brüder ihn nicht bei sich wohnen? 6. Was sagten sie ihm? 7. Warum erschrak er, als er unter den Bäumen saß? 8. Beschreiben Sie den unbekannten Mann! 9. Was für Füße hatte er? 10. Was sollte der junge Mann von ihm bekommen? 11. Warum wollte er wissen, ob der junge Mann Mut hatte?

PART (2). 12. Was sah der junge Mann hinter sich? 13. Was sollte der junge Mann während der nächsten sieben Jahre tun? 14. Was wollte der Fremde dem jungen Mann geben? 15. Wann sollte der junge Mann dem Fremden gehören? 16. Was geschieht, wenn er nicht stirbt? 17. Was wollte der Teufel wirklich? 18. Warum sagte der junge Mann schließlich zu allem ja? 19. Was sollte er mit der Haut des Bären tun? 20. Beschreiben Sie den Bärenhäuter im zweiten Jahr! 21. Warum wurde er von allen Menschen gemieden? 22. Warum wurde er von den Gasthäusern nicht fortgejagt?

PART (3). 23. Warum wollte der Wirt dem Bärenhäuter nicht einmal einen Platz im Stall geben? 24. Warum änderte der Wirt seine Meinung? 25. Was mußte ihm der Bärenhäuter versprechen? 26. Was hörte der Bärenhäuter im Nebenzimmer? 27. Wen sah er dort? 28. Was hatte den alten Mann sein letztes Geld gekostet? 29. Warum hatte er die Reise gemacht? 30. Was würde der Wirt tun, wenn der Alte seine Rechnung nicht bezahlte? 31. Was war alles, was der Alte noch hatte? 32. Was wird eine der Töchter tun?

PART (4). 33. Was tat die älteste Tochter, als sie den Bärenhäuter erblickte? 34. Was sagte die zweite Tochter? 35. Warum sah der zahme Bär besser aus als der Bärenhäuter? 36. Wann würde jeder den Ausdruck der Freude auf dem Gesicht des Bärenhäuters gesehen haben? 37. Was sollte die Braut in den nächsten drei Jahren tun? 38. Was für ein Kleid wählte sie? 39. Warum wird die Hochzeit lustig sein? 40. Warum wurde der Bärenhäuter jetzt von allen gemieden? 41. Warum wurde er jetzt von jedem Gasthaus fortgeschickt? 42. Was mußte der Bärenhäuter nun essen? 43. Wann würde Gott ihm vielleicht seine Sünden verzeihen?

PART (5). 44. Wann erreichte der Bärenhäuter sein Ziel? 45. Was verlangte der Teufel von ihm? 46. Was tat der Bärenhäuter, während der Teufel Wasser holen ging? 47. Was ließ er den Teufel tun? 48. Wie sah er in der Uniform aus? 49. Für wen hielt der Vater den Bärenhäuter? 50. Was erklärte der Bärenhäuter dem Vater? 51. Warum waren die zwei ältesten Töchter fortgelaufen? 52. Wie wußte die jüngste Tochter, daß der Fremde ihr Bräutigam war? 53. Was taten die zwei Schwestern, als sie sahen, daß der Bärenhäuter die jüngste gewählt hatte? 54. Was wollte der Bärenhäuter sehen, als jemand am Abend an die Tür klopfte?

QUESTIONS FOR 9A

PART (1). 1. Wo soll diese Geschichte passiert sein? 2. Wie modern war man noch nicht geworden? 3. In welchem Augenblick fing die Geschichte an? 4. Was hatte die Kusine gesehen? 5. Was machten die Geschäftsreisenden nach dem Abendessen? 6. Warum glaubte Herr Mampe die Geschichte, die er erzählt hatte? 7. Was möchte der ältere Herr gern über den Geist wissen? 8. Wie wäre die Geschichte interessanter geworden? 9. Warum glaubte der alte Herr an Geister? 10. Wann würde er nicht an Geister glauben?

PART (2). 11. Warum mußte er die anderen um Geduld bitten? 12. Was bedeutet es, Geschäftsreisender zu sein? 13. Wovon spricht man bei einem Glas Bier, wenn man nach langer Zeit jemanden trifft? 14. Was war Albert Moser passiert? 15. Was wußte man nicht über die Art seines Todes? 16. Beschreiben Sie das Zimmer, in dem Albert Moser starb! 17. Was stellte das Bild über dem Bett dar? 18. Beschreiben Sie Albert Moser, wie er vorher gewesen war! 19. Was geschah, als der ältere Herr nach der Nummer seines Zimmers fragte und um den Schlüssel bat? 20. Was war in jenem Zimmer geschehen?

PART (3). 21. Warum mußte er in seinem Zimmer bleiben? 22. Was tat er, als er in das Zimmer kam? 23. Wann würde er jemanden im Zimmer gefunden haben? 24. Warum hatte ihn das Dienstmädchen geweckt? 25. Warum machte er die Tür auf? 26. Warum rief er nicht laut nach warmem Wasser? 27. Warum würde es so lange dauern, bis er sich rasiert hatte? 28. Wann sah er, daß sich etwas in dem Zimmer bewegte? 29. Was sah er im Spiegel? 30. Wie wußte er, daß der Mann auf dem Bett lachte? 31. Warum strich der Mann mit dem Daumen leicht über das Rasiermesser? 32. Was tat der Mann auf dem Bett einen Augenblick später? 33. Was tat der Herr im Armstuhl?

PART (4). 34. Was hatte den beiden Geschäftsreisenden das Leben gekostet? 35. Wie hatten sie sich die Kehle durchgeschnitten? 36. Um wieviel Uhr war es geschehen? 37. Warum hatte der Herr die Geschichte gerade an jenem Abend erzählt? 38. Warum war Herr Mampe plötzlich blaß geworden? 39. Was hatte der Hoteldirektor dem Herrn versprochen? 40. Warum sollte Herr Mampe nicht weiter an die Sache denken? 41. Was tat Herr Mampe? 42. Wie kam es, daß der Herr im Armstuhl sich damals nicht die Kehle durchschnitt? 43. Warum entschuldigte er sich und stand schnell auf? 44. Wann erzählte er immer seine alte Geistergeschichte?

QUESTIONS FOR 9B

PART (1). 1. Was würden die jungen Leute aus dem Brief erfahren? 2. Warum war Lisels Erfolg nicht so sicher? 3. Wie hatten die anderen ihr geholfen? 4. Wo sollte das Picknick stattfinden? 5. Wann wurde die Burg niedergebrannt? 6. Wie wußten die anderen, daß Lisel ihre Examen bestanden hatte? 7. Beschreiben Sie Lisels neues Armband! 8. Warum war die Burg ein guter Ort, um Verstecken zu spielen? 9. Warum wird Lisel wahrscheinlich die erste sein, die gefunden werden wird? 10. Was schien ihr, nachdem die Schritte aufgehört hatten?

PART (2). 11. Warum wurde Lisel nervös? 12. Warum erschrak sie beinahe, als sie der Wand folgte? 13. Warum glaubte Lisel, daß der Raum eine Bibliothek gewesen sein mußte? 14. Woher kam das Licht? 15. Beschreiben Sie die Gegenstände im Raum! 16. Warum konnte Lisel das Gesicht der Gestalt nicht klar sehen? 17. Was schienen die hohlen Augen des Skeletts zu suchen? 18. Warum begann Lisels Furcht zu schwinden? 19. Was sah Lisel auf dem Tisch liegen? 20. Beschreiben Sie, wie der Brief aussah!

PART (3). 21. Wie wußte die junge Gräfin, daß der Kampf vorüber war? 22. Wie hätte sie gewußt, daß ihr Vater und ihre Brüder den Kampf gewonnen hatten? 23. Wer war Waldemar? 24. Warum zieht die junge Gräfin vor, zu sterben? 25. Warum kam die junge Gräfin nicht bis zum Knopf? 26. Welches ist ihr letzter Wunsch? 27. Wann wurde solch ein geheimes Zimmer in früheren Zeiten gebraucht? 28. Warum konnte Lisel nichts mehr mit ihren Händen fühlen, als sie den Knopf suchte? 29. Was sah sie durch das Loch? 30. Warum war seit Jahrhunderten niemand in den Hof getrehen?

PART (4). 31. Was war für Lisel jetzt sehr wichtig? 32. Warum waren klare Gedanken notwendiger als je? 33. Warum versuchte Lisel nicht mehr, den Knopf zu suchen? 34. Warum hatte es keinen Zweck, noch einmal durch das Loch hinauszuschreien? 35. Was erblickte sie auf der lezten Bücherreihe? 36. Wo lagen die Kätzchen? 37. Warum war das Zimmer ein sicherer Ort für die Kätzchen? 38. Warum konnte Lisel mit der Katze keinen Brief hinausschicken? 39. Was gebrauchte Lisel als Zeichen? 40. Was tat die Katze, als sie das Armband nicht loswerden konnte? 41. Was sahen die Freunde um die Ecke kommen?

QUESTIONS FOR 10A

PART (1). 1. Warum wollte die Dame der Krankenschwester nicht sagen, wer sie war? 2. Warum wurde die Dame nervös? 3. Was wußte sie, als der erste Herr aus dem Sprechzimmer nicht wieder herauskam? 4. Warum wollte sie, daß niemand von ihrem Besuch etwas erfuhr? 5. Was tat ihr Mann in der Nacht? 6. Wann würde die ganze Sache vielleicht nicht so schlimm sein? 7. Warum denkt die Dame, daß ihr Mann vielleicht an einer Geisteskrankheit leidet? 8. Worüber (*about what*) wissen die Ärzte nicht genug? 9. Was schlug der Doktor der Dame vor? 10. Was soll die Dame ihrem Mann inzwischen geben?

PART (2). 11. Was hatte der Geschäftsleiter sich zur Regel gemacht? 12. Was zeigte die Kleidung der Dame? 13. Was für ein Armband suchte die Dame? 14. Was stand in der Mitte des Ladens? 15. Was war der Dame von ihrem Mann für das nächste Jahr versprochen worden? 16. Welche Vorteile hat eine Perlenkette? 17. Was würde Dr. Freudenberg nie tun? 18. Was schlug die Dame dem Juwelier vor? 19. Was würde geschehen, wenn der Juwelier nein sagte? 20. Was tat der Juwelier mit den Perlen, bevor er ins Auto stieg?

PART (3). 21. Wann hielt das Auto vor dem Haus des Psychiaters? 22. Was sagte die Dame, als sie die Treppe hinaufstieg? 23. Worüber (*about what*) sollte der Geschäftsleiter mit dem Doktor lieber allein sprechen? 24. Wie war die Krankheit schlimmer geworden? 25. Warum müßte alles eigentlich gut gehen? 26. Warum hätte die Kette schon vor Weihnachten verkauft werden sollen? 27. Was tat die Dame, als die Tür zum Sprechzimmer sich öffnete? 28. Was fordert der diplomatische Dienst? 29. Woran dachte der Juwelier, als er das Wort „Diskretion" erwähnte? 30. Wann war die Kette praktisch verkauft? 31. Wie vollkommen waren die Perlen, die der Juwelier so lobte? 32. Wann wäre der Juwelier nicht zu Dr. Freudenberg gekommen? 33. Warum wurde der Juweiler plötzlich kreideweiß? 34. Wo war die Dame, als Dr. Freudenberg die Tür zum Nebenzimmer aufriß?

QUESTIONS FOR 10B

PART (1). 1. Was hatten die Truppen Napoleons nicht gestört? 2. Was hätte während der Kriegsjahre fast vollständig aufgehört? 3. Was brachte mehr Besucher als je auf das Schloß des Grafen? 4. Wann wären die Eltern überglücklich gewesen? 5. Was erfuhren die Eltern, als Maria Gabriele ihrer Mutter ihr Herz öffnete? 6. Warum wollten die Eltern nicht, daß ihre Tochter den jungen Leutnant heiratete? 7. Was taten die beiden jungen Leute, nachdem der Graf seiner Tochter verboten hatte, den Leutnant wiederzusehen? 8. Was versprachen sie einander? 9. Wozu (*to what*) wäre Rupert bereit gewesen? 10. Wann würde das Herz der Eltern gerührt werden? 11. Was wird Ruperts Diener Johann tun? 12. Was tat Maria Gabriele am Abend in ihrem Zimmer? 13. Warum war es gut, daß es zu schneien begonnen hatte?

PART (2). 14. Was hatte Rupert am Morgen zuerst gemacht? 15. Wozu (*for what*) brauchte er am Nachmittag mehrere Stunden? 16. Warum war seine Wohnung leer, als er zurückkehrte? 17. Von wem hatte er den Schlitten bekommen? 18. Was wußte Rupert nach kurzer Zeit nicht mehr, als der Schnee in dichten Mengen zur Erde fiel? 19. Was würde mit ihm in dem weißen Meer geschehen? 20. Warum fühlte er plötzlich einen stechenden Schmerz? 21. Was erblickte Rupert zwischen den Stämmen der Bäume? 22. Was tat er, als er das erste Haus erreichte? 23. Wann hörte er die Kirchuhr schlagen, und wie spät war es? 24. Wo mußten Maria Gabriele und die anderen zu (*at*) dieser Zeit sein? 25. Wie weckte Rupert den Pfarrer?

PART (3). 26. Warum schickte die Gräfin das Dienstmädchen in das Zimmer ihrer Tochter? 27. Was tat Maria Gabriele, nachdem sie ihren Eltern einen guten Morgen gewünscht hatte? 28. Warum mußte ein Arzt gerufen werden? 29. (a) Was erkannte der Arzt sofort? (b) Was empfahl und riet er? 30. Warum sagten der Pfarrer und die Trauzeugen nichts? 31. Warum hielt Johann den Mund? 32. Was fürchtete man, als der Zustand der Kranken schlimmer wurde? 33. Was hatte Maria Gabriele getan, nachdem sie aufgewacht war? 34. Was hielten die Eltern für den Grund von Maria Gabrieles Krankheit? 35. Was tat Rupert, als er die Einladung bekam? 36. Was hatte er getan, als die Eltern ihm zum zweiten Mal schrieben? 37. Was berichtete die Zeitung? 38. Was fürchteten die Eltern, als sie das bleiche Gesicht ihrer Tochter sahen? 39. Was schien Maria Gabriele heilig zu halten? 40. Was hätte Maria Gabriele vorgezogen, nachdem ihr Vater gestorben war? 41. Welches war der wahre Grund für den Wunsch der Mutter, mit ihrer Tochter in die Stadt zu ziehen (*move*)?

PART (4). 42. Warum galt Maria Gabriele als das reichste Mädchen der Provinz? 43. Was stellte sie dar? 44. Wonach (*for what*) strebten die jungen Männer? 45. Als was hätten Maria Gabrieles melancholische Züge und ihre blasse Farbe bei anderen Mädchen gegolten? 46. Was versuchte jede Mutter? 47. Wie taten sie das? 48. Wann schüttelte Maria Gabriele schweigend den Kopf? 49. Wann atmete ganz Europa wieder frei? 50. Was wollte Graf Burkhard tun, nachdem er einige Wochen lang die Vergnügen der Hauptstadt genossen hatte? 51. Was hatte Graf Burkhard früher getan? 52. Warum beobachteten ihn viele Eltern mit gemischten Gefühlen? 53. Wann hätten viele Mädchen ihm seine früheren Fehler verziehen? 54. Wo hatte Burkhard die junge Gräfin getroffen? 55. Worüber (*about what*) gab es für Maria Gabriele bald keinen Zweifel mehr? 56. Was mußte Burkhard gemerkt haben? 57. Was beschloß Maria Gabriele zu tun, um zu erfahren, warum Burkhard schwieg? 58. Worauf (*for what*) wartete sie mit Ungeduld?

PART (5). 59. Wo saß Maria Gabriele, als Burkhard in den Garten trat? 60. Was schien sie zu tun? 61. Was würde geschehen, nachdem Burkhard fortgegangen war? 62. Was sollte die junge Gräfin erfahren, bevor Burkhard sie verließ? 63. Welchen Trost brauchte Burkhard? 64. Warum hätte er die junge Gräfin nicht heiraten können? 65. Wo war Burkhard im Winter des Jahres 1812? 66. Warum war er unruhig? 67. Was tat er, obwohl man ihn gewarnt hatte? 68. Was mußte nach kurzer Zeit geschehen sein? 69. Was geschah, als der Bach plötzlich in eine andere Richtung bog? 70. Wie sah Burkhard aus, als er in die Kirche trat? 71. Warum halfen die zwei Männer der Braut? 72. Was tat Burkhard, als er die Braut wie tot zur Erde fallen sah? 73. Wie konnte Burkhard einschlafen, nachdem er die Kirche verlassen hatte? 74. Warum konnte er seinen Diener später nicht fragen, in welcher Kirche die Trauung stattgefunden hatte?

Vocabulary

The vocabulary does not list personal pronouns, possessive adjectives, or numerals.

Beyond giving the English equivalents which the words have within the context of this Reader, an attempt has been made to list all the key meanings.

Nouns are given with article and plural ending; the genitive singular is indicated in the case of weak masculine or otherwise irregular nouns [**der Junge, (–en), –n; das Herz, (–ens), –en**].

Uncompounded strong and irregular verbs are given with their vowel changes. With verbs that have a change of stem vowel in the present tense, the vowel change is indicated [**sehen, a, e, (ie)**]. An asterisk (*) after a compound verb indicates that the principal parts are to be found under the simple form. Separable verbs are divided by a hyphen after the prefix.

Words that can be used interchangeably as adjectives or adverbs are ordinarily listed as adjectives.

A

ab off, away; down
ab-drehen to turn off
der Abend, –e evening
  das Abendbrot supper
  das Abendessen supper
  der Abendstern evening star
  die Abendstunde, –n evening hour
  die Abendzeitung, –en evening newspaper
abends in the evening
aber but, however
abergläubisch superstitious
ab-fahren* to leave
die Abfahrt, –en departure
ab-nehmen* to take off; decrease
ab-schließen* to lock (up)
ab-schneiden* to cut off
die Absicht, –en intention
absolut absolute
der Abt, ⸚e abbot
das Abteil, –e compartment
  die Abteiltür, –en compartment door
ab-wischen to wipe off
ab-ziehen* to take off, remove
ach oh, ah; alas!
achten to esteem, respect
  achten auf + acc. to pay attention to, watch
der Acker, ⸚ field
ähnlich similar

der Akt, –e act
der Alkohol alcohol
all all
allein alone
allein however, yet
allerdings to be sure, it is true
allerlei all sorts of
als when; as; than
also therefore, thus, then
alt old
der Alte, (–n) the old man
der Altar, die Altäre altar
das Alter age, old age
(das) Amerika America; United States
amerikanisch American
das Amt, ⸚er office
an at, near, by, on, etc.
an-blicken to look at
ander other
anders different, else
ändern to change
an-drehen to turn on
der Anfang, ⸚e beginning, start
an-fangen* to begin, start
angenehm pleasant, agreeable
die Angst, ⸚e fear
Angst haben* (vor + *dat.***)** to be afraid (of)
an-haben* to have on
an-kommen* to arrive
an-lassen* to leave on
die Annonce, –n ad, advertisement
an-rufen* to call, telephone
an-sehen* to look at
anstatt instead of
an-treiben* to drive on, urge on
die Antwort, –en answer
antworten to answer
an-ziehen* to put, dress
an-zünden to light
der Apfel, ⸚ apple
der Apfelbaum, ⸚e apple tree
die Apfelsine, –n orange
die Apotheke, –n pharmacy, apothecary, drugstore
der Apotheker, – pharmacist
die Arbeit, –en work
arbeiten to work
der Arbeiter, – worker
der Arbeitsplatz, ⸚e place of work
der Ärger annoyance, vexation
ärgerlich annoying; annoyed, vexed
ärgern to annoy, vex, irritate
(sich) ärgern (über + *acc.***)** to be annoyed (at)
arm poor
die Armut poverty
der Arm, –e arm
das Armband, ⸚er bracelet
die Armbanduhr, –en wrist watch
der Armstuhl, ⸚e armchair
der Ärmel, – sleeve
die Art, –en kind, manner, way, sort
die Artillerie artillery
der Artilleriehauptmann artillery captain
der Arzt, ⸚e doctor, physician
das As, die Asse ace
die Asche ashes
atmen to breathe
auch also, too; even
auf on, upon; up, etc.; open
auf sein to be open
auf-blicken to look up
die Aufgabe, –n assignment, lesson; task; job
auf-halten* to delay, detain, stop
auf-hören to stop, cease
auf-machen to open
auf-passen to pay attention, watch, look out
auf-passen auf + *acc.* to pay attention to, watch
auf-reißen* to tear open
auf-setzen to put on
auf-springen* to jump up
auf-stehen* to get up, rise
auf-wachen to wake up, awaken
das Auge, –n eye

der Augenblick, –e moment
aus out of, from
aus-blasen* to blow out
der Ausdruck, ⸚e expression
aus-geben* to spend (money)
aus-gehen* to go out
aus-gleiten* to slip
das Ausland foreign country
(sich) aus-ruhen to rest
aus-sehen* to look, look like, appear
außen outside
die Außenwelt outside world
außer except, beside(s), apart from; outside of
außerhalb outside (of)
außerordentlich extraordinary
aus-steigen* to get out
aus-strecken to stretch out
auswendig by heart
aus-ziehen* to take off, undress
das Auto, –s car

B

der Bach, ⸚e brook
die Backe, –n cheek
der Backenbart whiskers, sideburns
die Backenknochen cheekbones
backen, u, a, (ä) to bake
das Bad, ⸚er bath
die Bahn, –en course, way; railroad
der Bahnhof, ⸚e station
das Bahnhofsrestaurant, –s station restaurant
die Bahnhofsuhr, –en station clock
der Bahnsteig, –e (station) platform
bald soon
der Ball, ⸚e ball
die Bank, ⸚e bench
die Bank, –en bank
der Bär, –en bear
das Bärenfell, –e bear skin
der Bärenhäuter "Mr. Bearskin"
der Baron, –e baron
der Bart, ⸚e beard
der Bau, die Bauten construction; building
die Baufirma construction firm
bauen to build, construct
der Bauer, (–n/–s), –n farmer, peasant
das Bauernhaus, ⸚er farm house
der Baum, ⸚e tree
der Baumstamm, ⸚e tree trunk
der Beamte, (–n), –n official
bedecken to cover
bedeuten to mean
(sich) beeilen to hurry
die Beere, –n berry
befehlen, a, o, (ie) to command, order
(sich) befinden* to be
(sich) begeben* to go
begegnen to meet
beginnen, a, o to begin, start
begleiten to accompany
behalten* to keep
behandeln to treat
behaupten to assert, maintain, claim, say
bei at, with, near, at the house of, etc.
beide both
das Bein, –e leg
beinahe almost
das Beispiel, –e example
beißen, i, i to bite
bekannt known, well-known
der Bekannte, (–n), –n acquaintance
bekommen* to get, receive
bellen to bark
beobachten to observe
bequem comfortable
bereit ready, prepared
der Berg, –e mountain
der Bergsee, –n mountain lake
berichten to report
der Beruf, –e profession
berühmt famous
beschließen* to decide, resolve

beschreiben* to describe
besitzen* to own, possess
besonder special
besonders especially
bestehen* to consist; to pass (an examination)
bestellen to order
bestimmen to determine, fix, set; destine, intend (for)
bestimmt certain, definite
der Besuch, –e visit
besuchen to visit
der Besucher, – visitor
beten to pray
das Bett, –en bed
das Bettuch, ¨–er bedsheet
bevor before
bewegen to move
beweisen, ie, ie to prove
bezahlen to pay
die Bibel, –n bible
die Bibliothek, –en library
biegen, o, o to bend, turn
die Biene, –n bee
das Bier beer
bieten, o, o to offer
das Bild, –er picture, image
bilden to form; educate
billig cheap
binden, a, u to bind, tie
die Birne, –n pear
der Birnbaum, ¨–e pear tree
bis until
bisher up to now, up to that time
ein bißchen a little
bitte please
bitten, a, e to ask
bitter bitter
bitterkalt bitter cold
blasen, ie, a (ä) to blow
blaß pale
das Blatt, ¨–er leaf; sheet, page
blau blue
bleiben, ie, ie to remain, stay
bleich pale
der Bleistift, –e pencil
der Blick, –e glance, look; view
blicken to look, glance
der Blitz, –e lightning
blitzen to lighten, lightning
blühen to bloom, blossom; flourish
die Blume, –n flower
das Blut blood
blutbedeckt covered with blood
blutig bloody
der Boden, ¨– ground, soil, floor; attic
die Bohne, –n bean
die Bombe, –n bomb
böse angry; wicked, bad, evil
braten, ie, a, (ä) to roast, grill, broil, fry
brauchen to need; (to use)
braun brown
die Braut, ¨–e fiancée; bride
der Bräutigam, –e fiancé; bridegroom
brav good; honest, upright
brechen, a, o, (i) to break
breit broad, wide
brennen, a, a to burn
das Brett, –er board
der Brief, –e letter
die Brieftasche, –n wallet, billfold
bringen, a, a to bring
das Brot, –e bread
die Brücke, –n bridge
der Bruder, ¨– brother
der Brunnen, – well
die Brust, ¨–e breast, chest
die Brusttasche, –n breast pocket
das Buch, ¨–er book
der Buchhalter, – accountant
der Buchmacher, – bookmaker, "bookie"
der Buchstabe, –n letter (of the alphabet)
die Bücherreihe, –n row of books
die Burg, –en (fortified) castle
der Bürger, – citizen
das Büro, –s office
der Busch, ¨–e bush
die Butter butter

C

die Chance, –n chance, opportunity
der Charakter, die Charaktere character
der Chauffeur, –e chauffeur, driver

D

da there; then; since; when
dabei in so doing, at the same time, etc.
das Dach, ⸚er roof
dafür for that, for it, for them; in exchange
dagegen against it; on the other hand
daher therefore, accordingly, consequently
da·liegen* to lie there
damals then, at that time
die Dame, –n lady
der Damenhandschuh, –e ladies' glove
der Damenstrumpf, ⸚e stocking, hose
damit with it, with that, with them; so that
danach after that, afterward
der Dank thanks, gratitude
danke! thank you
danken to thank
dann then
darauf after that, thereafter
dar·stellen to represent, present
darum therefore
daß that, so that
da·sitzen* to sit there
da·stehen* to stand there
das Datum, die Daten date
dauern to last, take
der Daumen, – thumb
davon away, off
davon·laufen* to run away
davor·stehen* to stand in front
dazu besides, in addition
die Decke, –n cover, blanket; ceiling
decken to cover
denken, a, a to think
denn for (=because); anyway, anyhow
dennoch nevertheless, still, yet
derjenige, welcher
diejenige, welche
dasjenige, welches
diejenigen, welche } he who, the one who, that which, those who, etc.
derselbe, dieselbe, dasselbe, etc. the same
deshalb therefore
desto: je . . . desto the . . . the . . .
deuten to point
deutsch German
(das) Deutschland Germany
dicht thick, tight, tense; close
dichten to write (poetry)
dick thick, fat
der Dieb, –e thief
dienen to serve, be of service
der Diener, – servant
der Dienst, –e service
das Dienstmädchen, – maid, servant girl
der Dienstag, –e Tuesday
dieser this, this one; the latter
diesmal this time
das Ding, –e thing, object
diplomatisch diplomatic
direkt direct, directly
der Direktor, –en director
die Diskretion discretion
doch yet, however; nevertheless; but; surely, after all
der Doktor, –en doctor
das Dokument, –e document
donnern to thunder
der Donnerstag, –e Thursday
doppelt double
das Doppelkinn double chin
das Dorf, ⸚er village
die Dorfuhr, –en village clock
dort there
dorthin there (direction-thither)

draußen outside
drehen to turn
dringen, a, u to penetrate, press, push, urge
drinnen inside
dritt- third
drittens thirdly
drücken to press, push, squeeze
dumm stupid
die Dummheit, –en stupidity
der Dummkopf, ⸚e blockhead, dumbbell
dunkel dark
das Dunkel darkness
die Dunkelheit darkness
dünn thin
durch through
durchaus by all means, quite
durch-fallen* to fail (an examination)
durch-lassen* to let through
durch(-)schneiden* to cut through
durch-stecken to put, get through
dürfen, durfte, gedurft/dürfen, (darf) may, to be allowed to
der Durst thirst
das Dutzend, –e dozen

E

eben flat
eben just; just a little while ago
ebenfalls likewise
echt genuine, real, authentic
die Ecke, –n corner
edel noble; precious
der Edelstein, –e precious stone
ehe before
die Ehe, –n marriage, married state
das Ehepaar, –e married couple
die Ehre, –n honor
die Ehrensache, –n affair of honor, point of honor
das Ei, –er egg
die Eiche, –n oak
der Eichentisch, –e oak table
der Eifer zeal, eagerness, fervor
eigen own
eigentlich actual(ly), real(ly)
eilen to hurry
einander one another, each other
der Eindruck, ⸚e impression
einfach simple
ein-fallen* to occur; collapse
einige a few, some
ein-laden* to invite
die Einladung, –en invitation
einmal once; some time
auf einmal suddenly
nicht einmal not even
noch einmal once more
einsam lonely, solitary
ein-schlafen* to fall asleeep
einst once, formerly, once upon a time; some day (future)
ein-treten* to go in, enter
einzeln single, individual
einzig only, sole
das Eis ice, ice cream
das Eisen iron
die Eisenbahn, –en railroad
der Eisenbahnwagen, – railroad car, coach
der Eisennagel, ⸚ iron nail
elegant elegant
die Eltern parents
empfangen* to receive
empfehlen, a, o, (ie) to recommend
empfinden* to feel, sense
das Ende, –n end
enden to end
endlich finally
eng narrow
(das) England England
enorm enormous
entdecken to discover
entgegnen to answer, reply
entlang along
entlang-gehen* to go, walk along
entlang-führen to lead along
entlang-rennen* to run along
entscheiden* to decide
die Entscheidung, –en decision
(sich) entschließen* to decide

entschuldigen excuse, apologize
die Entschuldigung, –en excuse, apology
entstehen* to come about, originate, start, arise
entweder . . . oder either . . . or
entwickeln to develop
entzünden to light, kindle, catch fire
der Erbe, (–n), –n heir
die Erbin, –nen heiress
erblicken to see (= catch sight of)
die Erbse, –n pea
die Erde earth
die Erdbeere, –n strawberry
erfahren* to learn, find out, experience
erfinden* to invent
der Erfinder, – inventor
der Erfolg, –e success
erfüllen to fulfill
erinnern to remind
sich erinnern to remember
(sich) erkälten to catch (a) cold
erkennen* to recognize
erklären to explain; declare
die Erklärung, –en explanation; declaration
erlauben to allow, permit
die Erlaubnis permission
ermorden to murder
ernst earnest, serious; grave, stern
ernten to harvest, reap
erreichen to reach, attain
erscheinen* to appear
erschrecken to frighten
erschrecken, a, o, (i) to be frightened, alarmed
erst first, at first; only, not until
erstens first(ly), in the first place
erstaunen to astonish
erwähnen to mention
erwarten to expect
erwidern to reply, answer
erzählen to tell, relate
die Erzählung, –en story, tale, narrative
erziehen* to educate, bring up
der Esel, – donkey
essen, a, e, (i) to eat
das Essen meal; food
etwa about, approximately, perhaps
etwas some, something; somewhat
(das) Europa Europe
ewig eternal
das Examen, – examination

F

das Fach, ⸚er subject; line of work; profession; drawer, compartment
der Fachman, die Fachleute expert
fahren, u, a, (ä) to drive, ride, go
die Fahrt, –en trip, ride, journey
das Fahrrad, ⸚er bicycle
der Fahrstuhl, ⸚e elevator
die Fahrstuhltür, –en elevator door
der Fall, ⸚e case; fall
fallen, ie, a, (ä) to fall
falsch wrong, false
die Familie, –n family
fangen, i, a, (ä) to catch, capture
die Farbe, –n color, paint
das Faß, ⸚er barrel, cask, keg
fassen to take hold of, grasp, seize, reach
fast almost
die Feder, –n feather; pen; spring
fehlen to be missing, lack, not to be there
der Fehler, – mistake, error; defect, flaw
feiern to celebrate
fein fine, elegant, refined; nice
der Feind, –e enemy
das Feld, –er field
die Feldblume, –n field flower
das Fell, –e fur, skin, hide
der Fels(en), (–ens), –en rock, cliff
das Fenster, – window
die Ferien (*plural*) vacation

die Ferienreise, –n vacation trip
fern distant, far, removed
von fern from afar, from far away
fertig ready, done, finished
fest fast, firm, solid
fest-halten* to hold fast
fest-machen to fasten
das Fest, –e feast, celebration, holiday
das Festmahl festive meal, banquet
der Festtag, –e day of celebration, holiday
fett fat
das Feuer, – fire; light
die Feuerwaffe, –n firearm
das Fieber fever, temperature
finden, a, u to find
der Finger, – finger
der Fingernagel, ¨– fingernail
die Firma, die Firmen firm, company
der Fisch, –e fish
flach flat, shallow
die Flamme, –n flame
die Flasche, –n bottle, flask
das Fleisch meat, flesh
fleischlos fleshless
die Fliege, –n fly
fliegen, o, o to fly
fliehen, o, o to flee
fließen, o, o to flow
flüstern to whisper
folgen to follow; obey
fordern to demand, ask
fördern to advance, promote
die Form, –en form, shape, figure
fort away, off, gone; on, farther
fort-fahren* to leave; continue, go on
fort-gehen* to leave, go away
fort-jagen to chase away, drive away, turn away
fort-laufen* to run away
fort-rennen* to run away
fort-schicken to send away, turn away
die Frage, –n question
fragen to ask, question
(das) Frankreich France
französisch French
die Frau, –en woman; wife; Mrs.
das Frauenherz, –en woman's heart
das Fräulein, – young lady; Miss
frei free; vacant, unoccupied
im Freien outdoors, in the open
ins Freie outdoors, into the open
die Freiheit freedom, liberty
frei-lassen* to set free
freilich to be sure, of course, certainly
(der) Freitag, –e Friday
fremd strange, unknown, foreign
der Fremde, (–n), –n stranger
fressen, a, e, (i) to eat (of beasts)
die Freude, –n joy, pleasure, delight
(sich) freuen (über + *acc.*) to be happy, glad (about)
(sich)freuen auf + *acc.* to look forward to
der Freund, –e friend (male)
die Freundin, –nen friend (female), girl friend
freundlich friendly
der Friede(n), (–ens) peace
friedliebend peace-loving
frieren, o, o to freeze, to be cold
frisch fresh, brisk, new
froh happy, glad, joyful, merry
die Frucht, ¨–e fruit
früh early
der Frühling, –e Spring
das Frühstück, –e breakfast
der Fuchs, ¨–e fox
die Fuchsjagd, –en fox hunt
fühlen to feel
führen to lead, guide, take
füllen to fill
das Fünfzigpfennigstück fifty-pfennig piece
für for

die **Furcht** fear, fright
furchtbar terrible
fürchten to fear
sich fürchten vor + *dat.* to be afraid of
der **Fürst, –en** prince, sovereign
der **Fuß, ⸚e** foot
der **Fußboden, ⸚n** floor (of a room)
das **Futter** food, fodder, feed

G

die **Gabel, –n** fork
der **Gang, ⸚e** corridor; step, walk, gait
der **Gangster, –** gangster
die **Gans, ⸚e** goose
die **Gänsefeder, –n** goose quill, goose feather
der **Gänsestall, ⸚e** goose pen
ganz quite; whole, entire, complete
gar at all; quite
der **Garten, ⸚** garden
das **Gas, –e** gas
der **Gasofen, ⸚** gas stove, gas oven
die **Gasrechnung, –en** gas bill
der **Gast, ⸚e** guest
das **Gasthaus, ⸚er** inn, tavern
das **Gastzimmer, –** common room, lobby; guest room
das **Gebäude, –** building
geben, a, e, (i) to give
gebildet educated, cultured
geboren born
gebrauchen to use
der **Geburtstag, –e** birthday
das **Geburtstagsgeschenk, –e** birthday present
der **Gedanke, –n** thought
die **Geduld** patience
die **Gefahr, –en** danger
gefährlich dangerous
gefallen* to please, like
der **Gefallen, –** favor
der **Gefangene, (–n), –n** prisoner
das **Gefängnis, –se** prison, jail
der **Gefängnishof, ⸚e** prison yard, court
das **Gefängnisleben** prison life
das **Gefühl, –e** feeling
gegen against; toward, about
der **Gegenstand, ⸚e** object; subject, topic, matter
gegenüber opposite
gegenüberliegend (lying) opposite
gegenüber-stehen* to stand opposite
die **Gegenwart** present; presence
das **Gehalt, ⸚er** salary
geheim secret
im geheimen in secret
geheim-halten* to keep secret
das **Geheimnis, –se** secret, mystery
gehen, i, a to go, walk
gehören to belong
der **Geist, –er** spirit; mind; ghost
die **Geistergeschichte, –n** ghost story
die **Geisteskrankheit, –en** mental illness
gelb yellow
das **Geld** money
der **Geldsack, ⸚e** money bag
das **Geldstück, –e** coin
der **Geliebte, (–n)** beloved, lover, sweetheart
die **Geliebte, (–n)** beloved; mistress
gelingen, a, u to succeed
gelten, a, o, (i) to be worth; to be considered (as)
gemein mean; common; vulgar
das **Gemüse, –** vegetable
genau exact, precise, accurate
genauso wie just as
genießen, o, o to enjoy; to eat, drink
genug enough, sufficient
genügen to be enough, suffice
das **Gepäck** baggage, luggage
das **Gepäcknetz, –e** luggage rack

gerade just, just then; straight, direct; precisely
die Gerechtigkeit justice
das Gericht, –e court (of law), tribunal; dish, course
gering small, little, slight
gern(e) with pleasure, gladly
das Geschäft, –e business, affair; store, shop
der Geschäftsleiter, – manager
der Geschäftsmann, die Geschäftsleute businessman
die Geschäftsreise, –n business trip
der Geschäftsreisende, (–n), –n traveling salesman
geschehen, a, e, (ie) to happen, take place
das Geschenk, –e present, gift
die Geschichte, –n story, tale; history
der Geschmack, ⸗er taste
die Gesellschaft, –en company; society; party
das Gesicht, –er face
die Gestalt, –en figure, shape, form
gestatten to allow, permit
gestern yesterday
gesund in good health, healthy; healthful
die Gesundheit health
die Gewalt, –en power, force, violence; authority
gewaltig powerful, mighty
das Gewehr, –e gun, rifle
gewinnen, a, o to win, gain
gewiß certain, sure
gewöhnlich usual, ordinary, customary
gießen, o, o to pour
das Gift, –e poison
der Gipfel, – peak, summit, top
glänzen to shine, glitter, sparkle
das Glas, ⸗er glass
glatt smooth, even; slippery
glauben to believe; think, suppose
gleich (= sogleich) at once, immediately, right away
gleich same, equal, like
gleiten, i, i to glide, slide
das Glied, –er member (of body), limb
das Glöckchen, – } little bell
das Glöcklein, – } little bell
die Glocke, –n bell
das Glück luck, good fortune; happiness
Glück haben to be lucky
glücklich lucky, happy, fortunate
gnädig gracious; merciful
gnädige Frau Madam
das Gold gold
die Goldmünze, –n gold coin
der Goldring, –e gold ring
das Goldstück, –e gold coin
Gott God
das Grab, ⸗er grave
graben, u, a (ä) dig
der Graf, (–en), –en count
die Gräfin, –nen countess
der Gram grief, sorrow
das Gras, ⸗er grass
grau gray
greifen, i, i to seize; reach
die Grenze, –n border, boundary, limit, frontier
groß large, tall, great, big, grand
die Großmutter, ⸗ grandmother
der Großvater, ⸗ grandfather
grün green
der Grund, ⸗e reason; ground, basis, bottom
die Gruppe, –n group
grüßen to greet, salute, to give regards, to say hello
die Gunst favor
gut good
das Gut, ⸗er estate; goods, merchandise
das Gymnasium, die Gymnasien "Gymnasium" (German secondary school)

H

das Haar, –e hair
die Haarwurzel, –n hair root
haben, hatte, gehabt to have
der Hafen, ⸚ harbor, port
die Hafenstadt, ⸚e port, harbor town
der Hahn, ⸚e rooster; faucet
die Hahnenfeder, –n cock feather
halb half
das Halbdunkel semidarkness
die Hälfte, –n half
der Hals, ⸚e neck, throat
halt! stop!
halten, ie, a, (ä) to hold; stop
halten* für to consider, believe
halten* von to think of
der Hammer, ⸚ hammer
die Hand, ⸚e hand
der Handschuh, –e glove
die Handtasche, –n handbag
die Handvoll handful
hängen, i, a to hang
hart hard
der Hase, –n hare
der Haß hate, hatred
hassen to hate
der Haufe(n), (–ens), –n heap, pile, lot, crowd
das Haupt, ⸚er head
der Hauptmann, die Hauptleute captain
die Hauptsache, –n main thing
die Hauptstadt, ⸚e capital (city)
das Haus, ⸚er house
die Hausarbeit, –en housework, domestic work
das Hauskonzert, –e private concert
der Hausschuh, –e slipper, house shoe
die Haustür, –en house door
die Hauswand, ⸚e wall of the house
die Haut, ⸚e skin, hide
heben, o, o to lift, raise
das Heer, –e army
das Heft, –e notebook
der Heide, (–n), –n heathen
das Heil salvation
heilig holy, sacred
der Heilige, (–n), –n saint
das Heim, –e home
heim-führen to lead home
der Heimweg way home
die Heirat, –en marriage
heiraten to marry
heiß hot; passionate, ardent
heißen, ie, ei to to be called; to mean
das heißt that is to say, i.e.
der Held, (–en), –en hero
helfen, a, o, (i) to help
hell bright, clear, light
das Hemd, die Hemden shirt
die Hemdtasche, –n shirt pocket
her here (= hither)
herauf up
herauf-kommen* to come up
heraus out
heraus-kommen* to come out
heraus-können* to be able to get out
heraus-nehmen* to take out
heraus-stecken to stick out
heraus-werfen* to throw out
heraus-ziehen* to draw out, pull out
herbei here, there, up, near, along, over
herbei-eilen to hasten there, to hurry up
herbei-rufen* to call there, to call together
der Herbst autumn, fall
das Herbstwetter fall weather
die Herde, –n herd, flock
herein in
herein-bringen* to bring in
herein-kommen* to come in
herein-lassen* to let in
herein-rufen* to call in

der Herr, (–n), –en gentleman, man; Mr; master
der Herrenhandschuh, –e man's glove
die Herrin, –nen lady of the house, mistress
herrlich wonderful, splendid
herum around
herum-blasen* to blow around
herum-drehen to turn around
herum-laufen* to run around
herum-reichen to pass around
herum-schwimmen* to swim, float around
herunter down
herunter-gehen* to go down
herunter-lassen* to let down, lower
herunter-schreiten* to walk, step down
hervor out, forward
hervor-kommen* to come out
hervor-kriechen* to crawl out
hervor-holen to take out
hervor-stehen* to stand out, jut out, protrude
hervor-ziehen* to draw out, pull out
das Herz, (–ens), –en heart
nach Herzenslust to one's heart's content, desire
heute today
heutzutage nowadays, these days
die Hexe, –n witch
hier here
hier-bleiben* to stay here
hierher here (= hither)
hierher-bringen* to bring here
hierher-führen to lead here, take here
hierher-leiten to lead here
hierher-schicken to send here
die Hilfe help, aid
der Himmel sky; heaven
hin there (= thither)
hin und her to and fro, back and forth
hin-fahren* to drive there, go there
hinauf up
hinauf-eilen to rush up, hasten up
hinauf-fahren* to drive up
hinauf-schicken to send up
hinauf-sehen* to look up
hinauf-steigen* to climb, walk, go up
hinaus out
hinaus-blicken to look out
hinaus-bringen* to take out, bring out
hinaus-eilen to hurry out
hinaus-gehen* to go out, walk out
hinaus-führen to lead out, take out
hinaus-jagen to chase out, to race out
hinaus-lassen* to let out
hinaus-lehnen to lean out
hinaus-reiten* to ride out
hinaus-schicken to send out
hinaus-schreien* to call out, scream out
hinaus-sehen* to look out
hinaus-treiben* to drive out
hindern to prevent, hinder
hinein in(to)
hinein-blasen* to blow into
hinein-blicken to look into, gaze into
hinein-führen to lead into, take into
hinein-gehen* to go into, enter
hinein-werfen* to throw into
hinten behind, in the rear, in the back
hinter behind, beyond
der Hinterfuß, ¨–e hind foot
die Hintertür, –en back door
hinüber over, across
hinüber-gehen* to go over
hinunter down
hinunter-blicken to look down

hinunter-fließen* to flow down, run down
hinunter-gehen* to go down, walk down
hinunter-gleiten* to slide down, glide down
hinunter-laufen* to run down
hinunter-rollen to roll down
hinunter-senden* to send down
hinzu in addition, to; to that place, there
hinzu-kommen* to come there, to join, assemble; add
hinzu-treten* to go there, join, approach
der **Hirt, (–en), –en** shepherd, –herd
hoch high, tall
hoch-heben* to lift, raise (high)
die **Hochzeit, –en** wedding
der **Hof, ⸚e** yard, courtyard; court; farm
die **Hofdame, –n** lady-in-waiting
hoffen to hope
hoffentlich I hope, let's hope, etc.
die **Hoffnung, –en** hope
hoffnungslos hopeless
höflich polite, courteous
hohl hollow
hold lovely (elevated style)
holen to get, fetch, go and get
das **Holz** wood
das **Holzbett, –en** wooden bed
der **Honig** honey
hören to hear
die **Hose, –n** trousers, pants
die **Hosentasche, –n** pants pocket
das **Hotel, –s** hotel
der **Hoteldirektor, –en** hotel director, hotel manager
das **Hotelzimmer, –** hotel room
hübsch pretty, nice
der **Hund, –e** dog
das **Hundeleben** dog's life
die **Hundenase, –n** dog's nose
der **Hunger** hunger
hungrig hungry
der **Hut, ⸚e** hat
die **Hutschachtel, –n** hatbox

I

die **Idee, –n** idea
der **Igel, –** hedgehog
immer always
immer noch, noch immer still
in in, into
indem while; by
indes meanwhile; yet, however
indessen meanwhile; yet, however
die **Indiskretion, –en** indiscretion
innen inside
inner inner
insofern . . . als insofar as
der **Inspektor, –en** inspector
das **Instrument, –e** instrument
intelligent intelligent
interessant interesting
das **Interesse** interest
interessieren to interest
inzwischen in the meantime, meanwhile
irgend- some, any
irren to be wrong, mistaken
(das) **Italien** Italy
italienisch Italian

J

ja yes; indeed, to be sure, in fact, etc.
die **Jacke, –n** jacket, coat
die **Jagd, –en** hunt, chase, race
jagen to hunt, chase, race
das **Jahr, –e** year
jahrelang for years
das **Jahrhundert, –e** century
je ever, at any time
je . . . desto the . . . the
jeder each, every, everybody
jedesmal every time
jedoch however
jemand someone, somebody; anybody

jener that, that one, the former
jetzt now
die Jugend youth
der Juli July
jung young
  der Junge, (–n), –n boy
  das Junge, (–n), –n young (of an animal)
der Juwelier, –e jeweler
  das Juweliergeschäft, –e jewelry store

K

der Kaffee coffee
der Kaiser, – emperor
  kaiserlich imperial
kalt cold
  die Kälte cold
der Kamin, –e fireplace; chimney
der Kamm, ⸚e comb; crest, ridge
der Kampf, ⸚e fight, battle, combat, struggle
das Kapital capital (money)
die Karte, –n card, postcard; map; ticket
  das Kartenspiel, –e card game
die Kartoffel, –n potato
der Käse, – cheese
der Kasten, ⸚ box, chest, case
die Katze, –n cat
kaufen to buy
  der Kaufmann, die Kaufleute merchant, shopkeeper
kaum hardly, scarcely, barely
die Kehle, –n throat
keinerlei of no sort, none whatever
der Keller, – cellar, basement
der Kellner, – waiter
kennen, a, a to know
  kennen-lernen to make the acquaintance of, meet
die Kerze, –n candle
die Kette, –n chain; necklace
das Kind, –er child
  der Kindergarten, ⸚ kindergarten
das Kinn, –e chin
die Kirche, –n church
  der Kirchhof, ⸚e churchyard
  die Kirchuhr, –en church clock
klagen to complain, lament
klar clear
  klar-machen to make clear, explain
die Klasse, –n class
das Klavier, –e piano
das Kleid, –er dress, clothes
die Kleidung clothing
klein small, little
  der Kleine, (–n), –n little boy
  die Kleinstadt, ⸚e small town
klingeln to ring, tinkle, jingle
klingen, a, u to sound, ring
klopfen to knock
das Kloster, ⸚ monastery; convent
  die Klosterbibliothek, –en monastery library
der Knabe, (–n), –n boy
  die Knabenkleidung boys' clothing
das Knie, – knee
der Knochen, – bone
der Knopf, ⸚e button
kochen to cook, boil
der Koffer, – suitcase, trunk
  der Kofferraum trunk (of a car)
die Kohle, –n coal
  das Kohlenfeuer, – coal fire
kommen, a, o to come
kompliziert complicated
der König, –e king
  das Königreich, –e kingdom, realm
  die Königstochter, ⸚ princess
können, konnte, gekonnt/können, (kann) can, to be able
die Kontrolle, –n control
das Konzert, –e concert
der Kopf, ⸚e head
  die Kopfschmerzen headache
  das Kopftuch, ⸚er kerchief
der Körper, – body
die Kosten (*plural*) cost, costs, expenses

kosten to cost; taste
köstlich delicious, exquisite
die Kraft, ⸚e strength, power, force, vigor
krähen to crow
die Kralle, –n claw
krank sick, ill
das Krankenhaus, ⸚er hospital
die Krankenschwester, –n nurse
das Krankenzimmer, – sick room
die Krankheit, –en sickness, illness
die Kreide chalk
kreideweiß white as chalk
kriechen, o, o to crawl, creep
der Krieg, –e war
die Krone, –n crown
krumm crooked, bent
Krummbein "Crooked Legs"
die Küche, –n kitchen
die Küchentür, –en kitchen door
der Kuchen, – cake
die Kuh, ⸚e cow
kühl cool
die Kunst, ⸚e art; skill
das Kunstwerk, –e work of art
kurz short, brief, curt
vor kurzem a short while ago
die Kusine, –n cousin (female)
der Kuß, ⸚e kiss
küssen to kiss

L

lachen to laugh
lächeln to smile
laden, u, a (ä) to load; invite
der Laden, ⸚ store
das Lager, – store; camp
das Lagerhaus, ⸚er warehouse
die Lampe, –n lamp
das Land, ⸚er country; land
das Landgut, ⸚er country estate
die Landschaft, –en landscape, scenery; region
die Landstraße, –n country road, highway
lang long
Langbein "Long Legs"
langsam slow(ly)
langweilen to bore
lassen, ie, a, (ä) to let; leave; to have, cause, make someone do something
die Last, –en burden, load
der Lauf course; race, run
laufen, ie, au, (äu) to run
laut loud, aloud
leben to live, be alive
das Leben life
die Lebensgeschichte, –n life story
lebenslänglich for life, lifelong
die Lebensmittel (*plural*) food, foodstuff
das Lebensmittelgeschäft, –e food store
die Lebensweise way of life
leb wohl! farewell
leer empty, vacant
legen to lay, put, place (horizontally)
lehnen to lean
lehren to teach, instruct
der Leib, –er body
die Leiche, –n corpse
der Leichenwagen, – hearse
leicht easy; light; slight
leiden, i, i to suffer
leider unfortunately
leid-tun* to be sorry (for)
leihen, ie, ie to lend, loan; borrow
leise soft, low, gentle
leiten to lead, guide
lernen to learn, study
lesen, a, e, (ie) to read
letzt- last
die Leute (*plural*) people
der Leutnant, –s lieutenant
das Licht, –er light
die Lichtrechnung, –en light bill
lieb dear
die Liebe love
lieben to love

lieber rather, preferably

am liebsten (to like) best

das Lied, –er song

liegen, a, e to lie, be situated, located

die Linde, –n linden tree

die Linie, –n line

link- left

links to the left

die Liste, –n list

loben to praise

die Lippe, –n lip

das Loch, ¨er hole

der Löffel, – spoon

lohnen to reward; to be worthwhile, pay

(-)los -less; rid of; going on; off, away

los-fahren* to drive off

los-reißen* to tear off, away

los-werden* to get rid of

lösen to solve; loosen; buy (a ticket)

der Löwe, (–n), –n lion

der Löwenkopf, ¨e lion's head

die Löwin, –nen lioness

die Luft, ¨e air

die Lust desire, pleasure

Lust haben to feel like (doing something)

lustig merry, gay

M

machen to make, do

die Macht, ¨e power, force, might

mächtig mighty, powerful

das Mädchen, – girl

das Mädchenherz, –en girl's heart

der Magen, ¨ stomach

das Mahl, –e meal; repast, feast

die Mahlzeit, –en meal

das Mal, –e time

man one, people, they

manch- many a

manche (*plural*) some

manchmal sometimes

die Manier, –en manner

der Mann, ¨er man

der Mantel, ¨ overcoat, cloak

die Mark mark (100 pfennig)

der Markt, ¨ market, market place

der Marktplatz, ¨e market place

die Marktpolizei market police

der Marsch, ¨e march

die Mauer, –n wall (outside wall, stone or brick)

das Maul, ¨er mouth (of an animal)

die Maus, ¨e mouse

das Meer, –e sea, ocean

mehr more

mehrere several

meiden, ie, ie to avoid, shun

meinen to mean; say; think

die Meinung, –en opinion

meist- most

der Meister, – master

melancholisch melancholy

die Menge, –n crowd; lot, quantity

der Mensch, –en man (in general), human being, person

die Menschenmenge, –n crowd of people

menschlich human

merken to notice, note

messen, a, e, (i) to measure

das Messer, – knife

(das) Mexiko Mexico

miauen to miaow

die Milch milk

der Milchmann milkman

die Minute, –n minute

mischen to mix; mingle; shuffle (cards)

mit with

mit-bringen* to bring along, take along

miteinander with one another

mit-fahren* to drive along, come along, travel along

mit-gehen* to go along, come along

mit-kommen* to come along

mit-nehmen* to take along

der Mittag, –e noon, midday
das Mittagessen, – lunch
die Mitte the middle, center
das Mittel, – means; remedy
mitten in, auf, an, etc. in the middle of, in the midst of
die Mitternacht midnight
(der) Mittwoch Wednesday
modern modern
mögen, mochte, gemocht/mögen, (mag) to like
möglich possible
der Monat, –e month
das Monatsgehalt, ⸚er monthly salary
der Mönch, –e monk
der Mond moon
(der) Montag Monday
der Mord, –e murder
der Mörder, – murderer
morgen tomorrow
der Morgen, – morning
morgens in the morning
die Morgensonne morning sun
die Morgenzeitung, –en morning newspaper
das Motto motto
müde tired
die Mühe, –n effort, trouble, pains
die Mühle, –n mill
das Mühlrad, ⸚er mill wheel
der Müller, – miller
der Mund, ⸚er mouth
murmeln to murmur
die Musik music
musikalisch musical
der Musiker, – musician
der Musikverein, –e music association
müssen, mußte, gemußt/müssen, (muß) must, to have to
der Mut courage
die Mutter, ⸚ mother

N

na well
nach after; to; according to; etc.
nach und nach little by little
der Nachbar (–n/–s), –n neighbor
das Nachbardorf, ⸚er neighboring village
das Nachbarskind, –er neighbor's child
nachdem after
nachher afterward
der Nachmittag, –e afternoon
die Nachmittagssonne afternoon sun
die Nacht, ⸚e night
das Nachtmahl supper
der Nachttisch, –e bedside table
die Nachtigall, –en nightingale
der Nagel, ⸚ nail
nah(e) near, close
die Nähe nearness, vicinity, proximity
sich nähern to approach, come closer
der Name(n), (–ens), –n name
namens by the name of
nämlich you see; namely
der Narr, (–en), –en fool
die Nase, –n nose
die Natur, –en nature
natürlich natural(ly)
der Nebel, – fog, mist
neben beside, next to
das Nebenzimmer, – adjoining room, next room
der Neffe, (–n), –n nephew
nehmen, a, o, (i) to take
der Neid envy
nein no
nennen, a, a to name, call
der Nerv, –en nerve
das Nervenfieber, – nerve fever
nervös nervous
das Nest, –er nest; village, "hole"
das Netz, –e net
neu new
neugeboren newborn
von neuem anew
nicht not
die Nichte, –n niece
nichts nothing, not anything

nicken to nod
nie never
nieder down
  nieder-brennen* to burn down
  nieder-fallen* to fall down
  nieder-lassen* to let down
niedrig low
niemals never
niemand nobody, not anyone
noch still, yet, in addition, etc.
  noch ein one more
  noch einmal once more
  noch nicht not yet
der Nord(en), (–ens) north
  der Nordwind, –e north wind
die Not, ⸚e need, distress, misery
  nötig necessary
  notwendig necessary
(der) November November
die Nummer, –n number; size
nun now
nur only
die Nuß, ⸚e nut
  der Nußbaum, ⸚e walnut tree

O

ob whether
  als ob as if
oben above; upstairs, on top
ober upper
obgleich although
das Obst fruit
  der Obstbaum, ⸚e fruit tree
obwohl although
oder or
der Ofen, ⸚ stove, oven
offen open
  offen-stehen* to stand, be open
  öffentlich open(ly), public(ly)
der Offizier, –e officer
  die Offiziersuniform, –en officer's uniform
öffnen to open
oft often, frequently
ohne without
das Ohr, –en ear
der Onkel, – uncle
die Oper, –n opera
optimistisch optimistic
das Orchester, – orchestra
die Ordnung order
organisieren to organize
der Ort, –e place, spot; village
der Ost (en), (–ens) east
  (das) Ostpreußen East Prussia
  ostpreußisch East Prussian

P

das Paar, –e pair; couple
  ein paar a few, a couple, some
packen to pack
der Papagei, –en parrot
das Papier, –e paper
der Partner, – partner
der Paß, ⸚e passport; mountain pass
  die Paßkontrolle passport inspection
passieren to happen, occur
der Patient, (–en), –en patient
die Pause, –n pause; intermission
die Pension, –en pension
die Perle, –n pearl
  die Perlenkette, –n pearl necklace
die Person, –en person
  persönlich personal(ly)
der Pfarrer, – pastor, parson
  das Pfarrhaus, ⸚er rectory, parsonage, vicarage
die Pfeife, –n pipe; whistle
der Pfennig, –e pfennig, penny
das Pferd, –e horse
  der Pferdefuß, ⸚e horse's foot; hoof
  das Pferderennen, – horse race
die Pflanze, –n plant
  pflanzen to plant
die Pflicht, –en duty, obligation
das Pfund, –e pound
pfui! pfui, fie, pooh, for shame

der **Philosoph, (–en), –en** philosopher
das **Picknick, –s** picnic
der **Picknickkorb, ⸚e** picnic basket
Pik spades (cards)
der **Plan, ⸚e** plan
der **Platz, ⸚e** place, room; seat; square
plötzlich sudden(ly)
die **Polizei** police
der **Polizeiinspektor, –en** police inspector
der **Polizeioffizier, –e** police officer
die **Polka, –s** polka
die **Post** mail, post; post office
der **Postmeister, –n** postmaster
die **Poststation, –en** stagecoach station
praktisch practical
der **Preis, –e** price; prize
die **Preisliste, –n** price list
(das) **Preußen** Prussia
der **Prinz, (–en), –en** prince
die **Prinzessin, –nen** princess
das **Problem, –e** problem
der **Profit, –e** profit
die **Provinz, –en** province
die **Provinzhauptstadt, ⸚e** provincial capital
das **Prozent, –e** per cent (%)
prüfen to examine, test, check
die **Prüfung, –en** test, examination
der **Psychiater, –** psychiatrist
das **Publikum** public
das **Pult, –e** desk
der **Punkt, –e** point, dot; period

Q

die **Qualität, –en** quality
das **Quartett, –e** quartet
die **Quittung, –en** receipt (for a bill)
das **Quittungsheft, –e** receipt book

R

die **Rache** revenge, vengeance
das **Rad, ⸚er** wheel; bicycle, bike
die **Rakete, –n** rocket
rasieren to shave
der **Rasierapparat, –e** safety razor
das **Rasiermesser, –** straight-edge razor
der **Rat,** die **Ratschläge** advice, counsel; council
raten, ie, a, (ä) to advise, counsel; guess
das **Rathaus, ⸚er** city hall
die **Rathausuhr, –en** city hall clock
der **Räuber, –** robber
der **Räuberhauptmann** robber captain
der **Rauch** smoke
rauchen to smoke
der **Raum, ⸚e** room, space
der **Realismus** realism
realistisch realistic
rechnen to figure, calculate, count, reckon
die **Rechnung, –en** bill, invoice
das **Recht, –e** right
recht right; quite, very
recht haben to be right
rechts to the right
die **Rede, –n** speech, talk
reden to talk, speak
die **Regel, –n** rule
der **Regen** rain
der **Regenschirm, –e** umbrella
das **Regiment, –er** regiment
reiben, ie, ie rub
das **Reich, –e** empire; kingdom; realm; nation
reich rich
reichen to hand to, pass; reach; to be sufficient, suffice; to last
der **Reichtum, ⸚er** wealth, riches
reif ripe, mature
die **Reihe, –n** row, line, rank

der Reim, –e rhyme
rein clean, pure
die Reise, –n trip, journey
reisen to travel
der Reisende, (–n), –n traveler; traveling salesman
der Reisesack, ¨e traveling bag
reißen, i, i to tear, rip
reiten, i, i to ride (horse)
reizen to irritate, annoy; charm
rennen, a, a to run, race
das Rennen, – race
der Rennplatz, ¨e racecourse
das Restaurant, –s restaurant
retten to save, rescue, salvage
der Revolver, – revolver
der Richter, – judge
richtig right, correct; real, genuine
die Richtung, –en direction
riechen, o, o to smell
der Ring, –e ring
der Ritter, – knight
der Rock, ¨e skirt; jacket
rollen to roll
romantisch romantic
Rom Rome
römisch Roman
die Rose, –n rose
der Rosenbusch, ¨e rosebush
rot red
rotbraun reddish-brown
der Rücken, – back
rückwärts backward
rufen, ie, u to call, shout; exclaim
die Ruhe rest; quiet, peace
ruhelos restless
ruhig quiet, calm, still
rühmen to praise
rühren to move, stir, touch
die Ruine, –n ruin
rund round; approximately
(das) Rußland Russia

S

die Sache, –n thing, affair, matter
der Sack, ¨e sack, bag
die Sahne cream
das Salz salt
das Salzfaß, ¨er salt shaker, salt cellar
sammeln to gather, collect
der Samstag, –e Saturday
der Satz, ¨e sentence; leap, bound; movement (music)
sauer sour
die Schachtel, –n box, carton
schade too bad, that's a pity
schaden to hurt, harm, injure
das Schaf, –e sheep
der Schafkäse sheep cheese
der Schaffner, – conductor (train)
sich schämen to be ashamed
scharf sharp
der Schatz, ¨e treasure; sweetheart, darling
das Schatzhaus, ¨er treasure house
der Scheck, –s check
das Scheckbuch, ¨er checkbook
scheiden, ie, ie to part, depart, take leave; separate, divide
scheinen, ie, ie to shine; seem, appear
schenken to give (as a present)
schicken to send
schieben, o, o to push, shove
schießen, o, o to shoot
das Schiff, –e ship
die Schiffahrtsgesellschaft, –en shipping company
die Schiffahrtslinie, –n shipping line
die Schiffskarte, –n steamer ticket
der Schinken, – ham
die Schlacht, –en battle
der Schlaf sleep
schlafen, ie, a, (ä) to sleep
das Schlafmittel, – sleeping potion, sleeping pill
der Schlafrock, ¨e dressing gown
das Schlafzimmer, – bedroom
der Schlag, ¨e blow, beat, stroke
schlagen, u, a, (ä) to strike, beat

schlank slender, slim
schlau cunning, sly, crafty
schlecht bad, wicked; poor
schleichen, i, i to sneak, creep, prowl
schließen, o, o to close, shut, lock; conclude
schließlich finally; after all
schlimm bad, wicked
der Schlitten, – sleigh, sled
das Schloß, ⸚er castle; look
der Schloßhof, ⸚e courtyard of a castle
der Schluß, ⸚e end; conclusion
die Schlußprüfung, –en final examination
der Schlüssel, – key
das Schlüsselloch, ⸚er keyhole
schmecken to taste
der Schmerz, –en pain, ache, grief
der Schmied, –e smithy, blacksmith
der Schmuggel smuggling
schmutzig dirty
der Schnee snow
schneiden, i, i, to cut
schneien to snow
schnell quick, fast
schon already
schön beautiful, handsome
die Schönheit, –en beauty
schrecken to scare, frighten, startle
der Schreck(en), (–ens), –en fright, terror
schrecklich terrible
schreiben, ie, ie to write
das Schreibpult, –e writing desk
der Schreibtisch, –e desk
schreien, ie, ie to scream, shout, shriek
schreiten, i, i to step, go, walk
der Schritt, –e step, pace
der Schuh, –e shoe
die Schuld fault, guilt, debt
die Schulden debts
die Schule, –n school
die Schularbeit, –en schoolwork
die Schulter, –n shoulder
schütteln to shake
schwach weak, feeble
schwarz black
der Schwarzmarkt black market
(das) Schweden Sweden
die Schweden Swedes
der Schwedenkönig King of the Swedes
schweigen, ie, ie, to be silent
das Schweigen silence
das Schwein, –e pig, swine
das Schweinefleisch pork
die Schweineherde, – herd of swine
der Schweinehirt, (–en), –en swineherd
der Schweinestall, ⸚e pigsty
der Schweiß perspiration, sweat
(die) Schweiz Switzerland
schwer heavy; difficult
die Schwester, –n sister
schwierig difficult
die Schwierigkeit, –en difficulty
schwimmen, a, o to swim, float
schwinden, a, u to disappear, vanish
der Schwindler, – swindler
schwören, o, o to swear, take an oath
der See, –n lake
die See, –n sea, ocean
die Seereise, –n (sea) voyage
die Seele, –n soul
sehen, a, e, (ie) to see, look
sehr very; much
die Seife, –n soap
sein to be
seit since
die Seite, –n side; page
die Seitenstraße, –n side street
die Sekunde, –n second
selber myself, yourself, himself, etc.
selbst even; myself, yourself, himself, etc.
der Selbstmord, –e suicide
selten rare(ly), seldom
senden, a, a to send
die Serenade, –n serenade
setzen to set, put, place

sich setzen to sit down
sicher certain; sure, safe, secure
der Sieg, –e victory
das Silber silver
silberhell silvery
silbern silver, of silver
das Silberstück, –e silver coin
die Silberware, –n silver goods
singen, a, u to sing
sinken a, u to sink
der Sinn, –e sense, meaning; mind
die Situation, –en situation
der Sitz, –e seat
sitzen, a, e to sit
das Skelett, –e skeleton
der Skeptiker, – skeptic
so so, thus, in this manner
sobald as soon as
sofort at once, immediately
sogar even
sogleich at once, immediately
der Sohn, ⸚e son
solange as long as
solch such
der Soldat, (–en), –en soldier
sollen, sollte, gesollt/sollen, (soll) shall, should, etc.
der Sommer, – summer
die Sommerferien summer vacation
das Sommerkleid, –er summer dress
sondern but (on the contrary)
der Sonnabend, –e Saturday
die Sonne sun
der Sonntag, –e Sunday
der Sonntagmorgen, –e Sunday morning
das Sonntagskonzert, –e Sunday concert
sonst otherwise, else; formerly
die Sorge, –n worry, care; anxiety
soweit as far as
spät late
spätestens at the latest
der Spaziergang, ⸚e walk, stroll
spazieren-gehen* to take a walk, go for a walk
der Spiegel, – mirror
das Spiel, –e play, game
spielen to play
der Spieler, – player
das Spielzimmer, – play room, card room, game room
die Spitze, –n point, tip, head
die Sprache, –n language, speech
sprachlos speechless
sprechen, a, o, (i) to speak
das Sprechzimmer – consulting room
springen a, u to jump, spring, leap
der Staat, –en state; government
die Stadt, ⸚e city, town
das Stadtgefängnis, –se city jail
der Stall, ⸚e stable, pen, barn
der Stamm, ⸚e stem, trunk; race; family; tribe
stark strong
starren to stare
statt instead of
statt-finden* to take place
stechen, a, o, (i) to sting, prick, stab, pierce
stecken to stick, put, place
stehen, a, a to stand
stehen-bleiben* to stop; to remain standing
stehlen, a, o, (ie) to steal
steigen, ie, ie to climb, rise, go, walk
der Stein, –e stone
der Steinhaufen, – pile of stones
die Stelle, –n place, spot; job
stellen to put, place (vertically)
die Stellung, –en position, job
sterben, a, o (i) to die
der Stern, –e star
stets always
still quiet, calm, silent, still
still-stehen* to stand still
die Stimme, –n voice
stimmen to be right, correct; to vote; to tune
die Stirn(e), –en forehead

der Stock, ⸚e stick, cane; story, floor
der Stoff, –e material, cloth
der Stolz pride
stolz (auf + *acc.*) proud (of)
stören to disturb
stoßen, ie, o, (ö) to push, thrust
stottern to stutter
die Strafe, –n punishment; fine, penalty
die Strafkolonie, –n penal colony
die Straße, –n street, road
streben to strive
strecken to stretch
streichen, i, i to stroke; strike, cancel; spread
das Streichholz, ⸚er match
die Streichholzschachtel, –n matchbox
streiten, i, i quarrel, fight
streng severe, strict, stern
das Stroh straw
der Strohhaufen, –e pile of straw
der Strohmann, ⸚er man of straw
der Strom, ⸚e large river; stream, current
der Strumpf, ⸚e stocking, hose; sock
das Stück, –e piece; play (stage)
der Student, (–en), –en student (male)
die Studentin, –nen student (female)
studieren to study
der Stuhl, ⸚e chair
stumpf dull, blunt
die Stunde, –n hour; lesson
stundenlang for hours
der Sturm, ⸚e storm
stürzen to fall, plunge; rush
suchen to look for, search, seek
der Süd(en), (–ens) south
(das) Südamerika South America
der Südosten southeast
die Südwand, ⸚e south wall
die Summe, –n sum, amount
die Sünde, –n sin
der Sünder, - sinner
die Suppe, –n soup
der Suppenteller, –n soup plate
süß sweet
die Symphonie, –n symphony
das Symphonieorchester, – symphony orchestra
das System, –e system
die Szene, –n scene

T

der Tag, –e day
das Tageslicht daylight
täglich daily
das Tal, ⸚er valley
die Tanne, –n fir tree
der Tannenbaum, ⸚e fir tree; Christmas tree
der Tannenzweig, –e branch of fir tree
die Tante, –n aunt
tanzen to dance
die Tasche, –n pocket; purse, bag, handbag
das Taschentuch, ⸚er handkerchief
die Tasse, –n cup
der Tau dew
das Tausend, –e thousand
das Taxi, –s taxi, cab
der Taxichauffeur, –e taxi chauffeur, taxi driver
der Tee tea
die Teegesellschaft, –en tea party
der Teelöffel, – teaspoon
der Teil, –e part, portion, share
teilen to divide, share
das Telephon, –e telephone
die Telephonnummer, –n telephone number
der Teller, – plate
teuer expensive, dear
der Teufel, – devil
der Text, –e text
tief deep, profound
das Tier, –e animal, beast

die Tinte ink
das Tintenfaß, ⸚er inkwell
der Tisch, –e table
die Tischlampe, –n table lamp, desk lamp
die Tochter, ⸚ daughter
der Tod death; Death
todmüde dead tired
der Ton, ⸚e sound: tone
der Topf, ⸚e pot
tot dead
der Tote, (–n) –n dead man
töten to kill
tot-schlagen* to beat to death
träge lazy
tragen, u, a, (ä) to carry, wear
die Träne, –n tear
trauen to trust; marry, join in marriage
die Trauung, –en marriage (ceremony)
der Trauzeuge, (–n), –n witness to a marriage
trauern to mourn, grieve
der Traum, ⸚e dream
träumen to dream
traurig sad
treffen, a, o, (i) to meet; hit
treiben, ie, ie to drive; drift; do
trennen to separate, part
die Trennung, –en separation
die Treppe, –n stairs, steps, staircase
treten, a, e, (i) to step, walk; kick
treu faithful, loyal, true
der Trick, –s trick
trinken, a, u to drink
trocken dry
trocknen to dry
die Trommel, –n drum
die Trompete, –n trumpet
der Trompeter, – trumpeter
der Trost consolation, solace, comfort
trösten to console, comfort
trotz in spite of
trotzdem nevertheless, nonetheless, anyway
die Truppe, –n troop, troops; troupe
das Tuch, ⸚er (piece of) cloth, fabric; kerchief
tun, a, a to do; make; put
die Tür, –en door

U

üben to practice, exercise
über over, above, about, across, etc.
überall everywhere (stationary)
überallhin everywhere (motion)
überglücklich overjoyed
überhaupt at all; altogether; in general
überlegen to think (over), consider
überraschen to surprise
die Überraschung, –en surprise
übersetzen to translate
übrig left, left over, remaining
das Ufer, – bank, shore
die Uhr, –en watch, clock; o'clock
um around, about, for, etc.
um . . . herum around
um so (+ *comparative*) all the (+ *comparative*)
um . . . willen for . . . sake
um . . . zu (in order) to
(sich) um-blicken to look around, to look back
um-drehen to turn around
umgeben* to surround
(sich) um-sehen* to look around, to look back
um-wenden* to turn (around)
unangenehm unpleasant, disagreeable
unbekannt unknown
unbezahlt unpaid
und and
unerwartet unexpected
unfreundlich unfriendly
ungebildet uneducated
die Ungeduld impatience
die Ungerechtigkeit, –en injustice
ungerührt unmoved, untouched

ungewöhnlich unusual
das Unglück, –e misfortune, unhappiness
unglücklich unhappy, unfortunate
unhöflich impolite
die Uniform, –en uniform
die Universität, –en university
unmöglich impossible
unnatürlich unnatural
unruhig restless, troubled
der Unsinn nonsense
unten below, downstairs
unter under, below; among
unterbrechen* to interrupt
unter·gehen* to perish; to set (sun)
unterhalten* to entertain, amuse
sich unterhalten* to have a good time; to converse, talk
die Unterhaltung, –en conversation; entertainment
unterrichten to instruct, teach, inform
untersuchen examine, investigate
die Unterwäsche underwear
unterwegs on the way, on my, your, his way, etc.; busy
unzufrieden discontented, dissatisfied
der Ursprung, ⸚e origin
urteilen to judge, give an opinion

V

der Vater, ⸚ father
verbieten* to forbid, prohibit
verdienen to earn; deserve, merit
der Verein, –e association, society, club
verfassen to write (= be the author)
die Vergangenheit past (time)
vergessen, a, e, (i) to forget
das Vergnügen, – pleasure, enjoyment
verhaften to arrest
verheiraten to marry
der Verkauf, ⸚e sale
verkaufen to tell
der Verkaufstag, –e day of sale
verlangen to demand, ask, require; desire, seek, long for
verlassen* to leave, abandon
verlieren, o, o to lose
der Verlust, –e loss
das Vermögen, –e fortune, wealth
der Vers, –e verse
verschieden different
verschwinden* to disappear, vanish
versinken* to sink
versprechen* to promise
das Versprechen, – promise
verstecken to hide
Versteck(en) spielen to play hide-and-seek
verstehen* to understand
versuchen to try, attempt; tempt
verurteilen to sentence
verwandeln to change, transform
verwandt related
der Verwandte, (–n), –n relative, relation
verzeihen, ie, ie to forgive, excuse
verzollen to declare (customs); to pay (customs) duty
verzweifeln (an + *dat.***)** to despair (of)
die Verzweiflung despair
der Vetter, –n cousin
das Vieh cattle
viel; viele much, a great deal of, a lot of; many
vielleicht perhaps
der Vogel, ⸚ bird
das Vogelnest, –er bird's nest
das Volk, ⸚er people, nation; common people, populace, mob
die Volksmenge, –n crowd of people, multitude
voll full
vollenden to complete, finish
vollkommen complete(ly), entire; perfect
vollständig complete(ly), entire(ly)

von of, from, about, etc.
voneinander from each other, from one another
vor before; with; ago, etc.; ahead, forward
voraus ahead, ahead of time, in advance
voraus-gehen* to go, walk ahead
vorbei past, over; along, by
vorbei-eilen to hurry past
vorbei-gehen* to go past, walk past
vorbei-kommen* to come by
vorher before, beforehand
vor-kommen* to occur, happen
vorn in front
vor-schlagen* to propose, suggest
der Vorteil, –e advantage
vorüber past, over; along, by
vorüber-gehen* to go by, walk past
vorüber-ziehen* to go past
vorwärts forward
vorwärts-kriechen* to crawl forward
vorwärts-schreiten* to step forward, walk forward
vorwärts-stoßen* to push forward
vorwärts-strecken to stretch out, forward
vorwärts-treiben* to drive forward
vor-ziehen* to prefer; to draw out

W

wachsen, u, a, (ä) to grow
die Waffe, –n weapon
der Wagen, – carriage, wagon, car, auto
wagen to dare; risk, venture
wägen, o, o to weigh
wählen to choose, select, elect
wahr true, real
die Wahrheit, –en truth
währen to last
während during; while
wahrscheinlich probably
der Wald, ⸚er woods, forest
der Walzer, – waltz
die Wand, ⸚e wall (of a room)
wandern to wander, travel, go; hike
die Wange, –n cheek
die Ware, –n merchandise, goods, ware
warm warm
warnen to warn
warten (auf + *acc.*) to wait (for)
das Wartezimmer, – waiting room
warum why
was what; which, that which
was für ein what kind of; what a
waschen, u, a (ä) to wash
der Waschtisch, –e washstand
das Wasser, – water
wechseln to change
wecken to awaken, to wake up
weder . . . noch neither . . . nor
der Weg, –e way, road, path
sich auf den Weg machen to leave, set out on one's way
weg away, off; gone
weg-fahren* to leave, go away
weg-gehen* to go, walk away, leave
weg-legen to put away, lay aside
weg-nehmen* to take away
weg-stehlen* to steal away from
weg-stoßen* to push away
weg-werfen* to throw away
wegen because of, on account of
weh tun* to hurt
das Weib, –er woman; wife; (contemptuously) woman, hag, old hag
Weihnachten Christmas
das Weihnachtsgeschenk, –e Christmas present
der Weihnachtsmann, ⸚er Santa Claus
weil because
die Weile while, short time
der Wein, –e wine

die Weinflasche, –n wine bottle
das Weinfaß, ⸗er wine barrel
weinen to cry, weep
die Weise, –n manner, way; melody, tune
weise wise
weiß white
weit far, distant; wide
weiter farther, further, on
und so weiter and so on, and so forth
weiter-eilen to hurry on, to hasten on
weiter-fahren* to drive on, continue to drive, go
weiter-gehen* to go on
weiter-laufen* to continue to run
weiter-leben to continue to live
weiter-lesen* to read on, continue to read
weiter-reisen to go on, travel on, continue on one's way
weiter-reiten* to ride on, ride off
weiter-schreiten* to walk on
weiter-spielen to continue to play
weiter-sprechen* to continue to speak
weiter-suchen to keep on looking
weiter-trinken* to continue to drink
weiter-wandern to continue on one's way
der Weizen wheat
das Weizenfeld, –er field of wheat
welch which, who, what
die Welt, –en world
der Weltkrieg, –e World War
wenden, a, a to turn
wenig little
wenige few
wenigstens at least
wenn if; when
werden, u, o, (i) to become, grow, get
werfen, a, o, (i) to throw
das Werk, –e work
wert worth
der Wert, –e value, worth
der Wertgegenstand, ⸗e valuable object
das Wesen, – being, creature; essence; manner, character
der West(en), (–ens) west
die Weste, –n vest, waistcoat
die Westentasche, –n vest pocket
die Wette, –n bet, wager
wetten to bet, wager
das Wetter weather
der Whisky whiskey
die Whiskyflasche, –n whiskey bottle
wichtig important
wider against
widersprechen* to contradict
wieder again, back
wieder einmal once again
wieder-erkennen* to recognize
wieder-finden* to find again
wieder-geben* to return
wieder-haben* to have again
wiederholen to repeat
wieder-kommen* to return, come again
wieder-sehen* to see again
wiegen, o, o to weigh
die Wiese, –n meadow
wild wild, savage
der Wille(n), (–ens) will, will power
um . . . willen for . . . sake
der Wind, –e wind
der Winter, – winter
wirken to have an effect, work
wirklich real, actual, genuine
der Wirt, –e innkeeper; landlord; host
wischen to wipe
wissen, wußte, gewußt, (weiß) to know
das Wissen knowledge
wo where (stationary)
woher from where (= whence)
wohin where (= wither)

die Woche, –n week
wohl well; probably
wohnen to live, dwell, reside
die Wohnung, –en apartment, residence, dwelling
das Wohnzimmer, – living room
die Wolke, –n cloud
die Wolle wool
die Wolldecke, –n woolen blanket
wollen, wollte, gewollt/wollen, (will) to want
das Wort, –e/⸚er word
das Wunder, – wonder, miracle
wunderbar wonderful
sich wundern to be surprised, astonished, amazed
der Wunsch, ⸚e wish, desire
wünschen to wish, desire
die Würde, –n dignity, honor
die Wurst, ⸚e sausage
die Wurzel, –n root

Z

zahlen to pay
zählen to count
zahm tame
der Zahn, ⸚e tooth
zart tender, delicate
das Zeichen, – sign, signal, token
zeichnen to draw, sketch
zeigen to show
die Zeit, –en time
die Zeitschrift, –en magazine, periodical
die Zeitung, –en newspaper
die Zensur, –en mark, grade; censorship
der Zeuge, (–n), –n witness
die Ziege, –n goat
der Ziegenbart, ⸚e goatee
ziehen, o, o to draw, pull; move, go, march; grow, cultivate
das Ziel, –e aim, goal, destination
ziemlich rather, fairly
die Zigarette, –n cigarette
die Zigarre, –n cigar
das Zimmer, – room
die Zimmerecke, –n corner of a room
zittern tremble
der Zoll customs; toll
das Zollamt, ⸚er customs house, customs office
der Zollbeamte, (–en), –en customs official
zollfrei duty-free
der Zollinspektor, –en customs inspector
die Zollkontrolle customs inspection
der Zorn anger, wrath
zu to, toward; too; close, shut
der Zucker sugar
zuckersüß sweet as sugar
zuerst at first, first
der Zufall, ⸚e accident, chance, coincidence
zufrieden satisfied, contented
der Zug, ⸚e train; trait, feature; draught; pull, tug; march, column, procession
zugleich at the same time
zu-hören to listen
die Zukunft future
zu-machen to close, shut
zunächst first, first of all
die Zündflamme, –n pilot light
zurück back; behind
zurück-bekommen* to get back
zurück-bleiben* to stay behind, remain behind
zurück-denken* to think back
zurück-drehen to turn back
zurück-eilen to hasten back
zurück-fahren* to return
zurück-fliehen* to flee back
zurück-geben* to give back, return
zurück-gehen* to go back, return
zurück-gewinnen* to win back
zurück-halten* to hold back
zurück-kehren to come back, return

zurück-kommen* to come back, return
zurück-lassen* to leave behind
zurück-laufen* to run back
zurück-reiten* to ride back
zurück-schicken to send back
zurück-schreiben* to write back
zurück-schreiten* to step back, walk back
zurück-stecken to put back
zurück-stellen to put back
zurück-ziehen* to draw back, withdraw
zusammen together
zusammen-bringen* to bring together
zusammen-reisen to travel together
zusammen-setzen to put together
der **Zustand, ⸚e** state, condition
zuvor before, previously
zu-wenden* to turn to
zwar to be sure, indeed
der **Zweck, –e** purpose, aim, object
zwecklos useless, pointless
der **Zweifel, –** doubt
der **Zweig, –e** branch
zweitens secondly, second
zwingen, a, u to force, compel
zwischen between